The Industrial Revolution has been, and continues to be, the focus of massive historiographical as well as historical enquiry. This collection includes reappraisals by Phyllis Deane and by François Crouzet of their classic accounts of industrialization in Britain and in France, and more generally broaches the wider issue of 'new approaches' which have been emerging for the understanding of the industrializing process in nations where it came somewhat later.

In addition to grappling with questions of technical skills, economic analysis and the process of industrialization, the authors also tackle questions of national politics and international relations. In addition to the roster of authors who examine individual national experiences, a general essay by Sidney Pollard takes into account the relative contributions of the distinct national experiences in Western and Eastern Europe, the USA and Japan, and assesses them as special cases of a more general phenomenon.

D0898248

THE INDUSTRIAL REVOLUTION
IN NATIONAL CONTEXT

THE INDUSTRIAL REVOLUTION
IN NATIONAL CONTEXT

Europe and the USA

EDITED BY

Mikuláš Teich

Robinson College, Cambridge

AND

Roy Porter

The Wellcome Institute for the History of Medicine, London

CAMBRIDGE
UNIVERSITY PRESS

Published by the Press Syndicate of the University of Cambridge
The Pitt Building, Trumpington Street, Cambridge CB2 1RP
40 West 20th Street, New York, NY 10011-4211, USA
10 Stamford Road, Oakleigh, Melbourne 3166, Australia

© Cambridge University Press 1996

First published 1996

Printed in Great Britain at the University Press, Cambridge

A catalogue record for this book is available from the British Library

Library of Congress cataloguing in publication data

The Industrial Revolution in national context: Europe and the USA /
  edited by Mikuláš Teich and Roy Porter.
      p.   cm.

    ISBN 0 521 40100 3. – ISBN 0 521 40940 3 (pbk.)
    1. Economic history – 1750–1918. 2. Industrial revolution – Europe.
  3. Industrial revolution – United States. I. Teich, Mikuláš.
  II. Porter, Roy, 1946– .
  HC53.153   1996
  940.2′8–dc20   95-25377   CIP

Contents

Notes on contributors

IVAN T. BEREND is Professor of History at the University of California Los Angeles, a corresponding member of the British Academy and former president of the Hungarian Academy of Sciences. He is author or co-author of more than twenty books, among others *The Economic Development of Central and Easten Europe in the 19th and 20th Centuries, The European Periphery and Industralization 1780–1914, The Crisis Zone of Europe* (Cambridge, 1986) and *The Hungarian Economic Reforms 1953–1988*.

LJUBEN BEROV is Professor of Economic History at the University of National and World Economy in Sofia. He is author of numerous books and essays on the economic history of Bulgaria and the Balkan countries (*The Material Situation of the Working Class in Bulgaria under Capitalism*, Sofia, 1962; *The Economy of Bulgaria during the Centuries*, Sofia, 1981; *Economic Development of the World since Antiquity till Our Time*, Sofia, 1994, etc.).

FRANÇOIS CROUZET (Hon. CBE) is Emeritus Professor of Modern History at the University of Paris-Sorbonne. He has published extensively on the origins and early stages of modern industrialization, in Britain and in France. His books include *Capital Formation in the Industrial Revolution* (London, 1972), *The First Industrialists* (Cambridge, 1985), *Britain Ascendant: Comparative Studies in Franco-British Economic History* (Cambridge, 1990).

PHYLLIS DEANE is Professor of Economic History, University of Cambridge and Honorary Fellow of Newnham College. She is co-author of *British Economic Growth 1688–1959* (Cambridge University Press, 1967); and author *inter alia* of *The First Industrial Revolution* (Cambridge University Press, 1979) and *The State and the Economic System* (Oxford University Press, 1989).

BRUNO FRITZSCHE is Professor of History at the University of Zurich (Forschungsstelle für schweizerische Sozial- und Wirtschaftsgeschichte).

His main field of research is the history of urbanization in the nineteenth and twentieth centuries. His most recent publication (as a co-author) is *Geschichte des Kantons Zürich,* vol. III (Zurich, 1994).

BO GUSTAFSSON is Professor of Economic History at Uppsala University and a director of the Swedish Collegium for Advanced Study in Social Sciences (SCASSS), Uppsala. He has published monographs and papers on the Industrial Revolution, public-sector growth, history of economic theories and historical modes of production. His publications include: *The Saw-Mill Workers of Northern Sweden 1890–1913* (Uppsala, 1965, in Swedish); *Marxismus und Revisionismus* (Frankfurt/Main, 1972); *The Silent Revolution. The Rise and Growth of a Local Welfare Community* (Stockholm, 1988, in Swedish); *Power and Economic Institutions. Reinterpretations in Economic History* (Aldershot, 1991).

HERBERT MATIS is Professor of Economic History at the University of Economics and Business Administration and head of the Boltzmann-Institute of Economic Process Analysis in Vienna. He is author of numerous books on economic and business history from the eighteenth to the twentieth centuries.

GIORGIO MORI is Professor of Economic History of Europe in the University of Florence. His main, recent works are the following: 'L'economia italiana dal fine della 2ª guerra mondiale al secondo "miracolo economico"', in *Storia dell'Italia Repubblicana* (Turin, 1994), pp. 131–230; 'Riabilitare la rivoluzione industriale', *Studi storici* (1994), pp. 61–72; 'L'industria italiana alla vigili della 2ª guerra mondiale', in *Festschrift für Hans Pohl* (Stuttgart, 1994).

ROGER MUNTING is Senior Lecturer in Economic and Social history at the University of East Anglia in Norwich. He studied at the University of Sheffield and did his PhD at the University of Birmingham. He has published numerous articles on Russian agrarian history, foreign trade and commerce as well as books on the economic history of the USSR and Europe in the twentieth century.

MILAN MYŠKA is Professor of Czech History at Ostrava University (Czech Republic). He is the author of several works dealing with the economic and social history of early capitalist industralization. They include *Die mährisch schlesische Eisenindustrie in der Industriellen Revolution* (1970); *Protoindustriální železářství v českých zemích* (Protoindustrial Iron-making in the Czech Lands) (Ostrava, 1990); *Opožděná industrializace* (Retarded

Industrialization) (Trutnov, 1991). He contributed to Sheilagh C. Ogilvie and M. Cerman (eds.), *European Proto-Industrialization: An Introductory Handbook* (Cambridge, 1995).

WILLIAM N. PARKER is Bartlett Professor of Economics and Economic History, emeritus, in Yale University. A two-volume collection of his essays appeared under the title *Europe, America, and the Wider World*, from Cambridge University Press in 1986 and 1991. He is now at work on a memoir on his first sixteen years, growing up in the American Middle West.

SIDNEY POLLARD, now retired, is a former Professor of Economic History at the Universities of Sheffield and Bielefeld. His special interests are the process of industrialization in Britian and on the continent of Europe, and the British economy in the late nineteenth and twentieth centuries.

CARLO PONI is Professor of Economic History at the University of Bologna. Previously he taught at the University of Trieste and at the European University Institute of Florence. He is a fellow of St Antony's College (Oxford), a member of the Institute of Advanced Study (Princeton), Mitglied of the Wissenschaftskolleg zu Berlin and a life member of Clare Hall (Cambridge). His first interest was peasant technology. Since the early 1970s he has moved to urban and industrial history. He is currently working on institutions, technology, standards and civil society.

ROY PORTER is Professor in the Social History of Medicine at the Wellcome Institute for the History of Medicine. He is currently working on the history of hysteria. Recent books include *Mind Forg'd Manacles. Madness in England from the Restoration to the Regency* (London, Athlone, 1987); *A Social History of Madness* (London, Weidenfeld and Nicolson, 1987); *In Sickness and in Health. The British Experience, 1650–1850* (London, Fourth Estate, 1988); *Patient's Progress* (Oxford, Policy, 1989) – these last two co-authored with Dorothy Porter; *Health for Sale. Quackery in England 1660–1850* (Manchester University Press, 1989); *Doctor of Society: Thomas Beddoes and the Sick Trade in Late Enlightenment England* (London, Routledge, 1991) and *London: A Social History* (London, Hamish Hamilton, 1994).

MIKULÁŠ TEICH is Emeritus Fellow of Robinson College, Cambridge, and Honorary Professor of the Technical University Vienna. His publications include work on the history of chemistry and biomedical sciences, social and philosophical aspects of the development of science, technology and the economy, and on the history of scientific organizations. His *A Documentary History of Biochemistry, 1770–1940* (with the late Dorothy Needham) was published by Leicester University Press in 1992.

RICHARD TILLY taught at the University of Michigan, Yale University, the University of Wisconsin and the University of Munster where he is Professor of Economic and Social History. He is the author of *Financial Institutions and Industrialization in the Rhineland, 1915–70* (Madison, University of Wisconsin Press, 1966); with C. and L. Tilly, *The Rebellious Century* (Harvard University Press, 1975); *Vom Zollverein zum Industriestaat. Die wirtschaftlichsoziale Entwicklung Deutschlands 1834 bis 1914* (Munich, 1990). He is co-editor of *Geschichte und Gesellschaft.*

GABRIEL TORTELLA, who has a PhD in economics from the University of Wisconsin, presently teaches at the Universidad de Alcalá de Henares (Madrid). He has taught and researched at the Universities of Pittsburgh, California (San Diego), Chicago, Valencia and the Colegio de México, and at the Institute of Advanced Study at Princeton, and written on monetary and banking history, business history, economic policies and human capital. He is President of the International Economic History Association.

HERMAN VAN DER WEE is Professor Emeritus of Social and Economic History at Leuven University (Belgium). He has taught at several other Belgian and foreign universities. He was also a visiting fellow at several international research Institutes. His publications include *The Growth of the Antwerp Market and the European Economy (Fourteenth–Sixteenth Centuries)* (Louvain–Paris–The Hague, 1963), *Prosperity and Upheaval: The World Economy 1945–1980* (Harmondsworth–New York, Berkeley–Los Angeles, 1986), *The History of European Banking* (Antwerp, 1990), *The Low Countries in the Early Modern Times* (Aldershot, 1994).

J. L. VAN ZANDEN is Professor of Economic and Social History at the University of Utrecht. His recent publications include *Rise and Decline of Holland's Economy 1350–1850* (Manchester, 1993) and *The Transformation of European Agriculture in the Nineteenth Century: The Case of the Netherlands* (Amsterdam, 1995). He is currently working on a study of economic growth in The Netherlands in the nineteenth century.

Acknowledgements

Since it was first planned in 1989 no other collection, in the sequence under our editorship, has been longer in the making. For the delay in getting it to press we offer our sincerest regrets to contributors who did their best to meet the agreed deadline, and may feel that they have been put at a disadvantage because of it. We record our special thanks to Sidney Pollard for his helpful copy-editorial suggestions. We are greatly indebted to Margarita Dritsas, Alison Hennegan, Sonia Kanikova, Michael Kaser, Lenos Mavrommatis, Alice Teichova and Chronis Tzedakis for aiding us in linguistic matters and to Jean Field for carefully copy-editing the text. Once again it is a pleasure to renew our warmest thanks to William Davies of Cambridge University Press for the support he has unfailingly continued to give us.

General maps and graphs

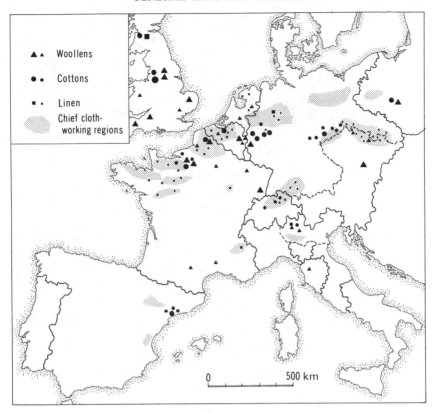

1 The European textile industry in the mid-nineteenth century

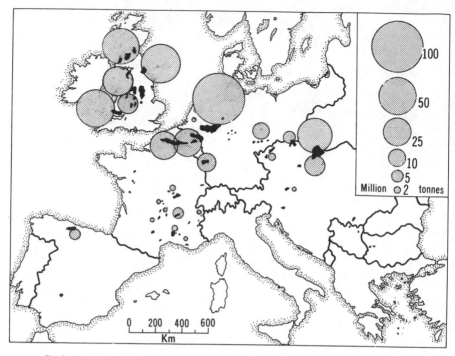

2 Coal production in Europe, 1912. The overwhelming importance of Great Britain and
Germany is apparent.

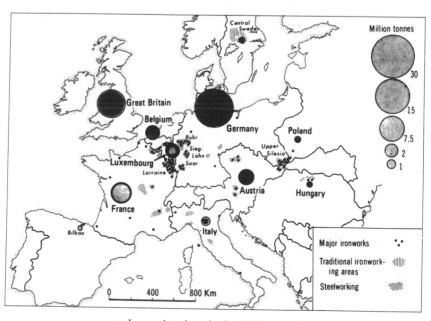

3 Iron and steel production in Europe, 1912

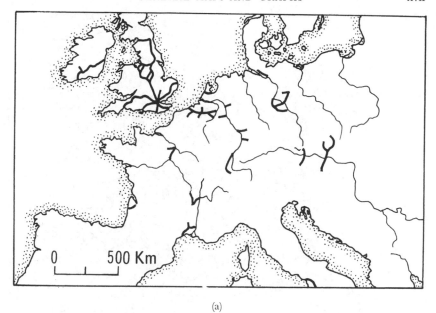

(a)

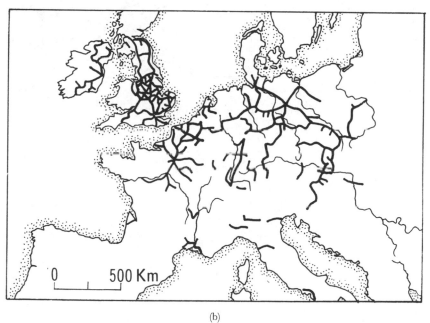

(b)

4 Railway development in Europe: (a) 1840; (b) 1850

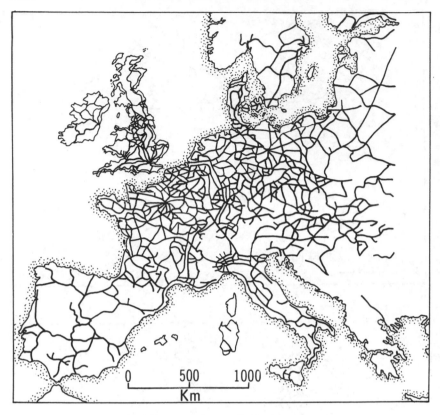

5 Railway development in Europe, 1880

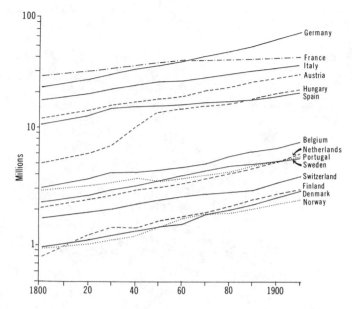

6 Growth of population in Europe by country, 1800–1910

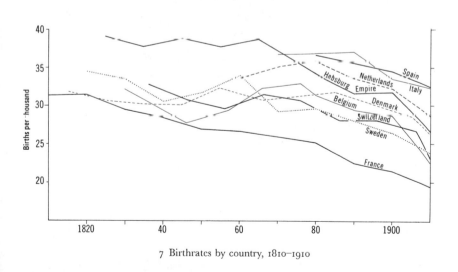

7 Birthrates by country, 1810–1910

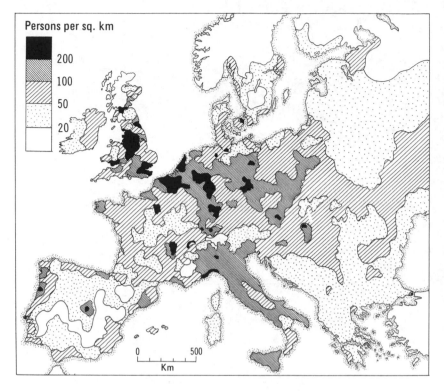

8 Population density in Europe, 1910

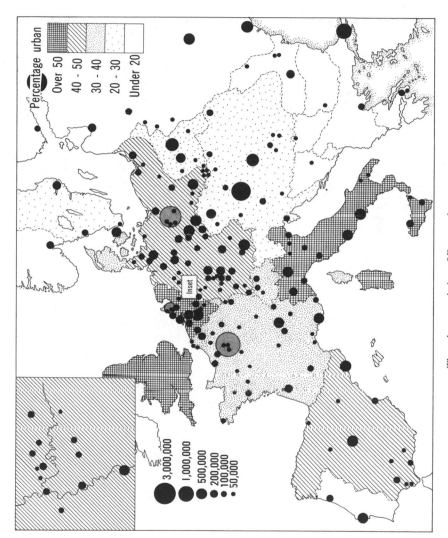

Percentage urban

Over 50
40 - 50
30 - 40
20 - 30
Under 20

Inset

3,000,000
1,000,000
500,000
200,000
100,000
50,000

9 The urban population of Europe about 1910

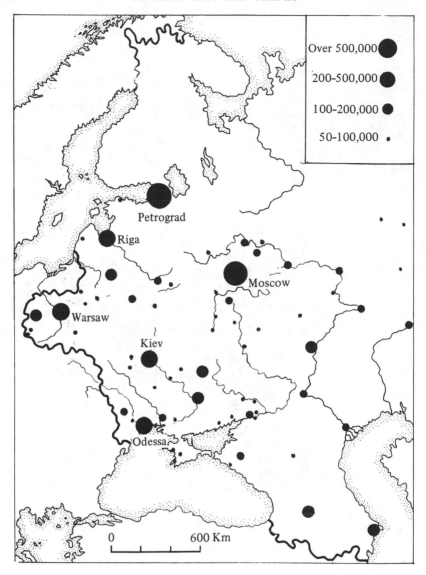

10 Urban development of European Russia, early twentieth century

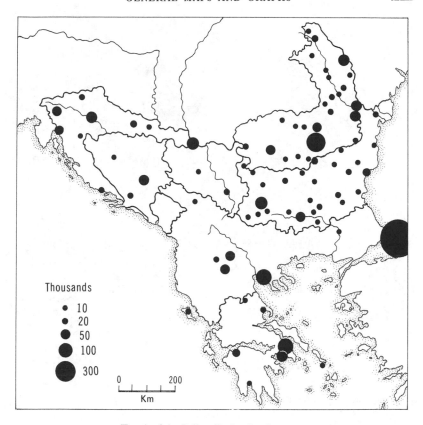

11 Towns of the Balkan Peninsula, about 1910

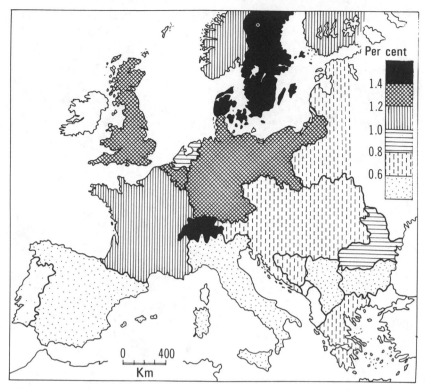

12 Increase in gross national product, 1830–1910, as percentage of 1830 figures, shown as per
cent per year

13 The Balkan states *c.* 1910. From J. R. Lampe and M. R. Jackson, *Balkan Economic History 1550–1950* (Bloomington, 1982)

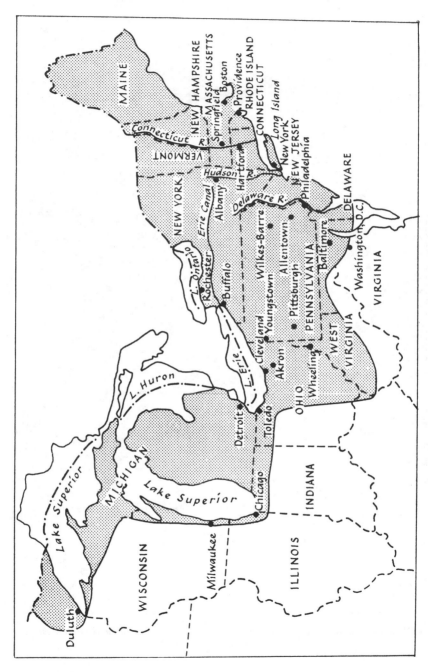

14 The north and north-east industrial-urban region of the United States. From J. Wreford Watson, *North America. Its Countries and Regions* (London, 1963). Scale 1:16 m.

Introduction

MIKULÁŠ TEICH AND ROY PORTER

THE THEME

THIS is the last of the explicitly 'National Context' collections of essays in the sequence which Cambridge University Press has been publishing under our editorship since 1981. Its purpose has been to bring together comparative, national and interdisciplinary approaches to the history of great movements in the development of human thought and action. What this book has in common with the preceding volumes is that we perceive in the Industrial Revolution a historical phenomenon of the same order as the Renaissance, Reformation, Scientific Revolution, Enlightenment and Romanticism. That is, movements which were brought about by and formed the development of bourgeois society in Europe since the end of the Middle Ages.

As goes without saying the Industrial Revolution has been, and continues to be, the centre of massive historiographical as well as historical inquiry. Both generally and specifically, the Industrial Revolution is about the changeover from economies based on agriculture (going back to the Neolithic Revolution) to ones based upon industry.[1] Twenty-five years or so ago, discussion of this complex historical process focused largely upon growth – both charting and explaining it. Thus R. M. Hartwell, as editor, introducing the well-known *The Causes of the Industrial Revolution in England* (1967), speaks of 'the great divide' between 'a world of slow economic growth' and 'a world of much faster economic growth'.[2] The titles of two articles (out of six) in that book give an indication of the preoccupation with this aspect of industrialization: 'The Industrial Revolution and economic growth: the evidence of early British national income estimates', and 'England and France in the eighteenth century: a comparative analysis of two economic growths'. How far has the accent changed? We have asked the authors of these two articles – Phyllis Deane and François Crouzet respectively – to re-examine their accounts and to reflect upon transformations in economic historians' thinking regarding industrialization in Britain and France.

This broaches the issue whether the industrializing process where it came later can be understood without taking into account specific national circumstances. How far was a 'knock-on' process at work, whereby industrialization in one national situation expedited economic progress in another next to it? Did the reverse happen, with inverse relationship between different adjoining national economies? What were the drawbacks or advantages of being late? How far was industrialization in any national context essentially a response to the local economic, social, cultural and political state of affairs? How far must we see industrialization, by contrast, as a transnational movement, with a relatively independent impetus of its own? To what degree were there transfers of skills, technologies, capital and outlooks from region to region? To answer these questions, technical skills in economic and econometric analysis are obviously requisite; but equally important is a willingness to grapple with larger questions of national history and international relations.

Matters such as these are variously explored in the essays by Roger Munting and Ljuben Berov on industrializing Russia/the Soviet Union and the Balkans respectively; as likewise in the contributions on Germany by Richard Tilly, Italy by Carlo Poni and Giorgio Mori, Sweden by Bo Gustafsson and Spain by Gabriel Tortella. A feature of this book is the separate treatment of the Industrial Revolution in the Czech Lands by Milan Myška and in Hungary by Ivan Berend, which supplement Herbert Matis's account of the Industrial Revolution in Austria in the framework of the multinational Habsburg Monarchy.[3] No less of special value is the separate attention given to the development of industrialization in Belgium by Herman Van der Wee, in The Netherlands by J. L. van Zanden and in Switzerland by Bruno Fritzsche.

It is well to remember that the Industrial Revolution in these parts of Europe, not unlike the Renaissance and the above-mentioned great movements, worked itself out in a sequence of non-simultaneous occurrences over a lengthy time-span. Can the concept of revolution be squared with a long-drawn-out historical event? It is this conceptual question which William N. Parker brings to the forefront in the essay on the USA. By taking into account the relative contribution of the distinct national experiences in Europe and the USA, and assessing them as special cases of a more general phenomenon, the essay by Sidney Pollard adds to the conceptual range and coherence of the volume. We have accepted and put great value on the fact that the articles express the individual view and approach of the authors.

HISTORY OF THE CONCEPT

In Eric Hobsbawm's striking characterization, the Industrial Revolution 'marks the most fundamental transformation of human life in the history of the world recorded in written documents'.[4] This perspective on the Industrial Revolution has not won universal acclaim. Indeed one critic, also taking a long view, has argued not long ago that the so-called 'Industrial Revolution' should be interpreted as a continuation of the division between town and country, which appeared first in Mesopotamia 5,000 years ago:

> Instead of having experienced an 'industrial revolution', England experienced an urban evolution, as part of an age-old process of a shift of population to the towns. This change was accompanied by changes in wealth, skill, commercial practices and transport facilities. It was part of a process which can first be observed to have occurred in the Sumerian cities of 3000 BC, in which some people got much richer, and other people got poorer (slaves in the earlier case, 'wage-slaves' latterly). It is a mistake to take the idea of 'revolution' over from political to economic and social history, in order to describe changes which are best thought of as cultural.[5]

Curiously, the history of the idea, including the variously written term (Industrial Revolution, industrial revolution), has attracted little interest. The *Oxford English Dictionary* registers the term in its *Supplement* of 1933 – under the word 'industrial' – for the first time as follows:

> *Industrial Revolution*, the rapid development of machinery, which took place in England in the eighteenth and early nineteenth century.

As to the lexicographic source, the reader is referred to Arnold Toynbee's posthumous *Lectures on the Industrial Revolution in England* (1884).[6]

In the 1971 *Supplement* the wording of the entry changes:

> *industrial revolution*, a rapid development in industry; *spec.* (freq. with capital initials) the development which took place in England in the late eighteenth and early nineteenth centuries, chiefly owing to the introduction of new or improved machinery and large-scale production methods.

Furthermore, J. S. Mill is shown to have employed the term in his *Principles of Political Economy* (1848) earlier than Toynbee.

Toynbee's paternity of the term has been widely accepted in Anglo-Saxon historiography since Paul Mantoux ascribed it to him in a footnote in the 'Introduction' to his classical work *La révolution industrielle au XVIIIᵉ siècle* (1906).[7] In the English version of the slightly revised French text, first published in 1928, Mantoux expanded the information in the footnote on

the authorship of the term. Giving William Rappard's *La révolution indus-
trielle et les origines de la protection légale du travail en Suisse* (1914) as his source
Mantoux pointed out that Friedrich Engels employed the term, before
Mill, in his famed *Die Lage der arbeitenden Klasse in England* (1845).[8]

In the meantime (1922) a short article appeared, by Anna Bezanson,
demonstrating the earlier usage of the term in French literature during
the years 1820–40. At the same time, she stressed that the understanding
of 'the meaning attached to the term' is more important than the establishment of 'the date of use' and concluded: 'discussion of the real significance of the term must be part of a description of the industry of the
period'.[9]

In 1952 the noted Oxford historian G. N. Clark maintained that the
idea of the Industrial Revolution, despite being bereft of substance in historical reality, was heuristically valuable.[10]

A comprehensive attempt to deal with this topic is to be found in
Jaroslav Purš's massive *The Industrial Revolution Development of the Idea and
Concept*, published in 1973 in Czech with Russian and English summaries.
Specifically, he argues that a historico-semantic analysis of basic categories (revolution, industry, manufacture, manufactory, factory, etc.) can
throw light on the origins, uneven development, gradual dominance and
social consequences of factory production. Generally, he insists that it was
Engels with Marx who between 1844 and 1867 evolved the first serious
theory of the Industrial Revolution, and that the positive or negative
coming to terms with it underlies the further developments in this area.[11]

To claim that Marx and Engels elaborated the theory of the Industrial
Revolution is to stretch a point. What they did was use their analysis of
economic, technical, social and political aspects of the Industrial
Revolution in Britain to evolve a general theory of social development.
And it has been the latter's message heralding that socialism and communism respectively will follow capitalism, which has influenced in one
direction or another the debate regarding the nature and consequences
of the Industrial Revolution, and its place in history.

TOYNBEE'S *LECTURES* REVISITED

It is in this context that Toynbee's *Lectures on the Industrial Revolution* which
'effectively began modern discussion of the subject'[12] deserve to be revisited. All the more so since there has been a tendency to sideline Toynbee's
scholarly endeavours and influence by perceiving him primarily as the
creator of the 'pessimistic' interpretation of the social costs of the
Industrial Revolution. This point was reiterated in a critical appraisal of
him as a historical economist not long ago:

[Toynbee's] catastrophic interpretation of the social consequences of the Industrial Revolution, however, was an original contribution that laid the groundwork for an historiographical tradition in economic history, the impact of which is still felt.[13]

There is more to Toynbee's *Lectures* than the accent on the dark aspects of the Industrial Revolution[14] and statements such as the one quoted do not convey a balanced assessment of the book which, though unfinished, enjoyed a long-lasting reputation. It went through five editions between 1884 and 1908 when a cheaper edition was published which, reprinted many times, served as a textbook of English economic history until it went out of print in 1927.[15] This information is put forward in the new edition, published in 1969, with an Introduction by T. S Ashton asserting that 'this remarkable pioneer work will be welcomed by economic historians of all shades of thought, in England and elsewhere'.[16] By then and afterwards, however, Toynbee's work has received undeservedly no consideration – or a marginal one – in writings dealing with the Industrial Revolution, including contributions to this volume.[17]

We shall not attempt to analyse the reasons for the vanishing interest in Toynbee's *Lectures on the Industrial Revolution*. It is evident that in the process sight was lost of the subject matter, including methodology, Toynbee wished to explore in the first place. That is, the relations between the ideas of Adam Smith, Malthus and Ricardo and the economic and social reality engendered by the Industrial Revolution. Toynbee approached the relations between them from a standpoint that was doubtlessly indebted to Hegelian dialectic. This harmonizes with Toynbee's closeness to the Oxford protagonists of Hegel's philosophy in England, Benjamin Jowett and Thomas H. Green. The following passage from the 'Reminiscence' by Alfred Milner (Lord Milner) (who in the words of Mrs Toynbee 'shared my husband's entire intellectual life')[18] gives an indication of the place of historical and relational dialectic in Toynbee's methodology:

> The facts of economic history and the theories of economists should be studied side by side, and thus studied, they would throw light on each other. Adam Smith, Malthus, Ricardo should be interpreted by a knowledge of the industrial and social conditions of their time. This was an essential feature of Toynbee's projected work on the 'Industrial Revolution'.[19]

It is in the introductory lecture that we find the relevance of dialectics to Toynbee's solution of contrasting problems and issues, such as nature, value and relation of the historical and deductive method; universality and relativity of economic policies and laws; continuity between the past

and the present. These questions are discussed, in general as well as concrete terms, and merit being referred to extensively in order to get closer
to Toynbee's viewpoint on how history ought to be done:

> The subject of these lectures is the Industrial and Agrarian Revolution at
> the end of the eighteenth and beginning of the nineteenth centuries ... I
> have chosen the subject because it was in this period that modern Political
> Economy took its rise. It has been a weakness of the science as pursued in
> England that it has been too much dissociated from History. Adam Smith
> and Malthus, indeed, had historical minds; but the form of modern text-
> books is due to Ricardo, whose mind was entirely unhistorical. Yet there is
> double advantage in combining the two studies. In the first place Political
> Economy is better understood by this means. Abstract propositions are seen
> in a new light when studied in relation to the facts which were before the
> writer at the time when he formulated them. So regarded they are at once
> more vivid and less likely to mislead. Ricardo becomes painfully interest-
> ing when we read the history of his time. And, in the second place, History
> also is better understood when studied in connection with Political
> Economy. For the latter not only teaches us in reading History to look out
> for the right kinds of facts, but enables us to explain many phenomena like
> those attending the introduction of enclosures and machinery, or the effects
> of different systems of currency, which without its assistance would remain
> unintelligible. The careful deductive reasoning, too, which Political
> Economy teaches, is of great importance to the historian, and the habits of
> mind acquired from it are even more valuable than the knowledge of prin-
> ciples which it gives, especially to students of facts, who might otherwise be
> overwhelmed by the mass of their materials ...

> The historical method pursues a different line of investigation. It exam-
> ines the actual causes of economic development and considers the influence
> of institutions such as the mediaeval guilds, our present land-laws, or the
> political constitution of any given country, in determining the distribution
> of wealth. Without the aid of the Historical Method it would be impossi-
> ble, for instance, to understand why one-half of the land in the United
> Kingdom is owned by 2512 persons.[a]

> And not only does it investigate the stages of economic development in
> a given country, but it compares them with those which have obtained in
> other countries and times, and seeks by such comparison to discover laws
> of universal application ...

> The Historical Method is also of value because it makes us see where
> economic laws and precepts are relative.[b] The old economists were wont
> to speak as if these laws and precepts were universal. Free trade, for
> instance, is a sound policy, no doubt, for England, and for all nations at a

certain stage of development; but it is open to anyone to say that free trade is only good under certain conditions. No English economist, it is true, has dared to say this ... I do not mean to assert, however, that there are not some laws which are universally true, such as the law of diminishing returns.

The discussion about method may seem barren, but it is not really so. Take such a question as the functions of the State ... The proper limits of Government interference are relative to the nature of each particular state and the stage of its civilisation. It is a matter of great importance at the present day for us to discover what these limits are in our own case, for administration bids fair to claim a large share of our attention in the future. It would be well if, in studying the past,' we could always bear in mind the problems of the past, and go to that past to seek large views of what is of lasting importance to the human race. It is an old complaint that histories leave out of sight those vital questions which are connected with the condition of the people. The French Revolution has indeed profoundly modified our views of History, but much still remains to be done in that direction. If I could persuade some of those present to study Economic History, to follow out the impulse originally given by Malthus to the study of the history of the mass of the people, I should be indeed glad. Party historians go to the past for party purposes; they seek to read into the past the controversies of the present. You must pursue facts for their own sake, but penetrated with a vivid sense of the problems of your own time. This is not a principle of perversion, but a principle of selection. You must have some principle of selection, and you could not have a better one than to pay special attention to the history of the social problems which are agitating the world now, for you may be sure that they are problems not of temporary but of lasting importance.[20]

From such an approach arose Toynbee's perception of the Industrial Revolution as a major socio-economic event, with salient intellectual consequences, in England's as well as Europe's transition from medieval feudalism to industrial capitalism:[21]

The essence of the Industrial Revolution is the substitution of competition for the mediaeval regulations which had previously controlled the production and distribution of wealth. On this account it is not only one of the most important facts of English history, but Europe owes to it the growth of two great systems of thought – Economic Science, and its antithesis, Socialism.

It is of more than passing interest that while the first sentence in this passage has often been quoted and critically commented on, the following one has hardly attracted attention. It is in the light of Toynbee's core thesis that his concern with the socio-political and ideological repercussions of the Industrial Revolution in England has to be viewed. Consider the dissolution of the patriarchal relationship between the employer and the employed which he described as follows:[22]

> Between the individual workman and the capitalist who employed hundreds of 'hands' a wide gulf opened: the workman ceased to be the cherished dependant, he became the living tool of whom the employer knew less than he did of his steam-engine ... The destruction of the old bonds between employers and workmen was not peculiar to manufactures; it came to pass in agriculture also. An agrarian as well as an industrial revolution had taken place.

Toynbee acknowledges that there could be no return to what he depicted 'as a state of feudal dependence', which, 'like all feudalism has its dark and light sides'.[23] But what was the nature of the worker's relationship with the employer in capitalist society? More specifically, was the worker really free to express his point of view (political independence) without jeopardizing his liberty to sell his labour (material independence)? The resolving of this issue is the theme of Toynbee's last lecture, 'The future of the working classes' and of the address 'Are radicals socialists?', which was 'delivered in the earlier part of 1882 to audiences of workmen and employers at Newcastle, Bradford, Bolton and Leicester'.[24]

At the heart of Toynbee's solution, much in agreement with contemporary liberal radical thinking, was social reform directed towards assimilating working-class political activism to middle-class political perspectives. The fostering of class collaboration was to be underpinned by giving workers adequate material rewards for which Toynbee called. Apart from general class consent, Toynbee admitted rather reluctantly that for setting such reform into motion and for making it function backing by the state was needed. While claiming that this represented English Radical socialism, which he espoused, he rejected what he took to be Tory socialism and continental (German) socialism on diverging grounds:[25]

> We differ from Tory Socialism in so far as we are in favour, not of paternal, but of fraternal government, and we differ from Continental Socialism because we accept the principle of private property, and repudiate confiscation and violence. With Mazzini, the worst feature in Continental Socialism is its materialism. It is this indeed which utterly separated English Radical Socialists from Continental Socialists – our abhorrence and detestation of their materialistic ideal.[26]

Toynbee's advocacy of a policy allowing workers in Britain to increase their earnings relates to her status as the leading colonial power. Indeed, the colonialist perspective made use of by Toynbee to strengthen his case for making the English worker in material terms better off comes through clearly:

> I repeat, we demand increased material welfare for those who labour with their hands, not that they may seize upon a few more coarse enjoyments, but that they may enter upon a purer and higher life. We demand it also that the English workman may take his part worthily in the government of this country. We demand it in order that he may have the intelligence and the will to administer the great trust which fate has committed to his charge; for it is not only his own home and his own country that he has to govern, but a vast empire − a duty unparalleled in the annals of democracy. We demand it, I say, in order that he, a citizen of this inclement island, washed by dark northern seas, may learn to rule righteously the dim multitudes of peasants who toil under the fierce light of tropical suns, in the distant continent of India. We demand that the material condition of those who labour shall be bettered, in order that, every source of weakness being removed at home, we, this English nation, may bring to the tasks which God has assigned us, the irresistible strength of a prosperous and united people.[27]

Recently one of the masters of historical scholarship, Keith Thomas, observed critically that: 'For the most part British historians remain a stolidly untheoretical lot ...'[28] This is in line with what John Hicks (Nobel Memorial Prize for Economics, 1972) noted a quarter of a century ago. Venturing to develop a theory of history 'nearer to the kind of thing that was attempted by Marx', he stated:

> What remains an open question is whether it can only be done on a limited scale, for special purposes, or whether it can be done in a larger way, so that the general course of history, at least in some important aspects can be fitted into place. Most of those who take the latter view would use the Marxian categories or some modified version of them; since there is so little in the way of an alternative version that is available, it is not surprising that they should. It does, nevertheless, remain extraordinary that one hundred years after *Das Kapital*, after a century during which there have been enormous developments in social science, so little else should have emerged. Surely it is possible that Marx was right in his vision of logical processes at work in history, but that we, with much knowledge of fact and social logic which he did not possess, and with another century of experience at our disposal, should conceive of the nature of those processes in a distinctly difference way.[29]

Toynbee's blending of interests in theoretical problems of economics and history with regard for practical social justice is not in doubt. Is it then far-fetched to suggest that his approach, differing as it did from Marxism ideologically and politically, echoed its orientation on the unity of theory and practice? Be that as it may, Toynbee's *Lectures* should rightfully be restored to the historiography of the Industrial Revolution and not merely for reverential purposes.

NOTES

1 Regarding the juxtaposition of the Neolithic Revolution and the Industrial Revolution, see C. M. Cipolla, 'Introduction' in C. M. Cipolla (ed.), *The Fontana Economic History of Europe: The Industrial Revolution* (London and Glasgow, 1973), pp. 7–8. See also, by the same author, *The Economic History of World Population* (Harmondsworth, 1962), chap. 1.

2 R. M. Hartwell (ed.), *The Causes of the Industrial Revolution in England* (London, 1967), 'Introduction', p. 1.

3 What emerged variously from the contributions on Central and Eastern Europe is the socio-economic significance of the feudal system of forced labour, lasting in the Habsburg Monarchy until 1848 and in Russia until 1861. Also the treatment of terms such as 'manufacture' and 'manufactory' is of interest. They are regarded – as by Adam Smith – as large-scale handicraft production based on division and combination of distinct operations, in contrast to production by machines ('machinofacture'). Cf. A. Smith, *An Inquiry into the Nature and Cause of the Wealth of Nations* (eds. R. H. Campbell, A. S. Skinner and W. B. Todd), 2 vols. (Oxford, 1976), i, chaps. 1–3.

4 E. J. Hobsbawn, *Industry and Empire* (Harmondsworth, 1969), p. 13.

5 M. Fores, 'The myth of a British industrial revolution', *History*, 66 (1981), pp. 181–98 (pp. 196–7).

6 The book's full title was: *Lectures on the Industrial Revolution in England. Popular Addresses, Notes and Other Fragments Together with a Short Memoir by B. Jowett* (London, 1884). According to Toynbee's wife (Charlotte Maria): 'Of all that is contained in the volume nothing was left by my husband in a form intended for publication; ... though he had industriously collected in note-books a mass of materials, at the time of his death [1883 – eds.] he left nothing ready for publication; a fact which will account for the fragmentary character and unequal merit of the contents of the present volume ... The lectures as they now appear have been prepared for publication by Mr W. J. Ashley, B.A., and Mr. Bolton King, B.A., of Balliol College, from their own excellent notes compared with those of others among his hearers and with such of his own as belonged to the course. They remain notes and notes only, those of the later lectures being much less full than those of the earlier ones; ...' See 'Prefatory Note', pp. xxix–xxxi. Ever since the book was published, it has been assumed that the edited printed text reproduced reasonably accurately Toynbee's thinking.

7 P. Mantoux, *La révolution industrielle au XVIIIᵉ siècle. Essai sur les commencements de la grande industrie moderne en Angleterre* (Paris, 1906), p. 1.

8 P. Mantoux, *The Industrial Revolution in the Eighteenth Century. An Outline of the Beginnings of the Modern Factory System in England*, rev. edn. translated by Marjorie Vernon (London, 1928), p. 25, n. 1. (The note occurs in what is ostensibly an altered 'Introduction to the First Edition'.) Engels's book is probably most accessible in *Marx Engels Werke* (Berlin, 1962), vol. 11, pp. 225ff. For a by-no-means unproblematic English version, see F. Engels, *The Condition of the Working Class in England*, translated and edited by W. O. Henderson and W. H. Chaloner (Oxford, 1958).

9 Anna Bezanson, 'The early use of the term industrial revolution', *Quarterly Journal of Economics*, 36 (1922), pp. 343–9 (pp. 348–9).

10 G. N. Clark, *The Idea of the Industrial Revolution* (Glasgow, 1953), pp. 32–3.

11 J. Purš, *Průmyslová revoluce Vývoj pojmu a koncepce* (Prague, 1973), cf. p. 694.

12 D. Cannadine, 'The present and the past in the English Industrial Revolution 1880–1980', *Past & Present*, 104 (1984), pp. 131–72 (p. 132).

13 G. M. Koot, *English Historical Economics, 1870–1926: The Rise of Economic History and Neomercantilism* (Cambridge, 1987), p. 89.

14 See also the one good book-length study of Toynbee's life and work by A. Kadish, *Apostle Arnold: The Life and Death of Arnold Toynbee 1852–1883* (Duke University Press, 1988).

15 A. Toynbee, *Lectures on the Industrial Revolution of the Eighteenth Century in England: Popular Addresses, Notes, and Other Fragments New Edition Together with a Reminiscence by Lord Milner* (London, 1908).

16 *Toynbee's Industrial Revolution. A Reprint of Lectures on the Industrial Revolution in England, Popular Addresses, Notes and Other Fragments, With a New Introduction by the late Professor T. S. Ashton* (Newton Abbot, 1969).

17 Indeed, T. S. Ashton does not include the book in the bibliography (revised 1968) in his celebrated *The Industrial Revolution 1760–1830* (Oxford, 1968). It appears not to be referred to by D. S. Landes, *The Unbound Prometheus. Technological Change and Industrial Development in Western Europe from 1750 to the Present* (Cambridge, 1969). It is not mentioned in the reading lists suggested by P. Mathias, *The First Industrial Nation. An Economic History of Britain 1700–1914* (London, 1969). It is missing from the bibliography given by D. Winch, 'The emergence of economics as a science 1750–1870', in Cipolla (ed.), *The Industrial Revolution*, p. 507. It is not referred to by P. K. O'Brien either in 'Agriculture and the industrial revolution', *The Economic History Review*, 2nd ser., 20 (1977), pp. 166–81, or in 'Do we have a typology for the study of European industrialization in the XIXth century?', *Journal of European Economic History*, 15 (1986), 291–333. It has no place in the bibliography supplied by N. F. R. Crafts, *British Economic Growth during the Industrial Revolution* (Oxford, 1985). It is not included in E. Jay and R. Jay (eds.), *Critics of Capitalism: Victorian Reactions to 'Political Economy'* (Cambridge, 1986). It is not brought up by M. Berg and P. Hudson, 'Rehabilitating the industrial revolution', *The Economic History Review*, 45 (1992), pp. 24–50. It is briefly referred to or discussed, apart from the already-mentioned writings by Cannadine, 'The present and the past' and G. M. Koot, *English Historical Economics*, by P. Deane, *The First Industrial*

Revolution (Cambridge, 1965), including her essay in this volume; M. W. Flinn, *The Origins of the Industrial Revolution* (London, 1966); W. W. Rostow, *The Stages of Economic Growth*, 2nd edn (Cambridge, 1971). More and critical attention has been given to Toynbee's work by R. M. Hartwell, *The Industrial Revolution and Economic Growth* (London, 1971), and recently by D. C. Coleman, *Myth, History and the Industrial Revolution* (London and Rio Grande, 1992), pp. 19–26. Coleman's discussion contains a rare, albeit brief, examination of the relationship between the notions of Industrial Revolution developed by Marx and Engels, and Toynbee respectively.

18 C. M. Toynbee, 'Prefatory Note' in Toynbee, *Lectures* (1884), p. xxxi.

19 Lord Milner, 'Reminiscence' in Toynbee, *Lectures* (1908), p. xxii.

20 Toynbee (1884), pp. 27–32.

Notes to the quoted text:

a The owners of properties over 3000 acres, and yielding a rental of at least £3000 are 2512; they own:

England and Wales	14,287,373 acres out of 34,344,226.
Scotland	14,118, 164 acres out of 18,986,694.
Ireland	9,120,689 acres out of 20,316,129.

b Comte was one of the first to recognise this truth, and it was from him that Mill learned that 'the deductive science of society will not lay down a theorem ascertaining in a universal manner the effect of any cause, but will rather teach us how to frame the proper theorem for the circumstances of any given case. It will not give the laws of society in general, but the means of determining the phenomena of any given society from the particular elements or data of that society.' – *System of Logic*, bk. vi. c. 9, 2.

c Toynbee was addressing an audience principally composed of men studying for the History Schools – Ed.

21 *Ibid.*, p. 85

22 *Ibid.*, p. 191.

23 *Ibid.*, p. 148.

24 *Ibid.*, p. 203.

25 *Ibid.*, pp. 219–20.

26 The question-mark hanging over Toynbee's acquaintance with continental writings on socialism is how deep it was. In the book Toynbee mentions Karl Marx and Ferdinand Lassalle, whom he describes as the best-known 'if recent European theorists' on communism (*ibid.*, p. 150). While Toynbee refers to the French translation of *Das Kapital* (the English version appeared after his death in 1886), he appears to have obtained knowledge regarding Lassalle's ideas second-hand. Toynbee wrongly associates Marx with Lassalle's 'brazen law of wages' (pp. 130–8). Indeed, Marx explicitly rejects this notion in the *Critique of the Gotha Programme* (K. Marx and F. Engels, *Selected Works*, vol. III (Moscow, 1973), pp. 22–4.) On the other hand, Toynbee understood and agreed with Marx's analysis of surplus value (p. 130).

27 Toynbee, *Lectures* (1884), pp. 220–1.

28 K. Thomas, 'The death of certainty', *The Guardian*, 6 Sept. 1994.

29 J. Hicks, *A Theory of Economic History* (repr. Oxford, 1973), p. 223.

ONE

The British Industrial Revolution

PHYLLIS DEANE

INTERPRETING THE INDUSTRIAL REVOLUTION

THE Industrial Revolution has been a familiar landmark in British economic history for most of the twentieth century. The first text to focus on it appeared as long ago as 1884, having been reconstructed posthumously from notes of lectures delivered in Oxford in 1880/1 by a 27-year-old Balliol don and aspiring Liberal MP, Arnold Toynbee. Since then, and especially after the Second World War, it has attracted intensive academic research on an international scale. For it has been conventionally depicted as the precursor of (and sometimes as the model for) a long line of later industrial revolutions ushering in the 'modern epoch of economic growth in today's developed market economies'.[1] That such a diligently researched, familiarly deployed concept should still require clarification might seem surprising; but there is no doubt that it does. Successive generations of twentieth-century scholars, each bringing new questions, new evidence and new analytical techniques to bear upon this watershed in national economic development have systematically reinterpreted it to match their contemporary problem situations. Some economic historians, repelled by the unscientific quality of a concept that adapts in chameleon-fashion to the circumstances in which it is used, regard it as an imprecise idea at best, and at worst a positive hindrance to objective analysis.[2] But, as the title of this volume illustrates, the notion of an industrial revolution, viewed as a major turning-point in the history of a national economy, continues to provoke serious discussion and research. Evidently, an author proposing to explore some aspects of the Industrial Revolution needs first to clarify his/her own vision of its substance and significance and to identify the current research context – the state of the art, as it were, conditioning that viewpoint.

Inspiration for the post Second World War escalation of research on the British Industrial Revolution stemmed largely from its apparent relevance to some of the leading analytical and policy problems then preoccupying social scientists generally and economists in particular. It was an era when theorists were excited by recent developments in the pure theory of economic growth; and when applied economists, seeking explanations for national economic progress and decline, were using the concepts and ideas of modern growth theory to provide an analytical framework for comparative analyses of the historical and contemporary records of developed and underdeveloped economies. At the same time, macroeconomic perspectives and quantitative techniques inherited from the Keynesian revolution in economic ideas were shaping the way most economists tended to formulate their research problems – at least until the late 1960s. Given that much of the new work on the British Industrial Revolution was then being conducted by economic historians trained in faculties of economics (rather than of history) it is hardly surprising that their research results have transformed pre-war perceptions of its substance, dimensions and chronology.

The first important postwar text on the topic was T. S Ashton's brilliantly fresh and original monograph which appeared in the late 1940s and focused broadly on the period 1760–1830 – then the conventional chronological benchmarks. After insisting that the changes involved in an industrial revolution 'were not merely "industrial" but also social and intellectual' he warned against overstressing the discontinuity of the processes he was describing: 'The word "revolution" implies a suddenness of change that is not, in fact, characteristic of economic processes. The system of human relationships that is sometimes called capitalism had its origins long before 1760, and attained its full development long after 1830; there is danger of overlooking the fact of continuity.'[3] However, some years later, after further research and exposure to the current ferment of ideas on economic growth, Ashton had sharpened his focus to favour a more precise starting point, on the macroeconomic quantitative grounds that: 'If, however, what is meant by the industrial revolution is a sudden quickening in the pace of output we must move the date forward, and not backward, from 1782. After 1782 almost every statistical series of production shows a sharp upward turn.'[4] A year later, in 1956, an American economist, W. W. Rostow, fired the opening shot in what became an influential debate by presenting his dramatic interpretation of the British Industrial Revolution as the first 'take-off into self-sustained growth'. This he claimed was 'a rather old-fashioned way of looking at economic development. The take-off is defined as an industrial revolution, tied directly to radical changes in methods of production, having their decisive consequence over a relatively short period of time.'[5]

There was, however, nothing 'old-fashioned' about the notion of the first Industrial Revolution as a major discontinuity in the process of industrialization during which the British economy was launched irreversibly into 'self-sustained growth' within a couple of decades (1783–1802); nor about the proposition that it was feasible to locate a period of two or three decades of industrial growth within which Rostow hypothesized that eight other currently developed countries had achieved the transition to modern economic growth by 1914. When the 1956 article was expanded into Rostow's Non-Communist Manifesto – *The Stages of Economic Growth* (1960) – the persuasive power of an imaginative metaphor was widely demonstrated.[6] For, considered as the prototype for 'that decisive interval in the history of a society when growth becomes its normal condition',[7] the term 'take-off' rapidly became synonymous with 'industrial revolution' in the textbooks. Hobsbawm, for example, was reflecting widespread academic opinion in 1962 when he defined the outbreak of the first Industrial Revolution in Rostowian terms: 'It means that some time in the 1780s, and for the first time in human history, the shackles were taken off the productive power of human societies, which henceforth became capable of the constant, rapid and up to the present limitless multiplication of men, goods and services. This is now technically known to the economists as the "take-off into self-sustained growth".'[8]

As critical reaction to, and empirical testing of, Rostow's take-off theory unfolded in the 1960s, direct estimates of some of the macroeconomic magnitudes that (implicitly or explicitly) underpinned it were beginning to emerge from an international research programme (originally launched by Simon Kuznets in the 1950s) into the long-term economic growth of nations.[9] These results provided little evidence to confirm such a sudden and massive discontinuity in national economic performance for any of the countries to which Rostow had assigned 'tentative approximate take-off dates'.[10] Indeed, as far as British experience was concerned, later and better-informed quantitative studies published in the 1970s and 1980s offered even less support than the earlier estimates had done for the hypothesis of a sudden acceleration in national productivity growth beginning in the late eighteenth century.[11] The data base for the relevant historical measures of British economic growth and structure is still extremely fragile; but more than three decades of systematic quantitative researches have yielded improvements in the quality both of the available data and of the processing techniques deployed by leading economic historians. The results so far published now point, still tentatively, to two conclusions: first that such acceleration as occurred in the national rate of British economic growth during the late eighteenth and early nineteenth centuries represented the culmination of a long-drawn-out process, an evolutionary rather than a revolutionary development; and second that the British experience of industrialization differed in significant respects from that of any of the countries which industrialized subsequently.

In thus emphasizing the evolutionary characteristics of British industrialization, most of today's active researchers in the field share Ashton's 1948 concern with the continuity of the underlying process of economic change.[12] Apparently the revolutionary significance of the set of interrelated innovations which spread through certain limited sectors of British industry during the last third of the eighteenth century lies more in its long-term social and economic consequences than in its instant impact on national economic performance. According to Mokyr, for example: 'The main reason why we think of the Industrial Revolution as a "revolution" is that its effects were so profound that even if we divide it by seventy the per annum change was far-reaching enough to dwarf any change in Britain since the Black Death.'[13] Evidently, locating the decisive economic changes in time and space hinges crucially on the historical perspective and hindsight of the analyst. Eighteenth-century observers were not themselves generally conscious of living through an industrial revolution, though the new spirit of innovation that characterized the later decades of the century did not go unnoticed. 'The age is running wild after innovation', scoffed Samuel Johnson, for example; 'All the business of the world is to be done in a new way: men are to be hanged in a new way; Tyburn itself is not safe from the fury of innovation.'[14] By the 1830s, however, observant contemporaries such as Babbage and Ure were wide awake to the fact that the innovations which had taken place in manufacturing industry had already had revolutionary consequences for national economic progress.[15]

ESSENCE OF THE FIRST INDUSTRIAL REVOLUTION

This chapter envisages the Industrial Revolution as a decisive shift in methods of industrial production, a historically unique breakthrough in an evolutionary process of technological change, rather than as a discrete event occurring in a brief, sharply demarcated time-span. At its heart lay the development and rapid diffusion of a set of dynamically interrelated innovations in manufacturing technology, together involving profound organizational changes and continuously rising productivity for a group of industries which became the expanding core of a modern industrial nation. The distinctive growing points of the process of British industrialization were in the cotton, iron, engineering, machine tool and transport industries. But even in its early stages, in the last three decades of the eighteenth century, when the pace of innovation in these sectors began to gather spectacular joint momentum, they carried along with them other less strategically significant industries (such as pottery and papermaking) which also began to modernize their modes of production. What was revolutionary about the gamut of technical changes that developed in Britain between the 1760s and the 1860s was that they generated a new technological system, based on the massive application to manufacturing processes of powerful, precise, continuously improvable machinery, having far-reaching organizational, structural and social consequences for the economy as a whole.

The cotton industry presented the most dramatic example of rapid transition from a traditional, loosely organized, geographically dispersed, putting-out system of production, dependent on hand-tool technology, to a centrally managed and centrally located factory system using large-scale machinery, powered by inanimate sources of energy. Three highly productive and progressively improvable machines – Hargreaves' spinning-jenny, Arkwright's water-frame and Crompton's mule – together transformed both the quantity and the quality of the yarn that could be delivered by an individual spinner. In so doing they were able to exploit an already substantial and price-elastic domestic demand for the fine calicoes and muslins that had hitherto been supplied by imports from India. To begin with, the new spinning mills could be (and were) operated by hand, horse and/or water power. However, they could not have raised productivity and lowered costs of production in the cotton industry so fast, or so continuously, had it not been for their chronological coincidence with a complementary set of equally remarkable innovations in iron-producing techniques and in the steam engine. In the long term, technical progress in the production of iron and of steam power was to prove crucial in maintaining the momentum of British industrialization generally. For it directly reduced the costs of, and enlarged the scope for, large-scale mechanized production, not merely in textiles but in a widening variety of other industries.

The patterns of interaction between these technological subsystems involved complex forward and backward linkages, and demonstration effects, which developed over nine or ten decades from the 1760s, and are not easily encapsulated in a brief account. The iron industry – itself the leading prototype for large-scale, heavily capitalized and integrated factory operations – supplied a wide range of durable construction materials for machinery (including steam engines) and machine tools of all types, for transport equipment (bridges, railways, wagons, ships and locomotives) as well as for the framework of multistorey, fireproof buildings designed to accommodate heavy plant and machinery. By the first decade of the nineteenth century the annual output of British pig-iron had grown eightfold compared with its level in the 1760s. Watt's steam engine contributed considerably to this expansion of output and to the rapid diffusion of late-eighteenth-century innovations in iron smelting and refining as well as to the progress in machine tool technology that characterized the 1790–1825 period. When used to power water-pumping and hoisting gear, for example, steam gave access to cheaper and better coal and iron ore from ever deeper seams. When applied to the ironworks furnace, it could generate a blast strong enough to burn coke (instead of charcoal) thus permitting continuous operation of plant and machinery wherever coal and iron were available in close proximity. Moreover, the economies of scale and locational flexibility associated with the use of steam power encouraged the ironmaster to integrate sequential stages of the manufacturing operation in massive ironworks equipped with the latest mechanical technology and power systems. Although industrialists were experimenting with steam to drive machinery in textile spinning, carding and weaving, in flour and paper mills, and in breweries, from the late eighteenth century onwards, they did so with limited and sporadic success until well into the nineteenth century, while water-power technology continued steadily to advance. Even in the leading sector, cotton spinning, up to the 1830s according to von Tunzelmann: 'The largest mills, in which one might have expected the greatest economies to be reaped, were still generally water-powered. The exception was provided by some fine spinning mills, so that steam supported the substantial cheapening of finer yarns that had begun in the late 1780s, with noticeable effects on both exports and clothing fashion in Britain.'[16] It was not until the 1840s and 1850s, when the development and diffusion of high-pressure steam engines appreciably reduced the costs of using steam, that textile industries generally began to find it the most economical source of power.

By the middle of the nineteenth century it was obvious that the technological advances taking place in certain limited sectors of late-eighteenth-century British industry, had triggered a continuing process of technological and organizational change that had already transformed the character, structure and productive potential of the nation's economic system. When the 1851 International Exhibition held at London's Crystal Palace demonstrated the technological superiority of 'the workshop of the world', Britain was evidently the richest nation (in terms of income per head), the fastest growing (in terms of total output and share in the value of world trade), the most industralized (in terms of the percentage of national product generated in industry) and the most urbanized. To quote McCloskey:

> In the eighty years or so after 1780 the population of Britain nearly tripled, the towns of Liverpool and Manchester became gigantic cities, the average income of the population more than doubled, the share of farming fell from just under half to just under one-fifth of the nation's output, and the making of textiles and iron moved into the steam-driven factories. So strange were

these events that before they happened they were not anticipated, and while they were happening they were not comprehended ... The British economy from 1780 to 1860 was unpredictable because it was novel, not to say bizarre. [17]

The British Industrial Revolution was of course novel because it was the first. But recent research into the experience of European countries which industrialized during the nineteenth century suggests that there were other respects in which it was a special case – in particular that it developed from a radically different starting point and followed an atypical path to modern economic growth.[18] O'Brien, for example, has emphasized its geographical position, in analysing the circumstances which gave it an edge over its leading commercial rivals in the eighteenth century:

> Located at the hub of a rapidly growing Atlantic economy, when waterborne transport was the cheapest way to conduct commerce, a small island was more likely to reap larger gains from oceanic trade than continental powers. That locational advantage was, moreover, safeguarded by persistently high levels of public investment in sea power which over the long run lowered transaction costs for British merchants, provided favoured access to imperial and foreign markets and weakened the economies of their Iberian, Dutch and French rivals.[19]

However, this is not the place to attempt a comprehensive analysis of the national environment within which the British Industrial Revolution developed its distinctive characteristics. Instead, I propose to focus on three broad facets of that environment which I judge to have been of critical importance in relation to the timing, pace and pattern of British industrialization, namely the political, the demographic and the agrarian context.

The first Industrial Revolution was as much a part of Scottish as of English or Welsh history. Accordingly, in this chapter, what is generally meant by the term 'nation' is the British nation. However, in discussing the political context one has to bear in mind that it was not until 1707 that the Act of Union united the polity and the economy of north and south Britain into a free-trade area governed by a single parliament.

POLITICAL AND FINANCIAL CONTEXT

Undoubtedly the most important feature distinguishing Britain from those European nations which had reached comparable levels of economic development by 1700 was the form of government that emerged when the constitutional conflicts of the seventeenth century were resolved in 1688.

For it was then that the English aristocracy won its long battle against absolutism 'whether of King or Protector, whether Anglican, Puritan or Catholic'.[20] The so-called Glorious Revolution established a contractual monarchy in which the authority for decisions on national economic policy – such as decisions to raise or spend public revenue, to formulate and implement legislation constraining private economic activity, or to wage wars with the aim of defending or extending imperial markets – rested on the consent of both houses of parliament. While most eighteenth-century European parliaments found their political role increasingly marginalized by an authoritarian state, the Westminster parliament met annually, and for more months in each year than ever before. The House of Commons in particular assumed an increasingly wide range of legislative or administrative functions. It initiated, or approved, or amended, a variety of national, local and private bills bearing on the policing and defence of the realm, or on matters of economic development – such as those relating to municipal or company charters, or enclosures or roads, or canals, or ports and eventually railways. It legitimated tax increases, investigated corrupt government officials and debated the management procedures of public departments as well as a swelling stream of petitions submitted to it by aggrieved citizens or ambitious interest groups.

In principle, the House of Commons was an elected body representing the national interest. In practice, its conception of what constituted the public interest was, throughout the eighteenth century and well into the nineteenth, dominated by the views of the landowners. Most of the eighteenth-century members of parliament were either considerable landowners themselves, or were the relatives or friends of landowners.

They were elected (on the increasingly rare occasions when elections were held or contested) by property holders subject to social or economic pressure from large landowners or their nominees – such as the Justices of the Peace or the Anglican clergy. They were manipulated by a Cabinet largely drawn from the House of Lords and able to dispense patronage over a wide range of offices, livings and sinecures. By 1760, according to Beckett, for example: 'English government was in the hands of an aristocratic oligarchy. Members of the great landed families controlled the offices of state, positions in the executive, the House of Lords and a considerable proportion of the House of Commons.'[21] Of the 65 individuals who held Cabinet office over the period 1782–1830, a total of 57 were either peers or the sons of peers.[22] The landed classes also dominated local government, for the Justices of the Peace were appointed by the aristocracy from among the gentry. Even after the 1832 Reform Act, a property qualification determined who might vote at local and central levels and the aristocratic grip on government remained strong. In short, the system of government established by the English Revolution of 1688 was entrenched in property, held together by patronage and inspired by an ideal of liberty, where liberty meant the freedom of the individual to dispose of his or her property with the minimum of autocratic interference. The levers of power were thus firmly held by a wealthy, but open, elite whose members had a tradition of public service and a well-integrated set of broad policy objectives in which the maintenance of public order and the security of property took absolute priority.

It is not surprising, therefore, that amongst the earliest legislative enactments of the post-Revolution government were two statutes (passed in 1689 and 1694) that gave the landowners exclusive rights to all the minerals under their land except gold and silver. They thus acquired a personal interest in promoting industrial as well as agrarian development. Harold Perkin, for example, has argued that the landowners favoured economic policies conducive to a spontaneous industrial revolution: 'They abolished most of the restrictions on internal industry, ignored those on building, forgot the anti-enclosure acts, and exchanged corn trade controls for bounties on coal exports. During the eighteenth century they allowed the wage-fixing and apprenticeship clauses of the Statute of Artificers to fall gradually into disuse.'[23] They also encouraged a shift in the weight of taxation away from direct and towards indirect taxes, so favouring the rich merchant or industrialist as well as the large landowner. By the 1730s the land tax accounted for less than a quarter of a much-increased and still increasing public revenue, most of which was raised by regressive customs and excise duties falling on consumer goods in inelastic demand.

As it turned out, the eighteenth-century legislative framework against which the first Industrial Revolution originated was coloured by a predominantly mercantilist ideology and shaped by parliament's reactions to the competing interest groups demanding its attention and support. A recent study of pressure-group activity over the period 1696–1774, for example, analysed legislation instrumental in the cotton industry's spectacular rise from relative insignificance to the leading mechanized, factory-based sector of British industry, and concluded that: 'In retrospect British pragmatism appears more productive than Dutch free trade or French-style mercantilism ... Parliament not only encouraged the dyeing and printing of [imported Asian] textiles to mature, its legislative enactments in 1736–74 helped to transform fustian into a mechanized cotton industry.'[24]

Ultimately, however, it is arguable that it was the financial implications of the relatively stable constitutional environment emerging from the late-seventeenth-century settlement that had most influence on the timing and character of the first Industrial Revolution. The indisputable authority of the king in parliament was the rock on which, over the first few decades of the eighteenth century, was erected a highly centralized and effective fiscal system that enabled the British government to fund smoothly and to wage successfully, a series of major wars against France – then the leading power in Europe, with almost two and a half times the productive capacity of Britain.[25] Central to that fiscal system was the Treasury, which by 1685 had gained political control over revenue collection, abolished the inefficient system of tax-farming, and centralized receipts at the Exchequer. When, in the following decade, it also assumed control over the spending departments, England became the first major European power to keep full annual accounts of public revenue and expenditure. These were the initial stages in a gradual professionalization of the British system of public finance. A relatively well-administered system of tax collection enabled central government to extract a substantially increased level of taxation per head of a growing population during the eighteenth century.[26] Customs and excise duties, for example, which constituted the bulk of central government's tax revenues, were collected by centrally appointed officials; land tax, which provided most of the rest, was administered by provincially appointed assessors and collectors, well-informed about the eligible taxpayers in their locality. Probably more important still, however, was the fact that public resistance to frequent wartime tax increases was minimized, on the one hand by the overwhelming authority of parliamentary consent, and on the other by the even-handedness of a uniform system of charges. In contrast to the situation in most European countries, no class in the British community could claim exemption from customs and excise and no landowner could avoid land tax.

The other source of finance open to a stable administration was the National Debt. Before 1689 the government's borrowing options were virtually limited to high-interest, short-term loans, secured on the annual yield of specified taxes and paid off when the taxes came in. During the 1690s, however, the government exploited its special access to Dutch financial expertise and experimented with various innovations in borrowing techniques. Substantial sums were raised from the general public, for example, through the medium of tontine or lottery loans. Long-term loans were negotiated with joint-stock companies which could be persuaded to charge relatively modest rates of interest in return for their charters of incorporation. The most powerful, privileged and durable of the new chartered companies, however, was the Bank of England, founded in 1694, which advanced the whole of its capital to the state in the form of bills that were readily acceptable to the government's creditors because they represented a liquid, interest-earning asset that was instantly convertible into cash (i.e. into Bank notes). In 1696 the Exchequer introduced its own negotiable interest-earning bill, designed to provide the government with instant short-term credit in emergency situations. Holders of Exchequer bills could either apply them directly to the payment of certain taxes when they became due, or convert them into notes at the Bank. It was soon plain that the Bank was more competent to take over the management of the National Debt than the Treasury's own officials. Indeed, by the time the Bank's charter was renewed in 1707, it had become the principal agent channelling short-term loans to the government as well as the manager of the long-term funded debt provided by the great trading companies. The result of these developments in public-credit machinery was a massive expansion in the National Debt during each period of war.[27] Significantly, the cost to the Exchequer of an almost eightfold increase in the value of the Debt between the end of the War of the English Succession (1698) and the end of the Seven Years War (1764) was not much more than a trebling of the net annual debt charges.[28]

The upshot of this transformation in the English (and after the 1707 Union with Scotland, the British) system of public finance was twofold. In the first place it strengthened the economic power of the central government by giving it virtual immunity from the financial crises that plagued most of its European rivals. In the second place, and as a by-product of the massive increase in the National Debt, it contributed directly to the modernization of the nation's credit institutions, to the integration of its capital market and to the development of a prosperous and efficient financial sector.

John Brewer has described the 'emergence of a peculiarly British version of the fiscal-military state, complete with large armies and navies, industrious administrators and huge debts'.[29] This, in effect, was what turned a divided and relatively insignificant military power under the Stuarts into one of the heaviest weights in the European balance of power by the 1760s. Of course there were economic costs involved in the incessant wars that dominated the activities of the British government over most of the period between 1689 and 1815. But it is notable that the direct and indirect costs of these wars were generally higher for Britain's military and commercial rivals, especially for France where they precipitated a series of financial and political crises. Moreover to the extent that they achieved their objectives of widening and deepening overseas markets, especially the fast-growing North American markets, at the expense of their foreign competitors, they made a positive contribution to the climate of industrial investment in the run-up to the first Industrial Revolution. According to Davis, for example, the population of the North American colonies 'rose

tenfold between 1700 and 1774 and their income even faster. They spent
the greater part of their export earnings on British manufactures, of all
kinds except for the coarsest woollens and linens made within the household and some simple wooden and iron wares.'[30] Meanwhile, the traditional European markets for British manufactured exports became
increasingly defensive through the eighteenth century. Thus, between
1699/1701 and 1772/1774 exports of manufactures from England to
America, Africa and Asia multiplied more than sevenfold, compared with
a rise of little more than 13 per cent to continental Europe, which had
taken over four-fifths of the total in the early years of the century and less
than 43 per cent by the early 1770s.[31] Nor did the war that Britain lost –
the American War of Independence (1775–83) – disturb her expanding
channels of trade with the fast-growing Atlantic economy for much more
than a decade. From 1783 onwards her traditionally large public investment in the Royal Navy continued to win a larger share in the American
market for manufactures than any of her competitors could command.
Indeed, during the late eighteenth and early nineteenth centuries Britain
had more to gain than any of them from the trading connection with the
United States. For not only did it offer a rising demand for the exports of
the cotton industry – a leading sector in the first Industrial Revolution –
it also provided that industry's essential raw material, at a rapidly falling
cost after Eli Whitney's invention of the cotton gin in 1793.

DEMOGRAPHIC CONTEXT

The linkages between demographic and socio-economic change are so
complex and mutually interactive that it is rarely easy to discriminate
conclusively between variant interpretations of the dynamic processes
affecting actual historical trends – even where the data are reasonably full
and reliable. Nor, if it does seem possible to identify patterns of association between economic change and population trends, can they be
presumed to constitute durable relationships. Ronald Lee, for example,
has distinguished between short, medium and long-term patterns of interaction, arguing that long-run shifts in the rate of growth of a nation's
population (and it is the long run that concerns us here) are generally
explicable in terms of changing trends in the demand for labour, which
in turn hinge on the combined effects of such factors as climate, natural
resources and technology, as well as the institutions governing prevailing
systems of production and trade.[32] On the other side of the coin, of
course, the size, density, age- or ethnic-composition, and rural–urban
distribution of a nation's population may have important consequences
for the character and pace of organizational and technological change.

At present the basis for estimates of English long-term population trends and structure is better than for any other western European country, largely as a result of recent work by Wrigley and Schofield.[33] Their reconstruction of the population history of England concludes that:

> Rapid population growth in the sixteenth century provoked a sharp fall in living standards, which in turn was followed by a falling away in population growth so pronounced as to produce a 30-year period during which population fell and a much longer period lasting 65 years during which population was below the peak total reached in 1656. After the early decades of the eighteenth century, however, the population growth rate accelerated and real wages first grew more slowly and then declined, paralleling closely events 200 years earlier.[34]

For Great Britain as a whole the best estimates currently available suggest a modest overall increase in the first half of the eighteenth century, from *circa* 6½ million in 1700 to 7½ million in 1750.[35] Then in the second half of the century, as the Industrial Revolution gathered momentum, British population moved into an exponential mode of growth which exceeded 10 per cent per decade for the period 1781–1911 – its peak rise of 17 per cent being reached in the decade ending in 1821.

From the standpoint of this essay then, two well-established features of the demographic context within which the Industrial Revolution unfolded are of particular interest. The first is that British population, having grown, up to the early eighteenth century, in the fluctuating fashion characteristic of pre-industrial communities, and having resumed an upward trend in the run-up to the Industrial Revolution, went on to accelerate through the period when the revolution gathered irreversible momentum. The other is that a marked shift in the nature of the linkages between population and economy developed in the course of, and indeed as part of, the Industrial Revolution.

According to Wrigley and Schofield, for example, for the whole of the pre-industrial period they covered, their results were consistent with the two simple propositions underlying classical population theory: namely, that (other things being equal) population increase can be expected to depress living standards, and that a rise in living standards tends to stimulate population growth. Thus, they found a positive relationship between rising population and rising food prices; and (since money wage rates tended to vary little in the pre-industrial era) between population growth and falling real wages. Ironically, however, as Schofield has observed, the positive relationship between population growth and rising food prices 'disappeared with industrialization, almost at the very moment that

Malthus so forcefully drew attention to its significance'.[36] In the early nineteenth century then – after a period of two to three generations (1731–1811) during which the population almost doubled and the price of a basket of consumables rose two and a half times – average real wages first declined and then rose, while population growth continued to accelerate as the process of industrialization gathered irreversible momentum. To quote Wrigley and Schofield again:

> The world viewed by a man of Marx's generation had changed fundamentally from that which Malthus had surveyed two generations earlier. The tension between population growth and living standards that had pinned men down in poverty gave way before a change in productivity so profound that an increase in poverty was no longer the price of an increase in numbers.[37]

Those who argue that a buoyant demand is needed to create a favourable climate for industrial innovation and development will see the marked rise in the number of British domestic consumers from the 1730s to the 1820s as part at least of the explanation for the breakthrough in industrialization that took place in the late eighteenth and early nineteenth centuries. Certainly eighteenth-century Britain's demographic experience diverged significantly from that of any other European country at a similar level of economic development. The population of Britain's closest economic rivals grew much more slowly. Between 1680 and 1820 when English population increased by 133 per cent, French population showed a rise of 39 per cent and Dutch of 8 per cent.[38] More interesting still, perhaps, when assessing the impact of changes either in the weight and pattern of overall market demand, or in the structural and organizational characteristics of the national economy, was the fact that urbanization was also proceeding at a faster pace in Britain than anywhere else in Europe in this epoch. In 1700 London was already the largest city in Europe, with about 575,000 inhabitants (roughly 5 per cent of the English population) compared with about half a million living in Paris. By *circa* 1800 the population of Paris had risen by about 10 per cent whereas London's had reached 960,000. Nor was London the only sizeable town in eighteenth-century Britain. In 1700, 17 per cent of the English population lived in urban areas and by 1801 the percentage had risen to 27½. The corresponding percentages for France were in the region of 11 per cent at both dates.[39] By 1871 almost two-thirds of the population of England were town-dwellers – a figure more than twice as high as the levels of urbanization in other European countries, at similar levels of income, in the second half of the nineteenth century.[40]

The relatively high and sustained rate of urbanization in eighteenth and nineteenth-century Britain was associated with a relatively high mortality rate and a relatively low quality of life for an increasing proportion of the working classes.[41] Nevertheless urban birth rates were relatively high and the towns continued to grow because they attracted from the countryside mobile young adults in the family-building age groups. During the early stages of industrialization British towns expanded more by attracting labour from the countryside than by natural increase. Between 1776 and 1811, for example, roughly 60 per cent of the increase in the population resident in British urban areas consisted of immigrants from the rural areas of Great Britain and Ireland; and although that proportion diminished through the nineteenth century it was still over 40 per cent in the period 1846–71.[42] The migrants were attracted by the prospect of higher wages and more continuous employment than was available in the rural areas from which they came. They generally had more money to spend than their rural counterparts and their demands for food, fuel (especially coal) and essential manufactures (many of which a rural family customarily provided as part of the subsistence production of the household) stimulated the development of industries producing, carrying and marketing their needs. In addition, the migrants could be expected to respond more positively to the new products and opportunities opened up by technological progress – for example, by adapting their consumption patterns and working practices more flexibly than those who stayed in their traditional environment.

The other striking feature of British urbanization was the extent to which the most rapidly expanding towns were themselves a product of the Industrial Revolution. As early as 1801 the urban hierarchy had been transformed by industrialization. Of the six towns that then had more than 50,000 inhabitants, two had not even been rated as towns forty years earlier, namely Manchester (second in size only to London) and Leeds; while the populations of Liverpool and Birmingham had more than trebled in forty years. Apart from London, only Bristol, which had increased from 50,000 in 1750 to 64,000 in 1801, figured among the top six towns throughout the eighteenth century.[43] In effect, the newer urban settlements, being comparatively free communities outside the controls exercised by the traditional urban guilds and corporations, became the growth centres for the modern market economy.

AGRARIAN CONTEXT

Had domestic agriculture not been able to supply the extra food, raw materials and surplus labour to meet the needs of a rapidly growing and urbanizing population, it is hardly likely that British industrialization would have developed the momentum that it did in the late eighteenth and early nineteenth centuries. When and how the undoubted advance in agricultural productivity occurred is a matter of debate. Apart from the scarcity of directly relevant records, which vitiates all attempts to arrive at firm historical estimates of overall product or productivity, the problem as far as agriculture is concerned is that it is a territorially dispersed, multiproduct industry in which the conditions of production (even of a single product) defy generalization, because they differ from region to region for a variety of geographical, climatic, institutional and other reasons. Recent research, using local primary sources, continues to enlarge our basis of information on the long-term course and character of agricultural change in certain localities. The results bring into question traditional interpretations of a so-called agricultural revolution, more or less contemporaneous with the Industrial Revolution, and suggest alternative dates for the period of maximum agrarian progress. But the evidence still falls far short of justifying direct estimates of long-term trends in agricultural product or productivity at the national level.

There does seem to be a consensus among economic historians that some British farmers were in the vanguard of agrarian progress over most of the seventeenth, eighteenth and early nineteenth centuries. For it is clear that the food needs of a growing, urbanizing nation were met with little or no increase in the size of the agricultural labour force and with no more than occasional, short-term or marginal needs for food imports. A sixfold rise in agricultural prices lasting from the early sixteenth century to the mid-seventeenth century had encouraged substantial capital outlays on land reclamation, clearance and drainage projects, plus associated improvements in farm roads and tracks. These heavy infrastructural investments extended the area of productive land and raised the potential real rate of return from relatively modest annual outlays on, for example, new crops and techniques, improved storage facilities or farm implements and additional farm animals. So it is not surprising that when the pace of population growth faltered in the late seventeenth and early eighteenth centuries, and agricultural prices dropped, English capitalist farmers were faced with a problem of overproduction. According to Thirsk, the problem was already so serious by the mid-1650s that 'the government was obliged, first to intervene to encourage all food exports, then to pay bounties to farmers on grain exported, and later to allow drawbacks of tax on exported malt'.[44] By 1750 the corn exported from England was equivalent to the subsistence requirements of roughly a quarter of its total population.

The overproduction was soon mopped up in the second half of the eighteenth century by the acceleration in the rate of population growth and increasing urbanization. It has been calculated, for example, that by 1800 approximately 90 per cent of the population of Great Britain was fed by domestic agricultural produce, compared with 101 per cent in 1700.[45] The traditional interpretation of the progress of British agriculture associates it with an upsurge of parliamentary enclosures, which are supposed to have facilitated diffusion of new farming techniques (originally pioneered in the seventeenth century), so that they became common practice for the majority of farmers in the second half of the eighteenth century.[46] Certainly, the conviction that enclosure was an infallible recipe for increased agricultural efficiency was well entrenched in the ideology of eighteenth and nineteenth-century landowners. A succession of contemporary observers and later economic historians – from Arthur Young to Lord Ernle and beyond – swallowed the conventional wisdom uncritically. Late-twentieth-century historians, however, have been increasingly sceptical of the impact of enclosures on agricultural productivity and recent attempts to trace the course of agrarian advance discredit the traditional interpretation. According to Crafts, for example, recent research 'suggests that for the eighteenth century, the fastest growth of agricultural output occurred before 1760';[47] while R. V. Jackson's analysis of trends in population, real wages and prices puts the deceleration back to 1740 – near the beginning, that is, of an acceleration in the rate of population growth.[48] Moreover, R. C. Allen finds that the data Young collected on his tours of English farms fell short of substantiating the conventional view of the efficiency-promoting role of enclosures; for he shows that, when account is taken of differences in land types, open and enclosed farms were apparently equally efficient. This finding is buttressed by Allen's own study of South Midland estate surveys and land-tax assessments indicating that the well-documented increase in average farm size applied at least as much to open field as to enclosed farms.[49]

There is little doubt that by the time the British Industrial Revolution took place, widespread improvements in husbandry techniques and storage facilities had substantially raised the domestic supplies of food for human and animal consumption.[50] It remains debatable, however, whether British farmers were appreciably more innovative, or were getting higher yields per acre than their continental counterparts working land of equivalent quality. There were other areas in north-western Europe – for example, in Holland, north-western France and Ireland – where similar levels of yield were obtained. British agriculture does seem, however, to have acquired a distinctive edge over its European rivals in respect of its high and steadily rising productivity, an advantage that was due partly at least to its unique structural characteristics. The aristocracy and gentry, who already, at the beginning of the eighteenth century, owned more than 70 per cent of the nation's arable resources (and perhaps over 75 per cent at the end), were evidently motivated by a combination of political, social and economic reasons to expand and improve their estates. Their political power and social prestige depended directly on the extent of their holdings, which the custom of primogeniture helped to maintain intact. Their incomes depended on their rents; that is, on their ability to lease their lands to tenant-farmers who had the necessary wealth to acquire an adequate stock of farm implements and animals, the knowhow to adopt and adapt the most profitable methods available to them and the managerial authority to attract and deploy a suitably skilled, round-the-year daily labour force. As population growth and urbanization accelerated and agricultural prices rose, ambitious landowners went on enlarging their estates by piecemeal purchase, marriages of convenience and negotiated or parliamentary enclosures, and seized their opportunities to consolidate farms, improve market communications and renegotiate leases with a view to attracting enterprising and efficient farmers as tenants and encouraging diffusion of agricultural innovation.

The fact is that, even before the run-up to the Industrial Revolution, a capitalist agriculture oriented towards profit and the market was in existence in Britain, operated by substantial tenant-farmers or by specialist smallholders such as market gardeners, fruit farmers, or hopgrowers, who supplied expanding urban areas. It is thus not surprising that the size of farms went on increasing or that by the end of the century 'England was overwhelmingly a land of tenant-farmers'[51] and that the rural labour force was largely wage-dependent. It was an agrarian structure unique in contemporary Europe. On the continent the typical owner-occupied peasant holding produced most of its own basic subsistence needs, depended largely on an unspecialized family labour force, spent any appreciable surplus on adding to its holding (often highly vulnerable to fragmentation as a result of relatively egalitarian inheritance customs) and was constrained from investing in new techniques or implements or storage facilities by the fact that the family capital was sunk irretrievably in land. To quote F. M. Thompson, for example:

> It would have been of fundamental importance if the England of the population explosion and industrial revolution had been a country of peasant owners. Not only would such a structure have responded tardily to increasing demands for food and raw materials and by its slowness in adapting to new levels of output and new techniques have damped down the population increase; but also through its likely spending and saving

habits, it would have substantially choked off a large part of the home market support for growth.[52]

In the last analysis, then, the most distinctive feature of British agriculture's role in the development of the first Industrial Revolution stemmed from its ability to meet all or most of the food needs of a fast-growing and urbanizing population using a steadily diminishing proportion of the national workforce. Implicit in this was a high and rising labour productivity. The currently available evidence suggests not only that the productivity of British agricultural labour was already high at the end of the eighteenth century by comparison with other European countries at similar levels of development, but also that it went on growing relatively rapidly through the nineteenth century. According to Bairoch's calculations, for example, in 1840 the physical productivity of British male agricultural labourers was 50 per cent above that of their French counterparts and more than twice that of those in Switzerland, Germany, Sweden or Russia.[53] O'Brien's comparative study of economic growth in Britain and France suggests that over the nineteenth century as a whole, productivity per worker in French agriculture grew at only about a quarter of the British rate.[54] The reasons for the relatively higher labour productivity of British agricultural workers are no doubt complex and various, both over time and as between the nations with which the comparison is relevant. According to O'Brien, for example:

> it is the allocation of so much land to pasture that seems peculiar to Britain. The accumulation of a stock of animals which provided British cultivators with more draught power and far greater quantities of organic fertiliser per hectare of arable land gave them superiority not only over French farmers but over farmers in other regions of Europe as well.[55]

Whatever the reason, the consequence was that Britain could release the labour needed for continuous industrialization sooner than any of its European rivals.

The broad question that inspired this chapter was 'what was it about the British national context that was particularly significant in determining the distinctive characteristics of the first Industrial Revolution?' From the outset it was evident that space would not permit more than a provisional and suggestive answer to such a wide-ranging question. But there were two reasons why it seemed to me worth addressing at this time. One was that within the last quarter of a century the results of much fruitful research and informed debate bearing on the topic have been published, and have shed revealing, if still shadowy, light on such areas of consensus as existed among yesterday's economic historians. The other is that an adequate interpretation of the distinctive features of the British experience calls for comparison with the relevant experience of other nations. I conclude then with the expectation that the other contributions to this volume will not only complement my own, but will also highlight the gaps that I failed to notice.

NOTES

1 See Simon Kuznets, *Modern Economic Growth* (New Haven, 1966), p. 8.
2 See e.g. R. Cameron, 'A new view of industrialization', *Economic History Review*, 38 (1985), pp. 1–23.
3 T. S. Ashton, *The Industrial Revolution* (London, 1948), p. 2.
4 T. S. Ashton, *Economic History of England: The Eighteenth Century* London (1955), p. 125.
5 W. W. Rostow, 'The take-off into self-sustained growth', *Economic Journal*, 66 (1965), p. 47.
6 W. W. Rostow, *The Stages of Economic Growth*, 2nd edn (Cambridge, 1971).
7 *Ibid.*, p. 36.
8 E. J. Hobsbawm, *The Age of Revolution* (London, 1962).
9 S. Kuznets, the founder of modern national income and product measurement, inspired and to a large extent raised the finance for historical national accounting research in a number of developed and underdeveloped countries. The results of these quantitative studies provided him with the empirical estimates deployed in his own analyses of comparative economic growth. See e.g. Kuznets, *Modern Economic Growth*.
10 See Rostow, *Stages of Economic Growth*, p. 38.
11 See especially N. F. R. Crafts, 'The new economic history and the Industrial Revolution', in P. Mathias and J. Davis (eds.), *The First Industrial Revolutions* (Oxford, 1989); and P. K. O'Brien, 'Do we have a typology for the study of European industrialization in the XIXth century?', *Journal of European Economic History*, 15 (Spring 1986), pp. 292–315 and R. V. Jackson, 'Government expenditure and British economic growth in the eighteenth century; some problems of measurement', *Economic History Review*, 43 (1990), pp. 217–35.
12 Cited above, p. 14.
13 J. Mokyr (ed.) *The Economics of the Industrial Revolution* (London, 1985) p. 3.
14 Recent research in the patent records confirms this passion for innovation by discovering a 'revolutionary watershed' in the growth of patentable inventions dating from *circa* 1757–62 onwards. See Richard Sullivan, 'England's Age of Invention during the Industrial Revolution', *Explorations in Economic History*, 26 (1989), pp. 424–52.
15 See Charles Babbage, *On the Economy of Machinery and Manufactures* (London, 1832) and Andrew Ure, *The Philosophy of Manufactures* (London, 1835). These reflected the optimistic interpretation of the so-called 'Age of Machinery'. Thomas Carlyle, who coined the term took the extreme pessimist's view of the 'huge demon of Mechanism'.

16 G. N. von Tunzelmann, *Steam Power and British Industrialization to 1860* (Oxford, 1978), p. 224. But if the forward linkages from innovations in steam-power technology to the textile industries were modest before the mid-nineteenth century, a significant backward linkage from cotton to steam showed up as early as the 1790s when large new fine-spinning mills accounted for a substantial fraction of the new Watt engines erected in that decade.

17 See *The Economic History of Britain since 1700*, eds. Roderick Floud and Donald McCloskey (Cambridge, 1981), vol. I, p. 103.

18 See e.g. J. A. Davis, 'Industrialization in Britain and Europe before 1850', in Mathias and Davis (eds.), *First Industrial Revolutions*, p. 67: 'There can be no returning to a single model of industrialization and we have become increasingly aware of the unusual and a-typical features of the English case with respect to the more general European experience of industrialization in the nineteenth century.'

19 P. K. O'Brien, 'Do we have a typology?', p. 296.

20 The phrase in quotation marks is from Lord Dacre of Glanton, 'The continuity of the English Revolution', *Transactions of the Royal Historical Society*, 6th series 1 (London, 1991), p. 124.

21 J. V. Beckett, *The Aristocracy in England 1660–1914* (Oxford, 1986), p. 434.

22 *Ibid.*, p. 408

23 H. Perkin, *The Origins of Modern English Society 1780–1880* (London, 1969), p. 65.

24 P. K. O'Brien, T. Griffiths and P. Hunt, 'Political components of the industrial revolution: Parliament and the English cotton textile industry 1160–1774', *Economic History Review*, 44 (1991), p. 418.

25 See P. O'Brien and C. Keyder, *Economic Growth in Britain and France 1780–1914* (London, 1978), p. 57. See also *ibid.*, p. 60: 'On the eve of its great Revolution the population and domestic output of France surpassed British aggregates by an even greater amount than they did at the death of Louis XIV. Looking at the two countries in crude mercantilist terms, appropriate for the eighteenth century, it is not difficult to see France as a far greater economic power than Britain.'

26 Between 1700 and 1750 Exchequer net receipts from taxation increased by about 70 per cent.

27 The nation was at war during the periods 1688–97, 1702–13, 1739–48, 1756–63, 1776–82 and 1793–1815.

28 At the end of the Seven Years War, in 1764, the National Debt stood at about £134 million, of which only £5 million was in short-term (unfunded) loans, compared with a total of £17 million in 1698 (at the end of the war of the English Succession) of which £12 million was in short-term loans. See B. R. Mitchell, *Abstract of British Historical Statistics* (Cambridge, 1962), pp. 389–90 and 401–2, for figures of total National Debt and annual debt charges.

29 J. Brewer, *The Sinews of Power: War Money and the English State 1688–1783* (London, 1989), p. 250.

30 Ralph Davis, *The Industrial Revolution and Overseas Trade* (Leicester, 1979), p. 13.

31 *Ibid.*, p. 14.

32 See Ronald Lee, 'Population homeostasis and English demographic history', in R. I. Rotberg and T. K. Rabb (eds.), *Population and History from the Traditional to the Modern World* (Cambridge, 1986).

33 See E. A. Wrigley and R. S. Schofield, *The Population History of England 1541–1871: A Reconstruction* (1981). This study provides estimates based on primary sources (mainly parish registers and nineteenth-century census returns) which are full enough and reliable enough to permit historical demographers to analyse long-run patterns of change in demographic variables (births, deaths, marriages, and migrations) and to relate them to economic and social patterns of change.

34 *Ibid.*, p. 412.

35 See estimates for Wales and Scotland in Robert Woods, 'Population growth and economic change in the eighteenth and nineteenth centuries', in Mathias and Davis, *The First Industrial Revolution* (1989), p. 137.

36 A. R. Schofield, 'Experiment in history', in Rotberg and Rabb, *Population and History*, p. 28.

37 Wrigley and Schofield, *Population History of England*, p. 412.

38 E. A. Wrigley, *People, Cities and Wealth* (Oxford, 1987), p. 234.

39 E. A. Wrigley, 'Urban growth and agricultural change: England and the Continent in the early modern period', in Rotberg and Rabb, *Population and History*, p. 128.

40 See J. G. Williamson, *Coping with City Growth during the British Industrial Revolution* (Cambridge, 1990), p. 4, for a comparative assessment of urbanization levels in Western European countries which industrialized in the nineteenth century.

41 Over the whole century from the 1770s to the 1870s, quinquennial rates of English urban growth seem rarely to have averaged less than 2 per cent, or more than 2½ per cent, per annum. See Williamson, *ibid.*, pp. 22–3.

42 *Ibid.*, pp. 23–4.

43 M. J. Daunton, 'Towns and economic growth in eighteenth century England', in P. Abrams and E. A. Wrigley (eds.), *Towns in Societies* (Cambridge, 1978).

44 Joan Thirsk, Introduction to vol. VI of *The Agrarian History of England and Wales, 1640–1750* (Cambridge, 1983), p. xxiii.

45 See E. L. Jones, 'Agriculture, 1700–1800', in R. C. Floud and D. N. McCloskey (eds.), *The Economic History of Britain since 1700* (Cambridge, 1981), vol I, p. 68. Jones has plausibly, if tentatively, estimated that the percentage increase in total output was roughly twice that of the two preceding centuries.

46 The 'new husbandry' – which included substituting fodder-crop rotations for traditional fallows, selective breeding of livestock, intensive application of green and animal manure – is conventionally associated with the so-called 'agricultural revolution'.

47 N. F. R. Crafts, *British Economic Growth during the Industrial Revolution* (Oxford, 1985), p. 44.

48 R. V. Jackson, 'Growth and deceleration in British agriculture 1660–1790', *Economic History Review*, 38 (1985), pp. 333–51.

49 See R. C. Allen, 'The efficiency and distributional consequences of eigh-

teenth-century enclosures', *Economic Journal*, 92 (1982), pp. 937–53 and his 'The growth of labor productivity in early modern English agriculture', *Explorations in Economic History*, 25 (1988), pp. 117–43.

50 It would appear that corn yields had more than doubled in the two and a half centuries before 1800 and Wrigley has argued that net corn yield (after allowing for seed corn and fodder needs) would represent an increase of around 185 per cent if the rise in gross yield was, say, 120 per cent. See Wrigley, *People, Cities and Wealth*, p. 112.

51 F. M. L. Thompson, 'The social distribution of landed property in England since the sixteenth century', *Economic History Review*, 19 (1966), p. 516.

52 *Ibid.*, p. 517.

53 See P. Bairoch in an article in *Annales* (1965) quoted by Crafts, *British Economic Growth*, p. 121.

54 O'Brien and Keyder, *Economic Growth*, p. 102.

55 *Ibid.*, p. 119.

TWO

France

FRANÇOIS CROUZET

AN essay on 'the Industrial Revolution in France' will be objectionable
both to those who maintain that the expression 'industrial revolution' is
a misleading misnomer, and to those who accept the concept but consider
that economic change was never fast enough in nineteenth-century
France to deserve the epithet 'revolutionary'. I, however, remain devoted
to 'industrial revolution' as the designation of a cluster of macro-inven-
tions and innovations, which, from the late eighteenth century onwards,
'revolutionized' the industry – and so the economy – of Western countries. The main features were mechanization (the French *machinisme* is
rather better), that is, the increasing and systematic use of machinery as
a substitute to human labour; the 'factory system', that is, the centralization of work in large establishments; the substitution of mineral for
organic materials, particularly as fuel; the use of a new form of energy –
steam-power. This definition is old-fashioned, because of its emphasis on
technology (and of the use, later, of categories such as 'backwardness' and
'catching up'), but retains its validity.

France was among the first countries – very few in number – where
such changes occurred, and the French Industrial Revolution – though it
has been called 'the most aberrant case' – has much in common with the
experience of other 'early industrializers', including Britain. Thus, the
cotton industry was the first to mechanize on a large scale; the family firm
or the small partnership were dominant; most of the new industrialists
had earlier been either merchants or merchant-manufacturers or involved
in traditional industry; the financing of firms' expansion was internal,
through ploughing back of profits.

Moreover, the basic trait of the French Industrial Revolution was
shared with other 'follower' countries: it was not spontaneous and it was
not started by endogenous forces, as had happened in Britain. During the
eighteenth century, France had industrialized, as the share of industry in
national product had steadily increased; some changes the country under-

went had been similar to British developments, for example, the spread of putting-out in the countryside and a mushrooming after 1759 of calico-printing works. Frenchmen had made a fair number of inventions, but, unlike in Britain, they had no wide consequences (the macro-invention of ballooning, in 1783, which had no economic effect at all, is typical). So the impulse for revolutionary change came from outside, from Britain, which provided both the example of the 'first Industrial Revolution' and competition from the 'first industrial nation'. France followed and had the second Industrial Revolution (or the third, if Belgium is granted priority); this simple fact was to determine many characteristics of French development.

To withstand competition by cheaper British goods, on third markets and even on their own home market, French manufacturers tried to adopt British machines and to imitate British ways of making things. And the threat by Britain to the prosperity and power of France led governments to encourage, support, even initiate such attempts. While the state had played no direct part in the British Industrial Revolution, things were different in France – and other continental countries. However, governmental intervention must not be overestimated; it was extensive during the last years of the *ancien régime*, but there was much more *laissez-faire* later, even under Napoleon: public competitions for inventions, prizes and honours to inventors, exhibitions for the products of French industry were then the main means of stimulating innovation. After 1815, the only significant interventions by government were its planning and financing of transport improvements, and the heavily protectionist system which prevailed up to 1860. The French Industrial Revolution developed behind high tariff walls, but, again, this was not peculiar to France; there is no example of a country which industrialized without protection.

France – and the other nations which industrialized after Britain – thus had an industrial revolution which was an imported 'transplant' or an imitation; its history is largely about the introduction and diffusion of technologies which had been developed in Britain (but 'diffusion' must be seen as a complex process of creative adaptation). Scholars like John Harris (1992) have stressed that transfers of technologies which were empirical and craft-based were by no means easy. As learning was only 'by doing', by on-the-job training, the way to acquire new techniques 'was to acquire men with the right skills'. This meant enticing English workers to come to France, to settle there, to teach the natives. However, British laws banned both the emigration of skilled artisans and the export of most kinds of machinery (the last such restrictions were only abolished in 1843). Actually such interdicts could never be fully enforced; Bourbon France had a well-established tradition of industrial espionage, which was intensified when new technological progress was achieved in Britain from the 1760s onwards. So French 'spies' toured the manufacturing districts to gather information and suborn craftsmen; blueprints, models, parts of machinery were smuggled out to France. Nonetheless, British efforts to preserve industrial secrets were not entirely ineffective and they certainly delayed technological transfers, even in the 1830s; on the other hand, they stimulated the development on the continent – and especially in France – of a machine-building industry.

Nonetheless, transfers took place; some of them were easy and fast (in cotton), others difficult and protracted, for example coal-fuel technology (and related fields such as iron and steel), which had developed in Britain for three centuries but did not exist in France and was only learned 'by doing'. A small number of British experts played a decisive role, specially at the end of the *ancien régime*. In 1771, John Holker Jr. (his father, an ex-Jacobite, masterminded French industrial espionage for thirty years) brought back from England drawings of the newly invented spinning-jenny; the first copies were soon built at Sens. In 1785, James Milne and his sons, from Lancashire, contracted with the French government to build water-frames at the Château de la Muette near Paris; from 1786 to 1797, they supplied 17 firms with 84 sets of carding, drawing, roving and spinning machines. Another Englishman, P. Pickford, also built sets of spinning machinery in Paris from 1788 onwards. Earlier, William Wilkinson had played a key role in the setting-up of 'modern' works at Indret, for cannon-founding, and at Le Creusot, for iron-making.

The war between Britain and France, which raged from 1793 to 1815, made technological transfers from the former to the latter much more difficult than in the 1780s. Still, recent research has revealed the 'surprisingly large number of British technologists to be found in France throughout the war period'. They included prisoners of war and civilian internees, who were put to work when they had expertise, but also men who came of their own volition. Their influence was critical in machine-making. William Cockerill settled in Verviers in 1799 and moved to Liège in 1807; his main line was machinery for wool-carding and spinning and half of his output was sold in France. William Douglas, who had been persuaded to come to Paris by Chaptal, one of Napoleon's ministers, also made wool-spinning machinery and gig-mills. Moreover, even in wartime, machinery was smuggled from Britain: in 1798, after some bizarre adventures, Liévin Bauwens managed to import most of the plant – especially some mules – for starting two mills, in Passy and in Ghent.

On the other hand, transfers of technology would certainly have been more intense but for the wars, as is proved by post-1815 developments. There was a rush of French industrialists and *ingénieurs* to British manufacturing districts. Government had given up industrial espionage, but private enterprise stepped in: there were agencies which obtained from England machines which it was prohibited to export and also procured English workmen. Indeed, in those years, there was an inflow of British skilled workers (especially puddlers) to the continent and firstly to France. During the 1820s, the number of those *Gastarbeiter* may have reached several thousand. Moreover, some British entrepreneurs settled in France, to set up mills and works (with a labour force which was partly British).

Special mention must be made of Aaron Manby and Daniel Wilson, who in 1822 established a large undertaking at Charenton (near Paris), to puddle and roll iron, and also to build machines and steam engines; in 1826, they took over the ironworks at Le Creusot. Though they failed in 1832, they had given an impetus to the iron and engineering industries (they had also established gasworks and river steamboat services here and there in France). The inability to make good steel was one weak point of French industry; this was finally remedied, thanks to James Jackson, from Birmingham, who came over in 1814 and imported the crucible process. However, the main British contribution was once more in machine-building, especially for the textile industry, although H. Edwards was important in steam engines and W. B. Buddicom and W. Allcard founded the first firm specializing in locomotives. T. and G. Attwood established, near Rouen, a factory which made cylinders for roller-printing of cottons; Job Dickson went to Alsace and, in partnership with the Rislers, made water-wheels and textile machinery. In 1826–8, Richard Roberts, the inventor of the self-acting mule, advised André Koechlin, who was building a large textile engineering works in Mulhouse; he went there three times and his firm supplied machine-tools for the new works. In 1816–17, some Englishmen had settled in Calais and introduced frames for making bobbinet-lace; this industry later spread to Saint-Quentin, where John Heathcote, the pioneer of its mechanization, established a large mill in 1827. This early example of bi-national enterprise was later followed by S. C. Lister and Isaac Holden, who founded in France three large mills for wool-combing (1849 and 1852); they used machinery of recent British and French invention (they had bought the patent of the Alsatian Josué Heilmann). The first jute-spinning mill in France was set up in 1845 by the Baxter brothers.

Britons – skilled mechanics, foremen, engineers, entrepreneurs – thus played a significant, nay indispensable, role in the modernization of French industry in the late eighteenth century and the first half of the nineteenth; this role, which W. O. Henderson (1965) and J. R. Harris (1992) have analysed, has been stressed again recently in S. Chassagne's book (1991) on the cotton industry: he points out that all innovations came from England, that the industry nowhere developed without the help of British technologists, that post-1815 imports of British machinery were large. On the other hand, British migrants were only a tiny minority among the mass of entrepreneurs and workers, even in the 'modernizing' branches of industry; out of 148 cotton-spinners who set up between 1785 and 1815, only 9 were English; among 24 builders of steam engines who were active before 1830, only 5 were wholly or partly English. British workers and foremen were used to train the local labour force, not to replace it.

Needless to say, there were difficulties. Transfers of technology only succeed when a whole matrix of related capacities has been built up. Harris (1992) has pointed out that Cugnot (with his steam-tractor, 1769) and Jouffroy d'Abbans (with his steamboat, 1783) were brilliant pioneers, but their bright ideas had no immediate practical application, mainly due to lack of proper technological back-up for the engineering work which was involved. Pollard (1981) has also observed that the new British technology had to be transferred whole, without adaptation: steam engines, mules, coke blast-furnaces which were installed on the continent 'were exactly like the British ones' (or those of ten or twenty years earlier). Now, British inventions had been answers to specific British problems, appropriate to specific British comparative advantages, which were not necessarily those of the continent. France had similarities with Britain, which made possible the new technology's diffusion, but there were also differences, especially in resources endowment. The major one was that, for geological and geographical reasons, coal was abundant and cheap in Britain, rare and expensive in France.

As 'cheap energy is beginning to reappear as Britain's most significant comparative advantage' (O'Brien, 1986) and as 'those regions of Europe endowed with plentiful coal deposits became the primary sites of heavy industry' (Cameron, 1985), the eagerness of some writers to deny the role of the 'coal factor' in French economic history is amazing. Still, France, with a small production of coal (1 million tons in 1820, 8.3 million in 1860), was the only one among the early industrializers (alongside Switzerland, which had no coal at all) which imported a significant share of her coal consumption – rising from 20 per cent in 1820 to 43 per cent in 1860. This was a specific handicap, which was made worse by long distances between the coalfields and many manufacturing districts and by the scarcity of good coking coal. This handicap explains some peculiarities of the French Industrial Revolution, especially the 'slow' introduction of the coke-smelting process in the iron industry: in many places and up to the mid-nineteenth century, charcoal-smelted pig-iron was cheaper than the product of coke-fired blast-furnaces would have been.

The high price of coal in France (to which deficiencies in the transport system contributed) also explains the slow penetration of the steam-engine, the use of water-power on a large scale and a special orientation of French technological progress towards fuel savings. The Woolf compound engine – which achieved 50 per cent fuel economy over Watt's machine – had far more success in France than in Britain; it was brought over in 1815 by Humphrey Edwards, who had been Arthur Woolf's partner and who built those engines at Chaillot; as early as 1830, 63 per cent of French fixed steam engines were high-pressure ones. Soon French-made engines and locomotives surpassed those made in Britain for fuel economy. The same factor was behind the recovery of hot gases from blast-furnaces (c. 1837) and later improvements in the efficiency of coke ovens.

As for water power, France relied upon it to a much greater extent than did her coal-rich neighbours. In the cotton industry, water was over-whelmingly dominant, steam marginal, up to the mid-nineteenth century. In 1861/5, of 100,163 industrial establishments, outside Paris and Lyons, 60 per cent used water power, 31 per cent steam. This was less a sign of backwardness than a function of the relative abundance of water and of the high price of coal. Moreover, in Britain itself, the use of water power was extensive during the Industrial Revolution and up to the mid-nine-teenth century; water-wheels were greatly improved. The new breast-wheels with buckets were introduced in France in 1802, particularly by William Aitken; after 1815, several other Britons made them, while a good deal of mill equipment was imported from England. On the other hand, building upon theoretical research which had been done in the eighteenth century, the French took the lead in improving water-power technology and achieved a major breakthrough. J. V. Poncelet invented an undershot water-wheel with curved vanes (1823–5) and B. Fourneyron patented in 1832 the prototype of modern turbines, which other men soon perfected; in 1869, A. Bergès was to succeed in harnessing a high waterfall to a turbine. Water power contributed to the small size of firms, geographical dispersion and rural location in French industry.

The French Industrial Revolution was not therefore a purely imitative process; unlike Third World countries today, France had reservoirs of scientists and skilled craftsmen. Indeed, up to 1840, she was the leading country in science – a dominance which she lost later, to Germany, because of an education and university system which was not geared to research. The skills of traditional artisans could serve the new technology. Thus France made a contribution of its own to technological progress; it was much smaller than Britain's but it included some 'epoch-making' inventions (Henderson, 1965).

The earliest were in the chemical industry: in the 1780s, Berthollet discovered the bleaching properties of chlorine and N. Leblanc invented the process for making artificial soda which bears his name; their discoveries were the basis of the heavy chemical industry for sixty years. Later on, in the 1830s, Gay-Lussac and the Perrets made important contributions to sulphuric-acid technology. In textiles, between 1801 and 1810 J. M. Jacquard, of Lyons, building upon a century of efforts by inventors, developed from 1801 to 1810 the 'Jacquard loom', 'one of the most sophisticated technological breakthroughs of the time' (Mokyr 1990); thanks to coding on perforated sheets of cardboard, complicated patterns of silk fabrics could be automatically woven by one man; soon the principle of the Jacquard was applied to other fibres. In the 1830s, L. Perrot invented the *perrotine*, for power-printing cottons by means of wooden blocks. The wool-combing machine, mentioned above, invented by Josué Heilmann (1845) 'ranks with the greatest textile inventions'.

Not surprisingly, the French were not prominent in iron and steel technology, until Emile and Pierre Martin, small ironmasters in south-western France, found in 1864 a new way to make steel, which used W. Siemens's gas oven and became the Siemens-Martin or open-hearth process. Among many miscellaneous inventions are the food-preserving process of F. Appert (1804) and photography (J. N. Niepce and L. J. Daguerre, 1839).

It is a cliché that important inventions by Frenchmen were neglected in France, but picked up and successfully exploited abroad, especially in Britain. Indeed, the paper-making machine of L. Robert (1798) was soon perfected and used in England, to return to France only after 1815. The 'wet spinning' of flax, which P. de Girard invented in 1810, was not taken up in France before the 1830s. B. Thimonnier is the inventor with the best claim to the sewing machine (1830), but his invention was not adopted in France, because of workers' hostility, and it was I. Singer's American machine which eventually prevailed. However, such inventors' misfortunes are explained not only by French distrust of novelties, but also by unfavourable circumstances, like the fall of the Napoleonic empire in the case of Girard's machine.

On the other hand, if some British engineers and entrepreneurs played a vital role in the creation of an engineering industry in France, they soon had French emulators. The 'self-taught mechanics of Paris' (as M. Daumas called them) and others in Alsace built at first spinning machines, then machine-tools, eventually steam engines (a few of them graduated to locomotives); they started by copying English models, but later made original contributions. This industry really took off in the 1820s, when some men (Cail, Farcot, Cavé, etc.), who later owned large works, did set up.

A different group of industrial leaders was made up of *ingénieurs*, who had received a formal scientific education in one *grande école* – that typically French institution; at the Saint-Gobain company (plate-glass and chemicals), there was a clear change in methods of management when *ingénieurs* were put in charge. The Ecole Polytechnique (1794) provided an abstract kind of teaching and most of its graduates became government *ingénieurs* or army officers; yet it also produced some prominent industrialists. The Ecole Centrale des Arts et Manufactures, a private college established in 1829, tried to be more practice-oriented and indeed supplied many leaders of industry. As for the Ecoles des Arts et Métiers (two were founded under Napoleon, a third in 1843), they were intended to train the NCOs of industry, but many of their graduates rose to top jobs. Even the many schools and evening classes, established by private or public initiative, which, at a lower level, gave elementary instruction in science and technology, had a useful impact, inasmuch as many of their pupils set up their own business.

The Industrial Revolution, which had started as a foreign transplant, was thus 'naturalized' (roughly, from the 1820s); technological progress became indigenous, built-in within the economy, even though Britain's example and competition remained influential. The time lag in the introduction of British innovations was reduced; some inventions were made almost simultaneously in both countries (e.g. the steam-hammer). By mid-century, France had become self-sufficient for most kinds of machinery. At least twenty-four builders of steam engines had been active before 1830 and as early as 1833 only 16 per cent of fixed steam engines in France were 'foreign'. The early French railways imported their locomotives from England; their manufacture started in France in 1838; by 1842, foreign and French engines were equal in numbers; there were no more imports after 1846 and in the 1850s France was an exporter of locomotives – to Italy, Spain and Russia. She had become, like Britain and Belgium, a pole of diffusion for modern technology.

The optimism of these remarks will, however, be severely qualified when another trait of the French Industrial Revolution is considered: it was a long, protracted process, which, moreover, was irregular, even discontinuous, with an alternation of spurts and setbacks. The Industrial Revolution has been defined as 'the period between the first introduction of new techniques and their predominance, together with an appropriate sound capital goods supply, within major productive sectors' (Pollard 1981). On this basis, the French Industrial Revolution started in the 1780s and was completed in the 1860s (needless to say, some writers select other dates). This was indeed a long, drawn-out revolution (many innovations were introduced fairly early, but their diffusion was often quite slow). However, in Britain, the usual dates are 1760–1830 or 1780–1850, and

recent writers have stressed the 'slowness' of growth between 1780 and
1820, for both industrial and overall output. In France, the process was
still slower (at Saint Gobain, for example, not much happened before 1830);
few – and possibly none – of the changes 'were sudden or dramatic'. The
major difference from Britain is the dissociation of technological change
and economic growth, at least in the early stages, up to 1800 or even 1815.
This was a period when mechanization and factories – the central ingredients of the Industrial Revolution – first took root in France, but the
increase in output was small, especially if compared with Britain.
According to the latest calculations, industrial production increased in
France at a rate of 0.56 per cent per year from 1781/90 to 1803/12, in
England at 2.1 per cent from 1780 to 1801 (and faster afterwards).

The reasons for this peculiarity are obvious: the French Revolution and
the Twenty-three years war; 'the industrial revolution in France began in
a period of … extreme and violent economic disturbance' (Milward and
Saul, 1973). Though Britain was also involved in the 'French wars', their
effects upon her economy were far less baneful than the disasters which
struck France. 'Therein lies an important difference that affected the relative performance of the two economies for much of the nineteenth
century' (Cameron, 1985) – and also their patterns of change.

There was thus a first phase of the French Industrial Revolution, up to
the start of war with England (1793); a phase during which a large amount
of technological transfer from Britain was achieved. The new machines
for cotton-spinning – jenny, water-frame, mule – plus those for carding
and other preliminaries, were introduced and several mechanics started
to make them in France. Some cotton-mills were built, specially a large
one in Orléans. In weaving, the flying shuttle was introduced, particularly
by the Scotsman J. MacLeod. Other industries were also affected; N.
Leblanc started making soda at Saint-Denis (1791); large works for rolling
copper sheets were established at Romilly-sur-Andelle (in Normandy).
The building of steam engines was started by J. C. Périer at Chaillot (i.e.,
in Paris): in 1779 he bought two engines from Boulton and Watt which
were imported in the midst of the American war and were the first
condenser engines to work in France (8 August 1781); then he built 'pirate'
engines – about forty of them up to 1791. However, the most spectacular
achievement was the ironworks at Le Creusot, where coke-smelted pig-
iron was first cast in December 1785; with their four blast-furnaces, they
probably were in technical terms 'the most advanced works of the time',
heralding 'a new world of industrial and social organisation'. Actually,
they soon ran into difficulties and for the fifty years which followed they
were a 'counter-example' more than a model; established with the help
of government funds and of foreign experts, they were the forerunners of

the steel mills and other mammoth (and loss-making) plants, which Third World countries have been so keen to acquire in our time. Actually, government support and the leading role of British technologists are typical of industrial progress at the end of the *ancien régime*, so that these developments – the scale of which must not be overestimated – were largely artificial.

The French Revolution – committed to *laissez-faire* and short of money – put paid to state support for the nascent Industrial Revolution, while war, inflation and the command economy of the Terror were uncongenial to technological progress. On the other hand, contacts with England were not completely interrupted (the basic mechanical concepts and the first spinning machines had in any case become established in France before war started). There is something in the Jacobin view that the sale of monastic buildings provided manufacturers with fixed capital at low cost. So the process of change went on during the 1790s, but it slowed down and was restricted to a narrow, though strategic, sector: cotton-spinning. It was also more spontaneous than in the 1780s, as government aid had faded away; it resulted from a shift of home demand towards cottons, the protection against foreign competition which war provided, and the profit opportunities which some entrepreneurs did see and take. The number of mechanized (but water or horse-powered) cotton-spinning mills rose from 8 in 1790 to 17 in 1795 and 37 in 1799.

'La révolution industrielle est commencée en France'; so wrote a French diplomat, Louis Guillaume Otto, in 1799 (the first known use of the expression), the date which J. Marczewski proposed for the start of a French 'take-off'; but the maxim that 'whoever says Industrial Revolution says cotton' was then fully justified, as there was no significant progress in other industries – rather, serious setbacks. Leblanc's soda works had to close and he was ruined; the Périer business was in jeopardy; the 'prodigious efforts' of the Committee of Public Safety and the eminent scientists it mobilized to make steel were as unsuccessful as those of the *ancien régime*. Indeed, French industrial production was lower in the late 1790s than it had been before the Revolution.

However it strongly recovered under Napoleon. The definition of a new set of property rights was completed, in a *laissez-faire*, capitalist spirit. Protection of the home market – much extended by French conquests – was strengthened and various encouragements (but not much money) were given to technical progress. The major development was once again in cotton-spinning, where growth was explosive: the number of cotton mills rose from 37 in 1799 to 119 in 1803, 234 in 1806 and 266 in 1810 (there was a slow-down from 1808). When the Empire fell, hand-spinning of cotton had been wiped out and cotton spinning had become a factory industry, with 1 million spindles (Britain had 5 million); meanwhile the flying shuttle and roller printing had progressed. Another development had been the beginnings of machine-spinning in the woollen industry, thanks to the machinery built by Cockerill and Douglas. In both cotton and wool, some large-scale enterprises and a new breed of captains of industry had emerged. The secondary metal trades (like hardware) and machine-building also progressed (in 1807, Paris had fifteen firms which made spinning machines). However, an important branch – the iron industry – was stagnant; its output had fallen in the 1790s and did not grow much under Napoleon; in technology, protection by war conditions was a cause of conservatism, not of innovations. Many experiments were made, but the only significant improvements were the use of coal in the chaferies of some works and the setting-up of a few rolling-mills. This might be seen as proof of the non-spontaneous character of the Industrial Revolution in France: nothing happened when there was no competition from and no contact with England. In steam power, likewise, everything effective had come from England; with the war, the source of innovation was lost, the French were able to add nothing of their own and 'steam engines were made in France in 1815 only to the state of the art as it had been in England in 1789'; France did have almost 200 engines (had the British economy, however, been forced in 1800 to do without Watt's engine, the cost would only have been 0.1 per cent of national product!).

The achievements of the Napoleonic period must not, therefore, be overestimated. Though the bases of a developed industrial economy had been laid, the period 1780–1815, taken as a whole, could be considered as a preliminary phase of a French industrial revolution, which would have its proper start only after 1815 (for Germany, K. Borchardt treats as 'preliminary' the period from the late eighteenth century to 1850). Moreover, the French position after Waterloo was most inauspicious. 'The technological gap between England and France had if anything increased by 1814 as compared with the mid-1780s' (Harris, 1989), and it was more difficult to fill: D. Landes (1969) has shown that best-practice British equipment (admittedly an ambiguous concept) was expensive and unsuited to narrow markets (actually, French firms were often to install machinery or plant which were obsolete in England). Moreover, France was dismembered and financially squeezed by her enemies, and the 'cardinal fact for most French producers ... was the existence of an over-whelmingly dominant and powerful' neighbour, which was by itself an obstacle to industrialization. The British super-power had conquered overseas markets by force during the wars and firmly held them (e.g. the former Spanish colonies, which had been vital for France in the eigh-teenth century); it had 'obtained virtually the whole of world trade in cotton goods' so that it was impossible for France to base a major industrial impetus upon foreign markets – at least for cotton, and iron; France had to rely only upon her home market. This situation created an inferiority complex and a feeling of hopelessness among businessmen which could be crippling; it largely explains the excessive caution and the poor entrepreneurship of which they have been accused. The legacy of a quarter of a century of revolution and war was indeed heavy.

Nonetheless, the post-1815 period was marked by an acceleration of both industrial modernization and economic growth. The causes are obvious: peace – external and internal (though the minor revolutions of 1830 and 1848 had some negative economic impact), renewal of technological transfers from Britain, sound currency and finance, mobility of capital, improvements in transport (which acted both on supply of inputs to industry and on demand for its output), plus the pronounced growth of agricultural production. In this new stage, industrial change was spontaneous, though it was spurred on by British competition and by the protectionist system (which did not prevent internal competition developing, especially because of the fall in transport costs).

Textiles were by far the largest industrial sector in France and the pursuit of their modernization was a dominant feature. Cotton retained the lead in mechanization, size of factories and speed of growth: raw-cotton consumption increased fivefold from 1820 to 1860. The wool industry, however, displayed much vitality and adaptability; it was much more successful than cotton in export markets and its worsted branch became as big as its British rival. There was much technical progress in cotton-spinning; the speed of spindles and their annual output greatly increased (the latter by a factor of three in Alsace, from 1815 to 1845); French spinners succeeded in producing the finest counts of yarn, which previously they had been unable to make; some very large mills, with eight or nine-storied buildings, emerged around 1840. On the other hand, the self-acting mule, which was invented in England in 1825, was adopted in France after a serious time-lag: it was expensive, needed a lot of power to drive it and was less profitable than in Britain, as wages were lower in France. It was introduced in 1836, but only spread widely in the 1850s. It was also adopted for the spinning of wool from 1844 onwards. The mechanization of the latter, which had started under Napoleon, went on after 1815 and was completed in the woollen branch by the 1830s; for worsted yarn, it only started in the 1820s. A new development of the 1830s was the mechanization of flax spinning; it followed an invasion of the French market by machine-spun linen yarn from Britain; in 1835, machinery was smuggled from Britain and several mills were soon erected in and around Lille; the number of flax spindles rose from 15,000 in 1838 to 700,000 in the 1860s.

The rise of power-weaving was a major new phenomenon; it came late and slowly, even in Britain, as the early power-looms were unsatisfactory, as the productivity gains they brought were much lower than those from spinning machines, and as hand-loom weavers were ready to work for lower and lower wages; in France, which had large reserves of cheap labour in the countryside, the success of power-weaving was even more belated. In the cotton industry, some power-looms were introduced from 1822 onwards, but Alsace alone adopted them in large numbers. In other parts of France, they only spread after the depression of 1847–9. Their total number (in cotton) rose from 5,000 in 1834 to 31,000 in 1846 and 80,000 in 1866, when they were still outnumbered by hand-looms. Their introduction came of course later in the wool and linen industries (not to speak of silk; see p. 55); in Reims, a progressive centre, they were first used in 1844 and by 1860 their number equalled that of hand-looms; much hand-loom weaving survived up to the 1870s, especially in the woollen branch; and also in linens, where power-weaving in large mills only started in the 1860s. In Germany, power-looms did not prevail in cotton before 1873, and later in wool.

Nonetheless, Chassagne (1991) maintains that, by 1840, capital-intensive production was gaining the upper hand in all branches of the French cotton industry (e.g. roller-printing had become general by 1830). Cottons had been luxury fabrics in the eighteenth century; by 1840 *blouses* (overalls) of coarse blue cotton cloth were the uniform of both peasants and town workmen. By 1850, spinning factories were the branch of industry with the highest number of steam-engines; in the 1850s, factories greatly progressed, to the detriment of domestic rural industry; the Industrial Revolution in textiles was not far from completion.

However, the big post-1815 novelty was in the iron industry, which hitherto had been static; on the other hand, those changes were long-drawn-out, for reasons which have been mentioned: the location and quality of coal and of iron ore deposits, the location of existing charcoal ironworks, the high cost of transport made it uneconomical (despite a rise in wood prices), except in a few districts, to substitute coal for charcoal, according to British technology. The conservatism of French ironmasters is often blamed, but actually many of them 'showed an astonishing alertness to technical developments in Britain', where they rushed, as soon as peace had been made, to inspect ironworks and suborn skilled workmen (at Alais, in 1829, a master-mason and five bricklayers from England were employed to build a blast-furnace). Still, mastering the new technology was not easy: in Belgium, where the resources endowment was much better, 'modern' works were not successful for years. On the other hand, the fact that change started shortly after 1815 is proof that war had hampered technological transfers.

As early as 1817/18, puddling and rolling of iron were successfully started near Grosrouvre (Cher) and then in other places (e.g. Fourchambault, Nièvre); by 1823, the new process was used in twenty-three works. Though a 'mysterious art', for which British experts were at first needed, puddling did not involve costly investment and brought large fuel economies; it could be adopted by small works, especially when, in the *méthode champenoise* (much used up to the late 1830s), it was combined with tilt-hammers for forging and not with rolling-mills (there were other 'intermediate technologies', e.g., in some blast-furnaces, various mixtures of coke, coal, charcoal and wood were used). The refining of pig-iron into iron was thus the first process to change on a large scale: as early as 1828, 32 per cent of the iron made in France was refined with coal; this proportion rose to over 50 per cent in 1837, to 70 per cent in 1846 and 82 per cent in 1860.

In the smelting process, in which plant was expensive and the chemical composition of materials mattered more, change was slower, though coke-fired blast-furnaces were started in 1818–19 at Hayange (Lorraine) and near Vienne; their number rose to 29 in 1830, but they only supplied 10 per cent of pig-iron production. Actually, in 1820–1, some newcomers to the industry had established large new works, where the whole set of British technology was applied – coke-smelting, puddling, rolling; but they had been over-ambitious, 'too ready to innovate'; they had overestimated demand for their products and underestimated costs; most of the new companies failed in the slump of 1828–32 and innovation was discouraged for some time.

However, the number of active charcoal blast-furnaces peaked in 1839 (at 445) and then declined. From c. 1840, the demand for iron for railway construction gave a new impetus (by 1855/64, it was to absorb 18 per cent of iron products – by value); transport improvements reduced costs, especially for coal; the large modern works at last became profitable. The proportion of pig-iron output which was coke-smelted rose from 21 per cent in 1840 to 46 per cent in 1846, over 50 per cent in 1852, 65 per cent in 1860, 91 per cent in 1869. By that year, further change had started: the Bessemer process (invented in 1856) had been introduced in France in 1858. Indeed, during the 1850s and 1860s, the 'responsiveness' of the French iron industry to technical change was 'very high'.

By 1869, the industry had thus undergone a complete transformation and greatly increased its production (by a factor of 12 for pig-iron, 1822–69, at a mean rate of growth of 5.5 per cent per year); it was the first producer on the Continent, but Germany was catching up fast and Britain made four times more pig! The scattered industry of 1815 (over 1,000 small undertakings) had become concentrated and – after 1850 – oligopolistic (the ten biggest firms made 54 per cent of French iron). On the other hand, there were still remnants of the dualism which had prevailed earlier; most of the increase in production had come from a number of large, progressive firms (Le Creusot had become one of the largest industrial complexes in the world); they were mainly sited on coal-fields – on the northern periphery of the Massif Central and in the *Nord* department. However, in Champagne, Franche-Comté and elsewhere, the charcoal iron industry held up – even grew – up to the 1850s and only collapsed in the 1860s; it survived thanks to 'geographical protection' and high transport costs, but also because it made innovations (bigger furnaces, cylinder blowing-engines, recovery of hot gases). So older and newer techniques coexisted, as in most of French industry.

For an overall view of growth, there is an embarrassment of riches, as several indexes of French industrial production (and of investment in industry) have been computed – but they are at variance. According to Marczewski (1965), Toutain (1987) – and also Lévy-Leboyer (1985), the highest rates of growth were obtained during the early period, from 1815 to 1845; I have suggested that the period of fastest growth started *c.* 1840 and peaked in the 1850s, though the new, dynamic industries display an accelerating growth from 1815 to the 1850s. Qualitative data suggest that change intensified, in several regions or branches, after 1830.

Anyhow, there is a consensus that the 1850s were exceptional years. After the deep depression of 1847–51 (a cyclical slump made longer and worse by political crises – a pattern typical of French history), there was a sharp upsurge in activity; various factors, including railway building on a massive scale (which created the long-delayed single national market, soon to be fatal to archaic producers), generated an unprecedented pros-perity. Between 1815 and 1846, growth had been extensive, Smithian, with consumption goods industries as its engine (textiles, of course, but also soap, candles, paper, ceramics, glass, beet sugar); these industries remained labour-intensive and the rise in output was based on the increase in firms' numbers and in manpower. On the other hand, the 1850s were years of intensive growth, led by capital goods industries, based upon substitution of capital to labour, redistribution of the work-force and increased productivity (which grew by 38 per cent between 1845 and 1866).

Some historians have therefore maintained that the 1850s are the true period of the Industrial Revolution in France. One would rather say that the latter was almost completed, that 'modern' industry had come of age, had reached Rostowian maturity (just as *Haussmannization* – urban renewal – transformed Paris and some other towns from 'medieval' into 'modern' cities). At any rate, Napoleon III considered French industry as strong enough to stand up to British competition; the moderate tariff, which the

Table 2.1. *Industrial growth in Britain and France*

	Mean rates of growth per year (%)	
	France	Britain
Consumption of raw cotton, 1815/17–1849/51	4.4	5.6
Production of pig-iron, 1815–1847	5.4	6.0
Industrial production, 1815–1850[a]	2.5	3.7
Industrial production, per capita	2.0	2.3

[a] 1815/24–1845/54 for France; 1811/21–1841/51 for Britain. The last two sets of figures from Roehl 1976; the first two from Milward and Saul 1973.

treaty of 1860 established, was intended to stimulate more modernization; unlike in 1786, the gamble came off.

Up to 1850, 'it is quite possible that the gap, both quantitative and technological between British production and production elsewhere in Western Europe was increasing' (Milward and Saul, 1973); this seems confirmed by the figures in table 2.1.

Roehl (1976) maintains that, in per capita terms, the rates of the two countries are indistinguishable (indeed, it is on per capita figures that the case of the 'revisionists' rests, who deny the 'backwardness' and 'retardation' of nineteenth-century France). On the other hand, in 1860, French per capita consumption of coal and raw cotton, production of pig-iron, fixed steam-power installed were only 16 to 21 per cent of British figures (admittedly such indicators, concerning fields where Britain was the strongest, are biased in her favour). A safe conclusion might be that French industry did not perform too badly between 1815 and 1850, in comparison with its powerful British competitor. In the 1850s and 1860s, the gap may have narrowed: output of pig-iron and total exports grew faster in France than in Britain, cotton consumption at the same rate. France was catching up – but not for long.

Indeed, the French Industrial Revolution was incomplete – and was to remain so for some time. In the 1860s, France was an industrial power – the second in the world (though not for long, as Germany was drawing near), but she was not an 'industrial nation'.

Table 2.2 *Four countries at an income per capita of 550 US $ of 1970*

	Urbanization %	% of male labour force		% of income	
		In primary sector	In industry	In primary sector	In industry
Britain (1840)	48	29	47	25	32
Belgium (1850)	–	51	34	27	24
France (c. 1870)	31	51	29	34	36
Germany (c. 1870)	36	–	–	40	30

The figures in table 2.2 (from Crafts 1984a, 1989) are significant; they compare countries at a similar per capita real income level, which is deemed characteristic of industrialization being well under way.

Roughly speaking, Napoleon III's France had half her labour force in agriculture, not much more than a quarter in industry and the rest in services (but non-agricultural labour may be underestimated). As for the shares of national income originating in agriculture and in industry, they did not alter significantly from 1830 to 1870.

France was also notorious for her low rate of urbanization; if defined as a percentage of the population living in localities with over 2,000 inhabitants, urbanization rose from 19 per cent in 1806 to 26 per cent in 1851 and 31 per cent in 1872. This percentage had been reached by Britain before 1800; and by 1851, just half her population was living in towns. Moreover, France only had a small number of industrial towns where population grew fast: Roubaix, Tourcoing, Mulhouse, St Etienne, Le Creusot and some smaller ones. The population of the countryside and the agricultural labour force went on increasing up to 1861.

If the Industrial Revolution is basically a 'redeployment of resources away from agriculture' (Crafts, 1984b), one could wonder again whether France had one during the period under consideration. However, a serious qualification is the unique character of Britain's development path: she industrialized and urbanized much earlier than the continent, with a fast and unusual transfer of labour from agriculture to industry. The percentage of the male labour force in the latter may have been 19 as early as 1700, then rose to 24 per cent c. 1760 and 30 per cent in 1801. This was exceptionally high by European standards and from 1800 to the

1860s the proportion of the labour force employed in British industry was roughly double the ratio so employed in France, which started from a very much lower level than Britain. A structural redeployment on British lines, within a few decades, would have been a formidable, unfeasible, unrealistic upheaval. Actually, almost a century elapsed between the date at which employment in industry overtook that in agriculture in Britain and the time when it happened in France (1911) – as well as in Germany, the paragon of successful industrializers. So French levels of industrialization were not especially low in the 1850s and 1860s, except by British standards, which reflected the uniqueness of the British experience, with an employment structure which was untypical in Europe.

However, many writers have been struck by the limited transfer of resources – especially of labour – from agriculture to industry; and they have seen in the structures of French agriculture (especially in the existence of a numerous class of small owner-occupiers) an explanation of that 'retention' of labour and therefore of slow industrialization. This is an immense problem which can not be discussed here; suffice it to say that, actually, there was an exodus from the countryside on a large scale: from 1821 to 1871, 3.5 million people left it (but many of them had been in non-agricultural occupations). Besides, there is not much evidence that industrialists had difficulties in getting together a labour force, because of an hypothetical reluctance to leave the land; the problem was that migrants from the countryside were not too suitable for factory work; also there was a chronic shortage of skilled labour. On the whole, the situation of agriculture was not an insurmountable obstacle to French industrial growth.

France had therefore a dual economy, with agriculture and industry having roughly the same weight in gross national product (GNP). This dualism was also obvious geographically. Most of the industrial changes and growth, which have been described, had taken place in the northeastern half of France, eastwards of a line which ran from Le Havre to Marseilles. This zone contained the few truly industrial regions which developed in France (but also large areas which were purely agricultural); five departments in that zone had half the steam engines in the country. The Nord-Pas-de-Calais steadily grew in importance and built up a diversified structure, based on coal, textiles, iron, plus food-processing; by the middle of the century it was the biggest industrial region of France and the only one which was comparable to Lancashire or Yorkshire – though less powerful. The other large, but looser concentration was the region of Lyons-Saint-Etienne ('the Birmingham of France'); the silk industry had spread from Lyons far into the countryside; the Loire coal-field and some smaller ones were the cradle of the modern iron industry; after 1830, there was much diversification, particularly in chemicals and engineering. Lyons was a regional metropolis, rich in capital, which extended its influence over most of south-eastern France. Alsace also was an important and dynamic district, and Paris had many industrial activities; but Normandy, despite its many cotton-mills, did lose ground.

On the other hand, westwards of the Havre–Marseilles line, de-industrialization prevailed; the woollen industry of Languedoc and the linen industry of Brittany and Maine steadily declined as textiles shifted north-eastwards; only some small coal-fields (e.g. Decazeville) and some sea-ports had any significant growth of 'modern' industry. However, such geographical dualism was not peculiar to France, though it may have been sharper than in Britain.

The dualistic character of the French economy and the incompleteness of the Industrial Revolution are also obvious in another respect: both *grande* and *petite* industry, both capital-intensive and labour-intensive forms of production, both centralized and domestic/workshop manufacturing developed, side by side.

The textile industries were for a long time typically dualistic (this was not special to France), with spinning and printing being done in mechanized, power-driven factories, while weaving was put out to domestic hand-loom weavers, mostly in the countryside – a practice which progressed during the nineteenth century's early decades. Of course, mechanization and centralization of weaving increased markedly, but they had not yet fully prevailed by the 1860s. Moreover, most textile factories were not large: in 1843/5, in cotton – the most advanced branch – only 44 establishments had 500 employees and more. Inside the factories, human labour retained an important role; F. Caron (1981) suggests that this incompleteness of technological change was more pronounced in France than in some other countries.

The small-scale, crafts, workshop industry was much larger than the centralized, capital-intensive sector; and it went on growing, up to the 1860s, though more slowly than the latter. It lost ground, but remained predominant: in 1851, out of 4.4 million 'industrial' workers, only 1.2 million were in establishments with over 10 employees. There was no major change in that structure of manufacturing; up to 1850, *petite* industry accounted for about three-quarters of 'industrial' production; by the 1860s, its share was still 60 per cent or more. However this dominance of small-scale production did not cause stagnation. Both J. Nye (1987) and P. O'Brien (O'Brien and Keyder, 1978) stress that small firms must not be equated with backwardness; before 1870, economies of scale were insignificant over a wide range of activities. Many artisanal producers improved productivity by means of increased division of labour and of machinery which was suited to their work; for example, cutting-machines and stan-dardized sizes for glove-making in Grenoble.

This large sector of 'small' industry included the making of most consumption goods, particularly food and clothing. P. Verley (1986) has recently proved the continued importance, in the 1860s, of such tradi-tional activities and their role as engines of growth. Most of this sector worked for local or regional markets, but some of its branches had a wider, even an international market: the cabinet-makers of the Faubourg Saint-Antoine, the producers of *articles de Paris* and jewellery and, last but not least, the silk industry of Lyons and its region.

Lyons had suffered badly from the French Revolution but its industry recovered fast and had its heyday from 1815 to 1875, the peak being in the 1850s. The number of looms in the city and its region rose from 16,000 in 1790 to 18,000 to 20,000 in 1815, 30,000 in 1825, 60,000 in 1853, 116,000 in 1861 (raw-silk consumption increased by 4.2 per cent per year, 1815–49). From the city, the industry had spread to its suburbs and – in search of cheaper labour – to the countryside. Silk was, by value, the first French industry and silks ranked first among French exports (like cottons in British trade). Exports were the engine of growth, the USA and Britain the major markets (the British silk industry had no superior technology to offset the skill of the Lyonnais). Lyons was the fashion leader for silks and constantly created new products; in the 1850s with St Etienne, it made 20 per cent of the European output of silks. The paradox was that this buoyant industry remained at an almost purely artisanal stage; its fabrics were made on hand-looms (the Jacquard was a splendid, but hand-oper-ated machine), in small workshops or in the homes of the *canuts* (silk-weavers). No power-loom was used before 1843 and there were only 7,000 of them by 1875; with a few exceptions, silk mills – hundreds of them were scattered around Lyons – only engaged in reeling and throwing. On the other hand, commercial capitalism prevailed: the many small masters worked for and were controlled by *fabricants* (merchant-manufacturers; 444 of them in 1853). There was no serious change before the 1870s in that structure, which was said to be very flexible and to help the finding of new products and new markets.

The traditional character of a major industry is special to France; on the other hand, dualism between *petite* and *grande* industry also prevailed in other countries in the mid-nineteenth century; even in Britain, most – say 60 per cent – of 'industrial' employment was not in factories, but in small-scale handicraft activities, where steam-power was unknown. Clapham (1939) pointed out long ago that, by 1851, Britain had more workers in building than in cotton, more shoemakers than coalminers. In Germany a large artisanal sector was to survive for a long time.

However, a French peculiarity was that a significant share of that sector made 'luxury' goods, with a high skilled labour content, intended for well-to-do and demanding customers. This contrasted with the British way, which concentrated on the cheaper ends of the textile – and other – markets, to which the new, mass-production methods could be applied. There was an international division of labour, in which England supplied loin-cloths to Indians and Africans, France ball-dresses to London débutantes and Southern belles. This division is often seen as unfavourable to France, which was forced into that part of the market which was less capable of expansion, as demand grew faster for plain articles than for luxury goods.

This contrast, however, did not result from 'national' characters, 'social preferences' or French aristocratic values and there was no central planning authority to select niches of specialization. The choice was made by market forces, according to comparative advantages. Already in the eighteenth century, France had luxury industries on a significant scale: she had an opulent court and many wealthy noblemen and bourgeois; as most courts had Versailles as their model, French luxuries also found ready markets abroad. Those exports were resumed after the Revolutionary interval and they had – rightly or wrongly – a reputation for quality, taste and elegance which helped their sale; they also had an advantage in costs over England, as their production could not be much mechanized, while labour was cheaper in France, and sometimes more skilful.

On the other hand, Britain had captured, thanks to technology and war, the markets for mass-produced goods, such as most cottons and hardware (and later rails and the like); she constantly improved her productivity and left few opportunities for rivals in such lines. The French cotton industry never succeeded in exporting more than one-fifth of its output (mainly quality printed cottons from Alsace), as against two-thirds in Britain; and its exports were pitifully low compared to the British. Likewise, the German cotton industry found export markets inaccessible. Indeed, up to the rise, in the twentieth century, of modern cotton industries in Asia, Lancashire was unbeatable.

As Milward and Saul (1973) observed, French manufacturers sold the goods they *could* sell, and in the markets which were open to them. This is why some branches of industry which were able to export grew faster than those which had to deal with the home market; those branches were mainly in luxury, fashion and fancy goods, the only ones in which the French could get the better of the British.

However, positions once conquered had to be defended, especially by frequent changes in the products which were offered; so the Lyonnais kept ahead of their competitors by designing new fabrics (crêpe de Chine, foulard, plush, taffeta, faille, etc.) and perfecting new dyes. Likewise, in the worsted industry, manufacturers started in the 1820s to make *nouveautés* – light clothes in bright colours and often-changed designs; they also mixed woollen, worsted and silk yarns. Later on, Roubaix and Reims produced many kinds of cheaper fancy goods, often on Jacquard looms; eventually, from the 1860s, they were to outperform Yorkshire for three decades, thanks to soft all-wool worsteds. So efforts towards volume-production and lower prices were not absent in France (e.g. the firm of Christofle, founded in 1845 to make semi-luxuries, silver-plated goods). Still, altogether, the French devised and developed new products, rather than new and cost-reducing processes of production.

On the other hand, the making of quality goods, with a high labour content and little mechanization, was compatible with non-centralized, domestic/workshop production. This is one reason why non-capital-intensive modes of production continued to grow during the first half of the nineteenth century and why dualism prevailed in French industry. Moreover, up to the 1850s, the available factor-mix – with abundance of cheap labour – did not stimulate the substitution of capital for labour, except in a few branches.

These few branches made up the 'modern' sector of industry. It largely owed its existence to protection from British competition, which came first from war and blockade, then, after 1814, from a succession of laws which established high duties on manufactured goods and prohibitions for some of them (e.g. cottons). This system was less rigorous than it is often thought and was mitigated from 1836 onwards. It has been branded with infamy by many writers, but it was a reflex of self-preservation: had there been no protection, France would have had no cotton, iron or engineering industries – or very little of them; she would have specialized in silks, fine worsteds and other luxury goods, plus her traditional pillars of exports, wines and brandies. However, the chances of development on these lines would have been limited by the protectionist systems of all major European countries, and especially of Britain, which – as is often overlooked – had prohibitions or discriminatory duties against French goods. Harris (1992) also observes that France could not have continued as a major power without a large iron industry and the heavy engineering based upon it. On the other hand, F. Caron (1981) has rightly pointed out the contradiction between the 'natural' way which comparative advantages created for French industrialization (that of quality production) and the artificial development, according to the English model, which protectionism stimulated. Likewise, Pollard (1981) observes that France was thus encouraged to compete with England rather than to be complementary, to concentrate on branches in which she was weak rather than on her strength. Protection also hampered the quality sector, by restricting imports of semi-finished and capital goods.

The main trouble was that the imitation was not a good one: it was smaller than the original, its equipment less up-to-date, its mills and works tinier; and its growth was slower, at least up to 1850. These shortcomings have often been explained by the incapacity of most French manufacturers, but market forces and comparative 'disadvantages' were more important. For the textile industries (except silk and part of the wool industry) and some others, the brake on growth was on the demand side; they were 'export restrained' (Trebilcock, 1981), prevented from exporting by the competition of cheaper British goods and the British domination of international trade. They depended upon the French home market, where incomes per capita were lower – roughly by 30 per cent – than in England. The home market was also heterogeneous, fragmented and did not expand fast, because population growth was decelerating and was slower than in other European countries: 31 per cent from 1800 to 1850 as against 46 per cent in Germany, 95 per cent in Britain; eventually zero growth occurred, in the late nineteenth century. One can, of course, wonder how a population of 100 millions – which France would have had by 1914, if she had grown at the same rate as Britain – would have found the fuel resources for industrialization! This narrow and fragmented home market may have forced manufacturers into a strategy of risk minimization. Though the cotton industry was helped by the high elasticity of demand for cottons to increases in incomes, it remained much smaller and less advanced technically than its British rival, with lower productivity of labour: in spinning, output per French worker in the late 1840s was two-thirds of the British level; it was still lower in weaving; despite lower wage rates, French prices were about 25 per cent higher. The deficiency of the home market also delayed progress in the iron industry, but supply difficulties, specially a shortage of suitable and cheap coking coal, were more important (the cost of coal also harmed the chemical industry).

The high price of iron was damaging to engineering, which also suffered from the tardiness in railway-building and steam engine diffusion, plus a shortage of skilled workers. Nonetheless, machine-building had at a time promising prospects; at the Great Exhibition of 1851, France won several prizes for machinery and scientific instruments and in the 1850s she exported three times more machinery than she imported. However, machinery never became a French speciality – though this would have been in line with her calling for skilled labour-intensive products; the narrowness of the home market and the lack of specialization by machine-builders are often seen as an explanation. But this does not hold for

Switzerland, which in 1860 had the highest machinery exports per capita in the world. She was, of course, a small country, to be compared, as Pollard (1981) writes, to some advanced region in large states. Actually, France had 'a Switzerland' inside her own borders: Alsace, which specialized both in quality goods (from printed cottons to locomotives) and in mechanized production, thanks to a constant search for technical innovation; according to M. Hau (1989), the poverty of an over-populated countryside had bred hard-working and careful workpeople. An index of Alsatian industrial production rises from 4.8 in 1816/9 to 60 in 1866/9, i.e. an annual rate of growth of 5.2 per cent (against 3.3 per cent for Champagne). However, Alsace was exceptional and her path of quality production by mechanized methods was too rarely followed in the rest of France.

There was thus a vicious circle for many French industries: the narrowness of their market made them grow slowly; and this slow growth was not conducive to modernization, though the latter, by lowering prices and possibly opening foreign markets, would have worked for faster growth. Moreover, the modern sector had a limited capacity to create employment outlets and so to transform and absorb the traditional sector. So much for the sempiternal theme of the slowness in French economic growth and of the resulting backwardness.

All things considered, and especially the disasters of the period 1789–1815 (Trafalgar, O'Brien writes (1978), 'condemned commercial enterprise in France to "domestic shopkeeping"'), the unsatisfactory factors' endowment (little coal, wages higher than elsewhere, but Britain) and the thankless role of being the second industrial country, the French performance, *up to the 1860s,* was not bad, even though her Industrial Revolution was unfinished and her potential for higher levels of output and consumption had not been fully realized. The only serious black spot was not economic, but demographic: the steady fall in marital fertility, birth and reproduction rates, which was preparing the zero growth of a later period; only after 1880 can one assume that the stagnation of population had a negative effect on investment and on mobility in factors of production.

The words 'honourable', 'respectable but not outstanding', 'not brilliant but quite creditable' have been used by Crafts (1984a) and myself (1974), about the French performance in the nineteenth century. In 1870, Britain was as far ahead – nay, more – as she had been in 1815. Bairoch's (1982) indexes of per capita levels of industrialization, on the basis of the UK in 1900 = 100, put France in 1860 at 20, that is, in fifth position after the UK (64), Belgium and Switzerland (28 and 26), the USA (21). From 1815 to 1869, French industrial output had grown at an annual rate of about 2.5 per cent; from 1825/34 to 1855/64, labour productivity in industry at 1.4–1.5 per cent; from 1833 to 1869, the horse-power of fixed steam-engines at 9 per cent. Moreover, the economy had become more open, the ratio of exports to industrial production had risen; export volumes grew at a rate of 5.1 per cent per year from 1820/2 to 1867/9; French exports were 9 per cent of world exports in 1846/8, 16 per cent in 1864/6.

Actually the major anomaly came *after* the period which has been considered here: the slowing-down, the protracted deceleration of French economic growth, which started in the 1860s and became obvious in the 1880s. Early on, a number of exogenous accidents could be blamed: the American Civil War, the disastrous Franco-Prussian war, the loss of Alsace, the crushing war indemnity. But later on, the crisis was obviously structural; it falls outside the scope of this chapter and has been recently studied in depth by M. Lévy-Leboyer and F. Bourguignon (1985). Suffice it to say that some of its roots are to be found in the pattern of French industrialization which has been described: in a structure of both industrial output and exports, where the share of metals, machinery and chemicals was far too low; and in a path of specialization in labour-intensive quality products, which eventually led into a dead-end. Many French exports were regressive or vulnerable to competition from countries which either had lower wages or succeeded in mechanizing the making of silks and other 'luxuries', at a time when France had ceased to have an abundant supply of cheap labour (which had dwindled from the 1850s). France was unable to retain the position on world markets she had reconquered during the second third of the century. The traditional sector of her dual economy partly collapsed and the modern one – a frail copy of the British model, as we have seen – was too weak to make up for this disaster. So France remained an incompletely industrialized country – and a declining power because of her zero population growth.

As a poor country, with a tragic history, France might be more akin to the countries of Southern Europe – Spain, Italy, Austria-Hungary, than to the successful and happy industrializers of the North: Britain, Belgium, Germany, the Scandinavians; but actually, in economic development, as in geographical terms, she belongs to both North and South. She was thus 'closer to the European average than was Britain' and 'comparisons of France and Britain that take Britain as a norm are misleading' (Crafts, 1984a). Each industrial revolution is different, with, as Gerschenkron suggested, a system of graduated deviations from the British model, which was copied, imitated, but never to perfection.

REFERENCES

L'acquisition des techniques par les pays non-initiateurs. Pont-à-Mousson, 28 juin–5 juillet 1970. 1973. (Paris); papers by P. Costabel, M. Daumas, B. Gille, J. Payen, F. Russo, J. Walch

Asselain, J. C. 1984. *Histoire économique de la France du XVIIIe siècle à nos jours*, vol. I (Paris)

Bairoch, P. 1982. 'International industrialization levels from 1750 to 1980', *Journal of European Economic History*, 11, no. 2, pp. 269–333

Beltran, A. and Griset, P. 1988. *La croissance économique de la France 1815–1914* (Paris)

Benoit, S. 1989. 'Les échanges de technologie entre la France et le monde anglo-américain à l'ère de l'industrialisation: le cas des moteurs hydrauliques', *Cahiers du Centre de Recherches Historiques*, 4, pp. 15–41

Bergeron, L. 1978. *Les capitalistes en France (1780–1914)* (Paris)

1979. *L'industrialisation de la France au XIXe siècle* (Paris)

Braudel, F. and Labrousse, E. (eds.). 1976. *Histoire économique et sociale de la France*, vol. III, *L'avènement de l'ère industrielle (1789–années 1880)* (Paris, 2 vols.)

Cameron, R. 1985. 'A new view of European industrialization', *Economic History Review*, 38, no. 1, pp. 1–23

(ed.) 1970. *Essays in French Economic History* (Homewood, Ill.); papers by C. Fohlen, F. Crouzet, T. J. Markovitch

Caron, F. 1981. *Histoire économique de la France XIXe–XXe siècles* (Paris; a revised edition of *An Economic History of Modern France*, New York, 1979)

Caycz, P. 1978. *Métiers jacquard et hauts fourneaux. Aux origines de l'industrie lyonnaise* (Lyons)

Chadeau, E. 1988. *Annuaire statistique de l'économie française aux XIXe et XXe siècles*, vol. I, *L'économie nationale aux XIXe et XXe siècles* (Paris)

Chaloner, W. H. 1990. *Industry and Innovation. Selected Essays* (London)

Chassagne, S. 1991. *Le coton et ses patrons. France, 1760–1840* (Paris)

Clapham, J. H. 1939. *An Economic History of Modern Britain*, vol. I, *The Early Railway Age 1820–1850* (Cambridge)

Crafts, N. F. R. 1984a. 'Economic growth in France and Britain, 1830–1910: a review of the evidence', *Journal of Economic History*, 44, no. 1, pp. 49–67

1984b. 'Patterns of development in nineteenth century Europe', *Oxford Economic Papers*, 36, pp. 438–58

1989. 'British industrialization in an international context', *Journal of Interdisciplinary History*, 19, no. 3, pp. 415–28

Crouzet, F. 1974. 'French economic growth in the nineteenth century reconsidered', *History*, 59, no. 196, pp. 167–79

1990. *Britain Ascendant: Comparative Studies in Franco-British Economic History* (Cambridge); especially chapters 8, 10, 12

Daviet, J. P. 1989. *Une multinationale à la française. Histoire de Saint-Gobain 1665–1989* (Paris)

Dunham, A. L. 1953. *La révolution industrielle en France (1815–1848)* (Paris)

Fohlen, C. 1973. 'France 1700–1914', in C. M. Cipolla (ed.), *The Fontana Economic History of Europe*, IV, *The Emergence of Industrial Societies*, Part 1 (Glasgow), pp. 7–75

1971. *Qu'est-ce que la révolution industrielle?* (Paris)

Fremdling, R. 1986. *Technologischer Wandel und internationaler Handel im 18. und 19. Jahrhundert. Die Eisenindustrien in Groszbritannien, Belgien, Frankreich und Deutschland* (Berlin)

Gille, B. 1959. *Recherches sur la formation de la grande entreprise capitaliste (1815–1848)* (Paris)

    1968. *La sidérurgie française au XIXe siècle* (Geneva)

Haber, L. F. 1958. *The Chemical Industry during the Nineteenth Century* (Oxford)

Harris, J. R. 1992. *Essays in Industry and Technology in the Eighteenth Century: England and France* (Aldershot)

    1989. 'The transfer of technology between Britain and France and the French Revolution', in C. Crossley and I. Small, *The French Revolution and British Culture* (Oxford), pp. 156–86

    1991. 'Movements of technology between Britain and Europe in the eighteenth century', in D. J. Jeremy (ed.), *International Technology Transfer. Europe, Japan and the U.S.A., 1700–1914* (Aldershot), pp. 9–30

Hau, M. 1989. 'Comparaison des croissances économiques de la Champagne et de l'Alsace', *Histoire, Economie et Société*, 8, no. 3, pp. 459–67

Henderson, W. O. 1961. *The Industrial Revolution on the Continent. Germany, France, Russia. 1800–1914* (London)

    1965. *Britain and Industrial Europe 1750–1870* (Leicester, 2nd edn)

Heywood, C. 1981. 'The Role of the Peasantry in French Industrialization, 1815–80', *The Economic History Review*, 34, no. 3, pp. 359–76

    1992. *The Development of the French Economy, 1750–1914* (Basingstoke)

Landes, D. S. 1969. *The Unbound Prometheus. Technological Change and Industrial Development in Western Europe from 1750 to the Present* (Cambridge)

Leleux, F. 1969. *A l'aube du capitalisme et de la révolution industrielle. Liévin Bauwens, industriel gantois* (Paris)

Léon, P. 1954. *La naissance de la grande industrie en Dauphiné (fin du XVIIe siècle – 1869)* (Paris)

Léon, P., Crouzet, F. and Gascon, R. (eds.). 1972. *L'industrialisation en Europe au XIXe siècle* (Paris)

Lévy-Leboyer, M. 1964. *Les banques européennes et l'industrialisation internationale dans la première moitié du XIXe siècle* (Paris)

    1968. 'Les processus d'industrialisation: le cas de l'Angleterre et de la France', *Revue historique*, no. 485, pp. 281–98

Lévy-Leboyer, M. and Bourguignon, F. 1985. *L'économie Française au XIXe siècle. Analyse macro-économique* (Paris; English translation: *The French Economy in the Nineteenth Century. An Essay in Econometric Analysis*, Cambridge, 1990).

Lévy-Leboyer, M. and Lescure, M. 1991. 'France', in R. Sylla and G. Toniolo, (eds.), *Patterns of European Industrialization: The Nineteenth Century* (London), pp. 153–74

Locke, R. R. 1978. *Les fonderies et forges d'Alais à l'époque des premiers chemins de fer 1829–1874* (Paris)

Marczewski, J. 1965. 'Le produit physique de l'économie française de 1789 à 1913 (comparaison avec la Grande-Bretagne)', *Cahiers de l'I.S.E.A.*, AF, 4, no. 163

Mathias, R. 1979. *The Transformation of England* (London)

Mathias, R. and Davis, J. A. (eds.). 1989. *The First Industrial Revolutions* (Oxford)

Milward, A. and Saul, S. B. 1973. *The Economic Development of Continental Europe 1780–1870* (London)

Mokyr, J. 1990. *The Lever of Riches. Technological Creativity and Economic Progress* (New York and Oxford)

Nye, J. V. 1987. 'Firm size and economic backwardness: a new look at the French industrial debate', *Journal of Economic History*, 47, no. 3, pp. 649–69

  1991. 'The myth of free-trade Britain and fortress France: tariffs and trade in the nineteenth century', *Journal of Economic History*, 51, no. 1, pp. 23–46

O'Brien, P. K. 1986. 'Do we have a typology for the study of European industrialization in the XIXth century?', *Journal of European Economic History*, 15, no. 2, pp. 291–333

O'Brien, P. K. and Keyder, C. 1978. *Economic Growth in Britain and France 1780–1914* (London)

Payen, J. 1969. *Capital et machine à vapeur au XVIIIe siècle. Les frères Périer et l'introduction en France de la machine à vapeur de Watt* (Paris)

  1985. *La machine à vapeur fixe en France* (Paris)

Pinson, M. 1965. 'La sidérurgie française', *Cahiers de l'I.S.E.A.*, no. 158, pp. 7–101

Pollard, S. 1981. *Peaceful Conquests: The Industrialization of Europe 1760–1970* (Oxford)

Reddy, W. M. 1984. *The Rise of Market Culture: The Textile Trade and French Society (1750–1900)* (Cambridge and Paris)

Roehl, R. 1976. 'French industrialization: a reconsideration', *Explorations in Economic History*, 13 (3), pp. 233–81

Thuillier, G. 1959. *Georges Dufaud et les débuts du grand capitalisme dans la métallurgie, en Nivernais au XIXe siècle* (Paris)

Toutain, J. C. 1987. *Le produit intérieur brut de la France de 1789 à 1982* (Paris)

Trebilcock, C. 1981. *The Industrialization of the Continental Powers 1780–1914* (London and New York)

Verley, P. 1986. 'Secteurs forts et secteurs faibles dans l'économie française des années 1860: une simulation économétrique', in P. Fridenson and A. Straus, *Le capitalisme français 19e–20 siècle* (Paris), pp. 151–73

  1989. *Nouvelle histoire économique de la France contemporaine, 2, L'industrialisation 1830–1914* (Paris)

Vial, J. 1967. *L'industrialisation de la sidérurgie française 1814–1864* (Paris, 2 vols.)

Woronoff, D. 1984. *L'industrie sidérurgique en France pendant la Révolution et l'Empire* (Paris)

THREE

The Industrial Revolution in Belgium

HERMAN VAN DER WEE

INTRODUCTION

BELGIUM was the first country on the European continent that system-atically took over and assimilated the British industrial innovations of the eighteenth and nineteenth centuries. However, the pattern of develop-ment was not identical. Because of the time-lag the path of technological progress was different. There were also significant differences in the trade position of Belgium, as compared with Britain, and in the geographical spreading of the mechanization process, which in both countries was determined by specific rural and urban traditions. Finally, there were important differences in government policy and in financial structures and development.

For clarity, therefore, it was decided to divide the essay into four parts. The first part will focus on the historical background of the Industrial Revolution. The second part will give a general, descriptive survey of the industrialization process as it was realized in three main industrial regions of Belgium. The third part will pay attention to the role played by the two main centres of tertiary activity in supporting the Belgian Industrial Revolution. The final part will examine the shifts in the regional dynamics of the industrialization process and the role of investment banking in the Belgian Industrial Revolution.

THE HISTORICAL BACKGROUND

The Southern Netherlands (later Belgium) could rely on a very old and important industrial tradition. The medieval towns of Flanders and Brabant had already been centres of production of woollen cloth, based on a far-reaching division of labour. They later became famous too for the production of all kinds of luxury goods, such as paintings, tapestries, musical instruments, diamonds and lace, which they exported, as was already the case with the Flemish and Brabantine cloth, to the whole of Europe and to the Middle East. Meanwhile mass production of woollens and linens spread over the countryside. From the fifteenth and sixteenth centuries onwards it grew into a flourishing cottage industry producing also for export, in particular to Spain and increasingly to Latin America. The cottage industry became the real basis of the industrial strength of Flanders in the seventeenth and eighteenth centuries at the very moment that the protectionist character of European mercantilism, focusing particularly on import substitution of luxury goods, affected adversely the production of the many specialized craft guilds in the Flemish towns; the towns were forced to return to mass production or to finishing processes of cheap textiles based on low wages and proletarianization of the urban masses.

The principality of Liège and the other Walloon provinces (later the south of Belgium) possessed rich deposits of lead, iron-ore and coal, which were already exploited successively in the Middle Ages. From the sixteenth and seventeenth centuries onwards the scale of production of these ores and minerals increased remarkably. Coal particularly became a crucial export item to Flanders, to the Northern Netherlands, and increasingly to France. In urban Wallonia from the Middle Ages onwards, iron and bronze processing, manufacturing of sophisticated weapons, and manufacturing of copper and brass for household purposes were important artisanal activities. In the countryside, during the same period, a flourishing rural armaments and nail industry emerged. Somewhat later, in the seventeenth century, in the region of Verviers, south of Liège, a rural industry producing woollen cloth was expanding.

The Southern Netherlands had also built up from medieval times a solid commercial and financial infrastructure: the harbours of Bruges and Antwerp, the Brabant Fairs, modern banking, transcontinental trade by land and by river to Central and Eastern Europe, to Italy and to Spain were the most remarkable highlights of it. The Eighty Years War (1568–1648) destroyed most of the infrastructure of the Southern Netherlands, but certainly not all of it: the seventeenth century indeed was not as dark as the traditional historian usually depicts. Moreover, from the second half of the eighteenth century, a clear revival of investment in infrastructural improvement was noticeable. The Southern Netherlands, which since the peace of Utrecht in 1713 were integrated into the Habsburg Empire, benefited from Austrian mercantilism: roads and canals were built, governmental administration was strengthened, the maritime expansion of Ostend was supported with vigour and transcontinental trade was re-stimulated by the growing political links between the Southern Netherlands and the Austrian Empire.

Economic revival also initiated a financial come-back. The leading bankers of Brussels and particularly of Antwerp participated again more actively in the money and capital markets of Amsterdam, concentrating – with respect to short-term credit – on the international trade in bills of exchange and – with respect to long-term credit – on the stock market and on European governmental loans. Unfortunately, there was probably a net outflow of capital as the Belgian bankers rarely invested in industrial ventures of the country and preferred to invest on behalf of their customers in long-term European bonds or in colonial stock.

Stimulated by the improving prospects of export-led growth during the eighteenth century, interest in technological progress became evident in the iron and coal industry of Wallonia. By 1720 a Newcomen atmospherical pump was installed in the Liège coal-mining area; it was the first experiment on the continent. Technological progress was realized in the woollen industry of the Verviers region too; although the sector remained essentially a rural cottage industry for spinning and weaving, new machinery for the finishing process was introduced during the second half of the eighteenth century and set up in special large factory buildings in town. At the same time, concentration of the Verviers textile sector took place at an accelerated pace. Organizational process thus accompanied technological progress here.

In the Flemish countryside proto-industrialization was gathering momentum in the linen sector in the course of the eighteenth century, generating some organizational improvement. Some technological progress was made in the urban textile industry with the introduction of new machinery for the finishing process. More crucial was the organizational progress realized in the industrial sectors of the towns, especially the setting up of special factory buildings for the finishing operations in the textile industry, for the introduction of cotton printing, for salt and sugar refinery, for diamond cutting and so on.

An important factor towards the advance of proto-industrialization during the eighteenth century was the demographical and agricultural development in the Flemish and Walloon countryside. There were remarkable gains in agricultural productivity. The systematic cultivation of the potato was introduced in the region of Bruges in 1708 and from the 1740s onwards it quickly spread throughout the whole country. The successful introduction of the potato allowed for a steep population increase. There is also proof of clearing of new land and of an important improvement of the rotation process, linked with the general adoption of clover-growing. And last but not least there was the increasing specialization in commercial agriculture, for example, grain for brewing in Hesbaye, specialized flax-growing and flax-processing in east Flanders: it favoured the intensification of agriculture.

Many of the initiating mechanisms for the new dynamism of growth in the rural economy were exogenous, for example the action by the Austrian government for stimulating the Walloon (i.e. Hainaut) nail industry against its Liège counterpart, the colonial upsurge of the eighteenth century, creating an extra demand for linens, the fall of food prices when the War of the Spanish Succession (1701–14) was over, generating an effort to increase agricultural productivity in order to cover the agricultural income losses. When the two later mechanisms were combined, population growth occurred. Indeed, when the terms of trade shifted in favour of textiles from one period to the next, the peasants, selling more linen and receiving a better price for it, were able to increase their income as productivity gains in agriculture compensated for the fall in food prices. Even the cottage dweller who was involved in industrial production only, was better off as his food became cheaper and the linen he sold became more expensive.

A clear correlation was found therefore between the trend towards a lower age at the first marriage and the long-term economic growth which occurred in the regions of rural industry in the Austrian Netherlands during the first half of the eighteenth century. Furthermore, with respect to short-run fluctuations it was convincingly shown by Franklin Mendels in his well-known book *Industrial and Population Pressure in Eighteenth-Century Flanders* (New York, 1981) that the rising linen:rye price ratio positively affected marriages with a one-year lag in six typical linen-producing villages of the interior of Flanders in the course of the eighteenth century. For some time population growth did not nullify the increase of per capita income in the countryside because the productivity gains in agriculture were determined to a large extent by the possibility of an increased labour input during the seasonal peaks of weeding and harvesting, while during the period of slackening agricultural activity the expansive rural industry absorbed the growing mass of hidden unemployment generated by the rising population.

THE FIVE GROWTH POLES OF THE BELGIAN INDUSTRIALIZATION

The annexation of the Southern Netherlands by France after the invasion of the territory in 1795 by the French Revolutionary army gave birth to an entirely new society. The traditional rigid framework of socio-economic organization was abolished. The introduction of a new, liberal order raised high expectations. Moreover, the French were willing to protect the mechanized infant industry against English competition and opened up for the Belgian entrepreneurs the attractive prospect of a large and homogeneous market. All this no doubt created a psychological climate in favour of taking the risks of industrial mechanization or of new investment in the industrial sector. The drive towards innovation converged around five main growth poles: the regions of Verviers–Liège and of Mons–Charleroi and the towns of Ghent, Antwerp and Brussels, the three first regions being industrial growth poles in the first place, the two latter ones being centres of tertiary activity.

In 1798 William Cockerill, a British emigrant technician, contracted with the Verviers merchant-entrepreneur Jean-François Simonis to build five mechanized wool-spinning mills. It was such a success that the new machines were very rapidly introduced into the other large firms of the region. In 1810 only six firms out of a total of 144 possessed complete machinery sets for the spinning of wool, but these six firms controlled more than 50 per cent of total output.

After the defeat of France in 1814, mechanization was resumed in the region of Verviers: weaving of wool now became mechanized, and new technology was introduced in the finishing sector, but very soon further growth in the woollen industry became determined much more by differentiation than by mechanization of the production. At that moment, linkages with the iron and coal industry, activated *inter alia* by the Cockerills, had already shifted the centre of gravity of economic growth from the Verviers to the Liège region.

In 1807 a factory for machinery construction was founded by the Cockerill family at Liège; it soon became the heart of a large, vertically integrated industrial enterprise, which included coal-mining, iron-ore smelting, pig-iron processing, metal construction and so on. The Cockerills were also the first to introduce the puddling method on the continent. They built the first modern blast-furnace, the first locomotives and the first iron ships on the continent, becoming moreover the first continental suppliers of iron rails. The *demonstration effect* led to the setting up of several other blast-furnaces along the Meuse River near Liège (four between 1832 and 1835 with the financial help of the Banque de Belgique); it also led to the opening of new coal mines and to the founding of numerous plants for pig-iron processing, machinery construction and other metallurgical manufacturing. The Liège case therefore was a typical example of forward and backward linkages within the boundaries of a regional growth pole.

A second Belgian growth pole was the Mons–Charleroi region. Its original growth path, however, was quite different from the Verviers–Liège one. The first acceleration in the expansion of the coal industry occurred in the region of Mons (the Borinage) in the course of the eighteenth century, when canal building eased the export of coal to Flanders and to France, especially to Paris. The French conquest of 1795 favoured still more the improvement of the transportation system: new canals were dug or rivers were canalized. The result was a continuity in the export-led growth, based on the French market, even after Napoleon's defeat in 1814 and the definitive political separation of Belgium and France one year later.

Notwithstanding the amazing growth of the coal-mining industry (the number of mines had risen to 400 and the yearly production already reached a million tons at the end of the reign of Napoleon), the economy of the Mons region remained static within the stages of proto-industrialization. Technological progress during that period was very limited indeed and no real process of forward and backward linkages set in.

Different again was the development of the Charleroi region. Charleroi itself was a small eighteenth-century town south of Mons and the centre of the rural nail industry north of the Sambre River, an industry which had been favoured by the Austrian government against the older more important nail industry in the principality of Liège and which in its turn had stimulated some other minor iron manufacturing activity in the area. The rural nail industry in the neighbourhood of Charleroi was a typical cottage industry which had to import its iron from outside, in contrast to the nail industry of the Liège region, and for that reason was at a disadvantage vis-à-vis Liège. This disadvantage increased when the Austrian domination ended and the compensatory protection measures were eliminated. The nail industry suffered a new setback when the end of the French domination in 1814 and the unification of Belgium and Holland in 1815 discriminated against the Charleroi in comparison with the Liège region, hindering the former in its access to the nearby French market and favouring the latter in its access to the nearby Dutch market.

Against the background of this challenge, it is not surprising to see, between 1820 and 1830, the introduction of heavy industry in Charleroi, based on iron-ore smelting and iron-processing, following the newest English techniques. The setting-up of local modern coal mining in order to feed the new iron industry soon followed and last but not least came the founding of new metal manufacturing firms, constructing inter alia modern transportation equipment. By 1831 nine modern blast-furnaces were in production; the one, although begun later than Cockerill's first blast furnace in the Liège region, was the first blast-furnace to operate on the continent.

Two remarks should be made in this context. First, the new techniques were introduced by individual local merchant-entrepreneurs, with the help of English engineers. The driving force was on the local supply side, not on the demand side, but there is no doubt that the existence of a flourishing commercial and financial infrastructure in nearby Mons was an important element in the supply of capital and in the setting up of an export-marketing system, which at a later stage would bring rising demand. The second remark concerns the importance of the backward and forward linkages. After a while the dynamism of the Charleroi growth pole had an influence upon the Mons region: it even stimulated the emergence of a new coal-mining area in the same region between Charleroi and Mons (*le Centre*).

The third industrial growth pole of Belgium was Ghent, located in Flanders. Modernization first remained limited to the town of Ghent itself. The first machinery of modern cotton-spinning was introduced by Liévin Bauwens, the son of a Ghent tanner sent across the Channel to learn the English tanning techniques, but more interested in the mechanization of the cotton industry. In 1801 Bauwens set up a mechanized cotton-spinning factory in Ghent, based on the English *mule jennies*. He also introduced many other English innovations. More modern factories were founded, often by entrepreneurs who had some familial ties with Bauwens, leading to the building of a cotton-spinning family empire.

A second stage in the modernization of the Ghent textile industry was marked by the action of the traditional calico-printers, who because of Napoleon's blockade were unable to import English calicoes. The printers now bought raw cotton in the Levant and, preferring to control the spinning and weaving of it themselves, they added mechanized cotton-spinning and traditional cotton-weaving to their printing factories. The new strategy led to a process of vertical integration and concentration. Both actions, by Bauwens and his imitators and by the printers, led to over-investment, which by the time of Waterloo (1814) had become a disaster. Moreover, after the Congress of Vienna in 1815, the Ghent industry, being not yet modern enough to resist British competition, was faced with the prospect of decline.

When the challenge of British competition became acute a third stage of modernization started in the Ghent textile industry with some leading merchant-entrepreneurs from the calico-printing sector investing in mechanizing their weaving and printing divisions. This third mechanization drive of the early 1820s was successful because the unification with the Netherlands had opened the Dutch East-Indian colonies for the import of Ghent calicoes. When Belgium separated from the Netherlands in 1830, Ghent, losing its Asian markets, faced a new, difficult time, but struggled through the crisis by introducing the mechanization of the linen industry and by further modernizing and differentiating its cotton industry. No forward or backward linkages leading to the emergence of new industrial sectors occurred. Growth was very irregular, and limited until 1850. Only when the traditional rural linen industry entered its phase of final decay, particularly after the famine of 1847–51, did mechanized spinning, weaving, and finishing of cotton, linen, jute and wool spread slowly but steadily over the whole region of East and West Flanders, employing the mass of cheap labour available there.

The textile industry therefore, although a dominant sector in the Belgian economy of the *ancien régime*, was not a leading sector in Belgium's Industrial Revolution. The basic industries in the south of the country, on the contrary, had a much more decisive impact upon the changes in the industrial structure. But even in the new sectors of heavy industry Rostow's concept of *take-off* and Gerschenkron's concept of *great spurt* are difficult to apply to the Belgian case. There was no immediate connection between the increase of the investment ratio and the increase in total output. The first real spurt in coal output in Hainaut, for example, occurred during the eighteenth and at the beginning of the nineteenth century without any big investment and without important mechanization. When mechanization of the Hainaut coal and iron industry led to an increase of the investment ratio, total output did not rise very much initially because the mechanized production of coal and iron only replaced the traditional one. The same remarks apply to the Liège region.

One should also mention two other important growth poles, namely Antwerp and Brussels. When Napoleon reopened in 1798–9 the Scheldt River, closed by the Dutch since 1585, new hopes arose for a revival of the old Antwerp harbour. New banks, new insurance companies and new firms in other tertiary sectors and in the processing industry were founded. The canals built by King William I to connect the Mons–Charleroi area via Brussels with Antwerp added momentum to the rising expectations. After independence in 1830 Liège too was connected by canal with Antwerp. Soon the railway would become a new link between the Antwerp harbour and the two industrial regions of Wallonia in the provinces of Liège and Hainaut. The Belgian government took the initiative of building an *Iron Rhine*, that is, a railway that connected the German hinterland with Antwerp in the hope of diverting the German transit trade from Rotterdam and Hamburg to Antwerp. The foundations were thus laid for a successful international transit activity via Antwerp and for the maritimization of the exports of the Walloon heavy and manufacturing industries. Antwerp became also a centre of industrial processing of imported colonial goods and grains, a centre of shipbuilding and ship repair and later a centre of imports of raw materials and even energy for the Walloon industries.

Brussels is the last emerging growth pole to be noted here. In the beginning its rise was not based on mechanized industry, but on Brussels' growing importance as the political, diplomatic, administrative and financial capital of the country. Handicraft industry and services developed, and at a later stage of the Industrial Revolution these were mechanized too and thereby laid the foundation of modern industry in the Brussels area.

CONCLUDING REMARKS

During the first stage of the Belgian Industrial Revolution the centre of gravity in the process of structural change was clearly situated in the Walloon part of the country. Within Wallonia the Mons–Charleroi area in Hainaut emerged as the most dynamic and most powerful industrial growth pole. Its expansion during the third quarter of the nineteenth century, based now mainly on a further widening of capital and a further rise of coal exports to France, surpassed distinctively the growth of the Liège basin. The real great success of the Walloon heavy industry at that time, however, was not only due to factors on the supply side and to a fortuitous export boom of coal to France, but also to other more dynamic factors on the demand side, particularly with respect to the export demand for pig-iron, for intermediate finished metallic products, for steam engines, locomotives and other transportation equipment, a demand which was determined to a large extent by the Railway Revolution and the ensuing railway boom. Because at that time Wallonia's heavy industry had an undeniable technological lead over its French and German counterparts, and because it had a clear locational advantage vis-à-vis British competition, the first industrialization phase of Germany and France became very dependent upon exports from Wallonia. Later, when the demand from Germany and from France slackened and the depression of the 1880s threatened the expansion of the iron industry, Wallonia reacted by shifting from iron to steel and by increasing the size of its basic industry. Wallonia now differentiated its production much more by multiplying steel construction goods; it also diversified its markets by moving through the harbour of Antwerp towards maritime transportation of its products and worldwide sales. The result of this evolution was a relative weakening of the industrial position of the Hainaut province, because the Mons basin in Hainaut had focused its expansion too exclusively on coal export to France, which slackened because of the rise of French coal mining and English competition. Meanwhile, the Liège region strengthened its relative position because of the spectacular growth of steel manufacturing in this area.

The Antwerp harbour benefited from the maritimization of Wallonia's exports and from the rising transit trade with Germany and France. At the end of the nineteenth century it started to attract autonomous industrial investment, based on her location advantages. But Antwerp's industrialization was not nearly enough, even together with the steady diffusion of the mechanized textile industry from Ghent to the rest of Flanders, to move the balance of industrial power from south to north. Only after the Second World War was there a clear-cut shift in industrial dynamism from south to north.

A final remark concerns the role of the Brussels mixed banks (combining commercial banking with long-term investment), that is, the Société Générale de Belgique, founded in 1822 and the Banque de Belgique, founded in 1835. Why did these two banks play such a dominant role in the industrialization process of Belgium, and why did this specific Belgian banking system remain so stable and viable afterwards?

Financial intermediaries in Brussels concentrated heavily upon the basic and capital goods industries, which were paramount in Belgian industrialization in the course of the nineteenth century. These industries had a larger need for venture capital to finance their fixed assets. Because of the high capital outlays needed for mechanization, most of the firms active in the above-mentioned industries did not have sufficient reserves at their disposal to finance the transition themselves. Moreover, because of the low writing off for depreciation of fixed assets they were not able to generate sufficient cash flow internally to finance further mechanization and expansion. They therefore had to attract external funds. The mixed banks, because of capital-market imperfections in Belgium in the course of the nineteenth century and the traditional concentration of wealth, took the opportunity of coordinating and controlling the accumulation and allocation of capital in Belgium. They became the suppliers of funds to the basic and capital goods industries and in return gained control of them. The institutions for organizing control in Belgian industry were consequently financial institutions, an organizational innovation of decisive importance for the success of the industrialization process in Belgium, and for its later success on the whole European continent.

This financial structure remained typical in Belgium even in the twentieth century, when in other countries – particularly the USA – the development of a mass-produced consumer durables sector led to a substitution of financial capitalism by managerial capitalism where the coordinating and controlling functions of the holding company structure were replaced by the more modern organization and control systems of the large industrial corporations. Why did Belgium preserve its nineteenth-century financial structure so long? First, because income distribution in Belgium remained quite unequal until a recent date; relative abundance of labour allowed for keeping wages low and services cheap and hindered –

together with the small geographical size of the domestic market – the appearance of a mass market for consumer durables. Second, because the building of a large transportation system, not only in Europe but also in the colonial territories, provided scope for a long time for the attention to investment in basic industries and in heavy transportation equipment.

Only when after the Second World War investment in colonial mining and transportation had ceased and Belgium had become a more affluent society did industrial investment shift towards the new sectors of consumer durables. The traditional Brussels holding companies at the same time were losing their overall grip on Belgian industry to the American multinationals, to the German mixed banks and to some other financial independent European companies. The need for external funds was not decreasing. On the contrary, it was increasing. But the structure of Belgian industry was changing, and the control of the new industrial sectors was no longer in the hands of the traditional Belgian holding companies, but increasingly in the hands of foreign investors.

SELECT BIBLIOGRAPHY

Books in English on the Belgian Industrial Revolution are scarce. The interested reader therefore should not limit his search for sources to books only but should also look at journal articles in English, at chapters in general works in English and eventually at some studies in French or even in Dutch.

As far as the pre-industrial period is concerned one should mention first the general study by Hubert Van Houtte, *Histoire économique de la Belgique à la fin de l'Ancien Régime* (Ghent, 1920). For studies in more detail, see Jan Craeybeckx, 'The beginning of the Industrial Revolution in Belgium' in Rondo Cameron (ed.), *Essays in French Economic History* (Homewood, Ill, 1970), pp. 187–200; Franklin Mendels, *Industrialization and Population Pressure in Eighteenth-Century Flanders* (New York, 1981); Pierre Lebrun *L'industrie de le laine à Verviers pendant le XVIIIe siècle et le début du XIXe siècle. Contribution à l'étude des origines de la révolution industrielle* (Liège, 1948); Georges Hansotte, *La métallurgie et le commerce international du fer dans les Pays-Bas autrichiens et la Principauté de Liège pendant la seconde moitié du XVIIIe siècle* (Brussels, 1980); Hervé Hasquin, *Une mutation. Le 'Pays de Charleroi' aux XVIIe et XVIIIe siècles. Aux origines de la Révolution industrielle en Belgique* (Brussels, 1971).

The best recent publication on the general history of the Low Countries (i.e. The Netherlands and Belgium) in the modern period is Ernst H. Kossmann, *The Low Countries, 1780–1980* (Oxford, 1978). As far as general studies on the Belgian Industrial Revolution are concerned one should mention: Pierre Lebrun, Marinette Bruwier, Jan Dhondt and Georges Hansotte, *Essai sur la révolution industrielle en Belgique, 1770–1847* (Brussels, 2nd edn 1981); Guido L. De Brabander, Jean Gadisseur, Romy Gobyn and Jacques Liebin (eds.), *L'industrie en Belgique. Deux siècles d'évolution, 1780–1980* (Brussels, 1981); Joel

Mokyr, *Industrialization in the Low Countries, 1795–1850* (New Haven, 1976); See also N. Briavoinne, *De l'industrie en Belgique. Causes de décadence et de prospérité. Sa situation actuelle* (Brussels, 2 vols., 1838); Robert Demoulin, *Guillaume Ier et la transformation économique des provinces belges* (Liège, 1938); Jan Albert Van Houtte, 'Economic development of Belgium and the Netherlands from the beginning of the modern era' in *The Journal of European Economic History*, 1 (Spring 1972), pp. 100–20; Jan Dhondt and Marinette Bruwier. 'The Industrial Revolution in Belgium and Holland, 1700–1914' in: Carlo Cipolla (ed.), *The Fontana Economic History of Europe*, vol. IV, part 1 (London, 1973), pp. 329–69; Guido L. De Brabander, *Regional Specialization, Employment and Economic Growth in Belgium between 1846 and 1970* (New York, 1981); Herman Van der Wee and Karel Veraghtert, 'De economie van 1814 tot 1944', in Max Lamberty, Robert Van Roosbroeck, Michiel Vandekerckhove and others (eds.), *Twintig Eeuwen Vlaanderen*, vol. VIII: *De Vlaamse Gemeenschap: bevolking, economie, sociaal-economische ontwikkeling* (Hasselt, 1978), pp. 129–211.

The best general information in English on the Belgian Industrial Revolution can be obtained from the chapters on Belgium in works on the European Industrial Revolution in general, in particular in Alan S. Milward and S. B. Saul, *The Development of the Economies of Continental Europe, 1850–1914* (London, 1977); Sidney Pollard, *Peaceful Conquest. The Industrialization of Europe, 1760–1970* (Oxford, 1981); David S. Landes, *The Unbound Prometheus. Technological Change and Industrial Development in Western Europe from 1750 to the Present* (Cambridge, 1969).

For bibliographical and statistical information, see the following general works: Derek H. Aldcroft and Richard Rodger, *The Bibliography of European Economic and Social History* (Manchester, 1984); Brian R. Mitchell, *European Historical Statistics, 1750–1970* (New York, 1975). For statistical publications concerning Belgium, see B. Verhaegen, *Contribution à l'histoire économique des Flandres* (Louvain and Paris, 1961, 2 vols.); Jean Gadisseur, *Le produit physique de la Belgique, 1830–1913. Présentation critique des données statistiques: introduction générale; agriculture* (Brussels, 1990); Daniel Degrève, *Le commerce extérieur de la Belgique, 1830–1913–1939. Présentation critique des données statistiques* (Brussels, 2 vols., 1982); Joseph Pirard, *Le pouvoir central belge et ses comptes économiques, 1830–1913* (Brussels, 3 vols., 1980–5).

For information on specific topics only the most important studies will be indicated. As far as demographical development is concerned one should mention Ron J. Lesthaeghe, *The Decline of Belgian Fertility, 1800–1970* (Princeton, 1979); René Leboutte, *Reconversions de la main d'oeuvre et transition démographique. Les bassins industriels en aval de Liège, XVIIe–XXe siècles* (Paris, 1988); Claude Desama, *Population et révolution industrielle. Evolution des structures démographiques à Verviers dans la première moitié du XIXe siècle* (Liège, 1988).

Two recent books on agricultural development in Belgium during modern times deserve special attention: Martine Goossens. *The Economic Development of Belgian Agriculture: A Regional Perspective, 1812–1846* (Brussels, 1992); Jan

Blomme, *The Economic Development of Belgian Agriculture, 1880–1980: A Quantitative and Qualitative Analysis* (Brussels, 1992).

On the history of the textile industry, see François-Xavier van Houtte, *L'évolution de l'industrie textile en Belgique et dans le monde de 1800 à 1939* (Louvain, 1949); Jan Dhondt, 'The cotton industry at Ghent during the French régime' in François Crouzet, W. H. Chaloner and W. M. Stern (eds.), *Essays in European Economic History, 1789–1914* (London, 1969), pp. 15–52; Hilda Coppejans-Desmedt, 'De Gentse vlasindustrie vanaf het einde van de XVIIIe eeuw tot de oprichting van de grote mechanische bedrijven', *Handelingen van de Maatschappij voor Geschiedenis en Oudheidkunde te Gent*, 22 (1968), pp. 179–202; Pierre Lebrun, 'Croissance et industrialisation. L'expérience de l'industrie drapière verviétoise, 1750–1850' in *First International Conference of Economic History, Stockholm, 1960: Contributions and Communications* (Paris and The Hague, 1960), pp. 531–68.

On the history of heavy industry, see Georges Hansotte, 'La sidérurgie belge du XIXe siècle avant l'acier', *Revue d'histoire de la sidérurgie*, 6 (1966), pp. 211–37; Conrad Reuss, Emile Koutny and Léon Tychon, *Le progrès économique en sidérurgie: Belgique, Luxembourg, Pays-Bas, 1830–1955* (Louvain and Paris, 1960); Ami Wibail, 'L'évolution économique de la sidérurgie belge de 1830 à 1913' in *Bulletin de l'Institut des Sciences Economiques*, 5 (1933–4), pp. 31–61; Rainer Fremdling, *Technologischer Wandel und internationaler Handel im 18. und 19. Jahrhundert. Die Eisenindustrien in Groszbritannien, Belgien, Frankreich und Deutschland* (Berlin, 1986); Hubert Watelet, *Une industrialisation sans développement. Le bassin de Mons et le charbonnage du Grand-Hornu du milieu du XVIIIe au milieu du XIXe siècle* (Ottawa, 1980); P. Darquenne, *Histoire économique du département de Jemappe* (Mons, 1965).

On the history of technology and innovation during the Industrial Revolution in Belgium, see Anne Van Neck, *Les débuts de la machine à vapeur dans l'industrie belge, 1800–1850* (Brussels, 1979); C. Caulier-Mathy, *La modernisation des charbonnages liégeois pendant la première moitié du XIXe siècle. Techniques d'exploitation* (Paris, 1971); Ginette Kurgan-van Hentenryk and Jean Stengers (eds.), *L'innovation technologique: facteur de changement (XIXe–XXe siècles)* (Brussels, 1986).

On financial history (in particular the history of mixed or industrial banking), see Rondo Cameron, 'Belgium 1800–1875', in Rondo Cameron, Olga Crisp, Hugh T. Patrick and Richard Tilly (eds.), *Banking in the Early Stages of Industrialisation* (Oxford, 1967), pp. 129–50; Herman Van der Wee and Martine Goossens, 'Belgium', in Rondo Cameron and Valeri I. Bovykin (eds.), *International Banking, 1870–1914* (Oxford, 1991); Herman Van der Wee, 'La politique d'investissement de la Société Générale de Belgique, 1822–1913', *Histoire, Economie et Société*, 4 (1982), pp. 603–19; Ben Serge Chlepner, *La banque en Belgique* (Brussels, 1926); Roland Durviaux, *La banque mixte. Origine et soutien de l'expansion économique de la Belgique* (Brussels, 1947).

On communication, see Urbain Lamalle, *Histoire des chemins de fer belges* (Brussels, 1943); Léopold Génicot, *Histoire des routes belges depuis 1704* (Brussels, 1948); Karel Veraghtert, 'The growth of the Antwerp Port traffic,

1850–1900', in Wolfram Fischer, M. Marvin McInnis and Jürgen Schneider (eds.), *The Emergence of a World Economy, 1500–1914* (Wiesbaden, 1986), pp. 573–91. On social history, see Ben Serge Chlepner, *Cent ans d'histoire sociale en Belgique* (Brussels, 1936); Michel Neirynck, *De loonen in België sedert 1846* (Antwerp, 1944).

FOUR

Industrialization in The Netherlands

J. L. VAN ZANDEN

BRIEF HISTORIOGRAPHIC NOTE

THE late and slow process of industrialization in the Netherlands is possibly the subject which has concerned economic historians the most during recent decades. In the 1950s and 1960s, the debate about this was based, in a certain sense, partly on a misunderstanding. Historians such as I. J. Brugmans, J. H. Stuijvenberg and J. A. de Jonge went looking for an 'industrial revolution' on the lines of the British model, for a short period in which the 'take-off' took place.[1] Almost every decade after 1850 – with the exception of the 1880s – was nominated, something which, as such, already clearly shows that there was *no* Industrial Revolution.[2] The second theme in this debate concerned the question of the explanation of the late emergence of large-scale industry. Writers who emphasized the unfavourable economic conditions for modern industry – for example, the lack of coal and the relatively high level of wages – were opposed to historians who saw the mental element – the absence of a group of powerful, innovative entrepreneurs – as the most important reason for the late start.[3] The first stage of this debate ended with J. A. de Jonge's thesis in 1967.[4] On the basis of extensive empirical research, he showed that the breakthrough of large-scale industry took place only after 1890. However, he did not give a satisfactory explanation for this late start.

The debate received new impulses in the latter half of the 1970s thanks to the contributions of a number of writers (J. Mokyr, R. W. J. M. Bos, R. T. Griffiths) who tried to explain the problem of late industrialization with the help of theories derived from economics.[5] In addition, the debate concentrated more and more on the first half of the nineteenth century. Irrespective of the theoretical starting point chosen – Bos's neo-classical approach or the theory of the dual economy used by Mokyr – the conclusion reached was that the development of the factor prices (wages, coal prices, prices of machines and steam engines) played a decisive role. Mokyr compared late industrialization in The Netherlands with the early and rapid breakthrough of industry in Belgium and concluded that the difference in wage levels between the two countries was the most important explanatory element.[6] According to his calculations, wages in Belgium were considerably lower than in The Netherlands, a proposition which was criticized in detail in 1980 by Kint and Van der Voort.[7] Bos and Griffiths did not confine themselves to wage costs and, furthermore, they also took regional differences between factor prices into account. In the Eastern and Southern Netherlands, for example wage costs were no higher than in Belgium but, because of the large distance to the (Belgian and British) coal mines and the poor transport system, coal prices were prohibitively high. As a result, the introduction of the steam engine was not profitable before the arrival of the railways in those areas. On the other hand, the Northern and Western Netherlands contended with high rates of pay. The transport system there was, thanks to water transport, reasonably well developed.[8]

In the 1980s, research concentrated primarily upon the working out and testing of the approach formulated by Bos and Griffiths. Case studies of the development of different branches of industry – the textile industry in Twente, copper mills in the Veluwe, paper-making in the Zaan area[9] – showed that, because of the relatively unfavourable factor prices, the transition from a traditional technology to modern steam technology was, until 1850, definitely not profitable, as a result of which industrialization did not get going.[10] At the same time, research was liberated from the British model and thereby from the search for *the* Industrial Revolution. By means of fundamental quantitative research into the development of the services sector and agriculture into the period before 1850, a new picture was gradually created of the development of the Dutch economy in the nineteenth century, a picture of *balanced growth*, fairly evenly spread across the sectors of the economy and characterized by periods of rapid expansion, alternating with years of slow growth or decline.[11] Following in the footsteps of Cameron, Pollard and Crafts, we can now state that the development of Dutch industry fits in well with the overall European pattern of steady industrial growth, clustered in a few industrializing areas, and that the British model rather tended to be exceptional.[12]

The change which has come about in the approach to slow industrialization can also be described as a shift of perspective. In the debate that was conducted in the 1950s and 1960s, The Netherlands was seen as a 'traditional agrarian economy' in the Rostow sense, which had to undergo an industrial revolution in order to become a 'modern, industrial society'. The basic assumption of the new approach is the *special* structure of the Dutch economy at the beginning of the nineteenth century, a structure which, to a large extent, was an inheritance of economic growth during the seventeenth century.[13] The slow development of the economy in the period between 1800 and 1850 is seen as the continuation of the relative stagnation of national economy during the eighteenth century. The factors which hindered industrialization, such as high wages in the coastal provinces, were closely linked to the socio-economic structure which emerged in the seventeenth century. The slow industrialization of the nineteenth century is therefore ultimately linked to the difficult transition from the economic structure of seventeenth-century commercial capitalism to industrial capitalism, a transition which was made more difficult by institutional rigidities on the labour market, the commodity market and in the apparatus of government.[14]

This essay is a first attempt, partly on the basis of this perspective – arguing on the basis of the special economic, social and political structure of The Netherlands at the beginning of the nineteenth century – to interpret the slow process of industrialization. To this end, we shall first take a closer look at this starting point.

THE NETHERLANDS AT THE BEGINNING OF THE NINETEENTH CENTURY

At the beginning of the nineteenth century, The Netherlands was different, in almost all respects, from the traditional agrarian society which is often the basic assumption of the development of theories about the Industrial Revolution. About 1800, it was probably the most highly developed – the most urbanized, learned and rich – country in the world, a position which it had acquired in the seventeenth century but which it gradually began to lose to Great Britain. In the seventeenth century, Holland was the commercial and industrial centre of the world economy of the time. The most important export industries which had experienced most growth in the seventeenth century – textile, shipbuilding and beer-brewing – had fallen into decline in the course of the eighteenth century but, partly because of the still sizeable domestic demand for (luxury) industrial products, The Netherlands still had a fairly sizeable industry.[15] In about 1810, according to estimates, approximately 28 per cent of the male labour force was working in industry, a percentage which was barely lower than in Britain.[16] However, the contribution of agriculture to the economy was more important. Agriculture in the coastal provinces was characterized by large, capital-intensive farms with a very high level of productivity.[17] Despite the fact that only approximately 44 per cent of the male labour force worked in agriculture – this was 40.8 per cent in Great Britain[18] – and the level of consumption was relatively high, agricultural exports exceeded the fairly sizeable imports of grain (whereas Great

Britain had a large deficit on the agricultural trade balance).[19] Finally, as of old, the international services sector – shipping and international trade – was relatively sizeable and a large part of national capital was invested abroad in, among other things, the British national debt.

A few figures will illustrate the above. According to the most recent estimates, gross domestic product (GDP) per capita in The Netherlands in 1805 was approximately 10 per cent higher than in Britain and certainly 50 per cent higher than in Belgium.[20] Characteristic are the perhaps more reliable figures about meat consumption per capita, probably a good indicator at this time of the average level of consumption. In The Netherlands, in about 1810, approximately 36 kg. of meat were consumed per capita per year. In Great Britain, this was 45 kg., in Belgium almost 19 kg., and in Germany only 14 kg.[21] The level of literacy was, especially in the Protestant north of the country, considerably higher than in Great Britain and Belgium, even though The Netherlands was surpassed in this respect by Germany and Scandinavia.[22]

These national averages can not, however, be viewed separately from the large regional differences in economic structure. In Holland, the most urbanized part of the country, the estimated income per capita was, in 1820, almost twice as high as in the 'periphery', the Eastern and Southern Netherlands.[23] Reasons for these large differences were, firstly, the concentration of capital ownership in the towns of Holland, secondly, the concentration there of activities with relatively high earnings (particularly international trade) and, thirdly, the relatively high level of wages in Holland. In Holland, almost 60 per cent of the population lived in towns. In the 'periphery' the figure was 15 to 30 per cent.[24]

These large regional differences in a relatively small geographical unit like The Netherlands are a key to a more detailed analysis of the economic structure. How could wages in the agriculture and industry of Holland (and the other coastal provinces) be – and remain – almost twice as high as in the 'periphery'? Why did workers in the periphery not leave for Holland *en masse* in order to earn twice as much there? How could Dutch entrepreneurs continue to compete with entrepreneurs from Overijssel and Brabant despite these differences in wages?

The answer to the last question must be different for the different sectors of the economy. In agriculture, high wages in the coastal provinces were compensated for by the much higher productivity there, as a result of which the wage costs per unit product were not very different from each other in the two regions.[25] In the capital-intensive export industry – in particular the 'processing industries' linked to the ports (sugar-refining, beer-brewing, paper-making, gin distillation) – the same pattern had probably emerged. In beer-brewing in Holland, for example, productivity was so much higher than in the rest of the country that the wage costs per ton of beer were lower than elsewhere.[26] In both sectors – agriculture and processing industries – the high wage costs were therefore compensated for by much more capital-intensive production technology, which was made possible by the capital riches of Holland.

In the labour-intensive export industry – especially the textile industry – there had been no transition to more capital-intensive production technology. In Holland, then, this industry had, in the period after about 1670, declined considerably and, in part, moved to the periphery – Overijssel, Brabant – where the wages were much lower.[27] Finally, the industry of Holland, which worked for the local market, was partly protected from competition from elsewhere by the fact that production could not be traded – or only with difficulty – as a result of which building contractors in Amsterdam, for example, did not compete with those in Arnhem. But the policies of regional and urban governments who wanted to protect local industry also played a role. Higher wage costs here which were not accompanied by higher productivity – the pressure of competition was, after all, absent – were passed on to the consumer. The high wage costs of the Dutch bakers were shifted entirely onto the consumers by means of the bread prices fixed by the government and the regulation of the bread market in the context of the levying of duty on flour, as a result of which it was possible for an effective bakers' cartel to grow up in most towns in Holland. The bread prices in Holland were, as a result, considerably higher than elsewhere.[28] The strict regulation of all sorts of local markets was, in addition, anchored in the complex tax system of the Republic with its numerous local and regional taxes.

As a result of this a dual market system arose. The wholesale trade in the products of the Amsterdam staple market – grain, tropical products, etc. – was left as free as possible. The regional markets for these products were integrated to a considerable extent and the Amsterdam market often dictated the movement of prices. The government only intervened with the aim of preventing transit trade without transhipment and marketing in Holland. The retail trade, especially in all sorts of products from local industry, was, however, severely curbed and its markets remained fragmented. Grain, for example, was traded almost without restrictions; however, the trade in flour and bread was so severely curbed that it scarcely existed.[29] The trade in skins flourished but, in order to protect the town's shoemakers, it was forbidden to sell shoes in Amsterdam.[30] Guilds and other corporative organizations played a major role in this structure. Domestic transport and crucial parts of domestic trade – the trade in peat, for example – were also in the hands of such organizations, which were supported by local government.

The industry working for the local market was characterized by small business size and artisanal labour relations which were maintained partly by the policies of urban governments directed towards the protection of local cartels and guilds and the restriction of competition. The wages here remained at the same level for a long time; in the towns of Holland, wages had hardly changed since about 1650![31] The high wage costs were passed on to the consumer, as a result of which the cost of living in Holland was much higher than in the rest of the country. The price of the staple food, rye bread, was, for example, 30 to 50 per cent higher in Holland than the bread price in Overijssel. Workers from the Eastern and Southern Netherlands did not leave *en masse* for Holland because the higher nominal earnings there were nullified by the higher cost of living.[32] In this way, the structure which has been sketched out, characterized by large regional differences in income, wage level and productivity, persisted between approximately 1650 and approximately 1850.

The fragmented economic structure of The Netherlands at the beginning of the nineteenth century was linked to the fragmented political structure, in which, until 1795, each province (*gewest*) was autonomous and, inside the *gewesten*, the towns in particular had acquired a position of virtual independence. This was expressed in, among other things, the fragmentation of the tax system: until 1807, each region had its own tax system and, until 1866, each town could levy its own duties. As a result, the political unification which got under way in 1795 was, in a sense, a condition for economic unification.

INDUSTRIALIZATION IN THE PERIOD 1800–1850

During the first quarter of the century, industry went through a deep depression and the decline in the export industry, which had already started after approximately 1670, reached rock bottom. Between the years 1809 and 1813, large sections of industry came to a standstill when The Netherlands, as a result of the Continental System, the continuing war and the loss of the colonies, was cut off from international trade over the sea and therefore from raw materials and a large part of the export markets.[33] Industry working for the local market was hit by the crisis because the market shrank as a result of the general economic malaise. The recovery after 1813 was, in addition, only partial. As a result of the events which took place between 1795 and 1813, Amsterdam definitively lost its position as the Central European staple market so that important branches of industry which were dependent on it either directly or indirectly – shipbuilding, sugar-refining, the tobacco industry, etc. – only recovered in part.

Extreme cyclical fluctuations and uncertainties about the new Kingdom which was called into existence in 1815 determined the picture of the development of industry until half way through the 1820s. The boom in international trade and shipping of 1816/17 was followed by a new depression (1818–21) which was intensified by a sharp drop in the prices of agricultural products (as a result of the resumption of Russian exports) and of industrial products (as a result of British competition). The question of what economic policy William I, the new sovereign of the United Kingdom of the Netherlands, would follow and the numerous changes of course in his policy to meet the wishes of the Northern and Southern Netherlands prevented for the meantime the restoration of normal economic relationships.[34]

Outside Holland, industry had prospered more between 1800 and 1825. As a result of the high agricultural prices between 1800 and 1817, the domestic market in the agrarian provinces flourished. The south of the country, Brabant and Limburg, benefited particularly from the large market which had arisen with the integration into the French Empire. The gradual growth of the proto-industry in these provinces continued undiminished; the textile industry in the province of Overijssel had also, on balance, benefited from the falling away of foreign (British) competitions.[35]

In the 1820s, a number of William I's reforms began to bear fruit. An important stimulus for the economy was the expansionary policy directed towards the construction of canals and roads with the ultimate objective of the economic integration of The Netherlands.[36] The Southern Netherlands in particular benefited from his industrial policy. Industry there received the lion's share of the funds which were made available for subsidizing industry and, in Brussels, the large 'industrial bank', the Algemeen Nederlandsche Maatschappij ter Begunstiging van de Volksvlijt (General Dutch Company for the Promotion of Public Industry) was founded.[37] By contrast with the industrial expansion in the 1820s in the Southern Netherlands, the relative stagnation in the Northern Netherlands stood out as unfavourable. But the 1820s were not without important innovations. In a significant number of branches of industry, the steam engine was introduced for the first time and the first factories were founded, in which steam engines and steam ships were built.[38]

Only after 1830 would industrial growth in The Netherlands genuinely break through. Two events were responsible for this. As a result of the Secession of Belgium in 1830, industrial policy started to concentrate entirely upon The Netherlands. The most important impulse, however, came from the colonies: the introduction of the Cultivation System in Java in 1831/2. Under this system, in which the Javanese peasants were forced to cultivate export products (coffee, sugar, indigo) for the colonial government, exports from Java increased sharply. The profits of this – the peasant was paid only minimally for his work – were, for the greater part, creamed off by the Dutch state and the Nederlandsche Handelmaatschappij (NHM – Dutch Trading Company), a semi-public trading house founded in 1824, which had been granted the monopoly on trade with Java.[39] Javanese export production was auctioned by the NHM in Amsterdam, as a result of which international trade in Amsterdam came to life again and the NHM obtained, thanks to the success of the Cultivation System, the means of reorganizing a number of branches of industry. The Amsterdam sugar-refining industry, which was intended to purchase the Javanese sugar and, after refining, sell it on the world market, was modernized at the instigation of the NHM.[40] This is where the first, large-scale steam factories in The Netherlands were set up. Ship-building grew spectacularly because the NHM only chartered boats built in the Netherlands for transport to and from Java.[41] The textile industry in Twente (Overijssel) was given the greater part of the subsidized export orders to meet the demands of the Javanese market. By means of subsidies and trade tariffs, the British competition was pushed out of the Javanese market. In addition, the NHM introduced new production techniques (the flying shuttle) in the – in technologically rather backward terms – proto-industry of Twente, as a result of which productivity increased sharply.[42] For the dyeing and bleaching of the fabrics, a number of large Belgian entrepreneurs were prevailed upon to move their factories to Holland (Haarlem).[43] In short, as a result of the success of the Cultivation System and at the instigation of the NHM, an industrial structure arose in the 1830s which depended to a large extent upon trade with Java. Various forms of protection and subsidies kept this structure in place.

The branches of industry associated with colonial trade dominated industrial growth in the period up till about 1855, even though growth did not remain restricted to those branches. For example, the paper industry and gas production, a new branch of industry, developed successfully.[44] The domestic market, however, stagnated in the long term because the living standard of the population tended to drop between approximately 1830 and approximately 1855.[45] This also made itself felt in the falling level of consumption per capita. The fragmented structure of the economy remained almost unaltered, despite the formal abolition of the guilds and the construction of roads and a few canals. The construction of railways proceeded very slowly and only got into its stride after 1860 when a forceful policy was finally implemented in this area.[46] The weak, one-sided basis for the growth of industry in the 1830s emerged as early as 1841–2 when a demand crisis in Java led to a depression in industry linked to the colonial trade.[47] Recovery was barely completed when the 'potato crisis' of 1845/7 put a stop to the upward curve. On balance, the 1840s consequently showed almost no economic growth.

THE PERIOD 1850–1880

The years 1850–80 are perhaps the most interesting period of Dutch industrialization. In almost all branches of industry – we will return to the few exceptions – production and productivity increased rapidly, partly as a result of the gradual spread of the steam engine.[48] However, in general, this was not accompanied by a rapid shift in industrial structure. In most branches of industry, small and medium-sized industries continued to dominate and the breakthrough of large-scale industry took place only after 1890 (or even later).[49] Only in the textile industry did cottage industry make way for large-scale industry between 1855 and 1880.[50] The technology used altered, in general, no more radically. Where the steam engine was introduced, it often replaced wind or water power without radically altering the rest of the production process. A clear-cut 'leading-sector' was also absent. The textile industry, which grew sharply during this period, did fulfil this role in a number of areas (Twente, Brabant). New agricultural industries for the production of beet sugar, potato flour, strawboard and, in a sense, even margarine[51] dominated the economy of other areas (Groningen, West Brabant) but no single industry dominated at the national level.[52] The metal industry, the branch which might possibly have fulfilled this role, actually developed quite slowly after a flourishing start in the period 1825–55.[53] In short, much more than in the second quarter of the century, when a few branches of industry associated with colonial trade determined industrial growth, the period 1850–80 was characterized by balanced growth.

Nevertheless, a little further below the surface, a great deal was changing in industry. Of fundamental importance was the fact that the previously fragmented market system of industrial end products began to disappear. As a result of the accelerated construction of railways after 1860 and the abolition of numerous local and national taxes which had interfered with trade, inter-local and inter-regional competition on the domestic market increased sharply. In addition, the reduction of import and export tariffs, undertaken in stages between 1845 and 1862, increased the pressure of international competition.[54] Local cartels, which had controlled domestic transport and the industry working for the local market, disappeared or declined in importance. As a reaction to the increased pressure of competition and the new opportunities which arose as a result of the liberalization of economic life, industry was reorganized. Three examples can illustrate these changes.

After the abolition of the assize of bread (1854) and the duty on milling (1855) fairly large, mechanized bread and flour factories were founded in Holland. These had not been under the old duty system and, by breaking the cartels of local bakers, they ensured a sharp fall in the price of bread.[55] The lower bread prices in the towns of Holland after 1855 were subsequently an important factor in the improvement of the living standard of the workers in the period 1850–80. A second example: beer-brewing in Holland came under considerable pressure in the 1860s as a result of the import of a new type of beer from Germany – 'Bavarian beer' – as a result of which the local beer cartels were undermined. Previously, they had divided the local market up between themselves. About 1870, a number of entrepreneurs, among them G. H. Heineken, reacted to this by founding new breweries where this Bavarian beer was produced. In order to build up a market share these newcomers broke the existing cartel agreements, as a result of which a highly competitive market was created.[56] The third example concerns the emergence of the Langstraat, an area in North Brabant, as a specialized area for the production of footwear. The urban governments had attempted to protect the local shoemakers against competition from outside the towns, among other places from the Langstraat. Under the influence of the improved transport possibilities and a more liberal government policy, however, shoes from Brabant conquered the market in Holland definitively after approximately 1860, as a result of which the shoemaking industry in Brabant grew rapidly.[57] This, however, took place at the expense of employment in urban shoemaking.[58]

Comparable processes of specialization and rationalization under the pressure of the increased national and international competition took place in almost all branches of industry. The artisanal labour relations made way for more 'business-like' relations, as is shown, for example, by changes in the system of remuneration: daily wages were replaced on a fairly large scale by hourly rates and piece rates.[59] The driving force behind this process was the rapid expansion and the integration of the domestic market. After touching bottom about 1855, the living standard of the population began to improve again. Tensions in the labour market ensured a sharp increase in wages during the period 1865–80 – in Holland, 'wage rigidity' which had characterized labour relations since approximately 1650 ended.[60] As a result of the sharp increase in competition on the domestic market and the abolition of duties, the cost of living in Holland increased relatively little – this increase was probably greater elsewhere. Furthermore, in the 1860s, the level of urbanization, which had remained virtually unchanged since 1700, started to increase again.[61] After 1873, the growth of the urban population led to a boom in the construction industry which further stimulated the urban economy. An important part of this wave of urbanization was the emergence of new industrial towns in Overijssel (Twente) and North Brabant as a result of the transition in the textile industry from cottage to large-scale industry.

In addition to expansion as a result of the development of the domestic market, the Dutch economy also flourished because of the increase in exports. The export of agricultural products to Great Britain grew very rapidly until 1865.[62] In the agrarian sector, high incomes were earned as a result of the increase in selling prices. The transit traffic to the German hinterland increased very quickly as a result of the emergence of the Ruhr area[63] – not just industry but also agriculture and international services therefore prospered and grew.

A number of branches of industry participated very little, or not at all, in this process of balanced growth. These were principally in the sector linked with colonial trade and shipping which had grown up after 1830. The protection from which sugar-refining, textile-bleaching and dyeing and shipbuilding had benefited disappeared as a result of the liberalization of economic policy after approximately 1850. Only the textile (weaving) industry was able to maintain its position despite the falling away of protection on the Javanese market. Especially noticeable was the pronounced absolute declined in shipbuilding after the last boom in the building of wooden ships between 1853 and 1857.[64] The metal industry which was associated with shipbuilding also developed much less successfully than between 1825 and 1855, among other things as a result of the sharp increase in international competition after 1862.[65]

THE PERIOD 1880–1914

Broadly speaking, the process of industrial growth continued until the crisis of 1882. The Dutch economy largely escaped the international depression of 1873–9. But the crisis of 1882 hit home hard in all sectors of the economy: agricultural prices only began to drop sharply after 1882, international trade was paralysed by the 'sugar crisis' in Indonesia and building collapsed after the speculative boom which took place between 1878 and 1882. The development of industry in the 1880s was, as a result of these problems in the rest of the economy, generally not very buoyant, even if there were exceptions to this rule. The growth of margarine production, an innovation from the beginning of the seventies, continued unabated. Isolated branches of industry, beer-brewing for example, benefited from the low raw material prices but the overall picture was not very bright: industrial growth stagnated.[66]

The turnaround came in the 1890s. From approximately 1895 onwards – a precise dating is not yet possible – a new stage of industrial expansion started. The breakthrough of large-scale industry which took place between 1895 and 1914 was dominated by 'heavy industry' – metal working, machine construction and shipbuilding.[67] The emergence of heavy industry after a fairly long period of relative stagnation between 1855 and 1895 can, broadly speaking, be attributed to two factors. Firstly, the competitive position had significantly improved. Wages in The Netherlands had increased less than in neighbouring countries. In about 1850, the Dutch level of wages was probably still considerably higher than the level of wages in Germany and Belgium; after 1900 this relationship had been reversed and The Netherlands had become a country with low wages.[68] With an important raw material for heavy industry, steel, the same had happened. In about 1850, iron and steel prices in The Netherlands were significantly higher than in neighbouring countries as a result of the relatively high transport costs. As a result of the dumping of steel onto the Dutch market by the German steel cartel, the price of steel dropped in The Netherlands to even below the German level – in about 1900, steel was nowhere cheaper than at the Rotterdam market.[69]

At the same time, in the 1890s, heavy industry was again incorporated in the (international) service sector on which growth in the period 1825–55 had also been dependent. After 1860 in The Netherlands, large joint-stock companies had emerged in shipping – the steam lines – and in the railways. These companies played a crucial role in the reorganization of heavy industry.[70] In the ports of Holland, large, modernized shipyards and engineering works were built by them and existing ones reorganized in the 1890s. Orders from these companies were of decisive importance in the early years. However, exports to the related markets – Indonesia and South Africa – soon began. In this way, there emerged, in a few years, a considerable number of large, capital-intensive companies which dominated heavy industry. In addition, metal working grew sharply in terms of breadth: numerous new companies emerged for the production of gas and electric motors, bicycles, cars, light bulbs, etc.

The spectacular growth of heavy industry was not imitated by the rest of industry; only coal-mining in the extreme south of the country developed as quickly thanks to initiatives from government for expanding mining.[71] The traditionally strong foodstuffs industry expanded by means of, among other things, the expansion of cocoa processing and the emergence of the dairy industry. In the textile industry, the rapid growth of cotton spinning was particularly noticeable. In the past, preference had been given to yarns imported from Great Britain but the large weaving mills of Twente now started to take over this part of the production process themselves.[72] However, the chemical industry, which emerged extremely rapidly abroad (especially in Germany) during this period remained modest in size in The Netherlands; this was only to change after 1914. On the other hand, the expansion of utility industries, in particular the production of electricity, did follow the international trend.

As a result of the introduction and diffusion of gas and electric motors, the mechanization of small and medium-sized industries was rendered profitable; the steam engine had only been profitable in the case of production on a relatively large scale.[73] The economic position of small and medium-sized industries was strengthened as a result. However, despite the breakthrough of large-scale industry in a number of branches, particularly in heavy industry, firms with less than fifty employees continued to predominate to a considerable extent. In 1909, more than 70 per cent of employees in industry still worked in firms of this kind (in 1889, this percentage had been 85).[74] Furthermore, in 1909, 55 per cent worked in firms with less than ten employees. The growth of industrial production and productivity was therefore, to a large extent, achieved in these small firms.[75]

CONCLUSION

Some nuances must be added to the description of the industrialization of The Netherlands in the nineteenth century as a process of 'balanced growth'. It is characterized by the sequence of three periods of industrial growth.[76] In a certain sense, three different industrial structures can be distinguished. It will be clear that a discussion about *the* beginning of *the* Industrial Revolution is not meaningful in view of this sequence of industrial structures. The three periods of industrial growth which can be distinguished all showed clear imbalances. The first (1825–50) was characterized by the expansion of industry linked to colonial trade while industry working for the domestic product stagnated. During the second period (1850–80), it was precisely industry working for the domestic market which started to develop but 'heavy industry', which in turn, dominated industrialization during the third period after 1890, stagnated. It is this discontinuous and somewhat unbalanced nature of industrialization which partially explains the fact that the literature speaks of its 'late start' and 'slow tempo'. Finally, it has been shown that this discontinuous and unbalanced nature can be explained in part by non-economic (social and political) factors. The industrial structure of 1825–50 was partly born of government policy and disappeared after 1855 as a result of the liberal shift in this policy. The growth-in-breadth between 1855 and 1880 was, to a significant extent, the consequence of the liberalization of economic life and the disappearance of the institutional and socio-economic structures which had arisen in the seventeenth century but which continued to have an influence upon economic life until late in the nineteenth century. On the other hand, growth between 1825 and 1850 had taken place with these 'commercial capitalistic' structures and had not, in fact, affected them.[77] The transition from this 'commercial capitalism' to 'modern' industrial capitalism therefore only took place after 1850. By studying this transition more closely, the particular development of the Dutch economy in the nineteenth century can probably be explained more satisfactorily.

NOTES

This chapter was written in 1991; no literature published since then has been included in the discussion of industrialization in The Netherlands.

1 I. J. Brugmans, *Paardenkracht en mensenmacht* ('s-Gravenhage, 1969), pp. 201–14; J. H. van Stuijvenberg, 'Economische groei in Nederland in de negentiende eeuw: een terreinverkenning', in P. W. Klein (ed.), *Van Stapelmarkt tot welvaartsstaat* (Rotterdam, 1975), pp. 52–93; J. A. de Jonge, *De industrialisatie in Nederland tussen 1850 en 1914* (Amsterdam, 1967); see for a review of the debate J. L. van Zanden, 'Dutch economic history of the period 1500–1940: a review of the present state of affairs', *Economic and Social History in the Netherlands*, 1 (1989), pp. 17–21.

2 Van Stuijvenberg, 'Economische groei', pp. 59–61.

3 J. G. van Dillen, *Omstandigheden en psychische factoren in de economische geschiedenis van Nederland* (Groningen and Batavia, 1949); W. J. Wierenga, *Economische heroriëntering in Nederland in de 19e eeuw* (Groningen and Jakarta, 1955).

4 De Jonge, *De industrialisatie*.

5 J. Mokyr, *Industrialization in the Low Countries, 1795–1850* (New Haven, 1976); R. W. J. M. Bos, 'Factorprijzen, technologie en marksstructuur: de groei van de Nederlandse volkshuishouding 1815–1914', *AAG Bijdragen*, 22 (1979), pp. 109–38; R. T. Griffiths, *Industrial Retardation in The Netherlands, 1830–1850* ('s-Gravenhage, 1979).

6 Mokyr, *Industrialization*, pp. 163–89.

7 Ph. Kint and R. C. W. van der Voort, 'Economische groei en stagnatie in de Nederlanden 1800–1850', *Economisch- en sociaal-historisch jaarboek*, 43 (1980), pp. 105–54.

8 Bos, 'Factorprijzen'; Griffiths, *Industrial Retardation*, pp. 185–8.

9 E. J. Fischer, *Fabriquers en fabrikanten* (Utrecht, 1983), pp. 269–74; S. W. Verstegen and A. Kragten, 'De Veluwse kopermolens in de negentiende eeuw; een raadsel voor historiografen?', *Jaarboek voor de geschiedenis van bedrijf en techniek*, 1 (1984), pp. 172–87; A. R. J. R. Callewaert, 'Keuze van technologie: een onderzoek naar de invoering van de papiermachine in Nederland bij Van Gelder Schouten en Compagnie', *Jaarboek voor de geschiedenis van bedrijf en techniek*, 7 (1990), pp. 83–97.

10 H. W. Linsten, 'Stoom als symbool van de industriële revolutie', *Jaarboek voor de geschiedenis van bedrijf en techniek*, 6 (1988), pp. 337–53.

11 R. T. Griffiths, *Achterlijk, achter of anders?* (Amsterdam, 1980). This 'reappraisal'

of economic growth in the nineteenth century shows marked similarities with the same 'reappraisal' of the development of the French economy in the same period.

12 R. E. Cameron, 'A new view of European industrialization', *Economic History Review*, 38 (1985), pp. 1–23; S. Pollard, *Peaceful Conquest: The Industrialization of Europe, 1760–1970* (Oxford, 1982); N. F. R. Crafts, *British Economic Growth during the Industrial Revolution* (Oxford 1985).

13 Mokyr, *Industrialization*, p. 201; J. de Vries, 'The decline and rise of the Dutch economy, 1675–1900', in G. Saxonhouse and G. Wright (eds.), *Technique, Spirit and Form in the Making of the Modern Economies* (Greenwich, 1984), pp. 149–89.

14 J. L. van Zanden, *Arbeid tijdens het handelskapitalisme* (Bergen, 1991); the analysis shows similarities to the analysis of the role of institutional rigidities in the relative decline of the British economy after 1870 made by B. Elbaum and W. Lazonick (eds.), *The Decline of the British Economy* (Oxford, 1987).

15 For the decline in the eighteenth century see Joh. de Vries, *De economische achteruitgang der Republiek in de achttiende eeuw* (Leiden, 1968).

16 According to Crafts, 29.5 per cent of the British male labour force was employed in industry in 1800. The European 'standard' was 18.6 per cent; Crafts, *British Economic Growth*, p. 62.

17 J. L. van Zanden, *De economische ontwikkeling van de Nederlandse landbouw in de negentiende eeuw 1800–1914* (Wageningen, 1985), pp. 41–55.

18 Crafts, *British Economic Growth*, p. 62.

19 Van Zanden, *De economische ontwikkeling*, p. 48.

20 J. L. van Zanden, 'Economische groei in Nederland in de negentiende eeuw, enkele nieuwe resultaten', *Economisch- en sociaal-historisch jaarboek*, 100 (1987), p. 68.

21 J. L. van Zanden, 'De mythe van de achterlijkheid van de Nederlandse economie in de 19de eeuw', *Spiegel historiael*, 24 (1989), p. 165.

22 A. M. van der Woude, 'De alfabetisering', *Algemene Geschiedenis der Nederlanden*, vol. VII (Bussum, 1980), p. 258.

23 Van Zanden, 'Economische groei', p. 55.

24 J. M. M. de Meere, *Economische ontwikkeling en levensstandaard in Nederland gedurende de eerste helftvan de negentiende eeuw* ('s-Gravenhage, 1982), p. 35.

25 Calculated from Van Zanden, *De economische ontwikkeling*, pp. 42, 117.

26 J. L. van Zanden, 'Ondernemerschap en techniek in de 19e eeuw', unpublished research-memorandum, Amsterdam, 1990.

27 N. W. Posthumus, *De geschiedenis van de Leidsche lakenindustrie*, vol. III ('s-Gravenhage, 1939).

28 J. L. van Zanden, 'Kosten van levensonderhoud en loonvorming in Holland on Oost-Nederland 1600–1850', *Tijdschrift voor sociale geschiedenis*, 11 (1985), pp. 313–18.

29 De Jonge, *De industrialisatie*, pp. 218–19.

30 C. Wiskerke, *De afschaffing der gilden in Nederland* (Amsterdam, 1938).

31 J. de Vries, 'An inquiry into the behaviour of wages in the Dutch Republic and the Southern Netherlands 1580–1800', *Acta Historiae Neerlandicae*, 10 (1978), pp. 79–97; L. Noordegraaf, *Daglonen' in Alkmaar 1500–1850* ('s-Gravenhage, 1980).

32 Van Zanden, 'Kosten', pp. 317–19; J. M. M. de Meere, 'Daglonen in Nederland en België – een aanvulling', *Tijdschrift voor social geschiedenis*, 6 (1980), pp. 376–8.

33 E. Buyst and J. Mokyr, 'Dutch manufacturing and trade during the French period (1795–1814) in a long term perspective', in E. Aerts and F. Crouzet (eds.), *Economic Effects of the French Revolutionary and Napoleonic Wars* (Leuven, 1990), pp. 66–9.

34 H. R. C. Wright, *Free Trade and Protection in the Netherlands, 1816–1830* (Cambridge, 1955).

35 Buyst and Mokyr, 'Dutch manufacturing', p. 69.

36 Griffiths, *Industrial Retardation*, pp. 67–71.

37 W. M. Zappey, 'De negentiende eeuw. De periode 1813–1848', in J. H. van Stuijvenberg (ed.), *De economische geschiedenis van Nederland* (Groningen, 1979), p. 216.

38 J. L. van Zanden, *De industrialisatie in Amsterdam 1825–1914* (Bergen, 1987), pp. 24–34; Griffiths, *Industrial Retardation*, ch. 5.

39 C. Fasseur, *Kultuurstelsel en koloniale baten* (Leiden, 1975).

40 Van Zanden, *De industrialisatie*, pp. 26–31.

41 Griffiths, *Industrial Retardation*, pp. 93–5.

42 Fischer, *Fabriquers*, pp. 65–73.

43 Griffiths, *Industrial Retardation*, pp. 142, 152–5.

44 De Meere, *Economische ontwikkeling*, pp. 25–6; Van Zanden, *De industrialisatie*, p. 32.

45 De Meere, *Economische ontwikkeling*, pp. 93, 96, 100–8.

46 Griffiths, *Industrial retardation*, pp. 71–4.

47 *Ibid.*, pp. 159–61.

48 Van Zanden, 'Economische groei', pp. 64–5; Lintsen, 'Stoom', p. 339.

49 For this reason, J. A. de Jonge dated the 'take-off' as only taking place after 1890; see De Jonge, *De industrialisatie*, p. 230–45.

50 De Jonge, *De industrialisatie*, ch. 7; Fischer, *Fabriqueurs*, pp. 77–83.

51 Margarine was made partially from inferior butter and, in fact, also arose from the international butter trade. See C. Wilson, *The History of Unilever*, vol. II (London, 1954), pp. 24–74.

52 De Jonge, *De industrialisatie*, pp. 343–6.

53 Van Zanden, *De industrialisatie*, pp. 37–41; G. van Hooff, 'De Nederlandse machinenijverheid 1825–1914', *Jaarboek voor de geschiedenis van bedrijf en techniek*, 3 (1985), pp. 179–80; de Jonge, *De industrialisatie*, p. 178.

54 Brugmans, *Paardenkracht*, pp. 214–25.

55 Van Zanden, *De industrialisatie*, pp. 43–4.

56 H. A. Korthals, *Geschiedenis der Heineken's bierbrouwerij maatschappij N.V. 1873–1948* (Amsterdam, 1948).

57 C. A. Mandemakers, 'De ontwikkeling van de factor arbeid binnen de Nederlandse schoennijverheid, 1860–1910', *Jaarboek voor de geschiedenis van bedrijf en techniek*, 2 (1985), pp. 109–11.

58 *Ibid.*, p. 108.

59 A. Knotter, 'De Amsterdamse bouwnijverheid in de 19e eeuw tot circa 1870',

Tijdschrift voor social geschiedenis, 10 (1984), pp. 138–41; A. Knotter, *Economische transformatie en stedelijke arbeidsmarkt* (Zwolle, 1991).

60 Knotter, 'Amsterdamse bouwnijverheid', p. 140; Noordegraaf, *Daglonen*, pp. 62–3.

61 H. P. H. Nusteling, 'Periods and caesurae in the demographic history of the Netherlands, 1600–1900', *Economic and Social History in the Netherlands*, 1 (1989), p. 105.

62 Van Zanden, *De economische ontwikkeling*, pp. 220–4.

63 H. P. H. Nusteling, *De Rijnvaart in het rijdperk van stoom en steenkool 1831–1914* (Amsterdam, 1974).

64 De Jonge, *De industrialisatie*, pp. 132–46.

65 *Ibid.*, pp. 343–6.

66 *Ibid.*, p. 245.

67 *Ibid.*, p. 244.

68 D. J. van der Veen and J. L. van Zanden, 'Real-wage trends and consumption patterns in the Netherlands, *c.* 1870–1940', in P. Scholliers (ed.), *Real wages in 19th and 20th century Europe* (Oxford, 1989), p. 224.

69 J. W. Bonebakker, *De scheepsbouwnijverheid in Nederland* (Haarlem, 1936), p. 47.

70 C. A. de Feyter, *Industrial Policy and Shipbuilding: Changing Economic Structures in the Low Countries 1600–1980* (Utrecht, 1982), pp. 205–14.

71 Griffiths, *Achterlijk*, p. 5.

72 De Jonge, *De industrialisatie*, 101–6.

73 Lintsen, 'Stoom', pp. 343–8.

74 De Jonge, *De industrialisatie*, pp. 231–3.

75 H. Lintsen, *Een revolutie naar eigen aard* (Delft, 1990), pp. 28–31.

76 Van Zanden, *De industrialisatie*, chap. 2.

77 Van Zanden, *Arbeid*, for a fuller treatment of this topic.

FIVE

German Industrialization

RICHARD TILLY

INDUSTRIALIZATION is a species of the larger genus, economic development. It is the specific historical form taken by the latter in many countries in the nineteenth century. German industrialization is an example. That industrialization is of course of intrinsic interest to historians, but it also offers a basis for discussing wider issues such as the welfare implications of economic development, its causes, its social and political consequences. The following pages attempt, therefore, to treat the German industrialization experience generally. The approach taken, however, is pre-eminently historical, not only in the mechanical sense of adhering to a chronological framework and explicit treatment of periodization, but also in the more fundamental sense of attempting to show that the pattern of change and development of a given period significantly influenced that of following ones.

LONG-RUN WELFARE IMPLICATIONS: AN OVERVIEW

No one can doubt the absolute and relative improvements in the material well-being of Germany's population over the nineteenth century. Drawing on development and growth economics, one can estimate levels of real income per capita as an indicator of such well-being. Germany had no national income statistics in the nineteenth century, so such magnitudes must be estimated. The basic technique is to take a relatively reliable estimate of real income per capita for the twentieth century, in Germany's case, say, for 1913, and extrapolate it backwards in time by means of available economic indicators presumed to be highly correlated with real income (such as iron consumption per head, letters posted per head, etc.). Tables 5.1 and 5.3 reproduce results of two such exercises, table 5.1 depicting the German case alone.

Note the movement upwards over the first half of the nineteenth century and the acceleration in the second half. These movements reflect

Table 5.1. *Real net national product per capita and real labour earnings in Germany, 1780–1913 (marks in 1913 prices)*

Year	Net national product per capita	Labour earnings
1780	240	–
1800	250	–
1825	260	639
1850	265	693
1875	427	704
1900	593	942
1914	728	1,083

Source: F.-W. Henning, *Die Industrialisierung in Deutschland 1800 bis 1914* (Paderborn, 1973), p. 25; Rainer Gömmel, *Realeinkommen in Deutschland. Ein internationaler Vergleich (1810–1914)* (Nürnberg, 1979), pp. 27f.

Table 5.2. *Life expectancy*

Age	Sex	1816–60	1865–7	1901–10
0	m.	26.53	32.49	44.82
	f.	28.70	34.93	48.33
5	m.	42.11	45.69	55.15
	f.	42.99	47.46	57.27
15	m.	37.97	39.45	46.71
	f.	38.83	41.45	49.00
30	m.	29.08	29.97	34.55
	f.	29.37	30.87	36.94

important structural changes to which I shall return shortly. Note also the movements of estimated real wages. They stay well behind per capita income until the 1870s or 1880s, fluctuating but without significant upward trend, thus suggesting (1) a redistribution of income towards property owners until the 1880s and (2) from then on the general sharing of labour in the fruits of productivity growth. This impression of a general improvement is corroborated by data on life expectancy (see table 5.2).

The upward trend in the second half of the century is unmistakable. The share of the poorer groups of society in this improvement lagged behind the average, to be sure, but here too progress was marked before 1914. Which raises the question of distribution once more – a point to which I shall return below.

Table 5.3. *Real income estimates for ten European countries (in $ 1970)*

	1700	1760	1800	1820	1830	1840	1850	1860	1870	1880	1890	1900	1910
Great Britain[a]	333	399	427	–	498	567	660	804	904	979	1,130	1,269	1,302
Belgium	–	–	–	–	–	–	534	637	738	832	932	1,013	1,110
Denmark	–	–	–	358	382	402	489	497	563	617	708	850	1,050
Germany	–	–	–	–	–	–	418	481	579	602	729	868	958
France	–	–	–	–	343	392	432	474	567	602	668	784	883
Sweden	–	–	–	–	–	–	–	292	351	419	469	597	763
Norway	–	–	–	–	–	–	–	420	441	486	548	605	706
Finland	–	–	–	–	–	–	–	300	390	407	458	529	561
Italy	–	–	–	–	–	–	–	451	467	466	466	502	548
Russia	–	–	–	–	–	–	–	236	252	253	276	342	398

[a] England and Wales prior to 1800.
Source: Crafts in *Explorations in Economic History* (1983), p. 389.

Table 5.3 suggests that progress of material well-being in Germany was also relative. According to these estimates. Germans enjoyed significantly lower incomes than the British and the Belgians, and slightly lower ones than the French up to the middle of the century. Within a generation, however, the German position had improved considerably. One might question the precision of such estimates, and even their ordering, for example, the lead over the French as early as 1870. Nevertheless, the general impression of relative advance harmonizes with other accounts of European industrialization based on other evidence – for example, that of David Landes[1] based on technological change – and the implied view that industrialization could yield broadly distributed benefits is not implausible.

THE PERIODS OF GERMAN INDUSTRIALIZATION

In spite of much well-deserved criticism, the old Rostow-authored stages of Preconditions, Take-Off and Drive to Maturity do have their merits and fit the broad contours of German industrialization.[2] For reasons of linguistic taste, I do not stick to exactly the same terminology, but the logic is similar. Most German historians would probably accept the following rough periodization:

1 A period of germination or preparation of the preconditions of modern growth (also called 'early industrialization') stretching from the late

eighteenth century to the 1830s and encompassing important institutional reforms, borrowing of industrial technologies from abroad and other manifestations of economic modernization.

2 A phase of growth acceleration or industrial breakthrough (also 'Take-Off') marked by a vast increase in railway and heavy industrial investment from the late-1830s to the 1870s, by a large movement of labour towards urban industry and by a substantial increase in productivity and real incomes per head.

3 A phase of ongoing industrial growth – called by Rostow the 'Drive to Maturity' and dated from the 1870s to around the First World War – in which new organizational methods and technologies spread from a small number of 'leading sectors' to cover a much wider spectrum of the economy, and in which rising productivity and incomes per head are almost matched by rising real wages.

Further subdivisions have been suggested, but the three main segments here identified can suffice for the purpose at hand. The following narrative, then, takes the form of successive analyses of phases of industrialization.

DEVELOPING PRECONDITIONS

Histories of this formative period have especially focused on two important themes: the role of foreign technology and its imitation in Germany; and the matter of institutional change. The author's personal preferences lead him to focus the present chapter on the latter. Even this specialization requires considerable self-limitation; in what follows just two aspects are singled out for discussion: the Prussian agrarian reforms and the creation of the German customs union, the Zollverein.

The institutional reforms which began in Prussia in the wake of military defeat at Jena (1806) – the Stein-Hardenberg Reforms – constituted an important, indeed, crucial, step forward in German industrialization. Most important were the agrarian reforms which established, via a series of measures enacted between 1807 and 1821, individual property rights in land and labour in agriculture. These measures had their greatest impact in the older, East Elbian territories, where near-feudal relationships had hitherto predominated. Three key features of these reforms deserve emphasis.[3]

First, peasants became personally free, free to leave their lord's estate, free to marry, etc. The obverse of this freedom was that the lords no longer had the legal obligation to support their peasants in times of need. Oversimplifying somewhat, one might say that a market relationship replaced the hierarchical, feudal one. Second, lords and most peasants gained clear title to the land which they had been using, though here a significant asymmetry emerged. The implicit theory was that all land save the commons was the property of the lords. Thus peasants had to purchase it from the latter. In addition, peasant land use had been contingent on labour duties, so that peasant ownership required that these dues be commuted. For the most typical range of holdings, the settlement of these claims involved a transfer to the lords of between half and one-third of the land previously worked by the peasants. Third, these landowners, lords and peasants alike, separated their holdings from what had hitherto been common land and, by elimination of the latter and appropriate exchanges, created consolidated, individualized units of ownership.

This 'revolution in property rights' contributed to German industrialization in several ways. First, individual property rights in land and labour presumably encouraged more efficient (or more intensive) use of those resources: peasants retained a larger share of the fruits of their labour than previously, while larger landowners, who increasingly used hired labour, were likely to employ it in a more cost-conscious manner. An important corollary of these relationships was that 'surplus labor' in agriculture would be more readily recognized as such and induced to move into non-agricultural employments. The 'payoff' was, at least in the long run, increased productivity in agriculture. Of course, the data on agricultural outputs and inputs for the first half of the nineteenth century are poor, but a substantial increase in land and labour productivity in Prussia – and especially in East Elbia – over this period seems most probable (see table 5.4). Had reforms not taken place after 1806, one may hypothesize, productivity increases such as these would have been much less likely.

Second, the reforms had significant effects on wealth distribution and social structure. The Prussian (and later German) agrarian reforms forced the peasantry to pay for emancipation and for their land. Assuming that pre-reform land use reflected true ownership claims – not the assumption of Prussian reformers – one could interpret the reforms as a vast redistribution of resources in favour of the aristocratic estate owners. Considerable sums changed hands between c. 1821 and 1850 (the period in which about 90 per cent of the relevant land claims were settled), according to one estimate:

| cash payments of | 243 million marks |
| land transfers worth | 84 million marks |

for a total of 327 million marks or about 10 million marks per year. That is more than the estimated annual net investment in Prussia's industrial sectors in this period.[4] Two consequences flowed from this transfer. One was the further impoverishment and marginalization of smallholders and

Table 5.4. *Estimates of agricultural productivity growth in Prussia, 1800–1861*
(annual rates of growth)

Period	Crop production[a] in tons	Period	Net output per worker[b] in 1913 prices	Period	Gross output[c] per worker in tons per ha[d]	
1820–30	1.32	1816–22	1.61	1800–40	0.44	1.29
1830–40	2.58	1822–31	2.59			
1840–50	0.12	1831–40	1.46	1840–60	0.79	2.13
1850–60	1.72	1840–49	1.09			

[a] *Source*: G. Helling, 'Berechnung eines Index der Agrarproduktion in Deutschland im 19. Jahrhundert', in: *Jahrsbuch für Wirtschaftgeschichte* (1965), vol. IV.
[b] *Source*: R. Tilly, 'Capital formation in Germany', in *Cambridge Economic History of Europe*, vol. VII (1978).
[c] *Source*: R. A. Dickler, 'Organization and changes in productivity in Eastern Prussia', in W. N. Parker and E. Jones (eds.), *European Peasants and their Markets* (Princeton, 1975).
[d] Agricultural land in hectares.

the landless whose existence had in part depended upon access to the now 'privatized' commons. This social stratum became the basis of a rural proletariat, as Knapp argued so long ago, and it also filled the ranks of migrants on their way abroad or into non-agricultural employment elsewhere in Germany.[5] A second consequence was the strengthening of the social and economic position of the aristocratic landed estate owners in Prussia. The putative effects of this on economic growth are ambivalent. On the one hand, insofar as those estate owners were less efficient than peasant farmers, the transfer could be said to have held back economic development compared to what a conceivable alternative institutional arrangement might have produced. On the other hand, as beneficiaries of the new system of property rights, those landlords became, at least tacitly, one of its most important supporters. That made them more likely allies of the ascendant urban bourgeoisie, and probably enhanced the country's social and political stability – a positive input into the industrialization process.

Commercial policy represents a second important form of institutional change which belongs to the first third of the nineteenth century and which powerfully shaped subsequent development. The story begins with the Prussian customs union of 1818. This eliminated internal customs barriers and was designed to foster the administrative and political as well as economic integration of Prussia's new western and central territories with its older, eastern base.[6] Fiscal motives, however, dominated further development. The new customs system generated larger net revenue gains than had been anticipated – gains which were all the more welcome since they were free of the political restraints that burdened changes in *direct taxes* (negotiations with those quasi-parliamentary bodies, the United Estates). This turned out to be important later when the Zollverein was launched. The Prussian customs union of 1818 led to shifts in the geographic pattern of trade and affected other German states whose trade routes crossed Prussian borders. Those states, especially in southern Germany, viewed Prussia's policy with suspicion, in particular, they saw that Prussia would seek to unite her geopolitically separate western and eastern territories and that such unification could place their access to north-western Europe in Prussian hands. They proved vulnerable to Prussian influence, however, for one of the great advantages of the larger Prussian customs union was its relatively high ratio of revenues to collection costs – there were substantial economies of scale in administering customs union systems at this time – and this was a net revenue advantage which Prussia's leaders promised to share with cooperative states. Since the smaller German states, and particularly their princes and political advisors, were hungry for revenues which could strengthen their domestic political positions, the promise became irresistible: in 1828 the Prussia–Hesse–Darmstadt union was formed and shortly afterwards an agreement reached with the Bavaria–Württemberg customs union which gave Prussia the coveted east–west connection. Road-building concessions to Thüringian states not only helped secure the latter but also served to win these states' accession and break up a counter union, the 'Handelsverein'. Further accessions were soon registered and the Zollverein established (in 1833) Since it was a system of treaties of limited duration between sovereign states, one cannot assume that the Zollverein's future was at once ensured. Nevertheless, the 1830s were a period of commercial expansion which yielded substantial increases in customs revenues to the member states (of about 5 per cent per year per capita, 1834–42). This, more than anything else, made renewal in the 1840s 'inevitable'.[7]

Such institutional change, one may argue, contributed powerfully to German industrialization. This is not the place for a precise assessment of the net benefits of the trade-creating versus trade-diverting effects of the union (i.e., the extent to which the expansion of internal German trade outweighed the reduction of trade with non-German lands). Nor is this the place for a discussion of the Zollverein's tariff protection of 'infant industries'. Two important influences do deserve attention, however. One concerns railroad building. The Prussian and the German-wide customs union influenced the regional flow of trade and called the attention of affected states – and, indeed, of local interests in the most important cities – to the importance of transport improvements to ensure one's own share of trade. The establishment of the Zollverein made the competition for trade more likely to result in increased transportation facilities, with railway building in the 1830s succeeding the road building of the 1820s, and proceeding more vigorously than it would otherwise have done.

A second lasting contribution of the Zollverein to industrialization was monetary integration.[8] In contrast to today's European Union, the Zollverein pushed monetary integration from the beginning. The immediate reason was that apportionment of customs revenues among the member states required fixed exchange rates among the different currencies (largely metallic ones) then in operation. Since revenues were the Zollverein's principal *raison d'être*, this was a serious issue, formally resolved in treaties of 1837 and 1838. When later banks of issue emerged as a supplementary source of currency, this too was formally regulated (1857). What happened was that Prussia's bank of issue became *de facto* the Zollverein's main means for regulating the money supply. This evolution made inter-regional trade less costly earlier, and made formal unification of the country, when it came in 1867 and 1871, less difficult than would have otherwise been the case.

It must be understood that the two concrete examples discussed here by no means exhaust the contribution of institutional change in the early formative period to long-run industrial growth in Germany. They are simply illustrative of the ways in which institutional changes set up a framework within which the basic elements of German industrialization – capital accumulation, mobilization of labour, and technological change through imitation and adaptation of innovations made abroad – could begin to work. In this sense, the 'preconditions period' laid the foundations of subsequent development.

THE INDUSTRIAL BREAKTHROUGH

In the second third of the nineteenth century German economic growth accelerated, largely spurred by industrialization. The main driving force behind this acceleration was railway building; for railway building not only represented a major innovation in its own right, but also brought with it, in turn, the expansion of heavy industry. That is, at least, a plausible hypothesis: the 'leading sector' hypothesis of German industrialization. It is a view of the development process reminiscent of Joseph Schumpeter (in *Theory of Economic Development*). A major innovation, initially developed abroad, presents itself for local exploitation and is quickly seized upon by 'dynamic entrepreneurs'. Established economic and political interests oppose and slow adoption of the innovation at first, but within ten years (i.e., by the late 1830s) commercial railways are being built and hitherto unheard of sums of money are being mobilized to finance them. Building costs are typically underestimated and cost over-runs endemic, related financial difficulties as well. A clear cyclical pattern of boom and bust emerges, but on an upward trend of investment activity which continues for decades. Industrialization in this 'breakthrough' period, that is, unfolds as a series of 'growth cycles' very largely domi-nated by railways (see figure 5.1).

The persuasiveness of the 'leading sector' hypothesis of German indus-trialization builds on three distinctive features about railways identified by historians of the period: the timing and nature of railway and heavy industrial investment: the size of railway investment: and the productivity and transport price implications of railway growth. The following discus-sion is oriented toward these three points.[9]

First, expansion of the leading sector syndrome (LSS) of railways, coal mining and iron and steelmaking, was largely a market-driven process, although its precise timing, paradoxically, was highly sensitive to political change, that is, to the role of the state. In Prussia, railway building depended on state approval for a number of good reasons (e.g. land expropriation rights) and it was not until the late 1830s that a fairly consis-tent set of procedures for the concessioning of private companies was developed.[10] This freed railway investment of one important restraint and it took off in the 1840s – until slowed down in 1844 by another state measure in the form of restrictive laws against speculative transactions in railway securities (as Kubitschek last described) and stopped by the commercial and financial crisis of 1847–8.[11] The Revolution of 1848–9 which immediately followed that crisis itself altered the conditions under which the LSS developed, and in two ways: (1) thanks to the stabilized political situation after 1849 the state was prepared to pour a much larger volume of financial resources into railways in the 1850s than had been forthcoming in the 1840s; (2) the state liberalized its policy towards the chartering of joint-stock industrial companies, and it also withdrew from close administrative control of coal mining.[12] The juncture of these changes permitted a strong promotional and investment boom to take place in German heavy industry in the 1850s – one of the most remark-able booms of the entire century.[13] It would be misleading, however, to view the expansion of the LSS as an offspring of state action. Against the background of the political shifts just described, market forces determined the development pattern. If we seek to identify, for example, the deter-minants of railway investment over the period, the best answer we get is: expected profits, for example, as measured by the rate of return on

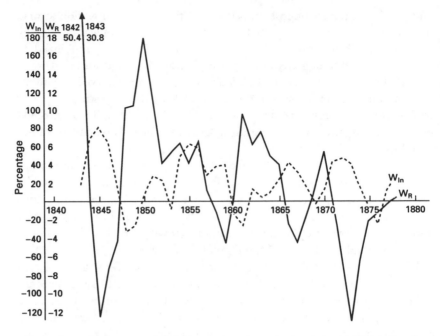

Fig. 5.1 Rate of return on capital (W$_R$) and rates of growth of capital stock (W$_{In}$) in Prussian railways, 1841–1879. Source: R. Fremdling, *Eisenbahnen und deutsches Wirtschaftswachstum 1840–1879* (Dortmund, 1975).

railway investment (see figure 5.1). Moreover, these expectations were not irrational, for they were related to realized revenues, which grew rapidly enough to suggest the presence of an adequate demand for railway services from the outset. Investment in coal and iron, in turn, appears to have depended on prices of these products in the previous period(s) and on demands emanating from (or sales to) the railways.[14] What we have, then, is a modern sector emerging within the larger, basically agrarian and artisan economy, a modern sector responding, not to the real income or consumption patterns of the economy as a whole, but to an initially small, but dynamically growing core of interdependent, modern industrial enterprises dominated by profit expectations. The cycles and crises of the 1840s, 1850s, 1860s and 1870s underscore the essentially unplanned, market character of the development of this period (see figure 5.1).

Second, railways were highly capital intensive, large-scale enterprises from the very beginning and, as such, soon began to exercise a perceptible influence on the rest of the economy. Their initial construction, and later, their operation, generated incomes and employment, both directly and indirectly. As early as the 1840s contemporary German observers, distressed by the poverty and underemployment around them, advocated

Table 5.5. *Indicators of railway development in Prussia, 1844–1881*

Years	Pfennigs per ton-km	Millions of ton-km	Length of network (in 1,000) km
1844–6	13.5	27.1	1.6
1854–6	7.5	643.7	5.3
1864–6	5.6	2162.7	8.7
1874–6	4.8	7600.0[a]	16.6
1879-81	4.2	9000.0[a]	20.7

[a] Rounded off to 100 million
Source: Rainer Fremdling, *Eisenbahnen und deutsches Wirtschaftswachstum 1840–1879* (Dortmund, 1975), pp. 18f., 48, 57.

Table 5.6. *Railway net investment in comparison with Gewerbe and the entire economy in Germany, 1851–1879 (annual average)*

Years	Railway (millions of marks in current prices)	Gewerbe	Entire economy	Railway as percentage of Gewerbe	Railway as percentage of entire economy
1851–4	88	113	738	78.3	11.9
1855–9	134	170	678	78.6	19.7
1860–4	142	246	1,204	57.6	11.8
1865–9	201	178	1,148	113.0	17.5
1870–4	425	718	2,282	59.2	18.6
1875–9	503	204	1,946	246.4	25.8

Sources: Rainer Fremdling, *Eisenbahnen*, p. 31; and W. G. Hoffmann with the assistance of H. Hesse and F. Grumbach, *Das Wachstum der deutschen Wirtschaft seit der Mitte des 19. Jahrhunderts* (New York, Heidelberg and Berlin, 1965), p. 259.

railway investment spending as a productive, long-run form of poor relief and job creation. Retrospectively, moreover, it is possible to identify railway investment as the economy's 'cycle maker', for most of the key (measurable) indicators of business-cycle movement tended to follow the former up and down over the cycles of this period (1840–80).[15] Tables 5.5 and 5.6 indicate some of the relevant long-run dimensions.

Of particular importance, however, are what economists have called *backward linkages*. These show how the railways' demand for inputs influences the sales, profits, production and, ultimately, investment in those branches of the economy which supply such inputs. The key branches affected were, of course, coal-mining and iron and steel-making. Economic historians have made some input–output calculations indicating the closeness of these linkages (see table 5.7). Note the asymmetry: railways influenced coal and iron much more than they were influenced by the latter. However, it is important to stress the dynamic and qualitative effects. As an example of the former, one may note the difference between the 1840s and the 1850s. In the 1840s Prussian railways grew at a rate of 20 per cent per year, iron and coal at rates of 4 per cent and 4.5 per cent, respectively. Prussian ironworks helped to supply the expanding railway sector with rails, but most of the supply was imported, and domestic rails were produced with pig-iron largely imported from abroad. For Prussian and German industry was far too small and backward to meet the huge demand. However, the profits for those who *could* satisfy part of it were large enough to induce considerable investment in iron and rail-making capacity and by the 1850s the picture was radically changing; in the 1850s we observe rates of growth as follows:

Railways	10%
Iron	30%
Coal	9%

By the 1850s, it can be seen (table 5.7 col. 6) that Prussia had become a net exporter of iron-rails, so thoroughgoing had been the transformation of her industry. This transformation reflects, though does not reveal, qualitative changes. For it is important to add that the largest, most modern iron and steel works by the 1860s were those which had grown by servicing the needs of the railways. Without the railways, the shift from the older charcoal technology to more efficient coke smelting and refining methods, would doubtless have taken much longer. Moreover, these were the enterprises which pioneered industrial use of such organizational forms as the joint-stock company. That was an important step forward in itself.

Railways, we have already noted, mobilized unprecedently large sums of capital. They did so largely through the banking system. For this reason, development of the latter can be viewed, in a sense, as a backward linkage generated by the former. The development of that particularly German phenomenon, 'universal' or 'mixed' banking practice, may be traced, at least in part, to the demands of railway finance.[16] At the founding of the first railway companies in the 1830s, in any case, we find private bankers playing an important role. They are members of the organizing committees, they subscribe a significant part of the company's initial share capital, both in their own name and on behalf of their customers. They serve as bankers or fiscal agents of the new companies, supply those companies with working capital, the employment of which they monitor by serving also as directors. Their election to such director-

Table 5.7. Input–output sectoral relations in Germany from the 1840s to the 1860s (coefficients in percentage of consumption)

Delivery (including trade) From/to	(1) Railways	(2) Coal-mining	(3) Iron-processing	(4) Blast-furnace production	(5) Agriculture	(6) Consumption = output + (imports − exports)
(1) Railways						
1840s	—	0	—	—	—	100
1850s	—	1	—	—	—	100
1860s	—	25	—	—	—	100
(2) Coal-mining						
1840s	0	7	5	—	—	100 = 106 − 6
1850s	2	7	12	—	—	100 = 102 − 2
1860s	3	7	30	—	—	100 = 109 − 9
(3) Iron-processing						
1840s	32	—	—	—	30	100 = 70 + 30
1850s	36	—	—	—	26	100 = 96 + 4
1860s	27	—	—	—	20	100 = 113 − 13
(4) Blast-furnace production						
1840s	—	—	84	—	—	100 = 72 + 28
1850s	—	—	88	—	—	100 = 72 + 28
1860s	—	—	92	—	—	100 = 85 + 15

Source: R. Fremdling, 'Modernisierung und Wachstum der Schwerindustrie in Deutschland, 1830–1860', Geschichte und Gesellschaft, 5 (1979), 201–27.

ships, in turn, is ensured by their control of proxy shareowners' voting rights at the shareholders' meetings. And they participate in syndicates or bankers which are formed to finance the railways' chronic needs for additional capital – not infrequently to 'fund' the short-term debt run up with bankers – whether in the form of shares, preferred shares, or in fixed-interest bonds. In short, virtually all of the practices which became well known as characteristic of German universal banking in the late nineteenth century, were pioneered in Germany's early Railway Age. Indeed, the principal motivation behind the creation of the joint-stock banks, whose growth eventually eclipsed that of the private bankers, derived in strong measure from limits those bankers experienced in financing railways while they themselves had no direct access to the instrument of limited liability. It is important to remember, finally, that the techniques and resources banks and bankers developed and accumulated in the railway business became available for the finance of other sectors, such as coal, iron and steel, or heavy machinery, when their needs reached appropriate levels.

Third, railways realized high rates of technological progress and productivity increase almost from their beginnings, partly through economies of scale (more intensive utilization of high fixed investment), partly through technical and organizational improvements (standardization of equipment, better scheduling, etc.). Competition for traffic among railway lines ensured that cost savings were passed on to railway users in the form of price reductions. Interestingly, the first railway companies set prices relatively high, apparently assuming an inelastic but sufficient demand for their product. As competition forced prices down, the companies were surprised by the increased revenues which followed – which suggested relatively high elasticity of demand. In a sense, therefore, cost reductions in railroading generated the observed demand. As figure 5.2 indicates, the cost savings were substantial.

E. Engel, a contemporary observer, compared pre-railway land freight rates with those realized by railways in the 1840–75 period and calculated how much revenue they would have generated at historically observed volumes of traffic. The difference represented the savings railways made possible, he thought: some 20 billion marks – or more than the cumulative costs of construction up to that time.[17]

Their significance for assessments of railways as a leading sector, however, lies in the *forward linkages* they might be presumed to have generated among rail transport-using branches: investment and productivity increases which would not have otherwise been realized. We do not know how large these were. We can observe many instances of rail transport supplanting water and other land transport, for example, in coal traffic,

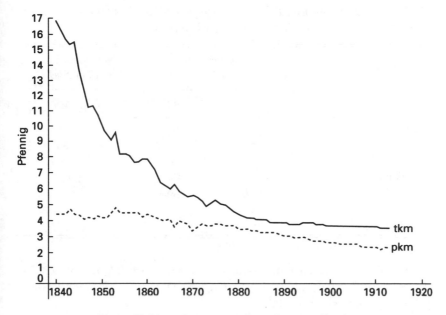

Fig. 5.2 Freight and passenger rates on German railroads.

and we have some evidence that industrial investment and urban-industrial growth responded positively to the availability of railway facilities, *ceteris paribus*. Germany's geography, finally – particularly its lack of major East–West rivers – makes it difficult to believe that a (hypothetical) modernized canal and river system could have rivalled railways as a form of German interregional transportation.[18]

A LABOUR SURPLUS ECONOMY?

The LSS-hypothesis sheds light on the breakthrough phase of German industrialization but it offers at best an incomplete interpretation, for it focuses on entrepreneurial motives, on innovation and investment, and *assumes* that the supplies of capital and labour essential to their realization were adequate. Since the latter deserve explanation, it makes sense to draw on yet another development theory for interpretation help: the 'classical' labour surplus theories as expanded by W. A. Lewis (and earlier by Marx). According to their ('dualistic') theory, large labour surpluses in the 'traditional' or backward part of the economy flow into the modern part in elastic response to the higher wages offered there. This supply of labour to the modern sector is so large and elastic that labour recruitment and production expansion can go on for an extended period without pulling wages significantly upward. The wage level remains largely determined

Table 5.8. *Estimated job supply and labour force potential and net migration in German regions, 1849–1865*

	Jobs per 100 workers		Net migration (cumulative)
	1849	1864	1849–65
North-east Germany	79.9	83.6	− 87,000
Kingdom of Saxony	74.2	73.5^a	− 48,000
Province of Saxony	80.1	88.1	+ 83,000
Rhineland	79.0	80.5	+ 3,053
Westphalia	85.6	90.4	− 52,000
Baden	95.2	105.9	− 135,000
Württemberg	93.7	105.9	− 203,000

^{a} 1861

Source: Wolfgang Köllmann, 'Bevölkerung und Arbeitskräftepotential in Deutschland 1815–1865', in W. Köllmann, *Bevölkerung in der industriellen Revolution* (Göttingen, 1974), pp. 69f., 73–7.

by the subsistence level and low productivity in the 'traditional economy'. With productivity rising much more significantly in the modern sector than wages, the share of profits or capital income is rising, and from this rising share stem increased savings, reinvestment, and − with 'embodied' technical progress − ongoing productivity increase and a high rate of economic growth.

The relevance of the labour surplus theory for German industrialization in this period lies in two or possibly three sets of facts. First, the historical literature has unambiguously documented the existence of 'population pressure' and underemployment as a chronic and widespread problem in Germany from the beginning of the nineteenth century well into the century's last third. Population growth seems largely to have represented growth of the poor and propertyless classes, generating increases in labour-force potential far in excess of jobs created. Table 5.8 indicates the nature and also some regional dimensions of this situation. Migration towards industrial growth centres alleviated, but could not eliminate the gap. One major response was overseas emigration. The roughly 2 million persons who left Germany (between *c*. 1840 and 1880) reduced the surplus significantly (by perhaps a quarter). For this same period the historical literature has recorded a massive collapse of rural industry, affecting something like 400,000 persons between 1850 and 1875.[19] This surplus was not so much demographic in origin as technological: foreign and domestic factory products undercut rural industry and forced its labour to seek other employment (for the textile industries a direct shift into factory employment is observable).[20]

Second, a consensus of sorts supports the thesis that aggregate real wages in Germany grew but little over most of the nineteenth century, fluctuating a great deal in connection with living costs, but without upward trend until the 1880s.[21] During the period discussed here – from the 1840s to the 1870s – real wages may have grown by as much as one-third of one percentage point while real net product per head probably grew by at least 1 per cent per year. This conforms to the notion of a 'labour surplus' economy, for it reflects pressure on wages leading to an increase in the share of income going to capital. Since capital incomes generate a disproportionately high share of a market economy's savings, this could help to explain the estimated increase in the investment rate in this period.[22]

The redistribution of income just noted is reflected in data on the personal income as collected and estimated for Prussia in the nineteenth century. One notes a marked increase in the inequality of this income distribution over the period with the driving force behind greater inequality clearly attributable to the rising share of high incomes – precisely those incomes whose size was significantly influenced by income from capital. These wealthy households – perhaps 5 per cent of the population – accounted for most of the economy's savings, as the historical evidence on stock subscription, saving deposits, mortgage holders, etc. shows. Many of them were entrepreneurs, and insofar as they were, their increasing share in income could have derived directly from the wage pressure of a labour surplus. Since most entrepreneurial investment was financed out of profits, the growth mechanism would also have been a direct one. Given the rapid development of the banking system in the period, however, such a direct connection between more savings and investment was not necessary for the latter to thrive. That is, positive 'labour surplus' effects on growth need not have been limited to direct advantages encountered in the labour market.

The foregoing reflection does raise a problem for interpretation of German industrialization, however. The historical literature strongly suggests that a number of important German industries in this period experienced considerable difficulties in recruiting skilled labour, especially where the basic technology was new (or imported), as, for example, in steelmaking or machine-building. Skilled workers' wages tended to be high relative to wages for unskilled work, and skilled labour recruits frequently travelled long distances.[23] In branches such as these the crucial entrepreneurial problem lay in mastery of new technologies and the related provision of adequate labour training, and not so much in a sufficient supply of capital related to advantageous wage bargaining. Part of the success of German industry in this period, seen absolutely and in relation to other countries, resulted from effective technical education and training and from the accumulation of human capital, both on the job and in special institutions created for that purpose. Cheap labour was no doubt an advantage, but high-quality labour may have been just as characteristic of Germany's successful industrial breakthrough.

ONGOING INDUSTRIALIZATION AND THE 'INDUSTRY STATE' (1870–1914)

The foregoing has I hope shown that, contrary to a frequently voiced opinion, German industrialization was well under way by the end of the 1860s and by no means a product of the imperial period. Industrial growth continues at about the same pace (see table 5.1) as in the previous period and with pretty much the same cyclical pattern. No doubt there was something special about the tremendous boom of 1867–73 (which anticipated but then, interrupted by war, also followed the founding of the Empire in the 1870s) and about the crisis and depression which followed it; but that, after all, could also be said for the earlier booms and crises of the 1840s and 1850s. Nevertheless, important changes did come after 1870 and this last period does deserve special attention. Not all important changes can be handled. In the following section, we take up three themes: (1) Industrial organization and the banks; (2) foreign economic relations and especially protectionism; and (3) urbanization and the 'social question'.

BIG BUSINESS

The emergence of large-scale business enterprise as a dominant feature in important segments of the economy was one of the period's most striking results. In branches like coal mining or steelmaking, heavy engineering, or chemicals, family firms increasingly gave way to enterprises organized as joint-stock companies (or as Kommanditgesellschaften or GmbH). This became obvious at the very top. In 1887 and 1907 four-fifths of the largest 100 industrial enterprises were joint-stock companies, and by 1907 c. 65 per cent of their total capital was owned by the latter.[24] Even when the family remained involved, as in the famous Krupp or Siemens enterprises, family influence receded and an important division between ownership and control became clearer. Note that this phenomenon was confined to only a few branches of the economy: most of the industrial joint-stock capital was in the four branches just cited, and enterprises with at least fifty employees accounted for 70 per cent of all occupied persons in these branches in 1907, as compared with only 45 per cent in all of industry. However, these *were* important branches, representing the most modern technologies, with a share in total value added of nearly 20 per cent, branches which grew rapidly and were unusually successful in export markets. Their success, absolute and in relation to those of other countries, raises a number of important, oft-debated questions.

The large size of these enterprises itself altered the character of inter–firm relations. Concentration, oligopoly and market-sharing agreements replaced many-firm competition. In Ruhr coal-mining, for example, the number of independent enterprises declined from 100 to 57, between 1880 and 1913, and the market share of the top ten producers grew from 24 to 53 per cent. In iron, concentration was rather less marked in this period, with corresponding shifts from 134 to 102 producers and an increase in the share of the largest five producers from 21 to 30 per cent. In the electro-technical industry on the other hand, concentration was still more extreme, at least in some of the most important products, where AEG and Siemens shared over half of the German market.[25]

Concentration affected competition by facilitating market-sharing agreements and especially cartels. It proved easier to negotiate the latter when the number of relevant parties was small. Thus the formation of the well-known Rhenish–Westphalian Coal Syndicate in 1893 followed on the heels of a wave of concentration. Cartels grew and spread in the 1890s, helped by a high court decision in 1897 which confirmed the binding legality of such contracts. By 1907, according to one contemporary estimate, around 25 per cent of all industrial production was so regulated. Interessengemeinschaften (IG) represented an alternative form of business corporation, favoured where small numbers of large firms predominated. The most notorious of these was the IG Farben, a capital and market-sharing agreement which bound together the largest three German dyestuff companies in 1906, but the institution also became typical in banking, as a veiled form of merger activity and concentration.[26]

The main reason for focusing on this aspect of Germany's large-scale industrial enterprise is that their role in the country's ongoing industrialization remains controversial. On the one hand, the potentially most severe restraints on competition appear to have favoured large enterprises and capital-intensive branches at the expense of smaller-scale and more labour-intensive ones (as Steven Webb has shown). Oversimplifying somewhat, this can be said to have represented a redistribution of income from labour to capital, from lower income groups to the wealthy. On the other hand these restraints – and even the transfer just mentioned – may have encouraged investment and accelerated technical progress and productivity growth in branches such as steel, where, for example, cartels may have encouraged vertical integration back into pig-iron and coal-mining. A full analysis of cartel effects, to be sure, requires joint consideration of tariff policy, a point to which I shall return below. Neither the historical record of these modern branches, nor the frequently noted comparisons with their less dynamic British counterparts, settles the question – which still deserves more research attention.[27]

THE ROLE OF THE BANKS

Economic historians have frequently sought to explain the success of German large-scale industrial enterprise in this period through the development of the large banks. It is in this period that the large joint-stock banks fully eclipsed the private bankers as suppliers of industrial finance. As indicated earlier, these large banks copied most of their operating procedures from the private bankers, including the close and continuing nature of their relations with industrial customers and also the 'mixed' or 'universal' orientation of their business, that is, they combined short-term credit and deposit with investment banking. The risks of 'mixed banking' induced the banks to maintain relatively large equity capitals. Thus, by 1913, the three largest German enterprises, and seventeen of the twenty-five largest ones, were banks. This, along with their other characteristics, gave the German banks a place in the economy which was unique among industrial countries in the period.

Prominence is not causation, however, and many economic historians have resisted the claim that these large banks had made German industrialization success possible. Apart from a few econometric efforts,[28] 'proof' has built largely on (a) the theoretical plausibility of a positive connection between enterprise growth and investment in risky innovations on the one hand and close links to the large banks on the other; and (b) the accumulation of histories of individual episodes in which banks helped or forced industrial enterprise to develop in certain directions. Space limitations confine our attention to (b). One example concerns the West German steel-rail cartel which was formed in 1876 largely at the behest of the powerful Berlin bank, the Disconto-Gesellschaft, which thus was able to limit – at least for a time – cut-throat competition among its debtors.[29] Another oft-cited example stresses the banks' support of the electrical engineering industry from the 1880s, initially permitting the upstart AEG to challenge and overtake Siemens and then, after a switch of sides by the Deutsche Bank, helping Siemens to recapture and maintain its leading position in the industry.[30] This example shows not only that banks played an entrepreneurial role in this industry but also that their interests were accompanied by a large-scale mobilization of funds in support of its expansion – this, as some historians have been at pains to point out, in sharp contrast to the attitude of British banks and other financiers towards the British electrical engineering industry.[31] And there is the famous example of the Deutsche Bank's support of the Mannesmann steel-tube manufacturer in the 1890s, an example which illustrates how long the banks were able and willing to continue their support and to wait before a financial payoff began to materialize.[32] These examples must suffice. Before closing the subject, however, the reader's attention is called to a pervasive influence of banking upon large-scale industry: by means of their great influence in the organized security markets in Berlin, Frankfurt and elsewhere, the banks were well situated for advising their industrial clients on how and when to finance their plans of expansion, including plans involving takeovers and mergers with other companies. Few important mergers in the period took place without bank intermediation, and quite a few followed directly from bank initiatives.[33] Since mergers and external growth were a very important part of the story of German industrial organization in the period, the banks' role in fostering the former was important. Only further research, to be sure, will be able to clarify the question of how well the benefits of such large-scale organziations – related to the exploitation of technological and organizational economies of scale – offset some obvious costs, such as market power.

PROTECTIONISM IN THE 'INDUSTRY STATE'

The economic depression of the 1870s brought to an end a long phase of secularly rising agricultural prices and prosperity in Germany.[34] A policy shift from free trade to protectionism accompanied this change, as is well known. Bismarck, in need of revenues for the Imperial government (Reich), offered the organized industrial and agricultural interests some protection from foreign competition in exchange for 'fiscal duties'. However, the initially moderate duties of the 1879 tariff rose considerably in the 1880s, not only for grain but for meat and livestock imports as well, the latter enjoying the even stiffer protection of non-tariff restriction based on health regulations. Bismarck's dismissal in 1890 marked the intensification of the debate in Germany concerning the policy priorities – the 'agrarian state' versus the 'industry state' – and the pros and cons of ongoing industrialization.[35] The debate actually transcended the question of protectionism,[36] but owing to space limitations, attention is restricted here to the latter.

Three implications of German protectionism deserve careful consideration. First, although German industrialization obviously continued over

the period observed (and even speeded up between the 1890s and the First
World War), agrarian protectionism was by no means trivial and almost
certainly slowed industrialization down (in comparison to what free trade
would have permitted). The economic weight of the duties for rye and
wheat alone have been estimated for the 1900–10 period at about 1 per
cent of the country's annual net national product![37] The prices and
incomes which owners of agricultural land, labour and capital could
realize were higher than they otherwise would have been and that braked
the movement of those factors out of agriculture. Moreover, one must
assume that tariff reductions would have especially benefited Germany's
internationally competitive industries and increased exports. Protectionism, that is, checked this pro-industrial mechanism as well. Second, industrial protectionism was more than negligible and had noticeable structural
effects. Duties on many iron and steel products, for example, proved
redundant in the 1880s as German firms became relatively low-cost
producers, but the cartels which emerged in these branches owed their
effectiveness to the existence of tariffs, which held foreign producers out
of cartellized domestic markets. In the long run, it is hypothesized, this
combination permitted export dumping abroad in free-trade countries
without fear of retaliation, and the stabilization of enterprise income over
the business cycle may well have called forth greater investment activity,
more innovation and higher productivity growth than would otherwise
have been achieved.[38] Since protection and cartels were stronger for the
heavy industrial branches of the iron and steel industry, the growth of
these sub-sectors was encouraged at the expense of the others. Given the
technology of the times, there is a presumption that German industrial
growth was on balance higher than it would have been with a different
tariff structure – but only a presumption. Third, protectionism, as just
suggested, had clear distributional implications. The chief beneficiaries
were the owners of large agricultural estates and the owners of the larger
enterprises of the steel, chemical and electro-technical industries.
Protectionism, in short, benefited capital-intensive branches and sectors.
It thus contributed to an increase in the share of property in the national
income. Since property income was (and is) much less equally distributed
than labour income, this contributed to an overall increase in economic
inequality in the country. Interestingly, however, it is at about this point
in time that the long-run trend towards increasing inequality in Germany
came to an end and reversed itself.[39] That is, other economic and social
forces must have been working to offset the effects of protectionism.

URBANIZATION AND THE 'SOCIAL QUESTION'

Urbanization and the 'social question' represent a joint product of German industrialization, one of its most significant social consequences, and one at the heart of the oft-cited debate on the 'Industriestaat'. The underlying theory is simple enough: industrialization generated agglomeration economies which made urban concentrations of population 'rational'. These largely working-class populations grew very rapidly, created social welfare problems (of public health, education, law and order) and social conflict, especially between 'labour' and 'capital'. The 'Social Question', that is, turned largely on the extent to which divergent economic and social interests and aspirations – which manifested themselves most dramatically in Germany's rapidly growing industrial cities – could be harmonized. This, in turn, depended on three difficult questions: (1) the question of the *objective* level of living of the population and its distribution; (2) the question of the attitude of the rich and powerful upper classes towards the social classes below them (especially their assessment of the need for meliorative, integrationist measures) and (3) the question of the attitude of the lower classes themselves, especially of their response to changes in the standard of living and to policy measures affecting their collective status. The rest of the chapter takes up these three questions.

First, however, a word on the rapidity of German urbanization. Table 5.9 shows the acceleration since 1870. Between 1871 and 1910 the annual rate of growth for cities with 20,000 inhabitants was 4.2 per cent for big cities (of at least 100,000 persons) over 5.0 per cent. This was nearly three times the natural growth rate in the period and implies considerable migration gains. For the largest cities, indeed, net migration did account for well over half of their growth (see table 5.10).

This increased the share of big cities in German population from *c*. 11 to 37 per cent (1871–1910). In no other European country was urban growth more impressive. Urban growth was not confined to industrial cities – an industrial economy engendered, after all, the development of cities specializing in financial, communication and administration services – but there was a strong correlation between the rate of urbanization of a region and the growth of its industrial labour force between 1870 and 1910, and the rough association industrialization–urbanization can stand.

The reference to city-bound migration can lead into discussion of the population's standard of living – one of the three critical questions just posed. For there can be no doubt about two major facts about the period: (1) aggregate real wages – incompletely corrected for shifts in the structure of employment – rose considerably; and (2) a real income gap between city and countryside, which grew in boom periods and correlated

Table 5.9. *Annual growth rates of Prussian urban population, 1819–1910 (in %)*

Year	Population[a] (1,000s)	Rate of Growth[b]	Annual rate of growth[b]
1819	637	–	–
1834	838	32	1.8
1837	875	4	1.3
1843	1,114	27	4.0
1849	1,319	18	2.7
1852	1,866	31	3.1
1871	2,712	45	3.9
1880	4,610	70	6.1
1890	7,189	56	4.6
1895	8,091	13	2.3
1900	10,480	30	5.1
1910	14,941	43	3.7

[a] Cities with at least 20,000 inhabitants
[b] Taking the previous population figure as base
Source: Author's calculations.

well with migration waves, persisted over the period, though declining since around the turn of the century. Real-wage indicators, that is, are probably lower-bound estimates of rising living standards.[40] The trend pattern is confirmed, moreover, by alternative indicators. A clear improvement in urban housing standards, as measured by the number of rooms per person, by the distribution of various qualitative characteristics, or by the share of sub-standard dwellings in the total number, can be demonstrated. Child and infant mortality also registered a decline, in urban areas more than in the aggregate, and this is no doubt related to the concurrent improvement in dietary standards.[41]

Distributional considerations are important, however. A closer look at incomes shows that the share of high-income households in total income rose over the period, and closely associated therewith the share of property incomes. All of this took place before 1900; thereafter the shares mentioned remained constant or fell slightly. The greatest gap in the distribution pyramid, however, seems to have been between the wealthy recipients of property income and the 'middle-class' groups below them. Between the latter and wage-worker households the differentials probably narrowed in this period. Housing conditions roughly corroborate the distributional picture just described. The greatest, most easily recognizable divisions were between the wealthy, residential areas and the rest. Visible and distinct from middle-class neighbourhoods were the working-class districts, but in housing a division also emerged between artisans and

Table 5.10. *Population growth and migration gains in Prussian cities, 1875–1905*

Type	Rate of population increase (1875 = 100)	Share of net migration gains (in %)	Population increase (in 1,000s)
Commerce and other services	264	73	1,410
Administration and military	210	70	280
University and rentier	208	73	229
Heavy industry	373	59	519
Textile industry	185	25	274
Other industry	327	59	784
Diversified (without Berlin)	225	60	1,346
Berlin	211	67	1,073
Total	240	64	5,015

Source: D. Laux, 'The components of population growth in Prussian cities, 1875–1905 and their influence on urban population structure', in Richard Lawton and Robert Lee (eds.), *Urban Population Development in Western Europe from the Late-Eighteenth to the Early-Twentieth Century* (Liverpool, 1989).

skilled workers on the one hand, and unskilled, casual workers on the other. In short, changes in material welfare in the period do not point automatically to intensification of the 'social question' in the sense of a two-class polarization.

Nevertheless, the German labour movement – the trade unions and the Social Democratic Party – was without doubt the essence of what middle and upper-class contemporaries meant when they spoke of the 'social question'. The labour movement itself was largely a big-city phenomenon, fostered by urban residential segregation and the social solidarity of working-class neighbourhoods. Its ranks were not filled by the poorest, but largely by skilled workers and artisans, who were also the main carriers of protest and strike activity in the period. In a sense, perhaps, rising living standards – including increased leisure – contributed to their ability to organize and challenge the social and political status quo. In retrospect, however, it is clear that despite significant gains since the 1870s, there was much for working-class organizations to challenge – the continual threat of being outlawed, the three-class suffrage system in state and local government, as well as the recurring risk of unemployment and sickness, in spite of the advent of social insurance.

Which takes us to our final point. The upper classes responded to the 'social question' by mobilizing the powers of the state – in the classic carrot-and-stick manner. Bismarck's Anti-socialist Law (1878) and social insurance measures are well-known examples. But there was much more, at the local as well as national level. What must be stressed is that the 'response' was not a matter of *perception* of the problem by a homogeneous 'upper class', but one of bargaining among factions of the latter and of the related weighing of alternative policy packages. Only two aspects of this complex problem – whose adequate treatment would require at least a book – can be mentioned here, and those only in illustrative form. One concerns the debate (on housing policy) between social reformers who stressed the need for government intervention to soften what they saw to be the market's negative effects on working-class living conditions, and adherents of economic liberalism whose position was essentially negative: they warned against the high cost of redistributive actions. Whereas, for example, the social reformers stressed the excessively high rents for working-class housing, the need for subsidizing the latter and for eliminating free-market pricing in urban land (which they saw as a primary cause of high rents), the 'liberals' saw high rents as a function of excess demand related to urban migration, and price controls and subsidies as instruments which would only fuel further excess demand, burden capitalist wealth and slow the voluntary flow of capital into urban housing construction.[42] In this important policy area, liberal free-market policy prevailed: government intervention remained largely confined to the role of setting basic rules: obligatory fire insurance, property registration, zoning laws, regulation of the mortgage banks, etc. Housing allocation remained largely a market result right up to the First World War. Why? Two reasons suggest themselves. First, the market worked pretty well. The secular improvement in housing conditions was sufficiently widespread to limit criticism to a minority position. Second, however, the virtual omnipresence of property owners in policymaking bodies, from the top of the Reich down to the local city councils, insured that their views were well heard.

A second aspect of upper-class response deserving consideration here is the role of local city municipal government.[43] As early as the 1850s and 1860s, but even more so during the 1870s, rapid growth, much of it immigration, created strong demands for public services – more and better streets and roads, water works and sanitation facilities and schools, to mention just a few – which the market could not be relied upon to supply. Under the prevailing electoral and local government rules, decision making was largely confined to property owners, well-to-do businessmen and professionals, part of the middle-class, and a growing corps of professional bureaucrats who exercised executive power. During the period most of the local tax revenues were paid by the well-to-do, though the benefits were widely diffused. Increasingly, to be sure, municipal enterprises began to generate supplementary revenues by selling services at a profit; but the willingness and ability of local city governments to provide a widening array of services to its largely working-class population in spite of rising tax burdens for middle and upper classes is a striking feature of the period. Municipal expenditures for public consumption purposes alone rose by 5.6 per cent per year 1870–1913 and reached *c*. 6 per cent of estimated net national product by 1913. Total per capita spending (including investment) rose in the period by 3–4 per cent per year – much more than the per capita social product. This expansion is a remarkable feature of the period. We have two explanations for it. (1) It can be interpreted in part as investment by propertied classes in social stability and social peace. Since 1890 the Social Democrats became increasingly visible in big-city politics, and in the Centre Party (Zentrumpartei) working-class interests had an additional, alternative focus of local policy representation. At this time, the upper classes – bankers, industrialists, managers, capitalists – sought cooperative arrangements with the middle classes, and became more interested in social measures which would help integrate the workers in local society and weaken the influence of the Social Democrats. In the Rhenish industrial city of Krefeld, for example, the business élite which ran the city created in 1893 a 'Commission for the Social Question' explicitly for his purpose. (2) Expansion could have resulted from the growing importance of municipal government. These administrators were appointed for long periods, dealt with technical questions which frequently transcended local interests and whose complexity gave them considerable autonomy *vis-à-vis* the local city councils. In a sense, moreover, they were representatives of the state in the local communities and frequently sought to achieve aims reflecting the interest of the entire community, not just those of the local élites. Many measures undertaken by city governments in this period, therefore, such as incorporation of neighbouring towns, municipalization of private works, etc., will have resulted from the independent power of the municipal executives. This was certainly one of the hallmarks of the German 'industry state'.

NOTES

1 David Landes, *The Unbound Prometheus*. (Cambridge, 1969).
2 W. W. Rostow, *The Stages of Economic Growth*. For a more detailed discussion see R. Tilly, 'German Industrialization and Gerschenkronian Backwardness', *Rivista di Storia Economia*, 6 (1989), pp. 139–64. An extended German version of this essay in which the periodization and other questions of German industrialization are discussed is available in paperback: R. Tilly, *Vom Zollverein zum Industriestaat* (Munich, 1990).

3 Progress and productivity increase in areas less affected by the reforms may have been greater than in East Elbia after 1820. This question deserves more attention. Still, that need not contradict the results discussed here. For recent discussions of the reforms see C. Dipper, *Die Bauernbefreiung in Deutschland* (Stuttgart, 1980); H. Harnisch, 'Die Bedeutung der kapitalistischen Agrarreform für die Herausbildung des inneren Marktes und die Industrielle Revolution in den östlichen Provinzen Preußens in der ersten Hälfte des 19. Jahrhunderts', *Jahrbuch für Wirtschaftsgeschichte* 4 (1977), pp. 63–82; H. Harnisch, 'Statistische Untersuchungen zum Verlauf der kapitalistischen Agrarreform in den preussischen Ostprovinzen (1811–1865)', *Jahrbuch für Wirtschaftsgeschichte*, 4 (1974), p. 1348–82; G. Franz, 'Landwirtschaft. 1800-1850', in W. Zorn (ed.), *Handbuch der deutschen Wirtschafts- und Sozialgeschichte*, vol. II (Stuttgart, 1976); R. A. Dickler, 'Organization and change in productivity in Eastern Prussia', in W. N. Parker and E. Jones (eds.), *European Peasants and their Markets* (Princeton, 1975), pp. 269–92; G. Helling, 'Berechnung eines Index der Agrarproduktion in Deutschland im 19. Jahrhundert', *Jahrbuch für Wirtschaftsgeschichte*, 4 (1965), pp. 125–43; H.-H. Müller, 'Landwirtschaft und industrielle Revolution – am Beispiel der Magdeburger Börde', in Toni Pierenkemper (ed.), *Landwirtschaft und industrielle Entwicklung* (Wiesbaden, 1989), pp. 45–62; H. Harnisch, 'Die Agrarreform in Preußen und ihr Einfluß auf das Wachstum der Wirtschaft', in Pierenkemper (ed.), *Landwirtschaft und industrielle Entwicklung*, pp. 27–44; also B. Vogel, 'Reformpolitik in Preußen, 1807–1820', in H.-J. Puhle and H.-U. Wehler (eds.), *Preußen im Rückblick* (Göttingen, 1980); H. Schissler, *Preußische Agrargesellschaft im Wandel, 1763–1847* (Göttingen, 1978).

4 See R. Tilly, 'Capital formation in Germany in the nineteenth century', in *Cambridge Economic History of Europe* vol. VII, pp. 388–96; also H. Harnisch, 'Bauerneinkommen, feudale Ausbeutung und agrarischer Fortschritt in der Mark Brandenburg gegen Ende des 19. Jahrhunderts', *Jahrbuch für Wirtschaftsgeschichte* I (1970), pp. 191–7; and Harnisch, *Statistische Untersuchung*.

5 G. F. Knapp, *Die Bauernbefreiung und der Ursprung der Landarbeiter in den älteren Teilen Preußens*, 2 vols. 2nd edn (Munich and Leipzig, 1927).

6 T. Ohnishi, *Zolltarifpolitik Preußens bis zur Gründung des deutschen Zollvereins. Ein Beitrag zur Finanz- und Außenpolitik Preußens* (Göttingen, 1973).

7 The most penetrating analysis of this entire early period of the Zollverein is that of Rolf Dumke, *Der deutsche Zollverein als Modell ökonomischer Integration*, in Helmut Berding (ed.), *Wirtschaftliche und politische Integration in Europa im 19. und 20. Jahrhundert* (Göttingen, 1984), pp. 72–101. See also H.-W. Hahn, 'Hegemonie und Integration. Voraussetzungen und Folgen der preußischen Führungsrolle im Deutschen Zollverein', in Berding, *Wirtschaftliche politische Integration in Europa*, pp 45–70.

8 On this see C.-L. Holtfrerich, 'The monetary unification process in nineteenth-century Germany. Relevance and lessons for Europe today', in M. de Cecco and A. Giovannini (eds.), *Monetary Regimes and Monetary Institutions – Issues and Perspectives in Europe* (Cambridge, 1989).

9 The basic studies are Rainer Fremdling, *Eisenbahnen und deutsches*

Wirtschaftswachstum 1840–1879 (Dortmund, 1975); C.-L. Holtfrerich, *Quantitative Wirtschaftsgeschichte des Ruhrkohlenbergbaus im 19. Jahrhundert* (Dortmund, 1973); R. Spree, *Wachstumszyklen der deutschen Wirtschaft von 1840–1880* (Berlin, 1977); H. Wagenblass, *Der Eisenbahnbau und das Wachstum der deutschen Eisen- und Maschinenbauindustrie 1835 bis 1960* (Stuttgart, 1973); also W. Hoffmann, 'The take-off in Germany', in W. W. Rostow (ed.), *The Economics of Take-off into Sustained Growth* (London and New York, 1963).

10 See D. Eichholtz, *Junker und Bourgeoisie in der preußischen Eisenbahngeschichte* (Berlin, 1962).

11 J. Bergmann, 'Ökonomische Voraussetzungen der Revolution von 1848. Zur Krise von 1845–1848 in Deutschland', in *GG*, 2 (1976), pp. 254–87; H. Kubitschek, 'Die Börsenverordnung vom 28. Mai 1844 und die Situation im Finanz- und Kreditwesen Preußens in den vierziger Jahren des 19. Jahrhunderts', in *Jahrbuch für Wirtschaftsgeschichte* (1962).

12 See W. Fischer, 'Die Stellung der preußischen Bergrechtsreform von 1851–1865 in der Wirtschafts- und Sozialverfassung des 19. Jahrhunderts', in W. Fischer, *Wirtschaft und Gesellschaft im Zeitalter der Industrialisierung* (Göttingen, 1972), pp. 148–60. See also Horst Blumberg, 'Die Finanzierung der Neugründungen und Erweiterungen von Industriebetrieben in Form von Aktiengesellschaften während der fünfziger Jahre des 19. Jahrhunderts in Deutschland am Beispiel der preußischen Verhältnisse erläutert', in H. Mottek (ed.), *Studien zur Geschichte der industriellen Revolution in Deutschland* (Berlin, 1960), pp. 165–208.

13 Hans Rosenberg, *Die Weltwirtschaftskrise 1857–1859* (Göttingen, 1974, originally as supplementary volume of *Vierteljahrschrift für Sozial – und Wirtschaftsgeschichte*, 1934); Spree, *Wachstumszyklen*.

14 Fremdling, *Eisenbahnen*; R. Fremdling, 'Railroads and German economic growth. A leading sector analysis with a comparison to the United States and Great Britain', *Journal of Economic History*, 37 (1977), pp. 583–604; Holtfrerich, *Quantitative Wirtschaftsgeschichte*; Spree, *Wachstumszyklen*.

15 *Ibid.*

16 See R. Tilly, *Financial Institutions and Industrialization in the Rhineland, 1815–1870* (Madison, 1966); and R. Tilly, 'Germany 1815 1870', in R. Cameron, O. Crisp, H. Patrick and R. Tilly, *Banking in the Early Stages of Industrialization* (New York, 1967), pp. 151–82.

17 E. Engel, 'Das Zeitalter des Dampfes in technisch-statistischer Beleuchtung', *Zeitschrift des königl. preußischen statistischen Bureaus* (Berlin, 1879). See R. W. Fogel, 'The social savings controversy', *Journal of Economic History* (1977), pp. 1–54.

18 Fremdling, *Eisenbahnen*.

19 F.-W. Henning, *Die Industrialisierung in Deutschland 1800 bis 1914*, Universitätstaschenbuch no. 145 (Paderborn, 1973) and R.-W. Henning, 'Industrialisierung und dörfliche Einkommensmöglichkeiten. Der Einfluß der Industrialisierung des Textilgewerbes in Deutschland im 19. Jahrhundert auf Einkommensmöglichkeiten in den ländlichen Gebieten', in Hermann Kellenbenz (ed.), *Agrarisches Nebengewerbe und Formen der Reagrarisierung im Spätmittelalter und 19./20. Jahrhundert* (Stuttgart, 1975), pp. 155–75.

20 G. Kirchhain, 'Das Wachstum der deutschen Baumwollindustrie im 19. Jahrhundert', doctoral dissertation, University of Münster, 1973; H. v. Laer, *Industrialisierung und Qualität der Arbeit* (New York, 1977); G. Adelmann, 'Strukturelle Krisen im ländlichen Textilgewerbe Nordwestdeutschlands zu Beginn der Industrialisierung', in Hermann Kellenbenz (ed.), *Wirtschaftspolitik und Arbeitsmarkt* (Vienna, 1974), pp. 110–28.

21 Wage data and underlying literature are in R. Gömmel, *Realeinkommen in Deutschland. Ein internationaler Vergleich (1810–1914)* (Nürnberg, 1979); A Desai, *Real Wages in Germany, 1871–1913* (Oxford, 1968) for the 1870–1913 period.

22 W. G. Hoffmann, with the assistance of H. Hesse and F. Grumbach, *Das Wachstum der deutschen Wirtschaft seit der Mitte des 19. Jahrhunderts* (New York, Heidelberg and Berlin, 1965), pp. 90ff. and 436ff.

23 On this see J. J. Lee, 'Labour in German Industrialization', in *CEHE*, vol VII; also H. von Laer, *Industrialisierung und Qualität der Arbeti* (New York, 1977) and W. Becker, 'Die Bedeutung der nichtagrarischen Wanderungen für die Herausbildung des industriellen Proletariats in Deutschland, unter besonderer Berücksichtigung Preußens von 1850 bis 1870', in Mottek, *Studien*.

24 On concentration see J. Kocka and H. Sigrist in Kocka, *Unternehmen*. W. Feldenkirchen, 'Concentration in German Industry 1870–1939', in Hans Pohl (ed.) *The Concentration Process in the Entrepreneurial Economy since the late 19th Century* in: *Zeitschrift für Unternehmensgeschichte*, 55 (Wiesbaden, 1988).

25 IG and cartels are discussed in Feldenkirchen 'Concentration', and in R. Tilly, *Vom Zollverein zum Industriestaat* (Munich, 1990).

26 M. Pohl, *Konzentration im deutschen Bankwesen. 1848–1980* (Frankfurt am Main, 1982).

27 Steven Webb, 'Tariffs, Cartels, Technology and Growth in the German Steel Industry, 1879 to 1914', *Journal of Economic History*, 40 (1980); U. Wengenroth, *Unternehmensstrategien und technischer Fortschritt. Die deutsche und die britische Stahlindustrie, 1865–1895* (Göttingen, 1986).

28 E. Eistert, *Die Beeinflussung des Wirtschaftswachstums in Deutschland 1880–1913 durch das Bankensystem* (Berlin, 1970); H. Neuberger and H. Stokes, 'German banks and German growth, 1883–1913', *Journal of Economic History*, 34 (1974), pp. 710–31; R. Fremdling and R. Tilly, 'German banks, German growth and econometric history', *Journal of Economic History*, 36 (1976), pp. 416–24; R. Tilly, 'Mergers, external growth and finance in the development of large-scale enterprise in Germany 1880–1913', *Journal of Economic History*, 42 (1982), pp. 629–38; R. Tilly, 'German banking, 1850–1914. Development assistance for the strong', *Journal of European Economic History*, 15 (1986), pp. 113–52.

29 Wengenroth, *Unternehmensstrategien*.

30 J. Kocka, *Unternehmensverwaltung und Angestelltenschaft am Beispiel Siemens. Zum Verhältnis von Kapitalismus und Bürokratie in der deutschen Industrialisierung* (Stuttgart, 1969); also A. Strobel, 'Die Gründung des Züricher Elektrotrusts. Ein Beitrag zum Unternehmergeschäft der deutschen Elektroindustrie 1895–1900', in E. Hassinger (ed.), *Festschrift für C. Bauer* (Berlin, 1974), pp. 303–32.

31 W. P. Kennedy, *Industrial Structure, Capital Markets and the Origins of British Economic Decline* (Cambridge, 1987).

32 F. Zeidenzahl, *100 Jahre Deutsche Bank, 1870–1970* (Frankfurt am Main, 1970); H. Wessel, *Kontinuität im Wandel. 100 Jahre Mannesmann 1890–1990* (Düsseldorf, 1990), pp. 55–80.

33 Tilly, 'Mergers'.

34 E. Klein, *Geschichte der deutschen Landwirtschaft im Industrialisierungszeitalter* (Wiesbaden, 1973).

35 K. Barkin, *The Controversy over German Industrialization 1890 to 1902* (Chicago and London, 1970).

36 The debate touched on the whole question of urbanization, emigration and 'land flight', on the vulnerability of a highly urbanized country to interruption in its foreign trade (imports of foodstuffs especially), on the question of concentration, cut-throat competition, cartels and threatened elimination of the 'Mittelstand', and on the need for a strong state policy of guidance and control of 'market forces' to protect the country from destabilizing influences. Tariffs played a central role in the debate since they were then the chief instrument of national government policy. For a *locus classicus* on this see S. Webb, 'Agricultural protection in Wilhelminian Germany. Forging an empire with pork and rye', *Journal of Economic History*, 42 (1982), pp. 309–26.

37 *Ibid.*

38 S. Webb, 'Tariffs, cartels, technology and growth'.

39 F. Grumbach, 'Statistische Untersuchungen über die Entwicklung der Einkommensverteilung in Deutschland', dissertation, University of Münster, 1957; R. Dumke, 'Economic inequality and industrialization in Germany, 1850–1913', unpublished manuscript 1988.

40 See Gömmel, *Realeinkommen*, Desai, *Real Wages*.

41 See, on this, H.-J. Teuteberg, *Stadtwachstum, Industrialisierung, sozialer Wandel. Beiträge zur Erforschung der Urbanisierung im 19. and 20. Jahrhundert* (Berlin, 1986); H.-J. Teuteberg and G. Wiegelmann, *Der Wandel der Nahrungsgewohnheiten unter dem Einfluß der Industrialisierung* (Göttingen, 1972); R. Spree, *Soziale Ungleichheit vor Krankheit und Tod* (Göttingen, 1981).

42 See H.-J. Teuteberg, *Stadtwachstum*; C. Wischermann, *Wohnen in Hamburg vor dem ersten Weltkrieg* (Münster, 1983) and 'Wohnungsmarkt, Wohnungsversorgung und Wohnmobilität in deutschen Großstädten 1870–1913', in Teuteberg, *Stadtwachstum*; T. Wellenreuther, *Wohnungsbau aund Industrialisierung. Eine ökonometrische Untersuchung am Beispiel Deutschlands von 1850 bis 1913* (Cologne, 1989).

43 On this see J. Reulecke, *Geschichte der Urbanisierung in Deutschland* (Frankfurt am Main, 1985); and esp. W. Krabbe, *Kommunalpolitik und Industrialisierung. Die Entfaltung der städtischen Leistungsverwaltung in Deutschland bis zum Ersten Weltkrieg* (Stuttgart, 1985).

SIX

⟫⟩·◇·⟨⟪

Switzerland

BRUNO FRITZSCHE

'WE set the take-off period between 1800 and 1820/25.'[1] Thus the statement of an economist in 1963 – shortly after the publication of Walt Rostow's seminal book.[2] In contrast to this is a text of 1974 by a historian and political scientist: 'The real take-off cannot very well have taken place before the middle of the century. Only then was the fifty years' struggle for a unified federal state over; the basis for a common market area was not laid before 1850.'[3] The two quotations go to show that the beginning of the Industrial Revolution has been dated quite differently, depending on the point of view and the scientific background of the author. Broadly speaking there are two schools of thought, the one insisting, with a certain national pride, that Switzerland was the first industrialized country in continental Europe,[4] the other pointing out that the existence of a national market was a prerequisite of industrial development that was not fulfilled until after 1848.

These two divergent opinions, based on conjecture rather than on fact, have so far coexisted peacefully. There has never been any widespread debate as to whether the take-off ought rather to be dated at the beginning of the nineteenth century or after 1850. Indeed, Swiss economic history has more or less avoided the first half of the nineteenth century. There are numerous and in part excellent studies on the demographic, agrarian and proto-industrial development in the seventeenth and eighteenth centuries.[5] Also, our knowledge with regard to the economic development after 1850 has greatly increased during the last twenty years or so.[6] But in between there lies not quite a *terra incognita* but, historiographically speaking, a barren land. Out of it emerge two quite remarkable monographs, both published a few years ago, both dealing with the leading sector of the era in question, the cotton industry.[7] To these works this chapter owes quite a number of insights. On the whole, however, we have to content ourselves with formulating hypotheses, posing questions and pointing out deficiencies.

THE SHAPING OF A MODERN STATE, 1798–1848

Unlike the economic history, the political history of the period is firmly established.[8] Up to 1798 the ancient Swiss Confederation consisted of thirteen *Orte* (states) and some associated republics (*zugewandte Orte*). Each of these small sovereign states, loosely held together by an inefficient governing body (Tagsatzung), possessed its own political structure. Each of them retained at least formally some of its medieval democratic traditions. In absolutist Europe, therefore, Switzerland used to be cited as a shining example of freedom. In fact the political systems were controlled everywhere by oligarchies of 'governing families', and without exception political rights were restricted to a minority of *Vollbürger* (full citizens). The majority of the people were *Untertanen* (subjects), living either in one of the several cantons or in one of the *gemeine Herrschaften* (subject territories under joint administration).

Invasion by the French army in 1798 brought an end to this medieval patchwork of tiny republics. It was replaced by the Helvetic Republic, whose constitution was based on the concepts of the Enlightenment and the Rights of Man. Although it was drawn up by two Swiss, César Laharpe and Peter Ochs, it followed the French tradition of a strong central government. The new regime, imposed by the French, strongly conflicted with the deep-rooted Swiss sentiments of local autonomy and traditional diversity. Widespread unrest and the ravages of war rendered the Helvetic Republic unworkable. In 1803 Napoleon, with his own interests at heart and an astonishing flair for Swiss sensibilities ('Fortune has put me at the head of French government, yet I should deem myself incapable of governing the Swiss ... I am myself a highlander and know the spirit arising therefore.'[9]), dictated the so-called Mediation. Switzerland saw itself reduced once again to a weak confederation of small states, this time under French tutelage. Some of the revolutionary achievements were taken up by the new cantonal constitutions (*Mediationsverfassungen*), for example, equality before the law, or the freedom of trade, but on the whole they remained dead letters. Six new cantons, cut out from former subject territories, were admitted as full members of the confederation, so that the country during the Mediation was made up of a total of nineteen small states.

After Napoleon's downfall conservative forces tried to reinstitute the *ancien régime*. The term *Restauration*, commonly applied to the period between 1815 and 1830 is in actual fact not altogether adequate. On the one hand it proved impossible to re-establish the old order fully. The new cantons, supported by the victorious Allied Powers, refused to subject themselves once again to their old masters. Even within their own jurisdiction the old cantons were forced to grant all male adults at least minimal, if unequal political rights.[10] On the other hand the *Bundesvertrag* (Federal Pact) of 1815 was in many respects simply a consolidation of restaurative tendencies that had already set in with the Mediation. The executive power of the confederation suffered still further impairment, the Tagsatzung (Diet), as of old composed of two delegates from each canton, was called upon to decide on matters of foreign policy but more often than not it lacked a quorum (three-quarters of the votes). In practically all other areas the cantons were free to do as they pleased. With regard to economic matters this meant that there were just about as many trade regulations, customs systems, monies, weights and measures in existence as there were cantons. The Congress of Vienna had decreed the return to Switzerland of its *zugewandte Orte*, or allies, Valais, Neuchâtel, and Geneva, which now took their place within the pact as full and equal members.

The French revolution of July 1830 triggered off a series of similar events in many European states. In Switzerland it led to the so-called 'Regeneration', that is, to a series of uprisings aiming at the revival, or regeneration, of the ideals of the Helvetic Republic. By 1831 twelve cantons had adopted 'regenerated' constitutions breathing the spirit of political liberalism (sovereignty of the people, representative government, civil rights, etc.). On the whole these revolts, most of them originating in the still underprivileged *Landschaft* (rural areas) ended up peacefully. Their leaders, predominantly members of the economic or intellectual rural élite (doctors, lawyers, inn-keepers, entrepreneurs, etc.) knew how to mobilize the masses. In the face of widespread mass-meetings the old autocrats simply withdrew. The French author, diplomat and gourmet Chateaubriand, who was at the time residing in Berne wrote: 'The horrible revolution happened on the quiet, by the peaceful smoke of a pipe, in a cosy corner of some pub.'[11]

A new federal pact, anticipating many ideas of the Constitution of 1848, was proposed in 1832 by the Liberals. The attempt, however, was doomed, mainly because in the meantime a reactionary movement had set in all over Europe. Switzerland came to be considered the very centre of revolutionary infection in the heart of Europe and was subjected to diplomatic and political pressures, and even to threats of intervention. The Liberals were thus obliged to move with caution. But even within the Confederation there was a growing resistance against the all too impetuous pace of change. The smaller and economically backward regions feared that they would be cornered by their bigger and more powerful rivals. The common people had been promised political rights, and – much more important in their view – economic betterment as well.

They were disillusioned since, contrary to their expectations, the new system had not produced immediate riches so that many wished that they were back in the old paternalistic regime. Also the new-fangled idea of a compulsory public education did not meet with universal approval: the opportunity costs involved in sending the children to school reduced the income of poor families to a critical level. But above all the people were greatly shocked by the growing anticlericalism of the left-wing Liberals or Radicals. Rabble-rousers of every political description started to abuse the profound attachment of the people to their respective churches for their own political aims. Presently the political conflicts between the regenerated progressive and the non-regenerated conservative cantons were turned into a religious strife between Catholics and Protestants.

In 1847 the Liberals at last, gained a majority in the Tagsatzung which resulted in a declaration of war on the Sonderbund (the Separatist League comprising the five cantons of Central Switzerland plus Valais and Fribourg). Fortunately mutual restraint and public spirit prevailed: the war lasted merely twenty-six days and did not turn into general bloodshed, as civil wars are apt to do (108 soldiers were killed in action). The surrender of the Sonderbund cleared the way for a renewed union. The federal constitution, drawn up within a few months in accordance with the principles of political liberalism, was adopted by the majority of the cantons in the late autumn of 1848. It put an end to half a century of political turmoil.

The basic conflict between the federalists who were jealous of cantonal rights and the centralists who were advocating a strong central state, was overcome by the adoption of a bicameral legislative body (Ständerat and Nationalrat) fashioned after the US constitution. In many areas (e.g. public education, raising of taxes, civil and criminal law, etc.) the cantons retained their sovereignty, whereas in economic matters they had to give up most of their old prerogatives, such as the coining of money, the definition of weights and measures, the regulation of trade, the customs sovereignty. They all passed to the union, so that now the way was cleared for the creation of a national market.

Alexis de Tocqueville summed up this birth of modern Switzerland succinctly: 'One people, composed of several races, speaking several languages, with several religious beliefs, various dissident sects, two churches both equally established and privileged, all political questions quickly turning into religious ones, and all religious questions ending up as political ones, two societies, one very old and the other very young, joined in marriage in spite of the age difference.'[12]

DEMOGRAPHIC AND ECONOMIC DEVELOPMENT, 1800–1850

A general but regionally widely varying population growth had set in during the second part of the eighteenth century.[13] No less a demographer than Malthus commented on the differences in reproductive behaviour between Leysin, a small Alpine and strictly agrarian community, and the region of the Neuchâtel Jura, where watchmaking and bobbin-lacemaking enlarged the means of subsistence.[14]

According to the first official census, instigated by the Helvetic Republic in 1798, 1.7 million people were living on Swiss territory; the first census of the Federal state numbered 2.4 million inhabitants. The mean growth rate in the first half of the nineteenth century (0.7 per cent per annum) is quite respectable, but by no means spectacular. Within the same period, the population doubled in England, whereas in Switzerland it did not even rise by half (42 per cent).

Official statistics on births, deaths and marriages do not reach back beyond 1870. Historic demography has yet to investigate the early nineteenth century,[15] so that precise data on the components of population growth are not available for the time being. We may however safely assume diminishing mortality rates and, by the same token, growing life expectancy: in 1850 mean life expectancy at birth was about forty years.[16]

The great famine of 1816/17 wrought tremendous havoc in Switzerland, particularly in the densely populated proto-industrial eastern part. The potato blight of the late 1840s made itself felt in Switzerland as well. It resulted in difficult food conditions but did not quite provoke the catastrophic nutrition problems of 1816/17.

Between 1800 and 1850 Switzerland, traditionally one of the emigration areas *par excellence*, appears to have suffered a remarkably modest decrease in population by migration. An estimated 100,000 persons emigrated from Swiss territories while, within the same period, Switzerland received around 50,000 immigrants, resulting in an actual loss by migration of approximately 50,000 persons, or merely 0.5 per cent. Within the subsequent period (1850–88) loss by migration was to live up to its reputation to a considerably greater extent (1.7 per cent).

Lack of famines after 1817, growth of life expectancy, relatively slight losses by migration: these combined demographic data imply that on the whole the expanding economy succeeded in providing for the population of the country. Population growth too in the first half of the nineteenth century varied to a noticeable degree according to individual regions. There is clear evidence for the growth of the population in regions with a predominantly rural economy, and especially so in the canton of Berne, while the more industrialized areas of eastern Switzerland now tended towards stagnation.

This marked population growth in rural areas is hardly to be interpreted as a result of immigration; rather, and in the first place it ought to
be looked upon as a consequence of the growing excess of births over
deaths. Together with the *ancien régime* the old marriage regulations disappeared, according to which the right of getting married depended on
ownership of means of production (usually a farmstead). This led to more
marriages, especially among the poor and, consequently, to more births.
Despite the fact that in agriculture the increase in productivity was considerable, mass poverty especially in rural regions became an ever increasing
phenomenon.[17] This, in combination with Malthus's gloomy prognostica-
tions, led to new matrimonial laws which, once again, made marriage
appreciably more difficult for persons without means.

The population of the cities, too, grew within this period. The traditional population policy had rigorously denied all but the most privileged
the right of residence in the cities. This became obsolete after 1830 at the
latest. In accordance with the newly introduced right of domicile and the
freedom for everyone to establish residence at will, the cities were obliged
to open their gates to an army of persons looking for employment within
their boundaries. But even though the urban population doubled in the
course of the first half of the nineteenth century (from 74,000 to 154,000
persons), it still supplied a mere 6.5 per cent of the total population in
1850. It must therefore be kept in mind that in Switzerland the Industrial
Revolution was an altogether rural phenomenon.

With regard to the distribution of the labour force, the available data
are even less substantiated than those referring to the population figures.
The earliest reasonably trustworthy statistics date from 1888; estimates
with respect to periods before 1888 which are used here have quite
frequently been called in question but have not been satisfactorily
corrected so far.[18] According to these estimates, the share of persons
employed in the agrarian sector would have run to some 66 per cent in
1800 and would have decreased to 57 per cent by 1850. By contrast the
percentage of persons employed in the secondary sector totalled 26 per
cent approximately in 1800 and increased to about 33 per cent by 1850.
In the services sector there occurred hardly any movement at all, the
number of persons employed moving up from 8 per cent in 1800 to 10
per cent in 1850. It is worthy of note that as early as 1800 the agrarian
sector appears to have comprised no more than two-thirds of the sum
total of the gainfully employed persons: which – more or less – corre-
sponds to the correlative proportional number in England in 1750.
Conversely, since there were no great shifts taking place in the course of
the following fifty years, the share of persons employed in the agrarian
sector in 1850 appears rather high in comparison with the corresponding

international data.[19] This reflects the fact that on the one hand
Switzerland in the eighteenth century, due to its exceptionally vigorous
proto-industry, was a progressive country economically speaking while in
the nineteenth century it stubbornly and for a long time retained the
traditional system of outwork combined with small-scale peasant farming.

The decision of the Helvetic Republic to abolish feudal duties in return
for compensation has never been revoked by any of the subsequent
governments; but ever recurring disputes regarding the respective sums to
be paid and the mutability of political affairs in general were apt to delay
the actual process of redemption so that the proceedings dragged on for
half a century. The coincident decline of the open field system released
the peasant farmers from their traditional duties towards the rural
community; the commons were divided and passed over into private
ownership. Once these changes had taken place, the new, individualistic
agrarian structures at long last permitted modernizations which the
economic societies (*patriotische Oekonomen*) had propagated as early as
the eighteenth century, orienting their theories according to the current
Dutch and English teachings of the day. These reforms were carried
through in the rural sections of the Swiss plain; they failed to touch the
Alps or the Alpine foothills where animal husbandry and dairy farming
had for a long time belonged to the most dynamic and prosperous
branches of the Swiss economy. Now however, stagnation set in, and the
small peasant farmers of the mountainous regions were confronted with
the gradually growing competition arising from cattle-keeping farmers of
the plain. The traditional distribution of landed property was, generally
speaking, hardly touched by reforms. Small peasant farmers remained the
vast majority in the whole of Switzerland so that, in 1850, some 80 per
cent of all Swiss households still owned some landed property. But more
than half of the peasants owned less than 10 hectares; homesteads of more
than 10 hectares were in fact considered to be large-size properties.[20]

The parcelling out into small, even tiny plots helps to explain why, up
to 1850, the use of agricultural machinery was practically unheard of.
Quite frequently, peasants did not even possess their own plough but were
obliged, if need be, to borrow one from a neighbour.[21] More intensive
cultivation was, as a rule, not realized by the use of machines but by the
employment of more manual labour. Even though the share of agricultural labour in Switzerland showed a downward tendency, absolute
numbers increased by little less than one-fourth: from some 500,000 agricultural workers in 1800 to a maximum of 620,000 in 1850. Statements of
all-round validity cannot possibly be made with regard to the growth of
agricultural production. While individual regions realized a doubling of
their calorific output, these findings may not be generalized.[22] On average

the growth in agricultural production and population growth appear just about to counterbalance each other, which would suggest an increase in agricultural production within the first half of the century of little less than 50 per cent.[23] But, as in the time of the *ancien régime*, Switzerland continued to be dependent on the importation of foodstuffs. Thus, in 1850, the domestic production of breadgrain supplied no more than 59 per cent of the demand. On the whole therefore, what is termed the 'agrarian revolution' in Switzerland turns out, in actual fact, to be somewhat less than spectacular. An investigation referring to the year 1860, covering nine European countries, puts the Swiss increase in agricultural production in eighth place; productivity is said to have worked out at 9 million calories per farm labourer, which would amount to less than half of the values reached in the United Kingdom (20 million calories).[24]

As early as the middle of the eighteenth century, Switzerland became one of the favourite tourist countries for intellectuals in search of an idealized pastoral republic and, incidentally, for an idealized pastoral people. The proliferating travel books of the time hardly ever failed to praise the proverbial industriousness of the Swiss, to refer to their prosperity and to mention the regional cottage industries. 'For a moment I thought I was in England', comments William Coxe in the 1770s.[25]

While watch- and clock-making, brought to Geneva by French Huguenots, gradually expanded to the Vallée de Joux (in the Jura) and to the northern part of the Jura attached to the canton of Neuchâtel, the textile industries, in the course of the eighteenth century, unmistakably moved to the eastern parts of Switzerland. At the same time, linen manufacture, situated in the Bernese part of what was later to become the canton of Aargau and in the regions adjoining Lake Constance, lost a great deal of its former significance: as far back as the Middle Ages, linen had been an important export commodity of the merchants of St Gall. Silk manufacture, on the other hand, introduced in Basle and Zurich during the Reformation, retained its importance in the eighteenth century, when it even succeeded in gradually expanding to central Switzerland.

At the beginning of the eighteenth century, Switzerland was struck by the phenomenon of the much-referred-to *Baumwollwut* (cotton mania), which caught hold of practically all the branches of textile production, involving spinning, weaving, cloth printing and embroidery alike. After 1760 at the very latest with the onset of intensive economic growth, the cotton industries became the leading branches in the economic structure of Switzerland.[26] Of an estimated total of some 200,000 persons employed in the whole of the secondary sector in 1800, a probable 140,000 were working in the textile industries, and of these again some 100,000 in the various branches of the cotton sector.[27]

In 1785, Swiss merchants started to import English machine yarn which, by 1800, already satisfied no less than one-quarter of the demand of the weaving mills.[28] The Golden Age of hand-spinning was therefore over and done with. Starting around 1750, wages had begun to move up in a striking fashion, due to a steadily growing demand for cotton yarn which could be met only with difficulty. But with the introduction of imported cotton yarn into the market, wages started to collapse rapidly. Between 1787 and 1799 the number of hand spinners declined from some 34,000 to some 20,000. Thus, to begin with, the bottleneck of production in the spinning sector was overcome by way of importation. Why did spinning not turn to mechanization at that early stage? One possible answer starts out from the sociopolitical conditions of the time. Cotton spinning, performed in outwork, was to a large extent organized and controlled by a class of small-scale rural merchants acting as intermediaries. Within the political system of the time these go-betweens were mere subjects deprived of political rights, whereas, economically speaking, they moved within a kind of no man's land, owing to the fact that entrepreneurial activities of any description were traditionally confined to the privileged full citizens residing in the cities. This being so, intermediaries could hardly be expected to go in for long-term investments, quite apart from the fact that they were permanently suffering from undercapitalization.[29]

The argument presented above appears all the more convincing when the development in cotton spinning is set against that in silk throwing. Silk-twisting was under the immediate control of the *Seidenherren*, the silkmen of the cities. Now in the silk industry, mechanical twisting machines were in wide use already: these were highly intricate, far more difficult to handle than the simple 'jennies' or the 'water-frames' of the day. One more supporting fact might be added, namely that mechanical spinning mills emerged after the Revolution of 1798, that is, at a time when the Helvetic Constitution granted full equality to all citizens.

Historiographic literature – excluding the most recent studies – frequently takes the year 1801 to be the crucial date for the beginning of the Industrial Revolution in Switzerland, referring to the fact that in that year the first mechanical spinning mill, boasting 26 'mules' with 204 spindles each, was put into use in St Gall.[30] According to Rostow's definition of the take-off, however, in the sense of 'starting point into self-sustained growth', the above dating is highly questionable. Undeniably, quite a number of mostly smallish spinning mills were to emerge in the years following 1801, but without exception they were frail little plants, capable of surviving only in the hothouse atmosphere created by the Continental Blockade.

After the end of the Napoleonic era cotton spinning was due for a comprehensive process of restructuring, whereby almost all the small mills were eliminated. In the foremost cotton region, the canton of Zurich, 99 mills – or a little more than four-fifths of the then existing spinning mills in the region – were equipped with less than 1,000 spindles each. In 1853 there remained no more than five of these small-scale mills, as opposed to the twelve largest establishments, provided with above 10,000 spindles each, and owning together 38.5 per cent of the totality of spindles then in use.[31] Compared to the heyday of hand-spinning, the gross value of production had gradually shrunk to a mere fraction, reaching its lowest level at 5 million Swiss francs in 1820, from which it recovered only very slowly in the years following.[32] The beginning of sustained growth in the cotton-spinning industry cannot therefore be set before 1820 at the very earliest.

First signs of the mechanization of cotton weaving occur only after 1825; the first weaving mill established with lasting success was founded in 1830.[33] Owing to the mechanization in the spinning sector, tens of thousands of workers had lost their livelihood. Now, what with the threatening mechanization in the weaving branch, the hand weavers were extremely apprehensive, fearing that they were going to suffer a fare similar to the workers in the spinning branch. The Liberals, making extensive use of the protest potential of the working classes during the revolutionary days of 1830, seemed to support the hand weavers' demand for a ban on all machinery. After having seized power the new Liberal governments did not, however, live up to the weavers' expectations. As a consequence, on the second anniversary of the Revolution the weavers, giving way to fear, fury and frustration, burned to the ground a barely completed weaving mill at Uster. This dramatic incident appears to have slowed down further mechanization considerably. At all events, in 1850 there existed no more than 3,000 mechanical weaving looms whereas, some fifteen years later (1866/7), their sum total amounted to about 13,000. By contrast, during these same years, the number of persons employed in hand weaving reached its highest level (some 45,000 workers).[34]

Assuming that the estimate for 1850, of about 150,000 persons employed in the textile sector as a whole, is roughly correct, the following findings would result with respect to the individual branches: 65,000 workers, or 44 per cent in the combined branches of the cotton industry; 46,000 workers, or 31 per cent, in the silk industry; the remaining 38,000 workers, or roughly one-quarter, would have to be assigned to the linen industry, to wool production and to the straw-plaiting branch. The cotton-spinning branch alone was fully mechanized: its estimated 16,000 workers may therefore be considered mill-hands, or industrial workers in the proper sense of the term. In all the other branches, mechanization was at best under way: if together they furnished another 10,000 actual mill-hands, then a sum total of 26,000 workers (or a little over 17 per cent) may be described as actual factory workers.[35]

Seeing that – from the point of view of the number of persons employed – the Swiss spinning industry is hardly of any great importance, surely it is not amiss to ask whether it ought indeed to be considered the leading sector in the Swiss Industrial Revolution. In recent historiographical literature it is especially Beatrice Veyrassat who blames researchers for having been fascinated with the merely technical aspects of the cotton-spinning industry, thereby neglecting the considerably more substantial numbers of persons employed in some of the remaining branches. In her view, some branches other than spinning were of far greater importance; according to her, the combined branches of cloth printing and embroidery acted as *industries pilotes*. Veyrassat furthermore argues that the process of industrialization in Switzerland followed the 'continental pattern': labour, by comparison with England, was relatively cheap and this in turn suggested to the Swiss entrepreneurs that they should avoid competition with superior English technology, concentrating on branches as yet untouched by industrialization in England, such as various kinds of specialties or small numbers of high-quality goods.[36]

Similar arguments may prove valid with regard to the watch- and clock-making industry. With the exception of textiles, watches were the most important Swiss export goods of the time. Manufacture was largely decentralized, either in the form of outwork or in very small *ateliers*. The decisive changeover to industrial manufacture did not take place before 1870 and is to be seen as a reaction to the steadily growing American competition. Up to then, inexpensive if very well-qualified labour, meticulous inspection and accurate assessment of the market situation, and a high degree of sensibility to fashion trends, had secured nothing short of spectacular success. As opposed to the textile sector, where Switzerland just about managed to keep pace, Swiss watches wholly controlled the world market. In 1850, a full million watches, that is, two-thirds of the entire world market, were manufactured in the regions of the Jura alone.[37]

If we accept as correct the fact that economic growth was indeed and in the first place due to manual skill, then there cannot have been any clear-cut turning-point in the development within the first half of the nineteenth century. As a matter of consequence, Veyrassat deals with the period between 1760 and 1840 as an entity. It is undoubtedly correct that manual labour continued for a long time to play a significant role. Not before 1880 did the number of industrial workers (130,000) outstrip that of the persons employed in the cottage industries (120,000).[38]

But it is of course misleading to draw conclusions regarding the significance of an economic sector based on the number of employed persons alone. It must be kept in mind that the declared aim of mechanized production consisted precisely in cutting down on labour. In the middle years of the nineteenth century, the cotton-spinning industry employed one-quarter of the labour available, while at the same time it contributed one-third to the value added by the cotton sector as a whole. Admittedly, the ratio is even more favourable in the dyeing and printing branches, which again tends to support Veyrassat's theory of the 'continental pattern', for in these branches, some 10 per cent of the labour force supplied roughly one-third of the value added.

Recent estimates of the gross value added with respect to the economic sector and branches suggest the following relative proportions for the average values in the years 1851–5: the agricultural sector is still clearly leading, with 358 million Swiss francs, or some 50–60 per cent of the national product. The respective contributions of the exporting industries look modest by comparison: 12 million Swiss francs from the watch and clock-making industries, 7 million Swiss francs from the silk industries, and 41 million Swiss francs from the cotton sector as a whole.[39]

PECULIAR FEATURES OF SWISS DEVELOPMENT

Applying the classical concept of the 'prerequisites' as a heuristic instrument, inquiries about particularities or peculiarities of the growth-path in Switzerland will yield the following results:

Raw materials. Even though Switzerland possesses iron as well as coal deposits, their exploitation entails unduly high costs. Owing to the transportation revolution, importation of both iron and coal became feasible and gradually less expensive. As a result, the mines in Switzerland disappeared, to be reactivated in times of supply difficulties as, for instance, during the Second World War. Heavy industry, responsible for areas of industrial concentration and conurbations elsewhere, is nearly wholly lacking in Switzerland. The demand for power of the early factories was, preferably, satisfied by means of hydraulic power. Instead of the congested areas abroad, there emerged a pattern of decentralized industries creating a series of industrial landscapes along the rivers.

Population and labour force. Even in pre-industrial times, Switzerland was a densely populated country. In the nineteenth century, population growth continued quite vigorously. Manpower was cheap; as far as the textile sector and the watch-and-clock industries were concerned, it was also well qualified. In comparison with the rest of Europe, the degree of literacy was remarkably high: there can hardly be any doubt that human capital was the mainstay and the most important stimulating factor of the economic growth.

Know-how. The multifarious and highly successful proto-industries of the eighteenth century suggest a high level of both technical knowledge and organizational competence. Thus the delay occurring in the mechanization of the cotton-spinning and cotton-weaving industries – a delay of some thirty to fifty years in comparison to England – need not be imputed to a lack of technical know-how. It seems more likely that, taking into account the economic situation at the time, it was thought more promising, at least temporarily, to specialize in branches not as yet touched by mechanized production.

Capital. Mechanization might of course also have been obstructed by shortage of capital. But, according to the concurrent view of researchers Switzerland at the end of the eighteenth century was a financially powerful country. While wars had ruined other nations, these same wars had been put to profit by the Swiss, who exported their mercenaries, true to their traditional maxim: 'Point d'argent point de Suissses.' Moreover, Absolutism with its costly apparatus of officials and its standing armies never had a chance to gain a foothold in the small Swiss republics. The problem in Switzerland therefore appears to have been not so much where funds were to come from, but rather how they had best be invested in the face of falling interest rates. Elsewhere, governmental demand for credit tended to stimulate the development of the banking system; in Switzerland, there was no more than a sprinkling of private bankers who, in the main, were concentrating on foreign business in order to export surplus liquidity.[40] The problem of financing industrial undertakings was therefore due much less to shortage of capital than to the absence of an institutionalized capital market. The possibilities of raising money through informal channels appears to have differed greatly according to individual regions, which may help to explain why the mechanization of the spinning and weaving industries remained confined to the canton of Zurich while the regions of St Gall, Appenzell and Glarus retained the traditional system of manufacture and domestic work.[41]

Foreign trade. Economic relations with foreign countries had played an important role long before 1800. To begin with, Switzerland had long since ceased to be self-supporting: thus, it depended on the importation of foodstuffs. On the other hand, the products of the several proto-industries were exported abroad almost without exception. After 1815, the European scene changed, inasmuch as the newly consolidated European nations were quick to introduce a policy of almost unmitigated protectionism, while Switzerland remained committed to the principles of free trade: conceivably rather from necessity than from conviction, since the tiny Alpine republics were of far too little account economically to lead a series of successful tariff wars. Confronted with this new situation, the Swiss entrepreneurs made efforts to open up new outlets outside Europe for their export goods: with the result that in 1845, three-quarters of all Swiss exports went overseas, and of these three-quarters again almost half went to the two Americas.[42] Which was indeed a remarkable achievement for so small a country that, into the bargain, lacked any direct access to the sea.

On the world market the Swiss found themselves face to face with keen English competition. But within this new context, the old Swiss strategy mentioned above – namely, to avoid direct confrontation with competitors, resorting to the production of special items instead – appears to have made sense once again. At the same time Switzerland turned English colonial expansion to its own advantage without being obliged to bear any share of the costs involved. In 1861, the German economist Emminghaus pointed out that the small, land-locked country had set up a sort of 'colonial system' without possessing a fleet, without maintaining any colonial administration, without having had to wage any wars, and without having been forced to resort to any kind of oppression.[43]

Undoubtedly, in the first half of the nineteenth century, foreign trade was of crucial importance for the development of the industrial sector. Both the textile and the watch- and clock-making industries exported over 90 per cent of their production, thereby furnishing some four-fifths of the totality of Swiss exports.[44] The most recent estimates with respect to the volume of exports, compared with a rough estimate of the national income in 1850,[45] suggests that exportation made up for something like one-third of the net national product: this would just about equal the findings for 1913, for which the available data are somewhat more exact. Possibly the above estimates are set rather too high;[46] but at any rate, it may be taken for granted that in the first half of the nineteenth century, the Swiss ratio of foreign trade exceeded that of England.

A totally different problem is that of the share contributed by the export-oriented industrial sector to the Swiss economic growth in its totality. So far, historians have assumed unquestioningly that the export sector has acted as the impulsive force of development. Until quite recently, this traditional view has never been challenged, which, by the way, tallies perfectly with the deep-rooted conception of the Swiss themselves regarding the economic structures of their country. It may be argued that the combined textile and watch industries contributed an enormous share not only to exports but also to imports, since their demand for raw materials amounted to some 40 to 50 per cent of the sum total of Swiss importation. Accordingly, the inland share of the value added was small (some 30 to 35 per cent); the share of the export industries in the national product is estimated at no more than 12 per cent.[47]

Of course, the notion that the 'leading sector' automatically contributes the main part to the total economic growth is mistaken in the case of other countries as well; of more decisive importance is the stimulus coming from interlinkages. There did indeed exist linkages within the cotton sector, for example, between the spinning, the weaving and the processing industries. But, since the products of the cotton sector were for the most part exported, they were satisfying a final demand that failed to set off any further stimulus on the domestic market. Backward linkages alike were of little importance: the raw materials had to be imported from abroad, and since the capital intensity involved was but small, the demand for products of the capital-goods industry was relatively small as well. The most noteworthy results were probably attained by the spinning industry, since it was responsible for the establishment of the first mechanized factories.

Assuming the above results of modern research to be correct, and assuming, consequently, that the significance of the export branches has so far been exaggerated, it would follow that, by contrast, the growth in the domestic sector has up to now been underrated. But we are here rather near the realm of mere speculation: precisely because it has been considered of little account, the amount of research done with regard to the domestic sector has been regrettably limited. Moreover we are confronted with perhaps the greatest oddity of the Swiss Industrial Revolution, namely the absence of a national market.

National market. Discussions concerning the 'prerequisites' invariably attach great weight to the existence of a well-developed and smoothly functioning domestic market. Until 1848 however, nothing resembling a home market existed within the Swiss territory. The two dozen cantons were, economically speaking, totally sovereign entities, every one of them possessing its own customs sovereignty. Article 15 of the Federal Pact of 1815 confined itself to the statement that the mutual exchange of goods was not to be impeded and that new customs duties would have to be approved by the Federal Diet.

The economic structures of the several cantons were disparate in the extreme. The cantons of the Alpine regions had hardly been touched by industrial development, but even major parts of the Swiss plain, such as the cantons of Berne, Fribourg and Vaud, retained a predominantly agrarian structure. The watch- and clock-making industries were confined to the canton of Geneva and to some Jura valleys attached to the cantons of Neuchâtel and Vaud, silk-ribbon weaving to Basle; the centre of cotton spinning and cotton weaving was situated in the canton of Zurich, extending to the neighbouring regions of the canton of Aargau; the textile-finishing industries were concentrated in the eastern part of Switzerland and the canton of Glarus. To summarize: even though there were a number of distinct areas of growth, they were practically incapable of giving impetus to the Swiss economy as a whole, as long as an efficiently working national market was missing.

The absence of a national market hardly ever hampered the textile or the watch industries, since almost the whole of their output went abroad. Conversely, because of its extreme restriction to purely local or regional markets, it is difficult to conceive how the home sector could have expanded at a reasonable pace. Undeniably, agricultural production displayed a considerable rate of growth in a number of regions; but a simple process of extrapolation would result in yielding highly fallacious values for the Swiss economy as a whole. So far, investigations concerning the growth of crafts and trade are almost wholly missing. But it may be assumed that up to the 1830s their growth remained badly hampered by the regulations of the various guilds, since these were not abolished before the Regeneration.

The dualism of growth- and export-oriented industries on the one hand, and on the other hand, of a traditional, locally structured domestic sector, exclusively covering local needs, may be observed both in Switzerland as a whole and within the individual industrialized cantons. It goes back to pre-industrial times, when the proto-industries, predominantly introduced by religious fugitives, did not supplant the traditional economic system, but rather established themselves beside and apart from them. Neither on the labour market, nor on the procurement and the outlet markets did they encroach upon the guild regulations: their raw materials were bought abroad, their products were sold abroad, and as a rule their labour was recruited from rural regions.[48] This pattern survived to a large extent up to 1850. That is to say, there was superimposed on the cantonal sovereignties a connecting network of pocket-size 'multinationals' as it were, and these, at least for some time to come, took precious little interest in what might be termed a properly national economic policy.

A comparison of the sums contributed to the federal war chest with the respective population figures yields a rough idea of the financial position of the several cantons.[49] It would appear that the cantons of Basle, Neuchâtel and Geneva, paying the amount of 50 rappen (half a Swiss franc) per capita, led the dance as the most prosperous Swiss cantons. Equally above the average of 32 rappen per capita ranged both the two industrialized cantons of Zurich and Aargau and the two fertile agrarian cantons of Berne and Vaud (40 rappen per capita). The opposite end of the scale was occupied exclusively by Alpine cantons; their payments to the federal war funds did not even reach one-third of the mean value.

The great disparities appearing in the level of economic development between the individual cantons allows for a further and at the same time new dimension in the assessment of the struggles for the constitution in the years 1847/8. It is striking that the Separatist League of 1847, bitterly opposing a centralized federal state, was made up of the poorest Swiss cantons – with the sole exception of Lucerne, heading the League, keeping a position somewhere near average in the financial hierarchy of the cantons. But Lucerne was in serious danger of losing its former political as well as its economic relevance: for, undeniably, both the historical and geographical centres of Switzerland had, economically speaking, become peripheral.

It has been argued that, conversely, the industrialized cantons insistently urged the establishment of a unified national market. It is true that the Constitution of 1848 formally ensured the economic unification of the country. But the process of welding together was to last for decades: its sluggishness may, for instance, be deduced from the very modest volume of goods transported by rail in the initial stages of the railways, whose construction was started in 1854.[50] Another pointer in the same direction is provided by the fact that the standardization of commercial law was by no means considered a matter of urgency, since only in 1874 did it come under the competence of the Federal Government.[51]

Of considerably greater immediate interest for the exporting industries than the rapid development of a national market was the submission of the external trade policy to central control. For a long time before there had been endless controversies over the matter in the federal Diet; but propositions directed towards the establishment of a unified foreign trade policy had always lacked a quorum. At long last, the Constitution of 1848 allowed pertinent decisions to be reached and, consequently, it permitted the formation of a unified front against the protectionism of the neighbouring countries.

But of greatest immediate significance was paragraph 21 of the new constitution, submitting the construction of 'public works' – meaning the railways – to the competence of the Federal Government. At that time, the railway route from Zurich to Baden (in Switzerland), a line some 23 kilometres long, was the only piteous remnant of a project which, originally launched by a handful of entrepreneurs from Zurich and St Gall, had come to nothing because of the diverging interests of the cantons involved. According to the original plans, the line was to lead from Lake Constance via Zurich to Basle, where it was to meet both the French railways and the German track on the right bank of the Rhine.[52] The intended route plainly reveals the interests of the exporting industries that were backing the scheme.

In 1852 the federal parliament decided against a national railway project, conceived by two English experts, and pronounced itself in favour of a railway system in private ownership. That decision ought not to be interpreted predominantly as a declaration of loyalty to the philosophy of economic liberalism: the parliament was, rather, giving way to regional interests and to the interests of the exporting industries. Clearly, the development of the domestic market was, by comparison, a matter of lesser importance. It was by no means a matter of chance that the first main line, opened in 1855, failed to lead from Zurich to the geographical centre of Switzerland. Instead, it led to the periphery of the country, in the direction of Lake Constance and, therefore, in the direction of southern Germany. Owing to the ensuing breakneck development of the railway network, the original direction of impact, was, admittedly, obliterated before long: in 1860, a network of over 1,000 kilometres was already open for use; two years later, in 1862, all Swiss cities north of the Alps were connected by rail.

SUMMARY AND OUTLOOK

To return to our initial question: at what particular point in time can the setting in of the Industrial Revolution in Switzerland reasonably be fixed? Obviously, the problem of the starting point of a sustained economic growth cannot be solved as long as a reliable computation of the national product for the first half of the nineteenth century is missing. On the other hand, it may safely be asserted that, within this period, the prerequisites were created for a thorough and extensive process of modernization, both politically and economically.

It may also be taken for granted that population growth, setting in around the middle of the eighteenth century, but periodically checked and retarded by famine (1771 and again in 1816/17), continued steadily from 1820 onwards. There is also a consensus among historians that in the cotton-spinning industry, the first branch to be fully mechanized, sustained growth was not achieved before 1820. Consequently, the year 1820 would have to be considered the earliest possible date for the 'take-off' of the Industrial Revolution in Switzerland. In point of fact, this dating would tally fairly well with the upswing in the building cycle, the only available long time-series of economic data reaching back as far as 1814.[53]

But it must be stressed once again that this early date is valid for only the most progressive cantons. To assume that the growth of the industrial sector in one canton or the development of agriculture in another automatically implies a similar growth or development either in other cantons

or in Switzerland as a whole would at best be problematic and very probably fallacious. It must be kept in mind that, until 1848, the cantons
formed individual, in some cases even almost self-supporting, economic
units; which is to say that, up to 1850, economic growth did not − nor
could it − take place within a national context in the accepted sense of
the term.

Hence, in 1850 the economic structure of Switzerland presents a rather
peculiar spectacle: on the one hand, a number of highly efficient light
industries, capable of meeting the much-dreaded English competition on
the world market; on the other hand a domestic sector lacking anything
more extensive than the traditional, purely local or, at best, purely
regional structures, the output or importance of which has not been
assessed to this day. The absence of a national market, acting as a
retarding element and, as such, by no means to be deemed negligible, is
formally coped with in the Constitution of 1848. Only from 1848 onward,
and after a considerable period of delay, could the construction of a
railway network be taken in hand; this in turn was to lead to the gradual
knitting together of the several Swiss regions, to the emergence of a
modern credit market, to the rise of investment banks, and to employment for tens of thousands of workers. Likewise, only from 1850 onward
was it possible gradually to overcome pauperism, an ever-growing and
ever more threatening problem in the first half of the century.

In the latter part of the nineteenth century, the railways were to play
an important part in the development of Swiss tourism. Scenic
Switzerland, discovered in the eighteenth century by intellectuals, had
since also become a favourite playground of the European aristocracy and
the very rich; it now came within reach of the merely prosperous of the
upper middle classes. After Thomas Cook's first 'conducted tour' to
Switzerland in 1863, the growth of Swiss tourism remained high
throughout the second half of the nineteenth century, reaching a peak in
the 'Belle Epoque', with 3.2 million registered guests from abroad and
12,000 hotels or a sum total of 385,000 beds in 1912.[54]

The 1860s also witnessed the emergence of the Swiss food-processing
industries, such as the Anglo-Swiss Condensed Milk Company (founded
in 1865) and Henri Nestlé's baby foods (1867). The first chocolate factories may be traced back as far as 1820, for example, Cailler to 1819 and
Suchard to 1826. But Swiss chocolate attained its worldwide fame and
became the trademark absolute of Switzerland only long afterwards,
thanks to a new and highly improved production process introduced
around 1880.

It has been shown above that the foundations for and beginnings of modern economic growth in Switzerland reach far back. It is, however, only with the long-term growth setting in about 1885 and ending on the eve of the First World War that Switzerland with its uneven patchwork character of regionally scattered industries was transformed into a truly industrialized nation. In 1882 the most difficult and most important line of the main railway system, the Gotthard route through the Alps, was completed. Between 1888 and 1910 the labour force employed in cottage industries declined from 110,000 to 70,000; during the same period the number of factory workers rose from 180,000 to 380,000 (including the administrative staff). Urban population grew as it had never grown before (mean growth rate between 1880 and 1910: 3.6 per cent per annum). In 1910 there were twenty-four towns with more than 10,000 inhabitants; Zurich, Basle and Geneva numbered more than 100,000.

The scales of the migratory balance tipped definitely in favour of immigration. In 1914 the foreign-born population amounted to no less than 15 per cent. The all-too-rapid pace of transformation led to severe social conflicts. The 1880s witnessed the birth of a new labour movement (1880 the Gewerkschaftsbund, 1888 the Sozialdemokratische Partei) which in turn grew more and more radical, adopting at least in theory if not in practice a Marxist view of society.[55]

Throughout the nineteenth century the textile industry remained the most important sector, employing more than a quarter of the industrial labour force and contributing nearly half of the total export value in 1910. In the latter part of the nineteenth century embroidery and lace-making, centred in the region of St Gall, came to enjoy enormous growth rates. After the First World War, however, this branch, dependent on the vagaries of fashion trends, collapsed almost entirely.

In the long run mechanical engineering and organic chemistry proved to be much more important. Both of them originated in immediate connection with the textile industries: the one providing dyestuffs for the silk-ribbon manufacture of Basle, the other producing mules, power-looms, turbines and similar equipment. And, owing to their intensive research work in the field of high technology, both of them acquired a worldwide reputation towards the end of the nineteenth century.

The chemical industry (e.g. Geigy, established in 1864, CIBA in 1884, Sandoz in 1886, Hoffmann-La Roche in 1894), producing aniline dyes and pharmaceuticals, held an important share of the international market. Swiss output in 1895 was almost one-fifth as large (by value) as the German and just about as big as that of all other countries combined.[56] Engineering works (e.g. Maschinenfabrik Oerlikon, 1876, Brown, Boveri & Co., 1891) were instrumental in developing new technologies in the fields of electric traction and of long-distance transmission of energy.

These two industrial sectors, then, proved instrumental in leading Switzerland during the years following 1885, an era occasionally referred to as the 'Second Industrial Revolution', incidentally thereby leading its economy to continued international success.

NOTES

1 Walter Wittman, 'Die Take-Off-Periode der schweizerischen Volkswirtschaft', *Zeitschrift für die gesamte Staatswirtschaft*, 119 (1963), p. 593.

2 Walt W. Rostow, *The Stages of Economic Growth* (Cambridge, 1960).

3 Erich Gruner, 'Wirtschaftspolitik und Arbeitsmarkt in der Schweiz im 19. Jahrhundert', in Hermann Kellenbenz (ed.), *Wirtschaftspolitik und Arbeitsmarkt* (Vienna, 1974), p. 130.

4 Jean-François Bergier, *Naissance et croissance de la Suisse industrielle* (Berne, 1974). Basilio M. Biucchi, *The Industrial Revolution in Switzerland*, in *The Fontana Economic History of Europe*, vol. IV (London, 1970), p. 655.

5 Ulrich Pfister, 'Protoindustrialisierung: die Herausbildung von Gewerberegionen, 15.–18. Jahrhundert', *Schweizer Zeitschrift für Geschichte*, 41, no. 2 (1992), pp. 149–60.

6 See Hansjörg Siegenthaler, 'Die Schweiz 1850–1914', in *Handbuch der europäischen Wirtschafts-und Sozialgeschichte*, ed. Wolfram Fischer und Hermann Kellenbenz, vol. V (Stuttgart, 1985), pp. 443–73.

7 Béatrice Veyrassat, *Négociants et fabricants dans l'industrie cotonnière suisse, 1760–1840* (Lausanne, 1982). Peter Dudzik, *Innovation und Investition. Technische Entwicklung und Unternehmerentscheide in der schweizerischen Baumwollspinnerei 1800–1916* (Zurich, 1987).

8 See *Handbuch der Schweizer Geschichte*, vol. II (Zurich, 1977).

9 W. Oechsli, *Quellenbuch zur Schweizergeschichte* (Zurich, 1818), p. 640.

10 'der Genuss der politischen Rechte [kann] nie das auschliessliche Privilegium einer Classe der Kantonsbürger sein' (Federal Pact of 1815, Art. 7).

11 *Geschichte der Schweiz und der Schweizer*, vol. II (Basle, 1983), p. 265.

12 Alexis de Tocqueville, *De la démocratie en Amérique, 1850*, cited from the English translation (New York, 1969), p. 736.

13 Markus Mattmüller, 'Das Einsetzen der Bevölkerungswelle in der Schweiz', *Vierteljahresschrift für Wirtschafts- und Sozialgeschichte*, 63 (1976), pp. 390–405.

14 Thomas Robert Malthus, *An Essay on the principle of population*, 2nd ed (London, 1803), chap. 5, 'On the checks of population in Switzerland'.

15 The standard reference work is still Wilhelm Bickel, *Bevölkerungsgeschichte und Bevölkerungspolitik der Schweiz seit dem Ausgang des Mittelalters* (Zurich, 1947).

16 My own calculations, based on Stefano Franscini, *Neue Statistik der Schweiz*, 2 vols. (Berne, 1848–51), vol. I, p. 87.

17 Erich Gruner, *Die Arbeiter in der Schweiz im 19. Jahrhundert* (Berne, 1968), pp. 26ff.

18 Francesco Kneschaurek, 'Wandlungen der schweizerischen Industriestruktur seit 1800', *Schweizerische Zeitschrift für Volkswirtschaft und Statistik*, 100 (1962), pp. 133–66.

19 In France (1856): 52 per cent, Belgium (1846): 51 per cent, England (1851): 22 per cent. Simon Kuznets, *Economic Growth of Nations* (Cambridge, Mass., 1971), pp. 250–1. Phyllis Deane and W. A. Cole, *British Economic Growth* (Cambridge, 1969), pp. 142–3.

20 Hans Brugger, *Die schweizerische Landwirtschaft in der ersten Hälfte des 19. Jahrhunderts* (Frauenfeld, 1956), p. 16.

21 *Ibid.*, p. 19.

22 Michael Bernegger, 'Die Schweiz und die Weltwirtschaft. Etappen der Integration im 19. und 20. Jahrhundert', in Paul Bairoch and Martin Körner (eds.), *Die Schweiz in der Weltwirtschaft*, Schweizerische Gesellschaft für Wirtschafts- und Sozialgeschichte, no. 8 (Zurich, 1990), p. 438.

23 Brugger, *Schweizerische Landwirtschaft*, p. 38.

24 Paul Bairoch, 'Niveaux de développement économique de 1810 à 1910', *Annales: Economies, Sociétés, Civilisations*, 20 (1965), p. 1096.

25 William Coxe, *Travels in Switzerland* (London, 1776), vol. I.

26 Ulrich Pfister, *Die Zürcher Fabriques. Protoindustrielles Wachstum vom 16.–18. Jahrhundert* (Zurich, 1992), p. 79.

27 Kneschaurek, 'Wandlungen', p. 155. According to recent research the number of embroiderers (30,000) is vastly overestimated.

28 Dudzik, *Innovation und Investition*, pp. 54–5.

29 Pfister, *Die Zürcher Fabriques*, pp. 110–11.

30 Walter Bodmer, *Die Entwicklung der schweizerischen Textilwirtschaft in Rahmen der übrigen Industrien und Wirtschaftszweige* (Zurich, 1960), p. 277.

31 Dudzik, *Innovation und Investition*, p. 107.

32 *Ibid.*, p. 550 (table 4.7).

33 Bodmer, *Entwicklung*, pp. 295ff.

34 Gruner, *Arbeiter*, pp. 54–5.

35 *Ibid.*, p. 64. (The number of embroiderers is estimated at 7,000, cf. note 27.)

36 Veyrassat, *Négociants et fabricants*, pp. 23–30.

37 David S. Landes, 'Swatch! Ou l'horlogerie suisse dans le contexte mondial', in Bairoch and Körner (eds.), *Die Schweiz*, pp. 227 36.

38 Kneschaurek, 'Wandlungen', p. 139.

39 Patrick Halbeisen, Roman Lechner, Erich Projer et al., 'Geldmenge und Wirtschaftswachstum in der Schweiz, 1859–1913', Nationalfonds-Projekt (unpublished).

40 Hans Conrad Peyer, *Von Handel und Bank im alten Zürich* (Zurich, 1968).

41 Veyrassat, *Négociants et fabricants*, pp. 278.

42 Béatrice Veyrassat, 'La Suisse sur les marchés du monde. Exportations globales et répartition géographique au XIXe siècle' in Bairoch and Körner (eds.), *Die Schweiz*, p. 302.

43 Arwed Emminghaus, *Die schweizerische Volkswirtschaft* (Leipzig, 1861), vol. II, pp. 1511ff.

44 Alfred Bosshard und Aldred Nydegger, 'Die schweizerische Aussenwirtschaft im Wandel der Zeiten', in *Schweiz. Zeitschrift für Volkswirtschaft und Statistik*, 100 (1962), p. 327.

45 Veyrassat, 'Le Suisse sur les marchés du monde', p. 312.

46 Michael Bernegger, 'Die Schweizer Wirtschaft, 1850–1913: Wachstum, Strukturwandel und Konjunkturzyklen', unpublished master's thesis, University of Zurich, 1983, p. 27. His estimate is 25 per cent.

47 Bernegger, 'Die Schweiz und die Weltwirtschaft', p. 436.

48 Hansjörg Siegenthaler, 'Die Bedeutung des Aussenhandels für die Ausbildung einer schweizerischen Wachstumsgesellschaft im 18. und 19. Jahrhundert', in N. Bernard and Q. Reichen (eds.), *Gesellschaft und Gesellschaften, Festschrift für U. Im Hof* (Berne, 1982), pp. 325–40.

49 Article 3 of the Federal Pact of 1815.

50 See Bernegger, 'Die Schweizer Wirtschaft', appendix, for statistical data.

51 Paragraph 64 of the Federal Constitution revised in 1874. The respective laws entered into force much later, e.g., law of obligation in 1881, law of bankruptcy in 1889, civil code in 1907.

52 Bruno Fritzsche, 'Eisenbahnbau und Stadtentwicklung in der Schweiz', in Hans-Jürgen Teuteberg (ed.), *Stadtwachstum, Industrialisierung, Sozialer Wandel* (Berlin, 1986), pp. 175–94.

53 Bernhard Beck, *Lange Wellen wirtschaftlichen Wachstums in der Schweiz, 1814–1913* (Berne, 1983), p. 26.

54 H. Gölden, *Strukturwandlungen des schweizerischen Fremdenverkehrs 1890–1935* (Zurich, 1939), pp. 25 and 32ff.

55 For more detailed information see Erich Gruner, *Arbeiterschaft und Wirtschaft in der Schweiz, 1880–1914*, 3 vols. (Zurich, 1987/8).

56 David S. Landes, 'Technological change and development in Western Europe, 1750–1914', in *Cambridge Economic History*, vol. VI/1 (Cambridge, 1966), p. 503.

SEVEN

━━━►·◄·◇·►·◄━━━

Italy in the *longue durée*:
the return of an old first-comer

CARLO PONI AND GIORGIO MORI

URBANIZATION occurred early in the history of Italy and remained one of its enduring characteristics, above all in central and northern Italy, even when the percentage of inhabitants in the towns declined in relation to the country (in the seventeenth and eighteenth centuries).[1] The relationship between town and country is worthy of special attention. The symbols and the palaces of the spiritual and temporal powers which ruled both the city and the surrounding countryside were concentrated in the cities and controlled by its most powerful families. Noble and non-noble landlords who made up the ruling political groups lived in the city, and it was to the city that the peasants (mostly sharecroppers) brought their rent (often in kind) to those who owned the land.

The social stratification of Early Modern Italian cities, as a consequence, was richer and more complex than that of other European cities. The cities were populated not only by merchants, lawyers, artisans, wage-labourers, domestic servants and beggars but also by the formal feudal nobility (which sometimes preserved some legal jurisdiction over their former lands) and the new nobility of the *nouveaux riches*: merchants, tax contractors, bankers and notaries who had bought or who were accumulating land and noble titles.

The upward mobility and ennoblement of the *nouveaux riches* has often been presented in a negative light, as if the commercial middle classes, in abandoning trade and industry for land, were somehow betraying their true historical role. But the transformation of rich commoners into land-holding nobles is a normal occurrence. The real problem, instead, is when the position they vacate in the business world is not taken by others moving upward in their turn.

It should be remembered, however, that ennoblement and the acquisition of land does not always indicate the abandonment of trade. By the end of the sixteenth century, for example, Florence had lost its role as Europe's leading financial centre, but as late as the eighteenth century a number of noble families were still investing in banking, while the noble Genoese bankers redirected their investments to what appeared the safer sector of the public debt of Italian and European states or cities.[2]

This picture is complicated by the fact that both established and new landowners often carried out improvements to the land they bought, by draining and ploughing hitherto uncultivated land, enclosing open farm land, creating more compact (or perhaps we should say less fragmented) holdings, extending viticulture, planting millions of mulberry trees and intensifying, specializing or diversifying the production of industrial crops such as flax, hemp or woad. By the sixteenth century or even earlier, the drained areas of the plain of Lombardy had farms run on wage labour which practised continuous crop rotation with forage.[3] The navigation canals of the Po valley were, at least in part, a response to the need to transport agricultural goods and construction materials (principally sand and gravel), but they soon came to constitute a key communications network for short- and long-distance trade. From the thirteenth century onwards, many cities of the Po valley such as Milan, Pavia, Padua, Reggio Emilia, Modena, Cento and Bologna built their own navigational canals linking them with the Po. Traffic reaching the river then continued its journey towards Venice (a large port with a huge hinterland) and the international markets. The Venice Arsenal, employing thousands of ship's carpenters and rope-makers, was just one of the industries that was supplied with raw materials via the canal system: hemp from Bologna and later from Montagnana for the sails and ropes, wood from Montello for planking.[4]

Investment in land and the construction of an elaborate network of drainage and navigational canals boosted agriculture and led to conditions that favoured growth. But few of the benefits of this process filtered down to the peasants. Rents were high and the burden of the oppressive tax system, which exempted to a greater or lesser extent the urban landowners, fell above all on the shoulders of the small independent landholders and the landless sharecroppers, whom the city governments forced to carry out heavy corvées for the maintenance of roads and canals. As a result, agricultural production (cereals, hemp, flax, raw silk, wood, must, wine and plants used to produce dye) tended to be marketed in the main city of each area, both to meet the demands of a growing urban population and those of its expanding industries.

This transformation would not have taken place, or would have been far less important, if the major cities of northern and central Italy had not been able to accumulate great wealth over the course of several centuries, principally through the monopoly of international trade between the East and Europe. This gave a considerable impulse to the urban industries, and in particular to fabrics (wool, cotton and silk), making the city states of Italy into the most highly developed area of Europe.

The peculiar social stratification of the cities, and the concentration of wealth inside their privileged walls gave rise, especially in the larger ones, to an unusual form of 'court society', often based (but not always) on princely courts. This new urban court society, made up of family groups, encouraged elegant conversation and a social competition based on quality consumption, refined taste and good manners. This in turn led to a growing demand for luxury goods such as silk, gold and silver jewellery, furniture, ceramics, musical instruments, books, paintings, mirrors, glass, statues, ornaments and the construction and decoration of palaces, gardens and villas.[5]

The change was not only quantitative. By means of a process which is as yet far from clear, although it goes under the general name of the Civilization of the Renaissance, luxury consumption underwent frequent, original and innovative stylistic changes. As early as the fourteenth century, the chronicler Giovanni Villani was writing that Florentine gold-smiths and silk entrepreneurs 'discover each day, to their advantage, new and different ornaments' (*Chroniche*, X, chapter CLIII).[6] These discoveries – which lasted for centuries and extended to many other luxury objects and goods, often in daily use – gave Italian or Italianate taste, defined by small, sophisticated and cultivated Italian elites, a strong long-term position on European and even Eastern markets.[7] The preponderance of Italian fashions reached as far as England, where Shakespeare celebrated the 'fashions in proud Italy / Whose manners still our tardy-apish nation / Limps after in base imitation' (*Richard II*, Act II, Scene I).

Alongside this aristocratic demand for luxury goods, there was another – on the part of the Catholic Church. The Church was a rich customer, requiring a range of materials for the decoration of churches, chapels, convents, oratories, sanctuaries and the adornment of religious cere-monies. This demand expanded in the period of the Counter-Reformation with the construction of countless new baroque churches and the widespread renovation of old churches to meet the new taste for rich and elaborate ornaments and decorations.[8]

This combined domestic demand, alongside a growing international demand, stimulated the production of luxury goods and led to the rise of the urban *Kaufmann* (merchant) and putting-out systems which often devel-oped from within the corporative guild system, using their rules and trade marks. The Italian textile guilds operating on the international market were essentially made up of merchant entrepreneurs (putting-outers) who tended to dominate the master craftsmen. The latter often were prevented from exercising autonomy within the guilds, except by using the putting-out system themselves to employ, outside the rules of the corporations, female and child labour.

Given the brevity of this chapter, we shall consider here the history of just one of these luxury goods, silk. This choice can be justified given that for centuries the production of cocoons, silk thread and silk fabrics involved huge amounts of capital and provided a livelihood for hundreds of thousands of men, women and children for different periods every year. Moreover, in terms of value, Italian silk represented a considerable proportion of the imports by Northern European countries and of the exports from the Italian states.

Towards the middle of the sixteenth century, Italian silks accounted for around 30 per cent of total French imports. In 1620, Scipion de Gramont wrote bitterly that France was paying Italy two million livres a year for its 'toile d'or et d'argent … et passemens de Milan, les velours, les satins et les bas de soyes d'Italie'. A few years later, the anonymous author of the *Advise au Roy et aux Monseigneurs de son Conseil* suggested promoting the development of an import-substitute silk fabrics industry in France to avoid spending 'douze millions de livres tous les ans' abroad (that is, in Italy). According to Cardinale Ludovico Guicciardini, Italian silks (thread and fabrics) accounted for 20 per cent of total Dutch imports in 1567. Another source estimates this figure to have been 36 per cent in the years before the revolt against Spain. Stanislaus Zaremba, a Polish mercantilist writing in the mid-seventeenth century, claimed that Poland imported annually Italian silk worth 9 million zloty, although this figure would seem to be an exaggeration given that it would be equal to the value of total Polish wheat exports over several years.[9]

These figures, while no doubt exaggerated, are indirectly corroborated by Italian sources. The second half of the sixteenth century witnessed a boom at all levels of silk production, including, weaving. In Genoa in 1580 there were 8,000 looms; in Bologna in 1591 the silk industry provided a livelihood for 25,000 people, half of whom were female weavers. In Milan and Venice about 40,000 people worked full- or part-time in the silk industry. In Genoa, according to P. Massa's calculations, about 35,000 thousand people – 60 per cent of the population – were involved in silk production. In Naples about half of the population worked in different sectors of the silk industry. To these data, inflated yet significant, one ought to add figures from Florence, Reggio Emilia and especially Lucca, where in the early 1500s about 12,000 people worked with silk.[10]

In this list we find the four great cities of the so-called 'quadrilateral': Milan, Venice, Florence (15,000 persons towards the middle of the seventeenth century) and Genoa. However, the network was much more complicated. Of course each city had its own peculiarities of organization, often managed by several guilds. But everywhere real power was in the hands of the great merchant-entrepreneurs. Some local studies are in the process of reconstructing the particular characteristics and transformations of a number of silk cities. However, the urban putting-out system seems to us the dominant one, at least as far as weaving is concerned.

The first silk-weaving centres of Lucca and Venice, set up in the thirteenth and fourteenth centuries, imported raw silk from Sicily, southern Italy and from the Middle East (which also supplied other luxury goods, including silk fabrics). Towards the end of the sixteenth century, Venice was still importing raw silk from the Middle East. By this time, however, the Venetian mainland was already producing as much as 600,000 pounds of raw silk a year, subsequently woven in Venice and in other cities of the Venetian Republic. By the end of the eighteenth century, the annual output of silk thread was 2,500,000 pounds. The growth of Piedmontese raw-silk production was even more spectacular, rising from a few tens of thousands of pounds in the mid-seventeenth century to around 1,200,000 to 1,600,000 pounds by the end of the eighteenth century. Production in the Duchy of Milan (Habsburg Lombardy) was much less impressive, increasing from between 700,000 and 800,000 pounds in the first half of the eighteenth century to 1,400,000 by the end of the century, and now including also production in the Duchy of Mantua. Silk production in the states situated south of the Po and in central Italy did not share in these increases, and in general output averaged around 700,000 pounds in this period. Production in the south of Italy, indeed, experienced a sharp decrease, although the precise extent of this decline is difficult to specify. According to Domenico Grimaldi, probably no more reliable than other sources, raw-silk production in the Kingdom of Naples amounted to around one million pounds in 1765, less than half the output of a previous, unspecified period.[11]

Increases in the production of cocoons, concentrated above all in northern Italy, was limited by the low technical level of silk reeling and throwing. This bottleneck in production was overcome by the import of advanced technologies developed in Bologna which had boasted, since the fourteenth century, several circular water-powered silk mills which could throw simultaneously hundreds and thousands of threads, integrated, in the sixteenth century, with mechanical winders. These silk mills, two or three storeys high and highly labour-saving, employed dozens of workers (mostly children), and the whole production process was mechanized. The workers' tasks were to feed the raw materials into the machines, knot the threads when they broke, regulate the twist points (a task given only to adults) and load the twisted thread into baskets. The Bolognese silk mill, producing a thread of a higher quality than that twisted by hand, constituted a factory system predating Arkwright's cotton mill.

By the sixteenth century, industrial espionage had taken the closely guarded secrets of the technology of the Bolognese silk mills to Modena, Faenza and Reggio Emilia. By the beginning of the next century, this technology had reached Padua, Treviso, Feltre, Mantua and Pescia. Some of these mills turned out to be failures, either because of bad construction of because they used unsuitable silk threads. In any case, they could not compete with the Bolognese manufacturers who were able, thanks to increases in supplies of raw silk, to expand in number and size. In 1683, there were 353 throwing machines in operation, driven by the same number of water-wheels located on the man-made canal network of the city. This constituted the highest concentration of urban water-wheels in Europe, in 112 small and medium-sized silk mills.

The situation changed radically between around 1650 and 1710, when a few hundred (and perhaps more) water-powered silk mills with mechanical winders were built in the hills and high plain area to the south of the Alps in Piedmont, upper Lombardy and the Venetian Republic. Several factors operated in favour of this new location in the countryside and in small walled towns: a plentiful water supply, cheap rural labour, the impressive growth of local production of raw silk, proximity to the rich European markets and the lack of corporation restrictions.[12]

This decentralization, though, cannot be seen as a single, undifferentiated process. It was also the result of the economic policies of the new regional states that were being formed by integrating the small and medium-sized city states into larger units (such as the Duchy of Milan and the Venetian Republic). These new regional states, whose power was based in the capital city, tended to create a new relationship between city and countryside, to the advantage of the latter.

The most important example that has been studied so far is that of the Duchy of Milan. An early reform was that of the tax system, with the introduction of a tax on merchant wealth (the *mercimonio*) in the sixteenth century and the land taxes later imposed by Maria Theresa, both of which hit the privileged urban classes.[13] Following the early collapse of silk weaving in the city (1620–40), the Milanese silk guilds were forced to accept, although not without resistance, the shift of manual silk-throwing works from the city to the countryside, where the cost of production was cheaper.[14] This move away from the city interlaced with the construction of the major water-powered silk mills of Varese and Como. The situation in the Venetian Republic was different. There the Senate passed a law on 5 January 1634 aimed at encouraging the water-powered silk mills on the mainland. The law granted the free use of running water, tax exemptions for all machinery, exemptions from all internal customs duties (thus permitting the free circulation of thread), the suppression of guild regulations preventing merchants from owning silk mills, and the exemption of foreign mechanics and throwers (the Bolognese technicians) from all corvée obligations, granting them at the same time the right to work without joining a corporation.[15] Urban employment suffered heavily from the stimulation that was given to industry in the rural areas. Of the 700 hand silk-throwing machines in Milan, only around 200 remained by 1680. The 550 hand silk-throwing machines in Venice in 1557 suffered repeated drops over the centuries.[16]

As the new technologies shifted north, they underwent further technical developments, especially in Piedmont where, as in the Venetian Republic, the size of the mills increased. No Bolognese silk mill had ever employed more than 100 workers, if we exclude the 'doublers' working at home. In Racconigi (Piedmont) by the end of the seventeenth century, Bolognese technicians were helping to build huge mills for entrepreneurs such as Gianfranco Peyron which employed around 300 workers and produced 26,000 pounds of thread a year. [17] It was in mills like that at Racconigi that John Lombe acquired the technical know-how that allowed him to construct his great Derby silk mill and introduce the first factory system to England. But the transfer was not limited to the technology of the silk mills. Italian entrepreneurs had also learnt the art of disciplining the workforce of the factories. This art was imported into England along with the throwing machines, and was later transferred to the organization of the workforce of the first cotton mills.[18]

The major technical and economic developments we have briefly mentioned might be expected to have given an important boost to the Italian silk-fabrics industry, which had dominated Europe since the fifteenth century. This, at any rate, would probably be the view of certain off-the-shelf theories on offer today. But this was not in fact the case, and it was during this period that the Italian silk-fabrics industry began to lose ground. This was to a considerable extent due to the appearance of new English and French competitors in the eighteenth century. Lyons, already the headquarters of Tuscan bankers operating in France, became the major weaving centre of Europe, at the beginning thanks to the contributions of Italian technicians. Lyons's dominance on the international silk-fabrics market throughout the eighteenth century would be based partly on its technological superiority, but above all on the annual changes in fashion, the 'modes de Paris faites à Lyon'.[19]

After major losses and defeats, both on the international and the home markets, the Italian silk-weaving industry survived only in the cities that were able to activate new, defensive strategies, either following French fashions with imitation fabrics or taking refuge in the safe havens of fabrics unaffected by the 'fashion empire'. Genoese velvet, for example, continued to satisfy the demand on the part of high-ranking public officials, lawyers and judges throughout the eighteenth century. Bolognese crêpe remained a versatile accessory used for trimmings in all new fashions, and enjoyed high sales during the frequent periods of Court mourning. Venetian brocade continued to be exported to Istanbul and to the Ottoman Empire in general.[20] The old industrial cities, then, although in decline, were still present on international markets. In Venice in around 1780 there were 6,650 silk workers; in Bologna in 1789 there were between 6,000 and 7,000; in Genoa in the decade 1780–90 there were 325 looms in the city itself (compared to 800 in 1772) and 1,625 in the surrounding countryside (compared with 4,353 in 1772). While the old centres of silk production were in decline, new ones such as Vicenza and Como were on the increase, each with around 1,000 looms at the end of the eighteenth century.[21]

In the north of Italy as a whole, the production and export of silk thread began to overtake the production and export of silk fabrics. Piedmontese thread was exported to Lyons, while Bolognese thread and Lombardy tram were sold on the markets of Amsterdam and London. All the regions and states of the Po valley, where around 60 per cent of the total European silk production was concentrated, exported silk thread to western and northern Europe. Given that the value added of the throwing process was much lower than that of weaving, it would appear that the radical international reorganization of labour within the silk sector which took place in the eighteenth century represented a fundamental shift of potential wealth from Italy to the new weaving cities north of the Alps.

This process can be described as a relative deindustrialization of the Italian silk industry, even though it was accompanied by an enormous expansion of throwing realized through the silk mills. This unusual combination of the diffusion of a factory system alongside the simultaneous deindustrialization of a weaving sector presents us with an embarrassing paradox which is, however, not the first to be found in the history of Italy. It suggests that we should be cautious in making mechanical links between the factory system and industrial expansion.

The scissor-like development, while it had a negative effect on the economy of important urban centres, did lead to the growth of a rich industrial system in the rural hill areas, of which the silk mills were only the most visible part, with the greatest concentration of capital. These mills did not, though, exist in isolation. The factory production of silk was dependent also on the land, where the mulberry trees were cultivated, and involved the peasant household, with the breeding of the silk worms. Women and children in the peasant families carried out the reeling, throwing, winding and doubling by hand; men, women and children of both sexes worked in the silk mills. Nor were the towns wholly excluded from the productive process. The urban nobility and middle classes, in fact, invested capital in rural factories, managed them, supplied the capital to cover production costs and marketed the thread.

It is tempting, but misleading, to classify these areas as examples of proto-industry. In the first place, the silk mills were already examples of a factory system. Second, although the reeling was initially carried out in the peasant households, from the eighteenth century onwards – and in Piedmont in particular – it began to be concentrated in one building (often adjacent to the silk mill) where hundreds of women and girls worked. Third, the industrial processing of silk was concentrated above all in the summer and the autumn, when major agricultural work had to be carried out.[22]

For these reasons we propose to put aside the term 'rural proto-industry' and use another: 'rural industrial districts'. This more flexible term can include a number of different types of organization (artisan production in the workshop or in the peasant household, the *Kaufmann* and putting-out systems, the manufacturing and the factory systems); numerous forms of interrelations with agriculture such as the work of women in industry during the summer months; and a series of complex network relations between firms which operated in different phases of production.

The rural developments of the silk industry's reeling and twisting sections were accompanied by the decline of other advanced technological sectors in which the Italian cities had long been dominant, partly, at least, due to the lack of competitors. A striking example of this is Venice, once the largest industrial city in Europe, which throughout the seventeenth century was plundered of its valuable know-how in the production of glass, mirrors, dyes, luxury soaps and, indeed, silk fabrics.[23]

Luxury goods were crucial in terms of the international market, capital, employment and the balance of payments, but they are not the only sector of interest to us. The dominance of Italy in the long term in these sectors was accompanied by a weak medium- and low-quality product sector, including industries such as the 'new draperies'. In this sector, there was strong competition from Dutch and English fabrics (the *londrine*), which penetrated the crucial Mediterranean markets in the course of the seventeenth century.[24] It was with these fabrics that the countries of northern Europe won the battle over the Venetian woollen products, in the Levant, in the Balkans and finally in the Venetian Republic itself.

The figures on the production of woollen fabrics in Venice are indicative, rising from 2,000 pezze in 1518 to 28,000 pezze by 1601, only to collapse over the course of the seventeenth century;[25] but new woollen districts were already developing in the hill and mountain areas of the mainland. Low-quality spinning and weaving grew up in the mountain valleys north of Bergamo, and became important in Europe in the space of just a few decades, although this primacy was to be temporary. As Domenico Sella has pointed out, the production of 40,000 pezze (1 pezza = around 50 metres) in this area put it 'very clearly in the forefront of the Italian wool industry'.[26]

Walter Panciera's extensive research into the woollen industry of the Venetian Republic has revealed the range and organizational diversity of the textile industries situated in rural hill areas, producing import substitutes. Here we shall mention just one example, that of wool production in the area north of Vicenza and of the hills above Schio which specialized in the production of import-substitute medium-quality carded fabrics. During the second half of the eighteenth century, these products were exempt from all domestic customs duties. They were part of an integrated production network that linked the decentralized spinning and weaving that took place in the peasant household to the centralized facilities in which the finishing operations took place (fulling, raising, dyeing and sometimes also weaving, with a dozen or so looms). They also took a share of the domestic markets away from their Flemish and English competitors and managed to enter neighbouring foreign markets, thanks to their tax exemptions and export subsidies.

Nevertheless, despite the fact that the wool production of Schio tripled within a few decades (from 1762–92), it appears that it never exceeded 14,000 pezze, and consequently there were never many more than 500 looms in operation. The most important entrepreneur of the Schio district was without doubt Niccolò Tron, a Venetian noble and ambassador for the Venetian Republic in London, who introduced new production techniques with the help of English workers and technicians. His innovations, including the introduction of the flying shuttle in around 1760, were exploited by his imitators and competitors, some of whom were former employees or business partners.[27]

Further east, in Tolmezzo, in an area just south of the Alps, there was the linen and mixed hemp 'factory' of Giacomo Linussio. This was another industry which enjoyed certain privileges, namely exemption from duties on the import of raw materials and from most of the duties on exports. In 1720 the firm produced 3,000 pezze, employing 200 master weavers and 2,500 spinners. By 1737, output had risen to 19,238 pezze, by 1748 to 26,667, and by 1752 to 32,117, peaking in 1776 at 42,739. This impressive performance was, however, followed by a rapid and unexpected decline in the 1780s due to the competition from German producers.[28]

The mountain valleys, and in particular those with iron mines, extensive woodland and waterfalls, were also the site of metalworking communities which produced, for relatively large markets, iron components for agricultural tools (in Val Sabbia and Val Camonica), wire (Lecco) and nails (Salò). Important also was the production of rifles and carbines in Val Trompia, divided into two sub-sectors. The barrels were produced in the ironworks of Gardone, the most important town of the valley, while the firing mechanisms (flints) were produced in Lumezzane. The guns were then assembled in Brescia by the town's armourers. This industry depended on government contracts, although hunting rifles were also produced for the export market. According to Ugo Tucci, Brescia sold 150,000 rifles to the King of Spain between 1794 and 1797,[29] and although this was an unusually large contract, other substantial contracts had been won from time to time throughout the eighteenth century. In 1743, the Kingdom of Naples bought 12,000 rifles and 6,000 pistols. In 1758, the Venetian Republic commissioned the production of 18,000 rifles.[30]

The hills to the south of the Alps also became the site of new paper mills such as the ones on Lake Garda Riviera; of the innovative Remondini printing works in Bassano which produced books, numerous popular prints and wallpaper; and of the porcelain and majolica manufactories in Bassano and Nove which, by 1770, had begun to imitate Wedgwood styles successfully. North of Milan, cotton and mixed cotton were spun and woven. This rural area was to become the centre of the Italian cotton industry in the nineteenth century. By 1767 in Busto Arsizio there were 7,000 people employed in spinning and weaving at home and producing around 60,000 pezze a year.[31]

By the end of the eighteenth century, then, some attempts at innovation can be observed. Overall, however, the economy of northern Italy was rapidly losing ground not only to England, already experiencing the radical transformations of the Industrial Revolution, but also to France, Belgium and the Rhineland. The gap was to widen during the French occupation and the Restoration.

In 1792, however, a careful observer such as the great English agronomist Arthur Young was still able to declare that northern Italy (Lombardy, as he called it) was, together with the Netherlands and England, 'the richest country in Europe'. In Piedmont and the area around Milan he found 'all the signs of prosperity: populousness well-employed and well supported; a great export without; a thriving consumption within; magnificent roads; numerous and wealthy towns; circulation active; interest in money low and the price of labour high'. Young put this prosperity down to agriculture alone, not to trade and 'certainly not to manufactures, because they possess hardly the trace of a fabric. There are

Table 7.1. *Patents granted by the Republic of Venice*

Years	Number of patents
1474–1500	28
1500–1600	593
1600–1700	605
1700–1788	670

Source: R. Berveglieri and C. Poni, 'Three Centuries of Venetian Patents (1474–1796)', in *Acta historiae rerum naturalium necnon technicarum*, special issue 17 (Prague, 1982), pp. 381–93.

few (of no consideration) in Milan; and there are in Piedmont the silk mills … but on the whole to an amount so very trifling that both countries must be considered without fabrics.' He did not, of course, deny the existence of manufacturing, but saw it as dependent on the prosperous agricultural economy ('it is agriculture which supports and nourishes them') and thus on the domestic market alone. Young's favourite theory, that agriculture produces enormous wealth and that industry could only grow at the expense of agriculture and the overall standard of living, seemed to find unconditional confirmation in the case of the economy of northern Italy. Nevertheless, earlier in his *Travels*, Young had attributed the lavish investment in palaces and churches in many Italian cities to the massive accumulation of 'national wealth' during the period when 'the Italian republics had all the trade of Europe'.[32]

But besides trade, Italian cities had encouraged innovation. In 1474 the Venetian Republic was the first in Europe to pass a bill on industrial patents, one which significantly weakened the power of guilds to control technical practices. The recognition of intellectual property for a limited period of time (up to fifty years) guaranteed a return to inventors. Once the patent had expired anyone could use the innovation.

Between 1474 and 1788 the Venetian Senate granted about 2,000 patents: for new kind of mills (grain mills, paper mills, silk mills, irrigation and drainage mills): for machines to recover ships which had sunk; for new technology and procedures for the manufacture of glass, ceramics and new dyes; for instruments to improve the quality of wool, silk and cotton cloth. Sometimes the inventors claimed that their inventions reduced the cost of production and increased productivity. Only occasionally a description of an actual experiment, with the result certified by a notary, can be found.

One should add that the Venetian patents, unlike the British ones, were granted free of payment, which explains their relatively high number.

Besides, in the eighteenth century no significant innovation was patented in Venice. Previous centuries had better records. According to R. T. Rapp, the changes in British industry between 1540 and 1640, described by U. Nef as 'the first Industrial Revolution' seem almost primitive compared to the panorama of technological sophistication of Venetian industries in the decades just before the crisis of the first half of the seventeenth century, when Venice excelled in the international market through her luxury products.[33]

The period which opens with the French occupation in 1796 witnessed important institutional innovations favourable to the development of a capitalist economy: the abolition of the corporations, the sale of ecclesiastical land and the creation of a large, customs-free market in northern Italy. But the frequent wars and political instability had a contrary effect, that of disrupting the structures of production and commerce and discouraging investments in new technology by putting outers, who were capable of organizing production networks based on the peasant household but as yet reluctant to risk even modest amounts of capital in new sectors. The quantitative growth in production of certain sectors and certain areas was caused partly by the disappearance of foreign competition due to the war and the continental block, and partly by large military contracts. This seems to have been the case, for example, in the production of wool fabrics which, in the years 1801–7 saw rapid expansion in the departments of Vicenza and Bergamo but serious decline in Padua and Verona.[34] The metal workshops of Val Trompia also benefited from military contracts. In 1808, the metalworkers of the valley presented government officials with 6,760 rifle barrels for inspection.[35]

The silk sector, though, was in the grip of a profound crisis due to the lack of outlets caused by the continental blockade and the war. Nevertheless, silk (mainly thread but also fabrics) still accounted for two-thirds of the exports of the Napoleonic Kingdom of Italy and was crucial to the balance of payments. The continuing importance of silk confirms once again the strong traditions of this industry. But it also reveals the lack of lasting industrial dynamics of other sectors in the richest parts of the country.

After the Restoration, which lasted in Italy until 1848, 'English-style' textile factories, including silk mills, were established in many Italian states, as they were throughout Europe and the United States. While these early signs of capitalist industrialization were few and far between, they nevertheless represented the *first vital stage* of the development of the new system. Over the next few decades they increased in number and improved in quality, thanks to the endeavours of local entrepreneurs – but also to the efforts of their Swiss, French and German counterparts.[36] By the time the various states of the country had been brought together to form the Kingdom of Italy in 1861, the number of factories had increased considerably and now employed around 200,000 workers, although they were involved almost exclusively in spinning (cotton) and throwing (silk). The silk sector, which had languished during the Napoleonic period and in the first few decades after the Restoration, experienced a period of considerable expansion until 1853, when it suffered the terrible crisis provoked by the pebrina plague. But by the mid-1860s, the industry was in full recovery, and could boast more than 500,000 throwing spindles and about 35,000 workers in Lombardy alone, only slightly lower numbers of both in Piedmont and a number of smaller mills in other areas of the country. Added to this, cotton mills had also been highly successful in Lombardy, Piedmont, Campania and Liguria, as had the woollen industry in Piedmont, the Veneto and the Liri valley, and hemp and linen production in Lombardy and the Salerno region.[37]

Mechanization started at first in the flour-milling industry, followed by the manufacture of locomotives in Naples, stationary steam engines in Genoa (although between 1839 and 1860 as many as 386 of the 426 locomotives in service were imported[38]), and later textile machinery, printing presses and agricultural machinery in Turin, Milan and Naples, and the 'continuous' presses in the paper industry in Naples, Tuscany, Lombardy and Piedmont.[39] On the other hand, in this early phase almost all the country's admittedly unimpressive mineral resources were exported, the metallurgical industry was in a state of almost total obsolescence and the chemical industry was reduced to workshops producing lighting gas (five in the Kingdom of Sardinia, eight in Lombardy-Veneto, two in Tuscany, two in the Papal States and two in the south).[40]

Taken as a whole, Italy's industrial resources were highly concentrated in only a few regions (Piedmont, Lombardy, Liguria and Campania) and from the development point of view were somewhere between the more industrialized countries of France, Belgium, Prussia and Great Britain and the rest of Europe. This half-way status raises one of the most frequent dilemmas regarding nineteenth-century industrial development: why did these early shoots of industry in the various Italian states manage to take root, unlike in many other areas, but find it exceptionally difficult to grow to maturity? At the time of unification, Italy lagged way behind Great Britain and the other second-comer nations mentioned above. Attempts to deny or minimize this question, moreover, by putting forward the teleological argument that Italy was to achieve results similar to those of its predecessors by means of other allegedly less difficult and less costly paths are not impressive.

We should first note that in this period Italy was in some ways similar to other industrializing countries. Production of consumer goods was higher than that of capital goods, and the reactions of the main social groups to the first signs of industrial growth were more or less the same. Intellectuals displayed extreme diffidence, the landowning and business classes were cautious, and the agricultural workers and artisans were reluctant to enter (or remain in) factories. Nor did the various governments in Italy show any great interest in the new forms of industry.

However, the degree to which industrial development varied throughout the Italian states was incontrovertible. These differences were clearly the result of endogenous variables such as access to raw materials, the culture and behaviour of entrepreneurs and workers, investments and labour markets. But it is also clear that a 'special case', however closely it is studied and analysed, must still be the result of an intricate series of interconnections between the past and the present: a synthesis of objective limits and choices, of external pressure and the different internal options available. It can only be entirely understood, then, if the object under examination is interpreted in the context of these disparate influences. Fundamental to this context are the commercial relations of the pre-unification states of Italy with the industrializing countries of central and northern Europe, whose demand for primary goods, as well as their supply of finished products, was increasingly rapid, at first to their advantage of the exporters of primary goods for several decades after 1815,[41] gave rise to a situation in which there were substantial profits for silk producers in the north of Italy, straw milliners in Tuscany, and wheat, oil, wine and citrus fruit producers in the south. They also benefited the bankers and merchants involved in this trade, as well as the exporters of finished products. The largest of these exporters was Great Britain which, with great determination and astute diplomacy, was seeking to establish 'a network of economic relations that would overcome protectionism in Europe', especially among these 'second-class' trading nations whose interests were not served by it. One such nation was precisely the Kingdom of Sardinia, the only Italian state that could follow an independent foreign policy.[42] Where no mutual advantage existed, the more powerful nations pursued their aims by other means, including the introduction of high customs duties and even the threat of military intervention, as in the case of Britian's opposition to the exclusive selling rights contract for Sicilian sulphur (the island had a natural monopoly of sulphur) stipulated between King Ferdinand II and a French company, resulting in the abandonment of the affair and of the latter's commitment to build a sulphuric acid plant on the island.[43]

The domestic situation of the individual states, moreover, was hardly conducive to industrial development, both for the reasons outlined above and because of the extremely limited domestic demand, itself a result of widespread urban poverty and the almost non-existent purchasing power of the peasants. These were conditions which could not be changed overnight. The overcautious attitude of the great aristocratic and bourgeois landowners, far from convinced of the validity of Say's law – according to which 'supply creates demand', was also important, as they owned most of the country's wealth. As Gerschenkron has written:

> the mere existence of accumulated wealth can only contribute to industrialization if it is in the hands of individuals disposed to invest in risky undertakings (or) able to entrust that wealth to individuals directly involved in industrialization.[44]

Lastly, we should not forget the state of the communications system. This concerned the quality of the road and canal links, particularly in the south, rather than shipping. From 1839 onwards there was also rail, but even by 1861 there was a total of little more than 2,000 km of track (75 per cent in the north, 19.5 per cent in the centre and 5.5 per cent in the south, concentrated in Campania).[45]

There were, however, some exceptions to this general trend. In the late eighteenth century, international demand had led to a recovery in the mining industry, in agriculture (which had been in the forefront of the reforming policies of the local absolutist monarchies), and in trade in general. The brief French occuaption of Italy had breathed new life into society and the economy in various parts of the country, and after 1815 there was a concerted effort on the part of the major landowners to introduce technical and cultural improvements into the countryside, with varying degrees of success. In the north, land under capitalist management spread, as did more rational crop-rotation methods. These in turn led to improvements in stabling and in the profitable milk and cheese industry. The first simple agricultural machinery came into use, and there was a striking expansion of the mulberrry plantations and the related silk industry in the foothills of the Alps. In central Italy, in the Grand Duchy of Tuscany, vast land-reclamation schemes were under way and the production of millinery straw increased, while in the north-eastern areas of the Papal States, hemp cultivation escalated and was rationalized. The south saw an increase in citrus orchards, vineyards and olive groves.[46] All this can be observed in the overall rise in exports, but it should be remembered that the 1861 figures show a per capita value of exports in the two northern states which far exceeded that of all the others.[47]

These improvements and innovations varied greatly in value and importance, not only due to the marked geographical and environmental diversity of the area but also to the unusual relationship between agriculture and industry. We have already mentioned the interest of the great landowners, in particular those in the two major northern states, in agricultural innovation (and especially, although not exclusively, with regard to sericulture) and the consequent search for new international markets. Fundamental, in this respect, was a simultaneous increase in the amount of work-time peasant families dedicated to non-agricultural activity. This question has recently resurfaced, following a model formulated by two economists on the basis of the fundamental historical research carried out in the late nineteenth century.[48] A large amount of careful research on a local level has recently been carried out using the notions of 'proto-industrialization' and 'pluriactivity', and the work has been able to correct previous imbalances and fill in certain gaps. Its principal aim is to use these notions to achieve a fuller understanding of economic and social development in various areas of Europe. An overall quantitative evaluation of these tendencies for the Italian states before unification is for the moment impossible. But it is also impossible for post-unification Italy given the shortcomings and taxonomic simplifications of the 1861 census, according to which, for example, the Kingdom of the Two Sicilies had the highest proportion of workers in industry (27 per cent), above Lombardy-Veneto (20.9 per cent) and the Kingdom of Sardinia (13.2 per cent). The officials in charge of the census were in fact well aware of these deficiencies:

> The manufacturing population in the southern provinces and in Sicily appears to be the most numerous, not because these provinces contain a greater number of industries but because almost all their inhabitants reside in large towns or cities so that whatever form of art or craft they engage in, they are considered industrial workers.[49]

The data might not, however, be all that far from the truth. It is in fact quite reasonable to suppose that the figures included those peasants living in urban areas and working at home, so that the real, and possibly insoluble problem is how to distinguish between production for personal consumption (without doubt very high in the south), cottage labour for putting-outers, and factory employment. The latter was important in Piedmont and Lombardy in the silk sub-sector, where the figure of the peasant-worker predominated.[50]

It would seem unlikely that these lukewarm developments could have given rise to a movement strong enough to demand the independence and unification of Italy. This was, instead, the somewhat romantic and confused programme of a handful of major intellectuals and an assortment of democrats and republicans. Although only a small section of the lower middle classes and urban intelligentsia supported it, unification became reality with Garibaldi's fearless expedition to the south of Italy which presented the courts of Europe with an ultimatum. The merit for the successful outcome of this situation must, though, go above all to Cavour, who sent the Piedmontese army to the south, thus ensuring the backing of both the international governments who were his allies (anxious to weaken the Austrian Empire and thus prevent events from taking a 'revolutionary' turn) and the major landowners (principally those in the south) also interested in avoiding any threats to the social order.

It was thus a *political* event, the birth of a new state, that created a new basis for the economic development of Italy. It was this that constituted the *second vital stage* of the history of Italian industrialization. In an unchanging socio-economic situation the state became Italy's 'principal financial operator',[51] using the huge domestic and foreign debt to finance the construction of crucial infrastructure. The burden of debt, by the end of the century, had grown to almost 100 per cent of gross domestic product (GDP).[52] The state became a key element alongside the others already in existence (great landowners, financiers and bankers, operators in international trade), in the new economic context within which industrial activity had to take place. The state was not neutral, however. From the start it was clear that its policies were totally consistent with the ideals and interests of the social classes which had presided over its creation and establishment – the great landowning classes[53] and the major Italian and European financiers. These policies consisted above all of a large public debt in order to keep down direct taxation on property and to concentrate instead on indirect taxation; the sale of state-owned and ecclesiastical property; the tendering of contracts for the tobacco monopoly and for tax collection; the guarantee of kilometre-based profits for the companies who were to build and manage the new railways; the crushing of the peasant rebellion in the south; the almost total opening to international trade; and the granting of controversial but wide-ranging powers to the Banca Nazionale (and in practice also to the private bankers who were its shareholders) to decide on credit policy and to perform the function of guarantor and intermediary between the country and the major European financiers involved in Italian affairs.[54]

These conditions, moreover, went hand in hand with the systematic and consistent reluctance of the private wealth to invest in industry, an understandable diffidence given the high degree of risk involved and the chronic stagnation of the domestic market. The influential politician De Cesare was in no way being unrepresentative when he declared before Parliament, perhaps without realizing that he was paraphrasing what Cobden had said many years before:

I believe that the climate, the air, the sun and the landscape of Italy will always prevent us from becoming as famous for our industry as the English and the French. We struggle in vain against nature and her laws.[55]

It is by no means evident that such an opinion was simply the result of a shortage of capital. In fact, even leaving aside the considerable investment in the railways, bank deposits in the first twenty years after unification rose from 300 to 1,300 million lire. Between 1867 and 1879 over 530 million lire were spent on buying ecclesiastical land and during the 1860s government bonds on sale on the *domestic* market usually encountered a demand that was five or ten times the supply. Purchases of foreign government stock, about which we know very little, were also substantial.[56] These few examples give some idea of the vast resources which had accumulated in Italy over the preceding centuries, part of which had perhaps been invested in real estate or squandered on luxury goods. All these elements raise considerable doubt as to the accuracy of the estimates of national wealth that are available to us.[57]

Progress was substantial, however. The financial infrastructure was modernized, the substitution of paper money for coins (but not credit notes[58]) proceeded apace; and the export of silk (over 25 per cent of total exports), agricultural produce and minerals helped to keep the trade deficit within reasonable limits (although the terms of trade were gradually worsening).[59]

The number of foreign entrepreneurs investing in industry dropped significantly after 1861, most preferring to invest their capital in mining activities or public services. Despite this fall, industry managed to survive, and, in certain sub-sectors actually flourish. This was due to the determination of the Italian industrialists, to lower wages than most other countries; to the indirect protectionism of the forced currency for the lira (introduced in 1866 and only abolished in 1883); to government contracts; and to the improvements made to infrastructure.

Production levels would constitute a good yardstick for evaluating the overall situation. But many attempts have been made so far to establish reliable figures for the period, and these:

> make interpretation of the overall pattern of industrialization more difficult rather than easier since they yield different results, while none of them is so clearly superior to the others from the point of view of data sources and method as to recommend itself for acceptance.[60]

We have no wish to quarrel with this view, but it seems to us that the most recent estimate, made by Albert Carreras, leaves a lower margin for doubt than the others. It indicates stagnation until the end of the 1870s, steady and moderate growth in the following decade and a marked surge between the mid-1890s and the First World War.[61] The apparently unimpressive growth over several decades may, in any case, conceal some important features. There may have been, for example, a 70 per cent rise in the number of industrial workers over the period 1861–81, and, even more importantly, an increase in fixed capital invested in industry. It is estimated, for example, that in 1881 there were 1,800,000 spindles in operation in the silk-throwing sector, 800,000 in the cotton industry, 300,000 in the production of wool, 60,000 in hemp and linen production. There was also a significant rise in the number of mechanical looms. A similar trend can be observed in paper production where the number of 'continuous' machines had reached ninety-five, and in the printing and engineering sectors (although over two-thirds of navy contracts were still awarded to foreign contractors), while estimates of the overall horsepower capacity of stationary steam engines (almost certainly an underestimation) was 35,000 (compared with 450,000 in hydraulic machinery). The first two Martin-Siemens furnaces were also in operation.[62] Industry, then, was growing more rapidly than the other secondary sectors (artisan production, cottage industry, manufacturing) but there was little change within the industrial sector itself, as textiles and foodstuffs still accounted for two-thirds of the workforce and probably a similar proportion of value added. At the same time, industry became even more concentrated in the north-west of the country and the gap between Italy and the other industrialized countries continued to grow in terms of volume and value production, specialization, technology and number of workers. This was despite the first experiments in the industrial sector in both limited companies, the most efficient institutions for the raising of risk capital (in 1880 the capital of the 189 limited companies in the sector amounted to 215 million, 18 per cent of the total for all limited companies[63]), and the first business and worker associations.

At the beginning of the 1880s, Italy's delicate equilibrium was profoundly shaken by an 'external' event and by a major, although not itself revolutionary, piece of government legislation: the crisis in agriculture and the 1881 decision to abandon the forced currency of the lira. The former was to give rise to enormous problems which, despite all efforts to the contrary, considerably weakened the power of the great landowners – particularly in the south but also in northern and central Italy. The latter ended a period in which the forced currency, the importance of which should never be underestimated, had increased the influence the already powerful banking and financial interests had over the economy and economic policy. Between 1861 and 1881 private and public-sector lending had risen by 190 per cent, far beyond any expansion of the GDP. Government lending and investment had grown from 27.3 per cent to

51.9 per cent and the lending of financial intermediaries had risen from 9.1 per cent to 18.5 per cent.[64] To back these operations, the government negotiated a 750-million lire cash loan with a syndicate of major English and Italian banks (including the Banca Nazionale). Although this was clearly a beneficial move, at least in the short term, it also caused a rise in inflation, resulting itself from the policies of the banks of issue, from a rise in local and central government spending and from a rise in the deficit budget, which had begun to increase again after a decline in the period 1870–80.[65] As in the decade after unification, this strategy did not on its own prove detrimental to the 'magic of credit', as one Italian economist wrote some time ago.[66] On the other hand it would not seem out of place to suggest that the policy was devised by Agostino Depretis, the Italian Prime Minister, as a means of ending the increasing conflicts between the principal ruling groups in Italy's economic and social structure, and to help him in his ambitious attempt to reorganize and concentrate the traditional parties in order to strengthen the government coalition, a strategy later known as *transformismo*.[67]

In terms of economic expansion at least, the operation seemed destined to succeed. A substantial proportion of local and central government spending was being channelled into a second, major series of public works which, while significantly increasing fixed capital investment, also resulted in a similar rise in general demand and wages. Military spending had been rising for some time, and contracts were now increasingly awarded to Italian firms, resulting in expansion in some industrial sectors. This general trend was reinforced by the government incentives granted in 1884 for the construction of the 'Terni' factory, the first major Italian steel-making plant producing rail track and ship hulls. A clause in the 1885 railway contracts was also inserted, according to which contractors were obliged to buy rolling stock and armaments from domestic suppliers when their prices did not exceed those of foreign competitors by more than 5 per cent. The new customs regulations of 1887, moreover, introduced protective customs barriers for steel and textiles (and for wheat: a success that was rather more apparent than real for the landowning classes). This encouraged foreign firms already active in the market to site their plants within Italy and there are some indications that this did happen.[68] The new tariffs also encouraged new initiatives and investment on the part of Italian entrepreneurs. The number of cotton spindles nearly doubled in the period 1880–91, the number of Martin-Siemens open-hearth furnaces rose to eighteen, the construction of locomotives increased and in 1883 the first electric power station opened in Milan.[69]

This new economic climate led to an increase in production in the secondary sector, and particularly in the more dynamic industrial sub-sector which was able to create a 'crack' in the economic system. This could have led to irreversible changes in the direction of the economy, although these changes could equally have been absorbed.[70]

The favourable industrial climate suddenly began to evaporate in 1888, the year in which the new customs tariffs came into force. Rather than the abolition of the forced currency, it was the overspending of central and local governments and the irresponsible overextension of large numbers of private businesses in construction speculation that began to have catastrophic results. These, together with other factors, led the country into a long period of political and institutional instability. There had been certain warning indicators from at least 1884, such as the repeated exchange premium on gold; the illegal rise in the volume of paper money and credit (the result of business needs and not without the tacit consent of the government); the steady transfer of deposits from the ordinary banks to the safer saving banks; the withdrawal of much of the foreign capital in the country in response to the new monetary regime; and the reduction of gold reserves due to the rising cost of the international servicing of the budget deficit. There is no single cause for this catastrophic situation, and it is simplistic to see it merely as the result of consistent errors on the part of those in government. It is nevertheless true that the banks had gone too far in 'giving credit to all' in order not to 'deprive shareholders of an acceptable dividend ... perhaps preventing due government authority being exercised over banking operations'.[71]

The trade war with France set off by the introduction of the protectionist customs tariffs brought the situation to a head. There was a total collapse in exports to France, in particular of agricultural products from the south, and this made it impossible for peasants and landowners to repay the loans they had contracted in investing in specialist crop production. This brought the banking system to a halt and disaster to much of the south. At the same time, the banks which had embarked on unbridled speculation in the construction industry, especially in Rome and Naples, found themselves in a similar situation due to the collapse of property prices. The two principal offenders, the Credito Mobiliare and the Banca Generale were soon to close, and the Treasury and the banks of issue were left to pick up the pieces of the debacle. The crisis spread quickly and dramatically, and seemed unstoppable. It is remarkable, moreover, that both the major landowners, also in difficulty, and the rising group of industrialists remained silent for so long and seemed not to realize the urgent need to protest against the policies of the government and the major financial groups. As an important London review warned as early as 1881, Italy needed:

a coalition of honest patriots and wise citizens, strong enough to free the country from the dead weight of a banking system which is suffocating production by draining it of its wealth.[72]

A hurried change in government policy (another *political* move which brought about important changes in the economy of the country) managed to avert a major banking crisis. The number of banks of issue was reduced to three, and the links between the newly created Bank of Italy, founded in 1893, and the private sector were severed. The fixed exchange rate was reintroduced. The major private banks, largely responsible for the crisis, were closed and, with the crucial support of German financiers, the Banca Commerciale Italiana and the Credito Italiano rose from the ashes to become Italy's most important short- and long-term lending banks.[73]

As a result of these measures, but also thanks to the international economic recovery which started in 1896 and renewed business confidence, Italy entered, without warning, the *third vital stage* in its industrial development. In the period 1898–1913, no economic indicator showed a downward trend, and those of the industrial sector were the most encouraging. An important cluster of process and product innovations occurred. The government decision to promote domestic consumption of the rich iron deposits on Elba convinced an Italo-French group to construct a coke-fired cast-iron plant in Portoferraio in 1902, the first such plant in the country, almost 200 years after its invention. The hydroelectric industry grew enormously, and calcium carbide, calcium cyanamide and rayon production began. The first bicycle, motorcycle and car factories were set up (Fiat was founded in 1899) and in Larderello Prince Ginori Conti built the only electricity plant in the world successfully operating on geothermal energy. But these examples do not give the whole story. They do not include the less capital-intensive sectors such as leathers and hides, clothing, wood, glass and ceramics, food and parts of the textile industry, all of which made advances in quality as well as quantity. Nor do they take into account the general tendency to growth in the total number of firms – with or without machinery – in the country as a whole, a tendency which was of course not a strictly Italian (or innovative) development. To some extent this was merely following the footsteps of the larger industries, but on the other hand it was actively promoted and the result of the wealth of human and natural resources available within the country. It was also the result of autochthonous factors such as family and regional loyalty, capacities for careful work and the readiness to work long hours and the potential for the harmonizing of different phases of production. This was a common inheritance which had grown in size and nature,

Table 7.2. *Limited companies in Italy: industrial and total; number and capital, in 1898 and 1914*

	Limited companies (industrial)		Limited companies (total)		Capital of industrial limited companies as a percentage of total capital of all limited companies
	Number	Capital (in millions of lire)	Number	Capital (in millions of lire)	
Year	1	2	3	4	2:4
1898	386	508	662	1,749	29.0
1914	1,988	3,131	3,138	5,756	54.4

Source: F. Coppola d'Anna, 'Le società per azioni in Italia', in Ministero per la Costituente, *Rapporto della Commissione Economica. Industria. II. Appendice alla relazione* (Rome, 1946), pp. 256–62.

and had not been lost in this period of rapid development. It was strong enough to resist, but it survived also due to the fact that it was one which was able to adapt to the realities of the new situation, one of new industrial giants (in particular in the electrical, engineering, sugar, car and rubber sectors)[74] that had already begun to aim at technical and productive concentration.

The rises in the workforce and investment are apparent although difficult to quantify. Reliable figures for the former appeared only in 1911, with the first industrial census. In this year, 2,043,609 workers were employed in manufacturing, 128,182 in construction, 24,187 in gas, water and electricity production and services, and a further 667,888 in some form of artisan production. There had also been a move towards trade unionism. The first national trade union, the Confederazione Generale del Lavoro (CGdL), was founded in 1905 and by 1914, together with other minor unions, it had 500,000 members. In 1910, the Italian Confederation of Industrialists was founded.[75] These too were signs of increasing modernization, and were to have important effects on the economic and social development of the country.

Trends in investment can to some extent be seen from the rise in the number and share capital of limited companies, data which also give some indication of the importance of this sort of company to Italy as a whole (see table 7.2).

Financing methods, which continued to be dominated by self-financing, began to diversity and become more specialized. The number of industrial companies quoted on the Milan Stock Exchange rose from

50 in 1897 to 188 in 1914,[76] and bond issues were becoming increasingly common. Indirectly, both cash remittances from emigrants – which rose from 225 million lire in 1897 to 727 million in 1913 – and foreign currency brought into the country by the expanding elite tourist trade grew in importance.[77] It was thanks to these indirect sources of finance that the balance of payments, struggling to meet the cost of importing the raw materials necessary for industry and not available in Italy, was able to maintain an equilibrium. Foreign capital, in particular but not exclusively German in origin, continued to play an important role.[78] It is also clear, however, that despite the somewhat over-enthusiastic and distorted view of one contemporary expert,[79] short- and long-term lending banks using a number of different techniques began to play a leading role in industry in this period. Types of involvement included share trading, medium to long-term company financing, contango, the placing of bank executives on a company's Board of Directors, unofficial presence at General Meetings by, for instance, the acquisition of blocks of shareholder proxies and the more or less secret involvement in risky, speculative ventures which contributed in no small manner to the major financial and stock-exchange crisis of 1907.[80] The result was the creation of a number of financial empires which, by 1914, controlled around 30 per cent of the capital invested in limited companies.[81] All this, however, did not alter the fact that:

> the tendency of the Banca Commerciale and the Credito Italiano to concentrate on the domestic market and on providing financing for Italian industry was of vital importance to the industrialization of the country.[82]

Industrialization had also been encouraged by a major shift in the economic policy of the government. Some early signs of this shift can be observed in certain policies of the late nineteenth century but they should really be seen as part of a different overall strategy followed in the early years of this century. This policy was able to build on the important modifications in the relations between the different social groups and classes. Its economic, financial and social policies overturned previous orientations and made industry its first priority. Examples of these policies were the decision to cut borrowing; the reduction of taxation on personal property; the 1906 law on public debt conversion; the special laws on Naples passed in 1904; and the legal recognition of workers' organizations and labour disputes which led to a rise in wages but also to rationalizing industrial investment. In line with this policy, the railways were nationalized in 1905, immediately after which a considerable proportion of the payments made to stock holders was invested in several major sectors, in particular electricity. At the same time, the government launched a refurbishment

Table 7.3. *World ranking of Italy in a certain number of industrial products in 1913*

Product	World ranking	Product	World ranking
Artificial textile fibres	3rd	Cement	7th
Silk	3rd	Electricity	7th
Calcium cyanamide	4th	Paper	7th
Phosphates	4th	Cotton (imported raw)	8th
Cars	5th	Steel	9th
Beet sugar	6th		
Calcium carbide	6th		
Sulphuric acid	6th		

Source: I. Svennilson, *Growth and Stagnation in the European Economy* (Geneva, 1954), *passim,* and ILVA, *Altiforni e acciaierie d'Italia. 1897–1947* (Bergamo, 1948), pp. 328–9.

programme for the entire rail network and rolling stock, most contracts being awarded to Italian companies.[83] Major military spending was also undertaken – over 300 million lire were spent ever year, approximately a third of the value of the output of the engineering industry.[84]

In line with international and public-sector demand, private demand too was rising steadily, although not booming. This was the result of growth in industrial employment and wages; the continued expansion of fixed capital investment; foreign remittances from emigrants; and the rise in agricultural production which, in the first decade of the century, was enjoying its best moment,[85] due in turn to important growth in the mechanization in the use of chemical fertilizer, in particular in the Po valley.

It is thus plausible that production in the secondary sector, a large part of which was now made up of industry proper, was developing at the rate suggested by Carreras's estimates, according to which, assuming the 1929 volume to be 100, it was 26.91 in 1897, 52.93 in 1907 and 61.45 in 1913. The quantitative leap had other important characteristics, not least of which was the shift to the second phase of historical industrialization according to Hoffman's model, in which there is a sudden disparity in the relation between the value of the production of consumer goods and that of capital goods, which in fact dropped from 4.82:1 in 1898 to 1.8:1 in 1912.

If we bear these radical and rapid changes in mind, along with comparative data on certain major Italian products in 1913 (see table 7.3), it cannot be denied that towards the end of the nineteenth century Italy began to undergo important changes, and that in 1914 she could call herself an industrialized nation. Her infrastructure and production capacity were without doubt clearly below the levels of the advanced countries, but were in line with those following her. It should be pointed out that 'industrialized nation' is by no means a synonym for 'industrial society', a status that could only be acquired after prolonged exposure to a world of machinery, factories, entrepreneurs and workers, together with their organizations and struggle for markets.[86]

Taking a long-term view, it would appear that Italy's 'economic miracle' took place not after the Second World War but in the first fifteen years of the twentieth century, when the country's industrialization played an important part in the decisive structural changes which pushed Italy along the path from the periphery to the centre.

With reference to the Industrial Revolution, it has been said that Great Britain and the generations which had the 'luck' to be the protagonists of this process, were the beneficiaries of a 'massive free lunch'.[87] This would seem unlikely, and in any case certainly did not occur in Italy. Its own 'leap' was not only carried out with incalculable social and human costs (as happened everywhere else, moreover) but was also the more or less direct cause of spectacular upheavals, splits, new conflicts which aggravated those already existing, and finally an inversion of Italy's traditional international alliances.

The industrial divide between the north-west and the rest of Italy increased enormously, as shown in table 7.4 on the industrial sector in 1911. Data and calculations such as these, although approximate and as regards value added purely speculative, are unequivocal. The entire south of the country, with the exception of Campania, was way behind the north-west, itself far ahead of the north-east, central Italy and Campania in terms of industrial development. This sort of divergence was not unique to Italy. But as several farsighted commentators predicted, while in the north, east and centre this gap could be made good, in the south this was impossible. The real 'Italian economic miracle' had probably already assumed its fundamental characteristics, and was to maintain this gap and the general difficulties that were associated with it. It is true, however, that siting considerations on the part of firms did play an important part, as did those regarding the volume of demand. Other factors such as the mass emigration of young workers and the economic policy of the government, without doubt 'northern' in orientation,[88] were also crucial, although the latter, it should be remembered, was decided by a parliamentary majority within which the southern lobby exercised a notable influence. This influence was used, in exchange for harsh repression of the peasant movement, to obtain substantial investment in public works in their constituencies, reductions in the land tax and a

Table 7.4. *The industrial sector in Italy in 1911*

	North-west	North-east	Centre	South (excluding Campania)	Campania	Italian totals
1. Surface area %	20.4	16.4	19.2	38.4	5.6	Km² 287, 764
2. Population %	27.3	17.9	16.3	29.0	9.5	No. 34,671,000
3. Employees %	50.2	15.7	14.2	13.3	6.6	No. 2,082,265
4. Horsepower installed (HP)	49.5	16.0	16.0	12.7	5.8	HP 1,186,526
3:1 (Employees/ surface area)	17.9	6.8	6.4	2.4	9.1	
3:2 (Employees/ population)	11.1	5.1	5.1	2.6	4.5	
4:1 (Installed HP/ surface area)	10.0	4.1	4.2	0.9	6.8	
4:2 (Installed HP/ population)	6.2	3.0	3.2	1.0	3.3	
Vallue added (per capita) (a) % per area	54.7	15.1	14.0	9.7	6.5	3,504 million
(b) Italian lire per inhabitant	204	84	85	34	69	101

Source: V. Zamagni, *Industrializzazione e squilibri regionali in Italia* (Bologna, 1978), pp. 226–31, 194–5 and 199.

slowing down in the completion of the new land register – to maintain, in short, the domination of the traditional ruling groups in the south.

Moreover, while profiteers and speculators had been forced more or less to abandon their happy hunting grounds of government bonds, government contracts and construction, the huge development of industry offered them new and inviting opportunities, from the stock market to big business and some of the large banks, in which they were to become inextricably entangled.

Finally, and this was probably the heaviest price the country had to pay, the 'change' which had brought Italy into the world of industry led to an intensification of the level of social and political conflict which went far beyond the norm. While conflicts between capitalist entrepreneurs and workers or between protectionists and free traders may be normal, this was not the case for the hostility between Catholics and non-Catholics, the deep-rooted conflict between Francophiles and Germanophiles, disputes between nationalists and their opponents and the general internal strife that characterized many of these movements (not excluding the workers' movement). This gave rise to a sort of *bellum omnium contra omnes* which indicated an accentuation of an old malaise within the governing groups. This was not *transformismo*, considered in its time as a therapeutic intervention, but the incapacity of ruling groups to conceive of themselves as a *real* governing class, 'able to think of itself as a general class'.[89] The moderates had been able to do so during the Risorgimento and the construction of the unified state. But it remained a task beyond the grasp of the industrial middle classes, if, indeed, it was recognized as a goal. This was particularly true of those in the north, despite the fact that they had proved themselves and achieved tangible success in the creation of a solid productive base and, in 1914, were in a position to be able to strengthen their hand further.

NOTES

1 Cf. Cattaneo (1858), 'La città considerata come principio ideale delle istorie italiane', in C. Cattaneo, *Scritti storici e geografici*, ed. G. Salvemini and E. Sestan (Florence, 1967; originally published in 1858), pp. 425–537. The cities came up against the obstinate resistance of the small rural towns and the areas still under feudal jurisdiction. For a general view of this period, see M. Aymard, 'La fragilità di una economia avanzata', in R. Romano (ed.), *Storia dell'Economia italiana*, vol. II (Turin, 1989).

2 P. Malanima, 'L'economia dei nobili a Firenze nei secoli XVII e XVIII', in *Società e storia*, 54 (1991), pp. 829–49; G. Felloni, *Gli investimenti finanziari genovesi in Europea tra il seicento e la Restaurazione* (Milan, 1971).

3 A. Ventura, 'Considerazone sull'agricoltura veneta e sull'accumulazione originaria del capitale nei secoli XVI e XVII', *Studi storici*, 3–4 (1968), pp. 674–722; C. Poni, 'Struttura, strategie e ambiguità delle "Giornate" di Agostino Gallo fra l'agricoltura e la villa', *Intersezioni*, 1 (1989), pp. 22–4.

4 As yet no comprehensive study exists of the construction, management and economic importance of the navigational canals in the Po valley.

5 R. A. Goldthwaite, 'The Renaissance economy. The preconditions for luxury consumption', in *Aspetti della vita economica medievale* (Florence, 1985), pp. 659–75.

6 G. Villani, *Croniche* (Venice, 1537), p. 204.

7 On the importance of the construction industry in the modern period, see D. Sella, 'European industries 1500–1700', in C. Cipolla (ed.), *Fontana Economic History of Europe*, vol. VIII (London and Cambridge, 1972).

8 One of the first economic historians to underline the importance of demand for luxury goods was C. Cipolla: *Storia economica dell'Europa preindustriale* (Bologna, 1974), pp. 44–70. Italy's economy under the *ancien régime*, as described here, is based on the excellent pioneering article published by Carlo

Cipolla forty years ago: 'The economic decline of Italy', in B. Pullan (ed.), *Crisis and Change in the Venetian Economy in the 16th and 17th Centuries* (London, 1988), pp. 127–45.

9 S. de Gramohnt (1620), *Le denier royal. Traicté curieux de l'or et de l'argent* (Paris, 1620), pp. 189–90; *Advis au Roy et aux Monseigneurs de son Conseil pour augmenter les manufactures des draps d'or, d'argent et de soye, et empescher le transport de plus de douze millions de livres tous les ans hors du Royaume* (Paris, 1627). Against the import of Italian luxury goods and for the development of a national silk industry in France cf. B. de Laffemas, 'Reiglement général pour dresser les manufactures et ouvrages en ce Royaume et couper les cours des draps de soye et autres marchandises qui perdent et ruinent l'Etat' (Paris, 1597); B. de Laffemas 'Response à messieurs de Lyon lesquels veulent empescher rompre le cours des marchandises d'Itali' (Paris, 1598); B. de Laffemas, 'La commission … et établssement du commerce général des manufactures en ce Royaume' (Paris, 1601); B. de Laffemas, 'Advis sur l'usage des passements d'or et d'argent (Paris, 1610). See also C. Poni, 'All'origine del sistema di fabbrica: tecnologia e organizzazione produttiva dei mulini da seta nell'Italia settentrionale (sec. XVII–XVIII)', in *Rivista storica italiana*, 3 (1976), pp. 492–3; A. Manikowski, 'Les soieries italiennes et l'activité des commerçants italiens de soieries en Pologne au XVII siècle', in *Mélange de l'Ecole Française de Rome*, 88 (2) (1976), p. 837.

10 Cf. P. Massa, *La fabbrica dei velluti genovesi da Genova a Zoagli'* (Genoa, 1981), pp. 86–7; C. Poni, 'Per la storia del distretto industriale serico di Bologna (secoli XVI–XIX)', in *Quaderni storici*, 73 (1990), p. 95; P. Massa, 'Tipologia tecnica e organizzazione economica della manodopera serica in alcune esperienze italiane (sec. XIV–XVIII)', in *La seta in Europa (sec. XIII–XX)*, Atti delle Settimane di Studi dell'Istituto Internazionale di Storia Economica F. Datini di Prato, ed. by S. Cavaciocchi (Florence, 1993), p. 215; C. M. Belfanti, 'Rural manufactures and rural proto-industry in the Italy of the cities from the sixteenth through the eighteenth century', in *Continuity and Change*, 8, 2 (1993), pp. 253–80. To understand these figures one must bear in mind that the aggregate data of employment in *ancien régime* sources almost never represent the span of one year. Work for a putting-outer could last a few weeks or many months. Moreover the length of the working day could vary from a few hours to fourteen or sixteen hours. In general these aggregate figures include the children who helped their parents with weaving, winding the thread on bobbins (or in other subsidiary work).

11 C. Poni, 'Schizzo di storia del setificio italiano nell'età di Antico Regime', *Annali della Fondazione Luigi Micheletti*, 3 (1987), pp. 63–4. From the sixteenth to the eighteenth century the increase of cocoon production was higher than any other sector of northern Italian agriculture.

12 C. Poni, 'All'origine del sistema di fabbrica', pp. 444–97; C. Poni, 'Espansione e declino di una grande industria: le filature di seta a Bologna fra XVII e XVIII secolo', in *Problemi d'acqua a Bologna in età moderna* (Bologna, 1983), pp. 211–88.

13 C. Vigo, *Fisco e società nella Lombardia del Cinquecento* (Bologna, 1979); D. Sella, *Crisis and Continuity. The Economy of Spanish Lombardy in the Seventeenth Century* (Cambridge, Mass., 1979); A. de Maddalena, *Dalla città al borgo. Avvio di una metamorfosi economica e sociale nella Lombardia spagnola* (Milan, 1982).

14 D. Sella, *Crisis and Continuity*. A. Morioli, 'La deindustrializzazione della Lombardia nel secolo XVII', *Archivio storico lombardo*, 2 (1986), pp. 167–203.

15 C. Poni, 'Archéologie de la fabrique: la diffusion des moulins à soie "alla bolognese" dans les Etats vénitiens du XVIe au XVIIIe siècle', in *Annales ESC*, 6 (1972), pp. 1475–96.

16 D. Sella, *Crisis and Continuity*; C. Poni, 'Piccole innovazione e filatoi a mano: Venezia (1550–1600)', in *Studi in memoria di Luigi dal Pane* (Bologna, 1982), p. 373.

17 G. Prato, *La vita economica in Piemonte* (Turin, 1908), pp. 217–21. In 1773 there were no more than 30 small silk mills in Venice which employed 82 men (adults and children). Probably 1,000 women and little girls worked at home as winders for the mills (Biblioteca S. Marco di Venezia, Ms. It. VII (1840), 9602).

18 P. Mantoux, *La révolution industrielle au XVIII siècle* (Paris, 1959), pp. 188–92; W. H. Chaloner, *People and Industry* (London, 1963), pp. 8–20; R. S. Fitton and A. P. Wadsworth, *The Strutts and the Arkwrights* (Manchester, 1958), pp. 226–7.

19 C. Poni, 'Fashion as flexible production. The strategies of the silk merchants of Lyon in the eighteenth century', in *A World of Possibility*, ed. Ch. Sabel and J. Zeitlin (Cambridge, forthcoming).

20 *Ibid.*

21 M. Costantini (1987), *L'albero della libertà* (Venice, 1987), p. 56; C. Poni, 'Per la storia del distretto industriale', p. 107; P. Massa, *La fabbrica dei velluti da Genova a Zoagli* (Genoa, 1981); G. Zalin, *Dalla bottega alla fabbrica. La fenomenologia industriale nelle provincie venete tra '500 e '900* (Verona, 1987), pp. 130–5; A. Dewerpe, *L'industrie aux champs. Essai sur la proto-industrialisation en Italie du Nord (1800–1880)* (Rome, 1985) p. 9; P. Malanima, *La decadenza di un'economia cittadina* (Bologna, 1982), pp. 322–4.

22 Cf. the observations of Dewerpe in *L'industrie aux champs*, p. 334.

23 R. T. Rapp, 'The unmaking of the Mediterranean trade hegemony; international trade rivalry and the commercial revolution', *Journal of Economic History*, 25 (1975), pp. 499–525.

24 R. Davis, 'England and the Mediterranean 1570–1670', in *Essays in the Economic History of Tudor and Stuart England*, ed. F. J. Fisher (Cambridge, 1974); Rapp, 'The Unmaking of the Mediterranean trade hegemony'.

25 D. Sella (1968), 'The rise and fall of the Venetian woollen industry', in B. Pullan (ed.) *Crisis and Change*, pp. 106–26.

26 D. Sella, Paper given at the conference Per una storia economica di Bergamo fra XV e XVIII secolo, *Bergamo economica* (December 1990), p. 37.

27 W. Panciera, *L'industria laniera della Repubblica di Venezia in età moderna* (forthcoming).

28 The relevant statistics have been published by G. Ganzer in *Arte e impresa nel Settecento in Carnia: Iacopo Linussio* (Udine, 1991), pp. 18, 21–2, 27, 29, 33, 35.

29 U. Tucci, 'L'industria del ferro nel settecento. La Val Trompia', in *Ricerche storiche ed economiche in memoria di Corrado Barbagallo*, vol. II, ed. L. De Rosa (Naples, 1970), p. 450.

30 Cf. D. Montanari, 'Produzione di armi su commessa pubblica. La vicenda di Gardone Val Trompia nei secoli XVI–XIX', in *Atlante Valprunino* (Brescia, 1982), pp. 178–180 and C. M. Belfante, 'Rural manufactures and rural proto-industries', 253–80.

31 I. Mazzotti, *Produzione e commercio della carta nello stato veneziano setttecentesco. Lineamenti e problemi* (Bologna, 1975); G. M. Zilio, 'L'arte della stampa', in *Storia di Bassano*, ed. G. Fasoli (Vicenza, 1980), pp. 271–91: M. Stringa 'La ceramica', in Fasoli (ed.), *Storia di Bassano*, pp. 317–27; R. Romano, *La modernizzazione periferica. L'alto milanese e la formazione di una società industriale 1750–1914* (Milan, 1990), pp. 4–38.

32 A. Young, *Travels during the year 1787, 1788 and 1789* ... (London, 1792), pp. 249, 467, 509–10. Young uses the geographical term 'Lombardy' in its widest sense, describing Bologna as 'the most industrial city in Lombardy' (*ibid.*, p. 164). For a rich and detailed survey of the industry of Lombardy in the second half of the eighteenth century see A. Moioli, 'Assetti manifatturieri nella Lombardia politicamente divisa della seconda metà del Settecento', in S. Zaninelli (ed.), *Storia dell'Industria Lombarda*, I (Milan, 1988), pp. 2–102.

33 R. T. Rapp, *Industry and Economic Decline in Seventeenth Century Venice*, (Cambridge, Mass., 1972), pp. 9–10

34 W. Panciera, 'Verso la crisi: i lanifici della Repubblica veneziana dalla fine del Settecento alla Restaurazione', in *Veneto e Lombardia tra rivoluzione giacobina ed età napoleonica. Economia, Territorio, Istituzioni*, ed. L. Fontana and A. Lazzarini (Bari, 1992), p. 260.

35 Dewerpe, *L'industrie aux champs*, pp. 104–5. Approximately one-third of the gun barrels were discarded by the French officials.

36 G. Mori, 'Industry without industrialisation' in J. Batou (ed.), *Between Development and Underdevelopment* (Geneva, 1991), pp. 315–16, 342–5.

37 B. Caizzi, *Storia dell'industria italiana dal XVIII secolo ai giorni nostri* (Milan, 1970).

38 M. Merger (1989) 'L'industrie italienne des locomotives (1850–1914)', *Histoire, économie et société*, 8 (1989), 364.

39 A. Dell'Orefice (1984), *L'industria della carta in Italia (1861–1914)* (Naples, 1984), p. 14.

40 G. Mori, 'La siderurgia italiana dall'Unità alla fine del secolo XIX', *Ricerche storiche*, 8 (1978), 11–14; A. Giuntini (1990), *Dalla Lyonnaise alla Fiorentinagas (1839–1989)* (Bari, 1990), pp. 8–10.

41 I. A. Glazier, V. N. Bandera and R. B. Berner, 'Terms of trade between Italy and the United Kingdom. 1815–1913', *Journal of European Economic History*, 4 (1975), 12.

42 F. Sirugo, 'L'Europa delle riforme', in C. Cavour, *Scritti di economia. 1835–1850* (Milan, 1962) p. lxxvi.

43 V. Giura, *La questione degli zolfi siciliani 1838–1841* (Geneva, 1973).

44 A. Gerschenkron, *Economic Backwardness in Historical Perspective* (Cambridge, Mass., 1962).

45 Merger, 'L'industrie', p. 363.

46 P. Bevilacqua (ed.), *Storia dell'agricoltura in età contemporanea* (Venice, 1989–91), 3 vols.

47 A. Graziani, *Il commercio estero del Regno delle Due Sicilie dal 1832 al 1858*, Archivio economico dell'Unificazione Italiana (1960), no. I, 10, 23.

48 S. Hymer and S. Resnick (1969), 'A model of an agrarian economy with non-agricultural activities', *The American Economic Review*, 59 (1969).

49 Statistica del Regno d'Italia. Popolazione. *Censimento generale* (31 December 1861, Florence, 1866), vol. III, p. xiii.

50 P. Corner, 'Il contadino-operaio dell'Italia padana', in Bevilacqua (ed.), *Storia*, vol. I, pp. 757–9.

51 F. Bonelli, 'Il capitalismo italiano', in *Storia d'Italia. Annali* (Turin, 1978), I, p. 1202.

52 V. Zamagni, *Dalla periferia al centro* (Bologna, 1990), p. 228.

53 P. Farneti, *Sistema politico e società civile* (Turin, 1971), p. 171.

54 G. Mori, 'L'economia italiana dagli anni Ottanta alla prima guerra mondiale', in G. Mori (ed.), *Storia dell'industria elettrica in Italia* (Bari, 1992), pp. 10–19.

55 Cited in G. Are, *Il problema dello sviluppo industriale nell'età della Destra* (Pisa, 1965), 48.

56 Banca d'Italia, *I bilanci degli Istituti italiani de emissione dal 1845 al 1936* ed. R. De Mattia (Rome, 1967), vol. I, pp. 945–6; M. Da Pozzo and G. Felloni, *La borsa valori di Genova del secolo XIX* (Turin, 1964), pp. 194–5; M. De Cecco, Preface to *L'Italia e il sistema finanziario internazionale* (Bari and Rome, 1990), p.25.

57 A. M. Banti, 'Una fonte per lo studio delle élites ottocentesche: le dichiarazioni di successione dell'ufficio del Registro', *Rassegna degli Archivi di Stato*, 43 (1983), pp. 112–18.

58 P. Masi, 'L'influenza del debito pubblico sulla costituzione dei sistemi finanziari. Il caso italiano. 1860–1893', *Rivista di storia economica*, 6 (1989), p. 75.

59 Glazier, Bandera and Berner, 'Terms of trade', p. 13.

60 G. Federico and G. Toniolo, 'Italy', in R. Sylla and G. Toniolo (eds.), *Patterns of European Industrialisation. The Nineteenth Century* (London, 1991), p. 203.

61 A. Carreras, 'La produccion industrial en el muy largo plazo: una comparacion entre Espana e Italia de 1861 a 1980', in L. Prados de la Escosura and V. Zamagni (eds.), *El Desarrollo economico en la Europa del Sur* (Madrid, 1992), p. 181.

62 V. Ellena (1880), *La statistica di alcune industrie italiane* (Rome, 1880) Dell'Orefice, *L'industria*, 55; L. De Rosa (1980), *La rivoluzione industriale in Italia* (Rome and Bari, 1980), pp. 160–7.

63 F. Coppola D'Anna, 'Le società per azioni in Italia', in Ministero per la Costituente, *Rapporto della Commissione economica. Industria*, III, *Appendice alla relazione* (Rome, 1946), p. 256.

64 A. M. Biscaini Cotula and P. Ciocca, 'Le strutture finanziarie, aspetti quanti-

tativi di lungo periodo (1870–1970)', in F. Vicarelli (ed.), *Capitale industriale e capitale finanziario: il caso italiano* (Bologna, 1979), pp. 92–3.

65 De Cecco, Preface to *L'Italia*, pp. 35–9; Banca d'Italia, *I bilanci*, p. 567; G. Brosio and G. Marchese, *Il potere di spendere* (Bologna, 1986), p. 178; Zamagni, *Dalla periferia*, p. 228.

66 *Sul classicismo economico in Italia: il caso Francesco Fuoco* (Florence, 1979).

67 G. Carocci, *Agostino Depretis e la politica interna dal 1876 al 1887* (Turin, 1956), chap. VI.

68 P. Hertner, *Il capitale tedesco in Italia dall'Unità alla prima guerra mondiale* (Bologna, 1984); L. De Rosa, *Iniziativa e capitale straniero nell'industria metalmeccanica del Mezzogiorno, 1840–1904* (Naples, 1968); M. Lungonelli, *La Magona d'Italia* (Bologna, 1991); G. Palmieri, *La Saint Gobain a Pisa* (Florence, 1979); M. Lungonelli, 'Dalla manifattura alla fabbrica', in G. Mori (ed.), *Prato. Storia di una città* (Florence, 1988), III, pp. 33-4; M. Gelfi, 'I cotonieri svizzeri a Bergamo tra il 1867 ed il 1888', *Padania*, 2 (1988), p. 11. On 'Terni', cf. F. Bonelli, *Lo sviluppo di una grande impresa in Italia* (Turin, 1978).

69 Mori, 'L'economia', pp. 36–40, 49.

70 A. Dewerpe, 'Verso l'Italia industriale', in *Storia dell'economia italiana* (Turin, 1991), p. 32.

71 Banca di'Italia. R. De Mattia (ed.), *Storia delle operazioni degli Istituti di emissione italiani dal 1845 al 1936* (Rome, 1990), vol. II, p. 465.

72 Cited in G. Berta, 'Un circuito finanziario dell'ottocento: gli Hambro e l'Italia (1851–1881)', *Annali di storia dell'impresa*, 6 (1989).

73 P. Hertner, *Il capitale*, pp. 10–76.

74 For a comprehensive and original account of this complicated issue, see G. Becattini, 'Il distretto industriale marshalliano', in G. Becattini (ed.), *Mercato e forze locali: il distretto industriale* (Bologna, 1987), pp. 7–34.

75 R. Chiaventi, 'I censimenti industriali italiani. 1911–1951: procedimenti di standardizzazione', *Rivista di storia economica*, 6 (1987), p. 47: A. Pepe, *Storia della CGdL dalla guerra di Libra all'intervento*, 1911–1915 (Bari, 1971), table VII, 2. For technical and productive concentration see V. Zamagni (1978), *Industrializzazione e squilibri regionali in Italia* (Bologna, 1978), p. 142.

76 A. Aleotti, *Borsa e industria* (Milan, 1990), p. 62.

77 *Sommario di statistiche storiche italiane. 1861–1955* (Rome, 1958).

78 Particularly in the electrical sector, see L. Segreto, 'Imprenditori e finanzieri', in Mori (ed.), *Storia*, p. 321.

79 R. Bachi, *L'Italia economica nel 1913* (Città di Castello, 1913), p. 300.

80 F. Pino Pongolini '*Il data-base* sui fiduciari della Comit nelle società per azioni (1898–1918)', *Rivista di storia economica* 8 (1991); F. Bonelli *La crisi del 1907* (Turin, 1977).

81 Zamagni, *Industrializzazione*, pp. 173–8.

82 Hertner, *Il capitale*, p. 155.

83 Mori, 'L'economia', pp. 72–3.

84 Zamagni, *Dalla periferia*, p. 215.

85 P. K. O'Brien and G. Toniolo, 'Sull'arretratezza dell'agricoltura italiana rispetto a quella del Regno Unito attorno al 1910', *Ricerche economiche* (1986).

86 *Sommario*, pp. 126–35.

87 D. N. McCloskey, 'The Industrial Revolution', in R. Floud and D. N. McCloskey (eds.), *The Economic History of Britain since 1700* (Cambridge, 1981), p. 117.

88 L. Cafagna, *Il Nord della storia d'Italia* (Bari, 1962), p. 357.

89 A. M. Banti, 'I proprietari terrieri nell'Italia centro-settentrionale', in Bevilacqua (ed.), *Storia*, vol. I, p. 70.

EIGHT

━━━▷•◇•◁━━━

A latecomer: the modernization of the Spanish economy, 1800–1990

GABRIEL TORTELLA

TWO CENTURIES OF SPANISH ECONOMIC HISTORY

THE question most frequently asked by Spanish economic historians dealing with the modern period is: why is the Spanish economy so backward in the comparative framework of modern Europe (Vicens Vives, 1959; Tortella, 1977; Nadal, 1975)? Similar questions, one may add, are asked, *mutatis mutandis*, by political and social historians (Carr and Fusi, 1981).

A thoughtful inspection of figures 8.1 and 8.2 will provide part of the answer to these questions. These graphs show, among other things, that the Spanish economy stagnated and remained backward with respect to Europe in the nineteenth century, while in the twentieth century it grew fast and recovered most if not all of its lost ground. They also show that the patterns of Italy and Portugal were strikingly parallel to the Spanish case.

Figure 8.2 compares the performances of six European countries with an abstract norm, the combined weighted British and French per capita income (this explains the almost mirror images of the British and French curves). Relative to the British–French norm, the Spanish economy sank precipitously during the first half of the nineteenth century, almost held its own during the second half, started to recover during the first third of the twentieth century, sank again in the 1930–50 period, and recovered vigorously after 1950. While in the nineteenth century the Spanish economy lost ground all the time, in the twentieth century the trend was reversed and it recovered partially.

Is there an explanation for this pattern? There may be, and an attempt in this direction will be our next line of enquiry. To start with, the fact that Italy's and Portugal's curves follow a path that is remarkably similar to that of Spain would lead us to wonder whether most of the explanations we might find for the Spanish pattern of retardation in the

184

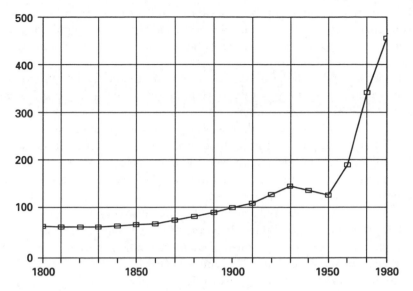

Fig. 8.1 Index of Spanish national income per capita, 1800–1980

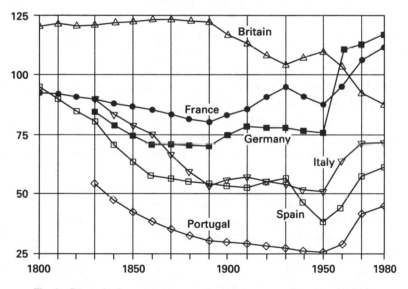

Fig. 8.2 Per capita income in six countries as percentage of combined British
and French income

nineteenth century and partial recovery in the twentieth should not be
examined in conjunction with what is known about the Italian and
Portuguese cases. Pollard (1982) has argued that the patterns of industrialization in Europe can be better understood if we adopt a regional rather

than a national standpoint. Should we not, in the case of Spain, a country with strong similarities to its western Mediterranean neighbours, be looking for regional, rather than national, patterns of development or stagnation (Tortella, 1991)?

If we accept that there is what we could call a 'Latin' pattern of modernization, a pattern of relative retardation *vis-à-vis* a European norm during the nineteenth century, and of rapid catching-up during the second half of the twentieth then we should look for possible explanations which may be applicable to the three countries in the region. If one were thinking only of the nineteenth century, one would be more inclined to concentrate upon the factors of retardation; however, since there seems to be clear recovery in the twentieth century, the explanation would not be complete unless we could account for this turnaround.

It would appear that Spain, Italy and Portugal share two traits which can explain the common features of their economic histories: their *culture* and their *physical endowment*. The culture of South-western Europe can be summarized in the oft-repeated word 'Latin' and dates back at least to its Roman heritage which has moulded so many of its features and institutions, from its languages and its religion to its legal systems. The physical, especially agricultural, endowment of the Mediterranean basin is quite homogeneous, and has determined the choice of techniques, of crops, even the shape of plots and of course the diets, of these countries for many centuries. These two elements, which in turn are interrelated, can explain the broad contours of the economic history of South-western Europe in the nineteenth and twentieth centuries.

The economic development of any human society is the result of the interplay of two main factors: the physical endowment of the area inhabited by the society and the technology available to it. Between these two elements, however, there is a crucial mediating factor: the institutional makeup of the society in question. If this standpoint is accepted, then the retardation of South-western Europe in the nineteenth century is a phenomenon whose origins date back to several centuries earlier. In fact, during the Middle Ages and the Early Modern period most technological innovations in agriculture were best adapted to the agricultural conditions and requirements of the lands of Northern Europe: this is the case with practically every single agricultural innovation mentioned in the textbooks, from the *heavy plough* to the many varieties of *convertible husbandry and farming*. Southern European agriculture, with only a few minor exceptions, remained tied to the two-field rotation of cereal cultivation, with the *light plough* scratching the sandy soil, much as in the time of the Roman Empire. This accumulation of agricultural innovations adapted to the moist, heavy, rich soils of northern Europe, the accumulation which culminated in the Agricultural Revolution of the Early Modern era first in the Netherlands and then in England, is the main explanation of the gap in incomes and in living standards between northern and southern Europe, which became increasingly apparent during the nineteenth century.

It is unnecessary to labour here the importance of agriculture in the early stages of the modernization of an economy. Those countries that were able to import the Agricultural Revolution during the nineteenth century could thereby become successful and early latecomers to economic modernity (such as Germany, Denmark and Sweden, for instance), whereas those countries which, for one reason or another, were unable to 'revolutionize' their agriculture remained backward. Such was the case of our Latin countries.

In Spain the physical obstacles to modernization were very strong, probably more so than in Italy or in Portugal. The sheer size and massive shape of the country, the dryness and altitude of the central plateau (the *Meseta*) made transportation expensive, isolated it from trade and innovation, and discouraged the transfer of human resources to more productive activities. For Spain, geography and culture reinforced each other as obstacles to modernization from the seventeenth to the mid-twentieth century. In the first place, the low level of agricultural productivity kept the diet of the average Spaniard at around the subsistence level, with little long-run improvement until well into the twentieth century. The stagnant agricultural sector also failed dismally as a market for industrial products, as a supplier of capital for modernization and as an exporter of labour for urban activities, due to high death rates and relatively low birth rates. The level of urbanization in Spain and in Portugal remained low throughout the nineteenth century. The failure of agriculture to produce a surplus population which would flock to the cities and man the factories before the very end of the nineteenth century is obviously typical of South-western Europe, in clear contrast with such northern countries as Britain since the mid-eighteenth and Germany since the mid-nineteenth century.

Agriculture must also produce an abundant flow of exports in the early stages of growth, and here Spanish agriculture failed partially; while it cannot be denied that exports were largely agricultural until well into the twentieth century – the main exception being mineral ores – the share of foreign trade relative to the size of the economy remained low, and therefore the contribution of agriculture remained small.

One could think, on a first approach, that a country with such poor agricultural conditions is ideally suited for industrialization, as the opportunity cost for its population to abandon one activity (agriculture) and take up another (industry) would be low. This idea may be considered simplistic, but it is not altogether wrong. The early and successful industrialization of Switzerland, where human, as contrasted with physical or geographical, factors appear to have played the key role suggests that this hypothesis has some merit. But, if this is the case, why was not Spain, as Switzerland was, another case of industrialization through comparative advantage?

There are several possible answers to this question, but the basic one is that the comparative disadvantage of Switzerland in agriculture was much greater. Due to the basic poverty of its subsistence agriculture its peasants and farmers have from very early on branched out and worked part-time in cottage industries. By the same token, Switzerland never had any pretence of self-sufficiency. The transition to industry, therefore, was facilitated by strong comparative advantage, early formation of human capital and also by relative free-trade policies. Most of these ingredients are missing in nineteenth-century Spain. Education and literacy in our Latin countries remained, as we shall presently see, among the lowest in Western Europe during the nineteenth century, while Switzerland was a pioneer in popular education (Bergier, 1983, pp. 177–9). And tariff barriers acted as buffers against trade-induced change, which in this case would chiefly have involved the transfer of resources from agriculture to industry (Prados, 1988; Reis, 1982; Lains, 1987).

Cultural factors are undoubtedly difficult to measure and therefore to subject to international comparisons. Fortunately, some parameters are amenable to measurement and comparison. Figure 8.3 reflects the evolution of illiteracy rates in six European countries. It is clear from figure 8.3 that Latin countries had literacy rates well below those of most other European nations. Around 1900, for instance, nearly 50 per cent of the adult population in Italy and Spain could not read (and *a fortiori* could not write). The Portuguese rate was even lower. In Belgium, meanwhile, one of the least literate among the 'developed' European countries, the proportion of those unable to read was less than one-fifth (19 per cent) of the adult population, and in France and England it was considerably lower.

In the light of these figures, it is almost impossible not to establish a relationship between literacy and economic development in Europe. This was done explicitly in an article by Lars Sandberg (1982) in which he showed that, if we arranged European countries by their literacy rates in 1850, this gradation almost exactly matched the list of these same countries ordered by per capita income *in 1950*, but not in 1850. His conclusion was that literacy rates were an excellent long-term (but not short-term) explanatory factor for economic development. This seems to fit very well our income and literacy data for Latin and non-Latin countries.

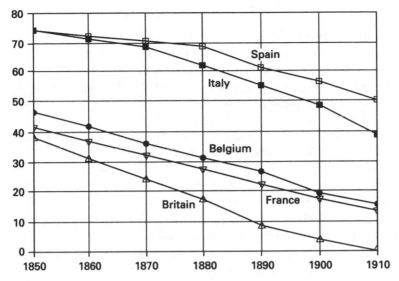

Fig 8 3 Illiteracy rates in five European countries

These views are supported by research carried out recently in Spain (Núñez, 1990, 1991); Italy (Zamagni, 1978) and Portugal (Reis, 1987, 1989). The work of Clara Eugenia Núñez (1990) shows that Sandberg's hypothesis for European countries is statistically confirmed for Spain's forty-nine provinces, although with a shorter time-lag. Using historical provincial data and allowing for a *time-lag* of about twenty-five to thirty years, roughly a generation, she has shown that there is strong correlation between literacy and per capita income in nineteenth- and twentieth-century Spain.

The correlation improves considerably when a second variable is included: the *gender gap*. This means that, other things being equal, the narrower the gap between male and female literacy rates, the stronger the positive impact of literacy on economic growth. Núñez's work has introduced a new variable into the analysis of the economic effects of literacy, and opened a host of new perspectives which we cannot examine here. Suffice it to say that the discovery of the importance of the gender gap in literacy suggests, among other things, that the diffusion of improved learning and reasoning skills, as opposed to the straight application of skills to the job at hand, is a potent contribution of literacy to economic growth, since women in Spain at that time were only a small fraction of the conventional labour force. The research that has been done for Italy, and to a lesser extent for Portugal, fully supports the general thrust of the findings about Spain.

FACTORS OF RECOVERY

We have to explain why, in spite of these strong physical and institutional factors of retardation, during the twentieth century the Spanish economy reversed or, at least, stopped the downward trend in relative income which was so obvious in the nineteenth century. Here again the parallels with Italy and Portugal are striking. Not only did the three economies modernize during the twentieth century, but the three countries were ruled by dictators during long and overlapping periods, thus intimating similar sociopolitical reactions to the strains of economic transition.

Before we proceed into a more systematic description I will sketch a few tentative explanations about the Spanish case. It seems obvious that to surmount the vicious circle which maintained the majority of the population tied to the soil at very low subsistence levels some sort of shock was needed, either of the 'pull' or the 'push' variety. By this I mean that population had to be either lured, *pulled* out of archaic agriculture by the attraction of urban industry and commerce, or *pushed* out of agriculture by deteriorating living conditions. I believe that the main stimulus for change was of the 'push' variety and was provided by the inflow of cheap grain exported by the USA and Russia, which depressed agricultural prices in Europe and pushed many farmers and field workers out of the land. (That this was a 'push' rather than a 'pull' is shown by the fact that a large part of the uprooted population migrated overseas, i.e., was not primarily lured by domestic cities and industry.) This overseas agricultural competition accelerated trends which inevitably led to the modernization of the Latin economies. These trends were in two main directions: (1) transfer of population from agriculture to other, more productive activities, such as industry; and (2) transfer of population and other resources from lower- to higher-productivity agricultural activities, that is, away from grains and legumes and into wine, fruits and vegetables, which were much better suited to Mediterranean soil conditions and also had much better markets in high-income Northern Europe. This transfer of human resources out of traditional agriculture, painful though it undoubtedly was, contributed vastly to economic modernization, by providing urban activities with cheap and abundant labour and also by helping to finance imports of capital goods and technology through the remittances of out-migrants.

The vicinity of a more developed Northern Europe and the existence of improved methods of transportation and refrigeration provided a ready market for the primary and semi-primary products of Spanish agriculture, which was reaping the benefits of low wages and Ricardian rent situation. If nineteenth-century agricultural technology had favoured cereal production, to the detriment of the Mediterranean basin, in the twentieth century the technology moved in favour of fruit and vegetable exporters, and this benefited the Latins. The unprecedented economic growth of Northern Europe after the Second World War produced spillover effects on Southern Europe, which by this time was also better prepared from a human-capital point of view.

Institutional barriers were removed slowly but effectively. Near-universal literacy was attained in Italy and in Spain by the mid-twentieth century, although functional, as opposed to official, illiteracy no doubt is still considerable. At the present income levels in these two countries, however, secondary and university education pose more of a problem than the teaching of the three Rs. The levels of state efficiency in the provision of services and the implementation of policies, although still quite low by European standards, have also improved.

HUMAN CAPITAL AND AGRICULTURE

Demographic variables may provide a clue to the pattern of economic development. In contrast with the European norm, Spanish population grew faster in the twentieth century than in the nineteenth (table 8.1). Birth and death rates remained high (at around 3.4 and 2.9 per cent respectively) until the turn of the century, when they started a process of sustained decline which has lasted until the 1980s. As a result Spain has never had anything resembling a population explosion: at its highest point, during the 1960s, yearly growth was barely above 1 per cent, and the average for the whole 1900–85 period was 0.87 per cent. While high within the twentieth-century European context, these figures are moderate by world standards, and, furthermore, growth in the last decades of the second millennium is fast approaching zero in Spain. These averages, in any case, mask considerable fluctuations: population growth has evolved in an M shape during the twentieth century. It went up and reached a peak in the 1920s, fell afterwards due to the Depression, the Civil War, and its aftermath, recovered and reached a maximum in the 1960s, and then fell as the economy and society matured.

Migration also has been mostly a twentieth-century phenomenon. We can distinguish two types of migration: domestic and international. Domestic migration, which is more difficult to quantify, shows a clear centrifugal trend. From the Early Modern period on, and accelerating recently, Spanish population has moved away from the interior and towards the coasts, mostly the Mediterranean littoral and the Canary Islands. There is a rational economic explanation for this: agrarian productivity, transportation conditions and weather are clearly better there. There is one main exception: Madrid, the central city where the

Table 8.1 *The population of Spain, 1787–1970 (thousands)*

Year	Population	Year	Population
1787	10,393	1910	19,927
1797	10,536	1920	21,303
1821	11,662	1930	23,564
1833	12,287	1940	25,874
1857	15,455	1950	27,977
1860	15,645	1960	30,431
1877	16,622	1970	33,824
1887	17,550	1981	37,617
1897	18,109	1987	38,606
1900	18,594		

Source: Censuses

pull of being the capital and the related external economies have compensated for the physical drawbacks of the interior. International migration was particularly intense in two periods: 1905–13, when the main destination was South America (Argentina and Brazil mostly) and to a lesser extent Algeria, and total net migration was around 600,000; and 1960–73, when the main destination was North-western Europe (mostly France, Germany, Switzerland, and Britain) and the total net estimated outflow was around 2 million.

This increasingly mobile population was incorporating increasing amounts of human capital, aided no doubt by longer lifespans, which evolved from a dismal thirty-five years in 1900 to some seventy-six in the mid-1980s. Censual literacy, which stood at 27 per cent (of age ten and over) in 1860, reached 45 per cent in 1900, 73 per cent in 1930, 86 per cent in 1960, and 94 per cent in 1981. Educational enrolments increased at all levels, but naturally at different rates of speed. While elementary-school enrolments grew during the late nineteenth and especially the early twentieth centuries, secondary and university enrolments did not grow very fast until the second half of the twentieth century. The number of university and technical school students relative to total population actually diminished between 1930 and 1940 (due to the civil war, no doubt), but it more than doubled between 1960 and 1970, and doubled again in the next decade.

Another sign of modernization was the gradual abandonment of agriculture. In the nineteenth century the proportion of active population engaged in agriculture had hovered at around two-thirds. This proportion started to diminish in the second decade of the twentieth century, although in absolute figures the decline did not set in until the 1950s. The civil war again marked an interruption in this modernizing trend, which continued after 1950. The proportion in 1981 was around 14 per cent.

There is a great deal of debate about whether agricultural output per capita stagnated or grew moderately during the nineteenth century, a debate which is hard to settle for lack of trustworthy data (Harrison, 1989). There is no doubt, however, that if there ever was an 'agricultural revolution' in Spain this took place in the twentieth century, and rather late at that. The most important process taking place in the Spanish countryside during the nineteenth century probably was the series of changes in the structure of land-ownership and land tenure loosely designated in Spanish by the term *desamortización* (the approximate English equivalent would be 'disentailment').

In its broad outlines, the Spanish disentailment followed the model of the French Revolution. It consisted essentially in the expropriation (with compensation) of a large fraction of the land and buildings belonging to the church, the municipalities, and the state, and in the auctioning of these 'nationalized' lands, the proceeds of which constituted a sizeable share of the budget revenues during the middle decades of the nineteenth century. In a milder version, however, disentailment had started in Spain prior to the French Revolution.

In an article surveying the disentailment issue in general, Herr (1974) stated that the most important effect of disentailment was neither political nor social, but economic. In his opinion, the main significance of disentailment lies in the fact that it brought into cultivation large tracts of land which had been idle or underutilized before. This increase in tilled acreage was required to feed a population whose numbers had been growing steadily since the beginning of the eighteenth century. Population pressure had brought about a steady increase in the prices of food, and thereby of land. Disentailment was thus the single stone which could kill two rather threatening birds: food scarcity and famine, on the one hand, and a state of chronic financial deficit on the other.

How did this gigantic real estate operation affect agriculture and its product? The massive import of the operation is undeniable: although very rough, the best estimates calculate that disentailment caused some 10 million hectares to change hands, approximately 40 per cent of all Spanish arable land. Herr puts the value of this land at between one-quarter and one-third of the total value of Spanish real estate. Even admitting that not all disentailed land was arable, a transfer of land on such a scale is generally assumed to have allowed for a considerable expansion of cultivation and growth of output. The most commonly held explanation for this is based upon the assumption that church, state and municipalities were not very efficient agricultural entrepreneurs.

What the most trustworthy estimates reveal, however, is modest growth in total agricultural output until the very end of the century. In per capita terms there was virtual stagnation until the last quarter of the century, when competition from abroad stimulated emigration, change and productivity increases. The pattern of change was not uniform for all products. Wheat production grew faster than total output until the 1870s, when foreign competition caused rearrangements in the output mix whereby other crops (maize, oranges and fruits in general) grew faster. Rye and other, less appreciated grains (spelt, millet), stagnated relatively and in some cases declined absolutely.

Although the output mix changed during the last quarter of the century, one can say with assurance that the basic structure of Spanish agriculture remained quite stable throughout the nineteenth century. It was a typically Mediterranean structure, based upon grains (mostly wheat), olive and the vine. Wheat output was between 25 and 30 per cent of agricultural production (in value terms) and between 35 and 40 per cent of the total cultivated area. The available data show a substantial decrease of livestock (all species, although horses and mules, work animals, fared less badly) during the second half of the nineteenth century; the first signs of recovery began in the 1890s (Garcia Sanz and Garrabou, 1985, pp. 229–78).

The most probable general cause for agricultural modernization has been the depopulation of the countryside. At the turn of the century this was due to the 'agricultural depression'. The *agricultural revolution* which took place in Spain during the 1960s must be related to the great exodus towards the cities and Northern Europe. There ensued an unprecedented process of mechanization and technification: machines and fertilizers replaced labourers. There had been 4,048 tractors in Spain in 1932, 12,798 in 1950 and 56,845 in 1960; the numbers shot up to 259,819 in 1970 and 611,433 in 1984; the great jump in the number of mechanical reapers took place in the 1960s: in ten years it went from 5,025 to 31,596. In chemical fertilizers, the average application per hectare went from 17 kg in 1950 to 102 kg in 1980. Productivity naturally grew by leaps and bounds. In constant pesetas per agricultural worker it actually went down between 1930 (1,656) and 1950 (1,472), the consequence of the civil war and the disastrous ensuing policies; but then it more than doubled in the next decade, and kept increasing at ever faster rates: 3,161 in 1960, 6,354 in 1970, 15,272 in 1980. The output mix also reflected the process of modernization. Income-elastic produce such as maize, milk, meat and oranges grew faster, at the expense of more traditional crops such as wheat, olive oil and potatoes.

THE PROCESS OF INDUSTRIALIZATION

One of the most active debates in Spanish economic historiography is about whether industrialization was brought about by tariff protection. This question cannot be settled here. The traditional opinion holds that, indeed, it was protection that produced industrialization, and points to the industrial surge which took place at around the turn of the century, coinciding with the steep increase in tariff duties (mainly in 1892 and 1906). However, Carreras (1984), the author of a long index of industrial production, states that there was no such industrial spurt. His index shows steady growth from the mid-nineteenth century to the 1920s. Then it accelerates, falls precipitously in the 1930s (the Great Depression and the civil war), hovers at low levels in the 1940s and then shoots up until 1974.

Aside from a few problems at some particular periods, Carreras's is the best long-term industrial series we have, and his description seems to fit the facts much better than the other versions which saw a 'big spurt' around the turn of the century, with the onset of highly protectionist tariffs. It remains true, however, that industrial diversification and fast growth are twentieth-century phenomena in Spanish history. The only two modern industries of any import in the nineteenth century were mining and textiles, mainly cotton and wool, located overwhelmingly in Catalonia, and mostly concentrated in Barcelona and its hinterland. Mining was scattered, predominantly in the coastal areas. Spain's mineral resources were abundant and varied: iron, copper pyrites, lead, zinc and mercury were the most in demand. Since the bulk of these ores was exported, the lodes near the coast were the most readily exploited (iron in Somorrostro near Bilbao, pyrites in Río Tinto near Huelva, lead in Aguilas near Murcia, zinc in Reocín near Santander). The exception to this rule was mercury, but it was exported in metal form and its high unit price made transportation cost from Almadén in the interior worthwhile. Unlike the textile industry, which was characterized by locally owned small-size firms, there were big foreign-owned firms in mining, the best known of which are Río Tinto and Tharsis (Checkland, 1967; Harvey, 1981; Avery, 1974; Flinn, 1955). Paradoxically, at the peak of Spain's ore-exporting activity (the 1890s) its metallurgical industry remained insignificant. During the twentieth century, as its mineral reserves dwindled, its metallurgy expanded, so that today Spain is a net importer of those ores it sold abroad a hundred years ago: iron, copper, lead and zinc.

Spain's industrial development followed the patterns predicted by Walther Hoffmann's (1968) theory: the weight of consumer industries was overwhelming (about two-thirds of all industrial output) until around 1900. From then on this proportion has steadily diminished, with especial intensity in the periods of fast industrialization: the 1920s and the 1960s. When can one say that Spain became an industrial country? Manufacturing plus mining output surpassed agricultural output around 1955; manpower engaged in these same industrial sectors became more numerous than agricultural labour in the mid-1960s. Labour productivity in industry, which had almost stagnated until around 1960, more than quadrupled in the following twenty years.

The main problem of Spanish industry is that it has developed behind a stout protectionist barrier. It is doubtful, as we just saw, if protection could have brought about industry. On the other hand, excessive government intervention no doubt has caused investment to flow into unprofitable sectors, developed for ideological or prestige reasons. This has been notoriously the case with the INI (National Industrial Institute), a typical Francoist creation, inspired by the Mussolinian IRI (Institute for Industrial Recovery). From its foundation in 1941, INI invested in heavy industry with little attention to productivity or comparative costs. The upshot of this kind of policy had been a wide array of smoke-stack industries (typically iron and steel, shipbuilding, coal mining) that were very vulnerable in the tough competitive atmosphere of the 1970s and 1980s. 'Industrial reconversion', therefore, became the tenet of the Socialist government in the early 1980s: a wise but painful loss-cutting policy.

One of the consequences of this forced industrialization may have been a deviation from the natural lines of 'comparative advantage'. Such could be the case with metallurgy, mentioned above, or with oil refining, which is, somewhat incongruously, one of the Spain's main industrial branches. Other large sectors are the automotive industry, iron and steel, chemicals and the mechanical industries. Clearly within the 'comparative advantage' logic, however, food and drink processing, and the textile, shoe, leather and tailoring industries remain substantial (their combined output was about 30 per cent of all industrial output in 1986).

THE TERTIARY SECTOR AND THE ROLE OF GOVERNMENT

The reasons for speaking of 'economic modernization' rather than simply of 'industrialization' is well known: at the end of the economic development process tertiary activities take over as the largest employer and source of output. In Spain this is even more so, since the tertiary has always had a greater weight than the secondary (construction excluded). The tertiary or service sector, however, is a mixed bag of *ancien régime* and space-age activities. In Spain one of the new service sectors has been tourism, which has boomed since 1960. Apart from 'commerce', also a mixed bag including no doubt tourism-related activities, hotel-keeping and catering is the largest employer within the service sector (on a par with the public administrations).

Spain's mountainous terrain had created a transportation bottleneck since very early on. The building of a rather thin railway network in the second half of the nineteenth century contributed to the partial alleviation of this handicap. The deficiencies of the network stimulated the development of road and motor transport in the twentieth century and the road soon surpassed the railway not only in passenger but also in bulk transportation, in larger proportions than in countries of comparable size such as France or Germany.

Government has naturally had a profound influence upon the course of economic development. Spain holds a long tradition of state intervention in the economy, which goes back at least to Ferdinand and Isabella in the late fifteenth century, and which Adam Smith described and decried in *The Wealth of Nations*. Spain has honoured this tradition in the modern era and most notably in the first twenty years of the Franco dictatorship. Some of the consequences of these policies have been referred to earlier. Another consequence has been the small relative weight of foreign trade within national income, a fact which reached extremes in the first period of Francoism (in 1950, for instance, imports plus exports were less than 5 per cent of gross national product (GNP)). During the 1950s, with the first stirrings of economic recovery, it soon became evident that foreign trade was becoming a serious bottleneck; against the regime's autarkic instincts, a stabilization plan was implemented in 1959 which included currency devaluation and a certain loosening of economic controls: an economic boom ensued, and with it rapid increases in foreign trade, which by 1985 was around 30 per cent of GNP. Traditional economic historians had assumed that near self-sufficiency had favoured economic development. Recent research has demolished this assumption (Prados, 1988; Fraile, 1991).

The tax system has evolved *pari passu* with the political and economic systems. In the nineteenth century indirect taxes predominated, with a rather primitive land tax (*contribución territorial*) as the main semi-direct exaction. Tax evasion by big landowners was the rule. In the twentieth century taxes on commerce and industry increased in importance, but their estimation and collection was similar to those of the old land tax. Serious reform did not come until 1978, after the end of Francoism, with the introduction of a modern *income tax*, and, a few years later, the *value-added tax*. Evasion, however, remains pervasive.

Spain is one of the few countries in Western Europe which has never, strictly speaking, been on the gold standard. Its abundant metallic stock was gradually depleted during the nineteenth century due to its chronic balance of payments deficit. Its bimetallic system was adapted to that of the Latin Monetary Union in 1868, became limping almost immediately, and was turned into a *de facto* silver standard (in fact a fiduciary standard, since the value of silver coins remained above the value of their metal content) in 1883. Silver was not officially abandoned until the Civil War, and a remarkable monetary discipline was maintained, so that the Spanish price level did not deviate greatly from those of its neighbours; but in fact Spain's *sui generis* monetary system was a further barrier which isolated its economy from the rest of the world. With the 1959 stabilization plan (which put an end to the extreme autarkic policies of early Francoism) a process was started that gradually decreased this isolation and led to the full entry of the peseta into the European Monetary System in 1990.

The fiduciary standard facilitated the development of a banking system of the mixed variety, similar in many ways to those of Germany, Italy or Japan. Although the first central bank (the Banco Nacional de San Carlos) in Spain goes back to 1782, and more than fifty banks existed in Spain by 1860 (Tortella, 1977, 1974), its modern banking system was established in the first decades of the twentieth century. The big banks (some seven in number) were able to promote industrial enterprises thanks to their especial relations with the government and the Bank of Spain. These banks often formed consortia to sponsor semi-public companies (the Banco de Crédito Industrial; CAMPSA, the official petrol monopoly); and they usually could count on the Bank of Spain as a lender of last resort, with the added elasticity of supply that a fiduciary monetary standard provided. It must be pointed out, however, that the Bank of Spain was rather discriminating in its help, and so a series of medium-to-large banks went under in the 1920s and 1930s. Under Franco the money-creating powers of the banking system were harnessed to the inflationary financing of industry until the men who put in place the 1959 stabilization plan imposed a limited amount of monetary discipline.

The result of all this has been undeniable economic growth and increasing standards of living, although whether and when Spain will totally recover the ground it lost in the nineteenth century is something that remains to be seen.

The following tentative conclusions can be proposed from the Spanish experience: (1) the physical endowment of a country, especially in relation with the available technology, can play a crucial role in the pace and shape of its economic modernization. (2) Cultural and historical factors, as they affect its stock of human capital and thereby its ability to apply and adapt techniques, have a strategic value and, unlike natural factors, can be moulded by policies. (3) Foreign trade has played the role of hand-maiden of economic growth; conversely, protection and attempts at autarky have hindered it. (4) The interplay of economic and political factors is evident in the history of modern Spain: a state of latent or open civil war has been the concomitant of economic backwardness and of the pains of economic transition. As in most of Europe, stable democracy took root when a measure of economic maturity had been achieved.

REFERENCES

Avery, David. 1974. *Not on Queen Victoria's Birthday. The Story of the Rio Tinto Mines* (London: Collins)

Bergier, Jean-François. 1983. *Histoire économique de la Suisse*, (Lausanne: Payot)

Carr, Raymond and J. P. Fusi Aizpurua. 1981. *Spain: Dictatorship to Democracy* (London: George Allen & Unwin)

Carreras, Albert. 1984. 'La producción industrial espanola, 1842–1981: construcción de un indice anual', *Revista de Historia Económica*, 2, pp. 127–57

(ed.) 1989. *Estadísticas históricas de Aspaña, siglos XIX–XX* (Madrid: Fundación Banco Exterior)

Checkland, S. G. 1967. *The Mines of Tharsis, Roman, French and British Enterprise in Spain* (London: George Allen & Unwin)

Flinn, M. W. 1955. 'British steel and Spanish ore: 1871–1914', *Economic History Review*, 8, pp. 84–90

Fraile, Pedro. 1991. *Industrialización y grupos de presión: la economía política de la protección en España, 1900–1950* (Madrid: Alianza)

Garcia Sanz, Angel and Ramón Garrabou (eds.). 1985. *Historia agraria de la España contemporánea. I. Cambio social y nuevas formas de propiedad (1800–1850)* (Barcelona: Crítica)

Harrison, Joseph 1989 'The agrarian history of Spain, 1800–1960', *Agricultural History Review*, 37, pp. 180–7

Harvey, Charles E. 1981. *The Rio Tinto Company. An Economic History of a Leading International Mining Concern, 1873–1954* (Penzance, Cornwall: Alison Hodge)

Herr, Richard. 1974. 'El significado de le desamortización en España', *Moneda y Crédito*, 131, pp. 55–94

Hoffmann, Walther G. 1968. *The Growth of Industrial Economies* (Manchester: Manchester University Press, 2nd edn)

Lains, Pedro. 1986. 'Exportaçoes portuguesas, 1850–1913: a tese da dependência revisitada', *Análise Social*, 22, pp. 381–419

(1987): 'O proteccionismo em Portugal (1842–1913): um caso mal sucedido de industrializaçao "concorrencial" ', *Análise Social*, 23, pp. 481–503

Martin Martin, Victoriano. 1980. *Los Rothschild y las minas de Almadén (El servicio de la Deuda Publica española y la comercialización del mercurio de Almadén)* (Madrid: Instituto de Estudios Fiscales)

Nadal, Jordi. 1975. *El fracaso de la revolución industrial en España. 1814–1913* (Barcelona: Ariel)

Núñez, Clara Eugenia. 1990. 'Literacy and economic growth in Spain, 1860–1977', in Tortella, 1990

　　　1991 *La fuento de la riqueza. Educación y desarrollo económico en la España contemporánea* (Madrid: Alianza)

Pollard, Sidney. 1982. *Peaceful Conquests: The Industrialization of Europe 1760–1970* (Oxford: Oxford University Press)

Prados de la Escosura, Leandro. 1988. *De imperio a nación. Crecimiento y atraso económico en España (1780–1930)* (Madrid: Alianza)

Prados de la Escosura, Leandro and Vera Zamagni (eds.). 1991. *El desarrollo económico en la Europa del sur: España e Italia en perspectiva histórica* (Madrid: Alianza)

Reis, Jaime. 1982. 'Latifúndio e progresso tecnico: a difusao de debulha mecanica no Alentejo, 1860–1930', *Análise Social*, 18, 2, pp. 371–433

　　　1987. 'A industrializaçao num país de desenvolvimento lento e tardio: Portugal, 1870–1913', *Análise Social*, 23, pp. 207–27

　　　1989. 'O analfabetismo em Portugal no século XIX: uma interpretaçao', *Nova Economia em Portugal*, pp. 95–125

Sandberg, L. G. 1982. 'Ignorance, poverty and economic backwardness in the early stages of European industrialization: variations on Alexander Gerschenkron's Grand Theme', *Journal of European Economic History*, 11, pp. 675–97

Toniolo, Gianni (ed.) 1978. *L'economia italiana 1861–1940* (Rome–Bari: Laterza)

Tortella, Gabriel, Dir. 1974. *La Banca española en la Restauración. I. Política y finanzas,* 2 vols. (Madrid: Banco de España)

　　　1977. *Banking, Railroads, and Industry in Spain 1829–1874* (New York: Arno Press)

　　　(ed.) 1990. *Education and Economic Development since the Industrial Revolution* (Valencia: Generalitat Valenciana)

　　　1991. 'La historia económica de España en el siglo XIX: un ensayo comparativo con los casos de Italia y Portugal', in Prados de la Escosura and Zamagni 1991

Vicens Vives, Jaime. 1959. *Manual de Historia Económica de España* (Barcelona: Teide)

Zamagni, Vera. 1978. 'Istruzione e sviluppo economico. Il caso italiano. 1861–1913', in Toniolo 1978

NINE

━━━━◈━━━━

The Industrial Revolution in Sweden

BO GUSTAFSSON

IN the history of economic history as a discipline, the debate about the nature, causes, significance and speed of the industrial transformation of Western Europe during the nineteenth century belongs, since Jéréome-Adolphe Blanqui with reference to Britain in 1837 coined the metaphor 'la révolution industrielle', to the favourite perennials of the discipline. It is easy to see why. Sometimes participants of the debate have approached the subject from different ideological and/or epistemological standpoints, some seeing only continuity or trees but no wood, while others have been seeing only discontinuity and wood but no trees; sometimes they simply referred to different aspects of the transformation, some stressing causes or technology, while others were stressing effects or industrial growth; sometimes they used different but never explicit criteria for what should constitute sufficient evidence for conclusions; sometimes they interpreted identical evidence differently; sometimes discord is explained by real scientific progress. But it is no easy task to define and delimit this last-mentioned element in a debate that sometimes transgressed the limits between Babel and babble. It must be handed over to the historians of the discipline.

Only true believers in the Marshallian motto 'Natura non facit saltum' could deny that the industrial transformation of Western Europe during the nineteenth century signified a qualitative transformation of the socio-economic structure deserving to be designated an industrial revolution. For the first time in human history a regime of *sustained* growth of output per capita was introduced. As Simon Kuznets once pointed out, such a regime cannot have existed earlier for the simple reason that the pure arithmetic of growth would lead us back to levels of per capita output below the physiological minimum necessary for human existence already obtaining in early modern Europe. Secondly, this transformation also introduced, for the first time in history, machine technology based on scientific principles and including working machines, energy machines as well as transmission machines and ultimately including also machines making machines, thereby increasing physical productivity to levels never before experienced. Thirdly, the interlinkage of machines and machinery systems in the processing of goods, in combination with new modes of work organization, gave rise to the modern factory, replacing handicraft shops, manufactories and primitive craft factories in industries catering for mass markets. Fourthly, the macro-structure of the economy was transformed insofar as agriculture was replaced by industry as the dominant sector with respect to employment as well as to value added. Fifthly, with the expansion of the wage-earning strata and their counterpart, property-owning industrial and financial capitalists, the labour–capital nexus became a focal point in the social structure and its transformation. In addition, the demographic structure and its mode of operation changed with the accompanying demographic transition, replacing the old regime of high birth and high death rates with a new regime of low birth and low death rates. A quite new socio-economic infrastructure comprising railways, harbours, telegraphs, etc., saw the light of day and urban civilization expanded radically. Parallel to all this and partly as a consequence there was a large-scale social and political mobilization resulting in the rise of professional organizations, trade unions, industrial associations, modern political parties and parliamentary democracy. Whatever view we may have on the development characteristics of nature: in the nineteenth century 'industria fecit saltum'!

THE STATE OF THE DEBATE

Swedish economic historians generally have taken for granted that there was an industrial revolution in Sweden during the nineteenth century, whatever meaning they may have put into the concept. The main disagreements have centred around timing and causes. Eli F. Heckscher, the doyen of Swedish economic history, tended to see the 1870s as the great divide, because by then the *ancien régime* belonged to the past with respect to legislation, technology and organization. The period 1815–70 was according to him 'the preparation for The Great Break-Through'. He did not go further into the subject although he had written a treatise devoted precisely to the Industrial Revolution in England and on the continent.[1] Heckscher's contemporary, Arthur Montgomery, was somewhat more explicit in his book, *The Rise of Modern Industry in Sweden*, published in 1939. For him it seemed 'convenient to draw a boundary line somewhere in the 1860s, marking off the initial stages from the full development of industrialization' and those years were 'something of a landmark in Swedish economic history'. He underpinned this view with four arguments: the dwindling of agricultural supremacy; the rapid growth of the sawmill industry playing 'somewhat the same role in the industrial revolution in Sweden as the cotton trade in England'; the incipient disappearance of surplus labour caused by overpopulation; and the spread of the factory organization in new branches of industry.[2] Torsten Gårdlund, writing a few years later, tended to side with Heckscher and characterized the 1870s as the watershed. The reasons he adduced were couched in terms of the diffusion of machine technology, the role of educated engineers, the development of communications, the spatial size of markets, etc. Like his contemporaries he found no need for presenting an analytical argument. To the extent that he did feel such a need, he seems to have put prime emphasis on the role of machine technology. But then the real breakthrough, according to him, occurred from the 1890s. For only then there took place 'within a short period of time a transition to production of material goods based on machine technology causing a fundamental change in the conditions of work and life habits of the people'.[3]

Lennart Jörberg, writing twenty years later, presented a more comprehensive view, which at the same time focused on the growth record and its causes. On the one hand he characterized the expansion of the 1870s 'as an industrial revolution, if by revolution is meant a rapid change in the economic structure' and by this he seems to have had in mind primarily the rapid change taking place in industrial growth, investments and railway building. But since he was mainly interested in the growth record he, at the same time, noted that the acceleration of the growth rate took place 'during three short periods', namely in the 1850s, the 1870s and the 1890s. Jörberg was also the first scholar to make some reference to the rapid industrial growth *before* the 1850s: in iron and textile industries (after 1830). But he was inclined to play down this finding, since the 'very large percentage increases' were explained by the fact that 'the initial position was very low'. With reference to causation, the rapid growth during the 1850s and the 1870s was ascribed to international demand, while the expansion of the 1890s 'reflected the bigger demand of the home market'. In fact, he came heavily down on the side of the theory of export-led growth: 'The Swedish industrialization was a reflection of an adaption to conditions outside Sweden.' Jörberg also pointed out that the rapid industrial growth in Sweden from the 1850s was made possible by the preceding transformation of agriculture, which created food supplies for the later growth of the industrial population and also reduced structural tensions with respect to investment demand.[4] Jörberg, thus, presented a more complex picture of the industrialization process during the nineteenth century and in accordance with new approaches within the discipline he focused his story on the growth record. With respect to the problem of the Industrial Revolution he regarded the 1870s as the crucial period, although his reference to a simultaneous 'rapid change in the economic structure' remained somewhat enigmatic.

In his dissertation 'From handicraft to mechanized factories. Textiles in Sweden 1820–1870' (1979), Lennart Schön followed up the hints of Jörberg as to the early industrialization before the 1850s and showed that the agricultural revolution in fact widened the home market for industrial consumer goods, especially for textiles. In his view the importance of export demand had been exaggerated and also the suggested qualitative change in industrial growth in the 1850s became in his investigation somewhat downplayed. Ten years later Schön presented a full overview of structure and change in Swedish industry from 1800 to 1980, which today is fundamental to facts and interpretations referring to the Industrial Revolution in Sweden.[5] Was there an industrial revolution in Sweden during the nineteenth century and, if so, when did it occur?

DEFINING THE TERMS

In order to be able to answer these two questions we need a preliminary definition of the concept of industrial revolution and reliable facts on the structure and growth of industries during the course of the century. Thanks to the investigations of Lennart Schön and others we now possess a tolerably clear picture of the structure and growth of industries. As to the proper definition of an industrial revolution, there seem to be two possibilities. Either we look for a period of time when the growth rate of industrial output decisively increased and was more or less sustained on a higher level than before the breakthrough. In this case we in fact use the *effects* of the transformation as a representation of what took place. Alternatively we define the Industrial Revolution in terms of the changes making this higher growth rate of output possible, that is, its *causes*. In that case important candidates are some of those changes mentioned in the introduction, like the large-scale utilization of machine technology or mechanization; the rise and spread of modern factories and new work organization; the rise and diffusion of the labour–capital relation; and the shift from agriculture to industry in the macro-structure of the economy. For these variables we would need to assign some kind of threshold values as defining characteristics. But if in addition we want to explain why the Industrial Revolution occurred we would need some explanatory model. This model should ideally link the changes registered to production functions, investment behaviour, markets for inputs and outputs, technology, innovation, business organizations, costs and prices, socio-economic infrastructure, prevailing institutions and their changes and economic policy. The list could easily be extended but the point is clear: we need a theory of industrial revolutions.

One might ask why we must choose between taking causes *or* effects as the point of departure for description and explanation of the Industrial Revolution, since there should by definition be a connection between them? There is a connection but it could be extremely complex. In the first place, it is evidently possible for the growth rate of industry to accelerate without large-scale technical transformation or diffusion of factories, if for example output expands mainly due to increase of labour power (ultimately related to demographic changes that could be autonomous due to increasing agricultural productivity or improved medical practices, e.g. vaccination). Nor is the capital–labour relationship a necessary precondition for an acceleration or an upward shift in the growth rate of industry, as testified by several instances of rapidly growing crafts or domestic industries. Also factories often multiplied during the industrialization of many countries before they were equipped with working-machines and power engines, since the mere centralization of labour made teamwork and, thus, increased productivity possible. What is more the diffusion of the factory system was never all-embracing and never came about in one big sweep. As long as traditional modes of production (crafts and domestic industries) existed in parallel with the new mechanized factories and production processes were not completely vertically integrated, the faster growth of factory production also implied a faster growth of non-factory 'pre-industrial' production. This seems to have been a general pattern in many countries at the time when the introduction of mechanized spinning gave a boost to hand-loom weaving. Lastly, while an increasing share of industry in total employment or total value added certainly could be used as an index of industrialization, a constant share does not necessarily imply the absence of industrialization. If productivity in industry and agriculture increases at the same rate, the share of employment in industry and agriculture, respectively, should remain constant, *ceteris paribus*. Given the existence of open economies, comparative advantage in agricultural production could motivate a country to expand agricultural output and employment, while at the same time – and perhaps as a precondition for this – technological progress and mechanization in industry could develop rapidly.

Unfortunately the complexities of the problem do not end there. As we noted earlier there is a considerable bewilderment among Swedish economic historians as to the timing as well as the causes of the Industrial Revolution in Sweden. This is probably explained by the fact that, on the one hand, the growth rates of industrial output are high throughout the nineteenth century although they are particularly high in certain periods;

and that, on the other hand, there were so many different conditions underlying these high rates of growth. Presented with these two sets of difficulties one may choose between two approaches to the problem. Either we may take a broad view and regard the Industrial Revolution as a comprehensive transformation of the socio-economic structure, drawn out in time, maybe for a century. Alternatively we focus on some specific phase of shorter duration, a 'take-off' during two or three decades, either because the growth rate of industrial output is exceedingly high or because we perceive at this junction the operation of one or several of those underlying causes which we believe are instrumental in effecting the change. If we are lucky, we may find a correlation between growth rate and causes. But taking into consideration the multitude of factors in operation as well as lagged responses between causes and effects we should not expect such a correlation (especially not in comparisons between countries with widely varying environments both in time and space and, furthermore, variations in available data and thus in units of observation.

In this chapter, I shall attempt to throw some light on more than one of the alternative approaches indicated, that is, the long-term course of industrial growth as well as its possible causes. But we shall also try to identify a crucial juncture, when the acceleration of industrial growth was particularly high, and correlate this 'take-off' with its possible specific causes.

THE EVIDENCE OF HISTORICAL STATISTICS

We do not know much about industrial growth in Sweden before the early nineteenth century. Judging from export statistics the most important 'heavy' industry, iron manufacturing, was growing only slowly because of the strict governmental regulations aiming at high export prices and long-run conservation of forest resources.[6] The output from traditional textile (woollen) manufactories may have increased by 0.5 per cent per year, although the output of domestic industry may add to this figure.[7] As for growth of industrial output after the nineteenth century, the rates achieved – with the exception of the 1950s and 1960s – never approached those of the late nineteenth century. *Between 1800 and 1910 there is a century of acceleration of the growth of industrial output in Sweden.*

During the first three decades of the twentieth century – and one should note that the second decade is exceptional because of the First World War – the growth rate varies between 2 and 17 per cent per decade and the accumulated yearly growth rate is 1 per cent. Between 1830 and 1880 the growth rate per decade rises to 20–34 per cent and the accumulated yearly growth rate is 3 per cent. Between 1880 and 1910 the

Table 9.1. *Growth rate of industry and handicrafts in Sweden, 1800–1910. Output value at constant prices (1910/12)*

Year	Growth rate per decade (%)
1800/9	1.7
1810/19	10.6
1820/9	16.9
1830/9	19.8
1840/9	24.7
1850/9	33.6
1860/9	28.4
1870/9	30.9
1880/9	59.8
1890/9	77.9
1900/9	53.5

Source: L. Schön, *Industri ach hantverk 1800–1980* (Lund, 1988).

growth rate per decade rises to 54–78 per cent and the yearly growth rate is 6 per cent.[8] On the basis of these figures three observations may be made. In the first place, there is a decisive turn taking place from the 1830s onwards, when a new regime of high and sustained industrial growth is ushered in. Secondary, *not one but two* long-run spurts in industrial growth take place, the first one lasting half a century and the second one during a thirty-year period. The question is whether there is a qualitative difference between these two periods or not. An answer to this question necessitates an investigation of the underlying causes. Thirdly, the much-debated importance of the 1850s is toned down in the picture of the growth record, even if the growth rate during the 1850s is the highest of the period 1830–80 and the growth rate is higher between 1850 and 1880 (28 to 34 per cent per decade) than between 1830 and 1850 (20 to 25 per cent per decade). Table 9.1 summarizes the evidence.

If we disaggregate total industrial output it emerges that the textile industry is the fastest-growing sector during the first two decades of the first phase of accelerating growth, that is, up to the 1850s. From then and up to the 1880s the wood industries (and especially the sawmill industry) is the leading sector, with mining and metal industries following suit. During the second phase (1880–1910) the growth rate of the wood industries slowed down because of increasing raw-material costs as well as increasing competition in the world market. But on the other hand the role of the wood industries is replaced by several other fast-growing industries: in the first place, the mining and metal (engineering) industries and, towards the end of the period, the pulp and paper industries. Secondly,

Table 9.2. *The structure of industry in Sweden, 1800–1910*

Year	Percentages of output value	
	Consumer goods industries	Capital goods industries
1800	73	27
1830	70	30
1850	67	33
1880	49	51
1910	36	64

Source: L. Schön, *Industri ach Lantverk.*

two important consumer goods industries, food and textiles, are also growing very fast. It is this concurrence of several fast-growing industries that statistically explains the exceptionally high rate of growth of total industry during this phase.

Since a changed structure of industries with respect to capital and consumer goods is often associated with the Industrial Revolution, a breakdown of total industry into these two categories is interesting. This is not easily done, but it is possible to indicate the rough proportions – see table 9.2

Two things are noteworthy. In the first place, the industrialization of Sweden clearly conforms to the classical 'Hoffman–Nurkse' pattern, that is, the period of sustained growth takes off in consumer-goods industries. But since the essence of industrialization is the enlargement of fixed capital (reflected also in an increasing share of investments in national product), this role is taken over by capital-goods industries. Secondly, table 9.2 discloses some information that remains hidden in table 9.1. According to table 9.1 there is a continuous acceleration of industrial output between 1830 and 1880. But table 9.2 shows that this growth, up to the 1850s, is mainly concentrated in consumer-goods industries. After 1850 the share of capital-goods industries increases dramatically and this is explained by the wood industry (sawmill industry) taking over the role of textiles between 1850 and 1880 and the mining, metal (engineering), pulp and stone and clay industries expanding still more between 1800 and 1910.

Export markets have, as indicated earlier, been assigned a crucial role in the industrialization of Sweden. However, this view must be qualified. Up to the 1860s the export share of industry was pretty much unchanged (10–15 per cent of total industrial output), although the export share of the sawmill industry increased from about 40 to 60 per cent between 1835 and 1860. This changed between 1860 and 1880, when the export share of total industrial output increased from 10–15 per cent to more than 25 per cent. Parallel to this, the export share of the sawmill industry increased from 60 to 70 per cent and this explains most of the increase of the share of exports in total industrial output. From 1880 to the middle of the 1890s the export share of total industrial output remained constant and during the ensuing tempestuous industrial growth the export share actually fell, from 28 to 21 per cent, because of the expansion of the home market and the stagnating or falling share of exports of the sawmill industry. Thus we can hardly say that the industrialization process was triggered off by exports and, during the period of the most rapid rate of growth of industry, the export share remained constant or even fell. The expansion of external markets for Swedish industry *as an engine of growth* was mainly limited to the sawmill industry between 1830 and 1880.

From this evidence it seems fair to conclude that an industrial revolution did in fact occur in Sweden during the nineteenth century. The two problems to be solved are, firstly, its timing and, secondly, its causes. Evidently there are two candidates for the answer to the first problem: either the half-century from 1830 to 1880 or the three decades 1880 to 1910. Both these periods were characterized not only by accelerating industrial growth but also by high rates of growth compared to the preceding century and partly also the following one. Mere comparisons of growth rates *per se* cannot decide the problem. First we have to investigate the causes behind the increased growth rates.

THE FIRST PHASE OF INDUSTRIALIZATION AND ITS CAUSES: 1830–1880

In order to make a systematic investigation of the causes of the increased rates of industrial growth we should ideally devise an explanatory model explicitly stating variables and relations and capable of having its predictions tested against empirical data. It would certainly be possible to construct such a model. But it would have to be very complex, allowing not only for the incorporation of structural change but also for institutional change and various policy variables, since we believe that the Industrial Revolution and its genesis, course and outcome were essentially associated with the transformation of the whole socio-economic and political structure. The construction of such models should be encouraged and properly utilized. But here a much more modest attempt will be made implying mainly – I hope – a plausible analytical story, where at least the component parts, if not the structure, are well known to Swedish economic historians.

By the second half of the eighteenth century the socio-economic structure of Sweden had begun to change. Since the middle of the century the Estate of peasants successively gained increasing political power at the expense of the nobility, especially since 1789, and used its power to acquire land formerly held by the Crown and the nobility and by means of lowered taxed on land gained control over an increasing share of the agricultural surplus. In northern and central Sweden large tracts of forests were simply transferred from the crown to the peasants in the early nineteenth century (the so-called *avvittringen* (alienation of crown forests)), whereby public forests were privatized. At this time the economic value of these forests was negligible. But when large parts of these holdings were bought by sawmill-industry companies these assets acquired tremendous value. Even if the sawmill industry often paid only low prices for these forests (or for long-term harvesting rights) some share of the windfall profits was also pocketed by farmers. These two large-scale transfers of landed property were an important precondition for the Industrial Revolution.

On the other hand, the state had initiated, since the middle of the eighteenth century, a process of enclosure of the common fields, whereby strips of arable land and meadows were redistributed and consolidated into private holdings. The reasons why the state had to take on this role in Sweden was partly because the big landowners (who were the ones most interested in the enclosure) were relatively few and partly because the peasant strata were not yet too differentiated. Even if some peasants favoured enclosure, majorities for cooperative solutions would have been costly. The state therefore decreed that any single peasant favouring enclosure in a village should have the right to get his strips enclosed (the so-called *skiftesförord* ('enclosure-recommendation')) and other villagers had to comply. The enclosure movement started in 1757 and was promoted by new and more radical enactments in 1803 and 1827. By the middle of the nineteenth century, approximately half of the land encompassed by the enactments was enclosed.

The enclosure movement had two main effects. In the first place it spurred a growing market for land and grain, and made possible large-scale improvement and enlargement of the cultivated area as well as an increasing prosperity among certain strata of the peasantry and increased demand for labour power and capital investment. In the second place it increased the debt burden of agriculture and contributed to an immense growth of proletarians and semi-proletarians.

According to official statistics, cropland increased by 140 per cent between 1800 and 1850 and the output of grain by 120 per cent, while the agrarian population increased by only 50 per cent. If the output of potatoes, which grew extremely rapidly, is added to the output of grain (rye, oats, barley, wheat, mixed grain and leguminous plants) the increase of the agricultural output is 210 per cent. As a consequence the supply of grain of the population in agriculture, which constituted nine-tenths of the population, increased from 217 kilograms per capita in 1800 to 314 kilograms in 1850. (If the harvest of potatoes is included, the corresponding figures will be 239 and 491 kilograms.) For future industrialization, this agricultural revolution had a threefold importance. First, it made possible a surplus of food for non-agricultural occupations. Secondly, it provided a market for agricultural implements and machines: iron ploughs, sowing machines, reaping machines and threshing machines. In fact the demand of improving farmers for those products constituted the most important market for the metal industries during the nineteenth century. Thirdly, agriculture also provided industry with raw materials, a fact which is reflected in the rapid growth of the sheep stock during the first half of the nineteenth century, when the textile industry expanded.[9]

But the agricultural revolution, based upon an increased productivity of land and labour, also set free labour power for industry. Land consolidation seems to have favoured mainly the rich peasants. Many villagers, who had to move to outlying fields, became indebted freeholders or tenants of the more wealthy farmer, while squatters on forest and waste land sometimes lost their livelihood. Maybe also the rapid population growth contributed to this, although there are indications that it was mainly the well-to-do farmers in need of more labour power who increased their family size.[10] On the other hand the increased output of agriculture, especially of potatoes, made survival easier for the poor and this fact is reflected in the decreased amplitude of death rates and also a decreasing frequency of harvest failures. Whatever the causes, we know roughly the main results. Between 1751 and 1850 the number of peasant-holders (bönder) increased by only 11 per cent, while the number of small-holders (torpare) increased by 247 per cent and the number of cottagers (backstusittare) and lodgers (inhysehjon) increased by 348 per cent. As a result the social structure of the countryside was completely transformed. In 1751 the peasant-holders had made up 80 per cent of the agricultural population and the proletarian or semi-proletarian population made up the remaining 20 per cent. In 1850 the shares were 50–50.[11] Recent research has shown that about 50 per cent of the unskilled workers in the new textile factories in the early part of the nineteenth century were recruited precisely from small leaseholders and cottagers, while self-reproduction among workers' families supplied labour in the following generation.[12]

As mentioned earlier, the textile industries were the leading sector in the early phase of the first period of accelerated industrial growth in Sweden

(1830–80), that is, from 1830 to 1850. This expansion was based, on the one hand, on the increasing purchasing power of the peasant-holders and, on the other hand, on the increasing needs of the agricultural poor for income and employment opportunities. Cotton-spinning factories were introduced from the late 1820s and the traditional woollen factories grew in size. This induced expansion in domestic industries as well. Between 1826 and 1849 the total output of woollen and cotton cloth turned out by domestic industries and factories for the market increased by 4.4 per cent per year. The respective shares of domestic industries and factories in total output changed only slightly during this quarter century, from 40:60 to 33:67. If we take into account that domestic industries made an important contribution to wool spinning, it is quite clear that this early upswing in industrial growth was a combined result of factories' and domestic industries' output. Only after the introduction of factory weaving on a large scale from the 1850s did factories become dominant in textile weaving. From 1849 to 1870 the share of factory weaving increased from 67 to 88 per cent (with a corresponding decline in the share of domestic weaving).[13]

We are much more in the dark as to the causes of the relatively rapid growth of the wood industries before the 1850s, that is, at a time when the timber trade was still restricted (although the efficiency of the regulations is not known), the British market was still reserved for the North American colonies and the technology of the sawmill industry was very primitive. The transformation of agriculture implied an increased demand for timber in construction work but most of this demand was probably not registered. Judging from export statistics for sawn and planed goods, however, the sawmill industry had started to expand by this time. Between 1832/5 and 1846/50 exports more than doubled and grew at a yearly rate of 5 per cent.[14]

We are on much safer ground with respect to the development of the iron industry, which at this time was trying to overcome the difficulties encountered due to the introduction of the puddling process in England for the manufacturing of bar iron. The invention by Swedish technicians of the Lancashire method for the manufacturing of charcoal iron at low costs had as yet no practical importance. But many small improvements of traditional methods contributed to a modest growth. Between 1825 and 1855 the output of cast iron and manufactured iron and steel doubled, while the output of bar iron increased by 60 per cent – in this case paralleled by a similar increase in productivity.[15]

From this we may conclude that the increased rate of growth of industrial output during the first two decades of the growth phase 1830–1880 was mainly conditioned by the agricultural revolution and its effects on the textile industries. From the 1850s to the 1880s the picture becomes more complex and the sustained and somewhat accelerated industrial growth rate is conditioned by a combination of various factors: continued growth of the textile industries due to mechanization, the explosive development of the sawmill industry, institutional reforms and − towards the end of the period − an outburst of railway building. Also the continued growth of mining and metal industries kept up the general industrial growth rate.

During these three decades the textile industries were mechanized on a large scale, especially the cotton industry, and mechanized weaving became more common. This, however, reduced the importance of the domestic textile industry and the textile industry as a whole lost its earlier momentum. The role as leading sector was instead taken over by the sawmill industry, which was favoured by new technological advances as well as by new external conditions. In the early 1850s steam power was introduced in this industry and around 1880 about 50 per cent of the more than 100 large sawmills in the country were run by steam engines. As a consequence, production was no longer constrained by the availability of water power and could be carried on also during winter time. At the same time the sawmill plants could be located at the coast, which favoured rapid shipment of the sawn products. The share of the wood industries in total industrial output increased dramatically from about 5 per cent in 1840 to about 20 per cent in 1880 and parallel to this the export share of the sawmill industry increased from 40 to 70 per cent.

During these decades also the improvement of communications had some impact on the growth rate of industry, especially in the 1870s when more railway track was laid down than in any other decade. The railways reduced transportation costs on land routes by three-quarters or even more for heavy and bulky goods. Railway building also increased demand from the iron and engineering industries.

The continued expansion of industry would probably not have been possible in the absence of institutional reforms. From the end of the 1840s to the middle of the 1860s free trade and deregulation were carried through, the guilds were abolished, restrictions in imports and exports were removed and customs duties were reduced. As for the sawmill industry, the repeal of the Navigation Acts and the introduction of free trade in England in the 1840s were instrumental in bringing about its expansion.

But even if a series of concurring events thus contributed to the sustained and even accelerated growth of industrial output, the continued growth of agriculture still exerted its influence on industrial growth, especially in the textile and metal industries. Mechanization of industry proceeded unevenly. Investments in industry increased but most investments were made in buildings rather than in machinery. In 1860 the proportions were 90:10 and in 1880 still remained 85:15. This distribution is an important index of the rate of technical progress, since technical progress is embodied and carried by machines rather than buildings.[16]

It is to be doubted whether investments in human capital made much progress. Real wages started to rise at a sustained rate only from the late 1870s and then mainly during periods of falling prices. Before the 1850s real wages may have been stationary since the end of the eighteenth century, even if there were long-term swings around the equilibrium. The large-scale emigration from the 1850s to the First World War (about 1 million people), which brought out of the country more workers than were employed in the whole of industry, indicates that Swedish industry, at least before the 1880s, may have enjoyed a more or less unlimited supply of unskilled labour. As for the supply of skilled labour, we may only note the low level of formal technical education and the perpetual complaints of many entrepreneurs, especially in mechanical engineering, that this was a problem.

A capital market did not exist in Sweden before the end of the nine-teenth century. Therefore the capital-using railway building had to be financed by foreign loans. In the early phase of industrialization capital was mainly supplied by merchants when enterprises were established. In the daily running of business, capital was secured by ploughed-back profits. When credits were necessary, personal loans, promissory notes and − increasingly − bills of exchange were used. Firms often had to wait a long time before they were paid for deliveries, especially for goods which were expensive and included construction work. A company law was issued in 1848 but the number of joint-stock companies increased at a slow pace before the last quarter of the century. Commercial banks appeared from the 1850s but it was only in the 1870s that deposits from customers became important for their business operations. In sum: Swedish industry went through great changes during the first phase of rapid growth of the industrial output. But still important elements associ-ated with a mature industrial revolution were missing. First, modern mechanized industries were still few and the diffusion of machinery in those industries that in fact were mechanized was very uneven. Secondly, the share of investment in national product was increasing but was only 6 per cent in the 1860s and still less than 10 per cent during the hectic upswing of the 1870s. Thirdly, modern business organization and accounting were also missing and organized labour had not yet appeared on the scene. Fourthly, as already indicated, modern banking had made only a modest beginning and the banking–industry nexus, which was to become such a crucial feature of Swedish industrial structure and performance, had so far not yet been conceived. Fifthly, the socio-economic infrastructure (railways, roads, harbours) was as yet undeveloped. As late as the end of the 1860s the northern parts of the country were hard hit by harvest failure and hunger. This was, indeed, the last famine in Swedish history. But the fact that it occurred was a sign of the immaturity and unevenness of the industrial transformation that had taken place so far.

THE SECOND PHASE OF INDUSTRIALIZATION AND ITS CAUSES: 1880–1910

From the 1880s Swedish industry entered its second phase of accelerated growth and it lasted more than three decades. What is distinctive about this phase is not only that the acceleration of growth rates continues but that it continues on a qualitatively new level compared to before (see table 9.1). The growth rate almost doubled from the 1870s to the 1880s from 31 to 60 per cent per decade; it rose to 78 per cent during the 1890s and remained at 54 per cent between 1900 and 1910. As a result, the accumulated yearly growth rate of industrial output doubled, from 3 per cent between 1830 and 1880 to 6 per cent between 1880 and 1910.

There were many factors which made this high rate of growth possible. In the first place *several* industrial branches grew in parallel at a rapid rate. Even if the rate of growth of the sawmill industry slackened, its role was replaced by mining and, towards the end of the period, also by the pulp industry. In addition the metal industries, especially mechanical engineering, entered a vigorous phase and expanded both in the home market and in foreign markets On top of this, the consumer goods industries, especially textiles and food, also grew fast due to the growth of the number of wage earners and their rising real wages.

Secondly, there was a secular rise of the price level from the middle of the 1890s up to the First World War, which made it possible for firms to reap the difference between purchasing and selling prices. This mild inflation contributed to a profit inflation the most visible sign of which was a secular rise in the share of profits in value added, while the share of wages fell. This was the general pattern before the war even if the increasing productivity of labour prevented falling real wages. Thirdly, the increasing profitability of capital propelled investments and as a consequence the share of investments in national product rose to 12 per cent during the two decades 1890–1910. Since the capital/output ratio in addition fell, that is, the productivity of capital investments in relation to output increased, the necessary result was an increasing rate of growth of output. Since the rate of investment activity increased, new technology was, fourthly, more rapidly embodied in the capital equipment of industry. This can be inferred also from the increasing share of machinery investments compared to investments in buildings. It increased from 15 per cent in the 1870s to more than 30 per cent in the 1890s and more than 40 per cent in the years 1907 to 1910. [17] Even if technical progress accompanied the accumulation of capital like a shadow, once the new and more productive investments had been made they in their turn contributed to the increase of the rate of growth. Fifthly, during this phase modern business organization – reaping the benefits of economies of scale and integration – as well as joint-stock companies and developed banking also saw the light.

Judging from the leap in the level of growth, the period between 1880 and 1910 could very well be designated as the period of *the* Industrial Revolution in Sweden. If we put the prime emphasis on mechanization and technological transformation on a large scale, this was certainly the case. Industry after industry experienced mechanization and technical innovation.

In mining a series of new methods like magnetic prospecting, machine boring with steel-drills, blasting with nitroglycerine, new methods of quarrying and raising of ore by rail and elevators run by electric machines, implied a complete revolution from the 1870s and the following decades. Thanks to these and other inventions, labour productivity in iron-ore mining increased from 122 tons per year between 1871 and 1875 to 598 tons between 1911 and 1915, that is, a yearly cumulative productivity increase of 4 per cent. In the further processing of iron ore, dressing by hand was replaced from the 1880s by mechanical methods. From the 1890s magnetic separators and calcination of iron-ore dust were also introduced. As a result of these and other changes, output of iron ore increased from 0.65 million tons in 1870 to 7.5 million tons in 1913, that is, a yearly growth of 6 per cent.

The main share of this growth took place from the 1890s and was conditioned by export demand, especially from Germany, where the rapidly increasing iron consumption necessitated increasing imports of iron ore. Output of pig-iron increased likewise (it more than doubled between 1870 and 1913) thanks to a continuous improvement of blast-furnaces (by increased size and recycling of gases), increased capacity utilization over the year and a spatial concentration of plants into larger units, which was made possible by the transportation of charcoal on the newly built railways. In pig-iron production, as well as in most other industrial branches using raw materials, raw-material intensity (inputs per unit of output) was also lowered.

Swedish industry was at the forefront in the development of the new ingot-steel production associated with the methods of Bessemer, Martin and Thomas, and Swedish inventors skilfully adapted them to specific Swedish conditions, even if the Lancashire method for the manufacture of bar iron (wrought iron) remained dominant until the 1890s. A large-scale centralization of ironworks took place (in Sweden called 'the Great Ironworks Death'), diminishing their number from 381 in 1870 to 140 in 1913, while output per ironworks increased tenfold. Still more impressive was the expansion of processed iron-and-steel products: the introduction of rolling mills for manufacturing plates, rails, tubes, wires and nails – further processed into a great variety of machine-made products such as files, locks, picks, spades, knives, etc., by means of forge hammers and forge presses.

Mechanical engineering, with a tradition reaching back to the 1830s, partly due to intensive stimuli from British mechanical engineering, entered an impressive trajectory after the 1870s. The core of this expansion was determined by the introduction and production of an almost infinite variety of manufacturing machines: drawing-engines, rolling mills, steam hammers, sawing machines, boilers, furnaces, larger and faster lathes (including the new rotary lathe), planing and boring machines. Still more important were the new and highly efficient cutting and grinding machines replacing hand filing and allowing a much more flexible shaping of metals at a much faster rate than before. This implied the disappearance of the armies of hand filers, whose presence had up to then characterized mechanical engineering. Both the rotary lathe and the cutting machine, equipped with heat-resistant steel alloys and high-speed steel, increased the scope and productivity of metal engineering enormously. In combination with the new measurement implements, invented by C. E. Johansson, machines and machine products could be manufactured much more precisely than before increasing their efficiency. This also paved the way for standardization and, thus, for mass production. The markets for the new products were provided by the demand from agriculture for ploughs, harrows, harvesting and threshing machines, but first and foremost by internal – and increasingly also external – industries which demanded steam engines, water-wheels and turbines for the transformation and transmission of energy, locomotives, coaches, iron ships for transportation, as well as the demand for processing machines originating within various industries, including mechanical engineering itself.

The hallmark of Swedish mechanical engineering became, from the 1890s, the foundation of new specialized branches based on highly successful Swedish inventions, which gave some Swedish multinational companies a prominent international position during the twentieth century. Among these were Gustaf de Laval's milk separator and steam turbine, L. M. Ericsson's many contributions to the electrical industry, the three-phase electric motor of Jonas Wenström, the spirit-stove of F. W. Linqvist, Gustav Dalén's contributions to lighthouse technology and the ball-bearings invented by L. J. Wingqvist. The key to success seems to have been a combination of inventiveness, efficient business organization and a conscious specialization on high-quality products for stable markets.

The pulp and paper industries also became a field of an intensive inventive activity. During the 1880s the Swedish inventor Alvar Müntzing successfully initiated the manufacturing of chemical pulp (according to the so-called sulphate method, but improved by a new cleaning procedure), which resulted in a very tough and cheap paper. But it was the improvement during the 1870s of the sulphite method – based on sulphuric acid and lime – due to the chemist C. D. Ekman, which became the dominant technology. In the 1880s fifteen factories were founded and in the following two decades another twenty-four and thirty respectively. Between 1892 and 1913 the output of pulp increased twelvefold, while labour productivity more than doubled. The pulp industry was also favoured by the ample supply of low-priced low-quality timber and waste products from the sawmill industry as well as by the fact that the technology admitted pronounced scale economies and vertical integration with the sawmill and papers industries. The output of the paper industry increased tenfold from the late 1880s to 1913 and the manufacturing process became more or less completely mechanized.

Even if the capital goods industries, as indicated by table 9.2, grew most rapidly, the consumer goods industries also expanded and became mechanized. In the cotton industry ring-spinning replaced throstle-spinning from the 1880s and in weaving the introduction of the Northrop power loom implied a technical breakthrough. The number of spindles per worker, which had increased slowly from 28 in 1845 to 36 in 1873 jumped to 62 in 1888 and to 88 in 1912. The most expanding market for this new technology was provided by mass consumer demand for fustian, calico, brown-cloth, etc. Also the woollen industry went through a comprehensive mechanization from the 1890s and this decade also saw the rise of the factory in the hosiery industry. Around the turn of the century factory-made products dominated products from domestic industries within textile manufacturing.

Parallel to this, shoe manufacturing was transformed from a craft to factory production: the number of factories increased from some ten in the early 1890s to almost ninety in 1913 and the work of shoemakers was reduced to the repairing of shoes. Likewise food manufacturing became mechanized and industrialized from the 1890s with the introduction of steam-powered flour mills, mechanized bakeries and – by the 1880s – sugar factories, which at the turn of the century supplied nearly the whole demand for sugar in the country. The growth may be gauged from the per capita consumption of sugar, which increased from 8 kilograms in 1880 to 27 kilograms in 1913. Breweries and distilleries were also mechanized.

Stone and clay industries present a similar picture. While the building and construction activity increased demand for bricks and cement, the increasing level of living allowed people to substitute for household implements made of wood tableware made of glass and china. In the glass industry, where the expansion started in the 1870s, the important technical innovations in processing were introduced from the 1880s with gas furnaces, which lowered inputs of fuel, made possible a higher and more even temperature and reduced the time of melting. The brick industry, which earlier was a rural side-line activity, was mechanized in the 1890s with machines for mixing clay, pressing bricks and burning bricks in large ring-furnaces. In cement manufacturing rotating furnaces were introduced and from the early 1890s up to 1913 the output of cement per worker quadrupled. The increasing demand for bricks and cement originated from urbanization, which started from the 1870s, and the construction of dwelling-houses, factories, walls, bridges, embankments, dams, tanks and roofs and replacing wood, stone and turf as building materials.[18]

Lastly, power industries were also transformed during this phase. From the 1880s electric light was successively introduced in industries, public institutions, restaurants, shops and also in the urban dwelling-houses of the middle class (electric light arrived in the countryside only in the 1930s). Electric engines were introduced in industry from the end of the 1880s and this was a fact of far-reaching importance. First, it implied that water power regained its earlier role as a power source. Secondly, the innovation by Jonas Wernström (patented in 1889) of the generation of three-phase alternating electric current implied that the large waterfalls in northern Sweden could be utilized for energy-intensive industries like pulp. Thirdly, electric engines were cheaper than steam engines and promoted the growth of small enterprises. Fourthly, they also freed factories from the costly, bulky and dangerous transmission mechanisms associated with one central steam engine which, in addition, caused large losses in energy utilization. Even if some energy was lost also in the transmission of electric current, electric motors – in contradistinction to steam engines – only used the exact amount of energy required by the operation of the working machines, while the remaining energy was transferred to other machines or discharged the generator.[19]

The striking element of innovative activity together with the general trend of mechanization during the industrial spurt between 1880 and 1910, resulting in a high level of productivity of labour and capital, can also be inferred indirectly from the trend of relative prices. The more marked the rate of technical transformation was, the higher the productivity of labour and capital, the more relative prices fell and markets expanded and the faster output grew. While total industrial output grew by 5.1 per cent between 1888/90 and 1910/12, mechanical engineering, pulp and paper, power and some other industries grew by 10.4 per cent, while, at the other end of the scale, glass and several food industries grew by 2.8 per cent. But there were also industries experiencing rapid technical transformation, which were characterized by rising relative prices – like ironworks, metal manufacturing, stone and clay and textile industries. In those cases the cost-reducing effects of technical progress were countervailed either by strong demand effects, as in the case of iron-ore production and in the industries just mentioned, or, by increasing raw material costs, as in the case of wood industry.[20]

During this phase business organization was transformed, too. At least in some large firms rational cost calculation and planning started to be applied and the joint-stock company emerged as an organization for mobilizing capital and spreading risk. The number of joint-stock companies increased from 657 in 1881 to 2,521 in 1908 and paid-up capital increased from 283 to 1,215 million crowns, that is, fourfold. Parallel to this development, the role of merchant capital for founding and financing firms declined. While the traditional *Verleger* disappeared, the financier entered the scene side by side with the captain of industry. Now commercial banking also started to have an impact on the financing of industry. The deposit business of the banks doubled during the 1890s and doubled again during the following decade, when also the stock exchange emerged as an institution in the capital market. Industrial enterprises increasingly raised money from the banks with industrial shares as security: on the average one-third of all bank loans to industry and as much as one half or more among the few big banks. Still, it would be an exaggeration to claim that banking capital at this time monitored industry. The important Swedish industry–banking nexus became a reality only after the First World War and the inflation–deflation experience.[21]

OUTCOMES OF THE INDUSTRIAL REVOLUTION

On the eve of the First World War the Industrial Revolution in Sweden was an established fact. The demographic transition had been consummated. Agriculture had been modernized and partly mechanized (the large-scale mechanization of agriculture took place in the 1930s). Industrialization had to a large extent taken place in the countryside. In fact more industrial workers, absolutely as well as relatively, lived in the countryside in 1913 compared to 1870. Still, urbanization meant that every fourth citizen in 1913 lived in a town compared to every eighth in 1870. While only 15 per cent of the gainfully employed population had been employed in industry in 1870, the share had increased to 32 per cent in 1913. Within industry a large-scale mechanization had taken place with respect to power engines and transmission and working machines. The share of investments in national product had increased and was well above 10 per cent. Capital goods industries had taken over the earlier role of consumer goods industries as the dominant sector in the industrial structure. Industrial relations were no longer dominated by crafts or patriarchical domestic industry but by the capital–labour nexus.

Working hours, which around 1870 were still largely set by the traditional twelve-hour day inherited from agriculture and pre-industrial habits, decreased to ten hours on the average around the turn of the century and remained more or less at that level until the introduction of the eight-hour day in 1919. Real wages, which before the 1860s had shown no marked long-term tendency to rise – and even declined for extended periods – increased on the average by 1–2 per cent per year after the 1870s, although with wide variations between industries, between permanently and seasonally employed workers – we know little about the wages of the last-mentioned category – and between periods of upswing and depression. In fact, real wages increased (for those employed) mainly during periods of depression and stagnation when costs of living were lowered. Housing conditions for industrial workers in Sweden were poor and most families had at their disposal only one single room, a combined kitchen-living-room-bedroom, while skilled and permanently employed workers sometimes were provided with one room and a separate kitchen. The usual fare of the pre-industrial age, consisting of porridge, gruel, potatoes, salted herring and rye bread, still dominated food habits. But wheat bread, sugar, margarine and salted pork and even milk, butter and occasionally cheese and meat were new ingredients in the quarter of a century before the First World War.

The years after the 1880s also witnessed the rise of organized labour and organized capital (between 1889 and 1902) and what Strindberg, the novelist, christened 'The New Society' (Det Nya Riket) had been ushered in by the first industrial mass strike among sawmill workers in 1879. This strike was wholly defensive and so also was the General Strike of 1909, which was the largest strike ever experienced up to then in the industrial world. Even though both strikes ended in defeat, organizing activity among workers during these decades completely transformed the nature of the labour contract. Collective agreements had not yet won the day in all industries (agricultural workers had to wait until the 1930s). But before the outbreak of the First World War most big industries were covered. Thereby working conditions were normalized; minimum wages underpinned the whole wage structure; wage rates no longer varied over the year; and piece rates were fixed in written contracts, as were dates for pay-day. Also rates for overtime work were agreed upon. First and foremost, collective agreements normalized working hours. None of this was realized in one big sweep and the transformation was uneven as between industries and between large and small firms. But the rate of change was distinctive and the trend was clearly set. Also, with respect to industrial relations the phase of industrial revolution between 1880 and 1910 brought something fundamentally new and lasting. Modern industrial society was institutionalized.

CONCLUDING COMMENTS

Was there an industrial revolution in Sweden during the nineteenth century? If so, when did it take place? What were its causes? What was specific about the Industrial Revolution in Sweden? In conclusion I would like to answer these questions. I have commented earlier upon the difficulties encountered in trying to define the meaning of the concept 'industrial revolution'. But whatever (reasonable) meaning we assign to the concept, it is clear that an industrial revolution did take place in Sweden. When the rate of growth of industrial output started to accelerate from the 1830s it was mainly conditioned by the preceding agricultural revolution providing a market for simple industrial implements and consumer goods, like textile products. Around the 1850s internal and external liberalization of trade provided the sawmill industry with a great opportunity which was seized. Parallel to this and since the 1830s a slowly and unevenly proceeding mechanization and a process of technical improvement were preparing the ground for a more comprehensive industrialization, which also was conditioned by a growing supply of labour power and savings and improved communications. From the 1880s the rate of growth of industrial output increased markedly compared to the first wave of industrialization. Several industries grew rapidly in parallel, all-round mechanization affected industries, the share of investment increased, the capital stock of industry – especially machinery investments – was thus renewed more rapidly, a series of epoch-making industrial innovations were made, new sources of rich raw materials were tapped and external and internal demand expanded. In this phase, the preceding industrialization was transformed into a real industrial revolution. At its core was the large-scale mechanization of industry and the increased rate of capital accumulation, which took place in a favourable environment provided by a unique innovative activity, exploitation of natural resource rents and expanding markets. These conditions gave Swedish industry the leading role in the Western European growth league from the 1870s.

The specific attribute of the Industrial Revolution in Sweden is, first, that it took off in a country which was one of the poorest in Western Europe with respect to the level of living. Secondly, that its course was so compressed in time after a lengthy period of preparation. Thirdly, that its success was made possible by a combination of favourable internal and external conditions. The favourable external conditions were provided by an industrially more advanced Western Europe in need of what Swedish industry could supply: sawn products, iron ore, pulp and engineering products. The still unsolved puzzle is how it came about that Swedish industry was capable of utilizing those favourable external conditions and adding an internal engine of growth to the external one. The *histoire raisonnée* – to use a felicitous concept coined by Schumpeter – given here has mainly summarized the descriptive features of the process within a low-brow analytical framework. There are still many empirical questions that remain unanswered. And the systematic rigorous causal analysis of the process is a still more difficult issue for future research.

NOTES

1 Eli F. Heckscher, *Industrialismen. Den ekonomiska utvecklingen sedan 1750* (Stockholm, 1953); Eli F. Heckscher, *Svenskt arbete och liv* (Stockholm, 1941), p. 23.

2 Arthur Montgomery, *The Rise of Modern Industry in Sweden*. Stockholm Economic Studies, no. 8 (London, 1939), p. 41.

3 Torsten Gårdlund, *Industrialismens samhälle* (Stockholm, 1942), p. 60.

4 Lennar Jörberg, 'Structural change and economic growth: Sweden in the 19th century', in *Economy and History* (Lund, 1965), vol. VIII.

5 Lennart Schön, *Från hantverk till fabriksindustri. Svensk textiltillverkning 1820–1870* (Lund, 1979), chap. 6, pp. 75–83 and *passim*.

6 Karl-Gustaf Hildebrand, *Swedish Iron in the 17th and 18th Centuries. Export Industry before the Industrialization*, Jernkontorets Bergshistoriska Skriftserie, 29 (Stockholm, 1992). See also Artur Attman, *Svenskt Järn och Stål 1800–1900*. Jernkontorets Bergshistoriska Skriftserie, 21 (Stockholm, 1986).

7 Olle Krantz 'Production and labour in the Swedish manufactories during the 18th century, I–II', in *Economy and History*, Ekonomisk-historiska Institutionen (Lund, 1976), vol. XIX: 1–2. Since out-work, organized by manufactories, was not included, Krantz's estimates refer only to centralized production carried on in manufactories covered by the specific legal-administrative definition of what a manufactory was. On this point, see Klas Nyberg, 'Köpes: Ull. Säljes: Kläde. Yllemanufaturens företagsformer i 1780-talets Stockholm'. Doctoral Dissertation, Ekonomiskhistoriska institutionen, Uppsala 1992. Nyberg shows

that out-work dominated in the preparatory processes in woollen manufacture; in wool-spinning more than half and in worsted-spinning the whole output was manufactured by out-workers.

8 Lennart Schön, *Industri och hantverk 1800–1980, Historiska Nationalräkenskaper för Sverige.* Skrifter utgivna av Ekonomisk-historiska föreningen i Lund, vol. LVIX (Lund, 1988).

9 *Historisk statistik för Sverige, II. Väderlek, Lantmäteri, Jordbruk, Skogsbruk, Fiske t.o.m. 1955.* Statistiska Centralbyrån, SCB (Stockholm, 1959).

10 Christer Winberg, *Folkökning och proletarisering. Kring den sociala strukturomvandlingen på Sveriges landsbygd under den agrara revolutionen* (Lund, 1977).

11 *Ibid.*

12 Anita Göransson, *Från familj till fabrik. Teknik, arbetsdelning och skiktning i svenska fabriker 1830–1877* (Lund, 1988), especially chap. 7, pp. 207–40.

13 Schön, *Från hantverk till fabriksindustri.* The shares tabulated in the text are calculated on the basis of the historical statistics presented in the Appendix, pp. 205–6.

14 Montgomery, *The Rise of Modern Industry in Sweden*, p. 89.

15 Yngve Fritzell, 'Yrkesfördelningen 1825–1835 enligt Tabellverket och andra källor', *Statistisk Tidskrift* (Stockholm), Årg. 14 (1976), 3.

16 Olle Krantz and Carl-Axel Nilsson, *Swedish National Product 1861–1970. New Aspects on Methods and Measurement* (Lund, 1975), p. 170.

17 *Ibid.*

18 Gårdlund, *Industrialismens samhälle*, especially chap. 2, which gives a superb overview of mechanization and innovation in Swedish industry after 1870.

19 E. Linder, *Den svenska mekaniska verkstadsindustrins utveckling intill krigsutbrottet* (Stockholm, 1923).

20 Jonas Ljungberg, *Priser och markandskrafter i Sverige 1885–1969.* Skrifter utgivna av Ekonomisk-historiska Föreningen, vol. LXIV (Lund, 1990).

21 Karl Gustaf Hildebrand, *I omvandlingens tjänst. Svenska Handelsbanken 1871–1955* (Stockholm, 1971). See also Ernst Söderlund, *Skandinaviska Banken i det svenska bankväsendets historia 1864–1914* (Stockholm, 1964).

NOTE

In addition to the references in the notes, I would like to mention some additional works, which have influenced my approach to the Industrial Revolution in Sweden: (1) Mats Isacson, *Ekonomisk tillväxt och social differentiering 1680–1860. Bondeklassen i By socken, Kopparbergs Län,* Uppsala Studies in Economic History, 18 (Stockholm, 1979). In this regional study the author shows not only the tremendous agricultural progress that took place in this parish in middle Sweden before the Industrial Revolution but also how this progress conditioned and was conditioned by the incipient proto-industrialization in domestic industries serving agriculture. (2) The close connection between agriculture and the early expansion of textile industries is vividly put forth in Christer Ahlberger, *Vävarfolket. Hemindustrin i Mark 1790–1850,* Institutet för lokalhistorisk forskning. Skriftserie no. 1 (Göteborg, 1988). This study is focused on the leading textile districts in south-west Sweden.

(3) The causes of the decline of domestic pig-iron production in a leading mining district in middle Sweden after the 1830s and its replacement by large-scale iron works are investigated by Ture Omberg, *Bergsmän i hyttelag. Bergsmannanäringens utveckling i Linde och Ramsberg under en 10-årsperiod från mitten av 1700-talet*, Jernkontorets Bergshistoriska skriftserie 28 (Uppsala, 1992). Omberg shows that the structural shift was conditioned by the fact that domestic producers could not put up with the quality requirements on more competitive export markets. (4) For the early history of industry financing in Sweden during the industrial revolution Torsten Gårdlund, *Svensk industrifinansiering 1830–1913* (Stockholm, 1947) is still indispensable. Gårdlund was the first economic historian who showed the instrumental importance of merchant capital for the rise of industrial firms. (5) Income distribution including wage:profit ratios is described and analysed in Karl-Gustaf Jungenfelt, *Löneandelen och den ekonomiska utvecklingen* (Uppsala, 1966). (6) Johan Söderberg, Ulf Jonsson and Christer Persson, *A Stagnating Metropolis. The Economy and Demography of Stockholm 1750–1850* (Cambridge, 1991) summarizes much useful information on pre-industrial and early industrial Sweden. It also lends support to the received view of Sweden as a poor country around the 1850s, compared to other Western European nations. (7) With respect to wages in industry and agriculture from 1860 to 1930 we still have to rely on G. Bagge, E. Lundberg and I.

Svennilsson, *Wages in Sweden*, I–II. Stockholm Economic Studies, 3 (London, 1933). Recent economic-historical research has added to and in some respects modified the general picture arrived at in this work. But no new overall assessment has as yet been made. The problem with *Wages in Sweden* is that the series mainly refers to permanently employed workers, who represented an insignificant minority. Very little is known about casual labour or unemployment before 1900.

TEN

Austria: industrialization in a multinational setting

HERBERT MATIS

IN his last longer book the late Alexander Gerschenkron wrote: 'the Austrian case enriches our general approach to, and our comprehension of, industrial history and, beyond it, of problems of economic development in which not just the economists but all social scientists maintain keen interest' (Gerschenkron, 1977, p. 3). This fact is perhaps one of the reasons why research into the economic history of the Habsburg Monarchy has made such remarkable progress during the last decades. This geographic area has attracted the attention not just of Austrian scholars (März, 1968; Sandgruber, 1978; Matis, 1972; Matis and Bachinger, 1973), but also of (primarily) American 'cliometricians' (Gross, 1966; Rudolph, 1976; Huertas, 1977; Good, 1984; Komlos, 1983 and 1989) who have published a number of works on the subject – not least out of an interest in comparing the historical and economic process of growth. Indeed, it is possible to use this body of work as the basis for drawing some preliminary conclusions. It also clearly emerges, however, that the assessment of the Austrian phenomenon of industrialization remains controversial.

Anyone dealing with Austrian history is first confronted with the difficulty of defining their terms of reference, because not only is the concept of 'Austria' itself so diverse, but also its geographic delineation: the size of the state changed considerably over the years, as did its form of government, and even the various terms used to refer to it. As a result, constructs like 'Habsburg Empire' and 'Danube Monarchy' have to be used to describe the chronological developments of the 'multinational' empire. Initially included were the so-called German hereditary dominions (*Erblande*) which included the Alpine region up to where it joined the Karst district, a small portion of the Adriatic coast and the territories under the Bohemian crown. The collapse of the Holy Roman Empire in 1804 and the subsequent creation of the Austrian Empire extended the term 'Austria' to define the sum of the complex of different countries under Habsburg rule. Following the Ausgleich – or Dual Compromise – with Hungary in 1867, the term 'Austria' was used for the western 'Cisleithanian' half of the Austro-Hungarian Monarchy, whilst terms like 'Habsburg Monarchy', 'Danube Monarchy', 'Dual Monarchy' or 'Austria-Hungary' were used to refer to the state as a whole.

The Habsburg Monarchy was, on the one hand, a European great power and an important political factor in the centre of Europe, and, on the other, an extremely complex historical structure, on account of its complicated conception of national convivium and internal socio-economic disparities. This multinational Empire – the second largest in geographic area, and possessing the third largest population in Europe (Bolognese-Leuchtenmüller, 1978, p.1) – was mainly held together by dynastic ties. The Habsburg Monarchy, however, was not only extremely heterogeneous in terms of geography, religion, ethnicity and culture, but also socially and economically. As such, it reflected, rather like a microcosm, the diversity of the European situation and 'the simultaneity of dissimilarities'. This applied both to the state as a whole and, more narrowly, to the western 'Cisleithanian' half of the Empire which, after the Dual Compromise with Hungary in 1867, bore the complicated official definition of the 'Kingdoms and Lands represented in the Reichsrat' (Imperial Parliament). The unofficial territorial designations for the western and eastern halves of the Empire, 'Cisleithania' and 'Transleithania', were derived from the Leitha, a river in eastern Austria and north-west Hungary, flowing about 180 km north and east to the Danube.

Within the confederation there lived no fewer than eleven different peoples who had been frequently intermixed as a result of various historical phases of settlement and migration: within its borders, at the intersection, as it were, of the north–south and west–east European economic divide, were united regions with starkly varying levels of development. To this day, historians cannot even agree on whether the internal regional inequalities actually increased or decreased in the nineteenth century. Whilst some regions, for example northern Bohemia and northern Moravia, but also the Vienna Basin, Styria and, westernmost, Vorarlberg, were able to participate, almost from the very beginning, in Western developments and the European process of industrialization, by far and away the largest area – in particular all the eastern provinces, but also parts of the southern crownlands – maintained, for the most part, traditional pre-industrial agrarian forms of life. This resulted, on the one hand, in that contradictory overall impression which can no doubt best be described in terms of Alexander Gerschenkron's concept of 'relative economic backwardness' (Gerschenkron, 1965), whilst, on the other, we can discern in the economic history of the Habsburg Monarchy numerous

phenomena characteristic of the mutual interplay between the 'centre'
and the 'periphery', as described by, amongst others, Immanuel
Wallerstein (1974). In this context the relationship between Austria and
the more advanced regions of Western Europe, as well as that between
Austria and Hungary, must be taken into consideration, as must the
domestic dependence of the 'Cisleithanian' regions on the political and
commercial centre of Vienna. In most European countries, both the
struggle for a bourgeois-liberal constitutional state and the collective social
phenomenon of nationalism were closely bound up with the socio-
economic structural change which took place in the wake of the process
of industrialization and which, in turn, provided the modernization
process with additional impetus. In the Austrian dynastic and multinational state, however, nationalism, in particular, with its centrifugal
tendencies, had a corrosive and destabilizing effect. Industrialization as a
national goal, which the Magyars, who did not have to consider their own
national minorities to the same extent, were able to pursue as a weapon
in the struggle to increase their own level of independence, was absent in
the western half of the Empire. In addition there were obstacles to a
speedy process of modernization which can mainly be attributed to
natural geographic factors and historically determined socio-economic
deficiences. Above all, it was the social dominance of the traditional aristocracy and the minimal presence of commercial capital which hindered
the internal integration of the economic area and slowed the pace of the
modernization process.

A further factor of importance was that the process of modernization,
and the social and economic change which accompanied it, was inevitably
directed against the same traditional forces whose devotion and ties to the
hereditary ruling dynasty ultimately kept this highly complex state
together. In view of the increasing nationalism, the internal political and
socio-economic balance became an existential necessity for the maintenance of the multinational Empire. In the context of state financial and
economic policy this naturally resulted in a kind of 'dispersion of
resources' (Wysocki, 1975). This also provides the framework in which the
Imperial policies of Austria-Hungary in its role as a major power are to
be viewed, and which took on a new quality in the era of so-called 'organized capitalism'. It was these policies which served as a necessary safety
valve to reconcile national and social friction, although they proved themselves to be incompatible with financial forces.

ECONOMIC GROWTH IN A MULTINATIONAL SETTING

More recent studies based on the methods of national accounting revealed that modern economic growth had already begun as early as the second quarter of the nineteenth century, and that it can be dated to the period 1825–30. According to Anton Kausel's calculations (1979), the average annual rates of increase in the national product in the period 1830–1913 oscillated between 1.1 per cent and 2.2 per cent. His calculations for the period 1830–70 revealed a growth in the gross domestic product (GDP) (measured in 1913 prices) of 1.11 per cent annually, and of 2.16 per cent between 1870 and 1913, which correspond to an annual rate of growth of 1.89 per cent for the whole period of eighty-three years. Real per capita income increased between 1830 and 1913 by 2.1 times (0.9 per cent annually). Whereas the annual rates of increase of 0.45 per cent in the years 1830 to 1870 were relatively modest, they rose to 1.32 per cent in the period 1870–1913. By comparison, the nominal income (GDP nominal) rose between 1830 and 1913 by 8.5 times (2.5 per cent annually) and per inhabitant by 4.6 times (1.9 per cent annually), whereby almost exactly half was accounted for by increased prices. David Good (1984) gives for the period 1870–1910 an annual rate of growth in Austria of the real per capita national product of 1.5 per cent, in Hungary 1.3 per cent, and 1.4 per cent for the Habsburg Monarchy as a whole. According to these figures Austria's pace of growth would have put it in third place in Europe behind Sweden (with 2.0 per cent) and Norway (with 1.6 per cent) and therefore ahead of the 1.3 per cent of Russia, Germany and Switzerland.

These quantitative statistics and macroeconomic indicators of economic development, however, have been challenged, and Komlos and Sandgruber, amongst others, have drawn attention to the fact that the data used by Kausel, essentially taken from Rudolph and Gross, are fraught with problems, such that the quantitative basis for the assessment of economic development up to the First World War remains extremely unreliable. Whilst, all things considered, the Habsburg Monarchy as a whole corresponded to the model of an 'industrialized agricultural state' (Koren, 1961, p. 234), the process of industrialization commenced in the major parts of the western half of the Empire in the first half of the nineteenth century, and this often led to the backwardness of the agrarian hinterland being overlooked; this 'partial modernization' is also expressed in the change in the contribution of the individual sectors of the economy to the national product. Whilst in 1850, agriculture was still able to contribute 57.1 per cent, industry 27.7 per cent, and services 15.2 per cent to the net national product (NNP), the corresponding figures for 1911 to

Table 10.1. *The distribution of income 1911 to 1913*

Region	Percentage of income per capita	Austrian crowns
Alpine Lands	33.8	790
Bohemian Lands[a]	42.8	630
Galicia	13.7	250
Southern Tyrol, Trieste and Istria	4.8	450
Slovenia and Dalmatia	3.3	300
Bukovina	1.6	300
	100.0	520

[a] Bohemia, Moravia, Silesia – known also as the Czech Lands
Source: Kausel, Németh and Seidel, 1965, p. 31

1913 are agriculture 33.65 per cent, industry 46.69 per cent, and services 19.66 per cent (Kausel, 1979, pp. 689–91).

The regionally disparate development referred to in the foregoing can be equally impressively documented with reference to the retrospective estimates of national income for 1911/13 (see table 10.1).

The quantitative analyses do prove that the development of the infra-structure promoted the inter-regional flow of financial and human capital brought a narrowing of regional differences in commodity prices, interest rates and wage-levels. The data show, however, that the economic union inherent in the reforms during Absolutism and neo-Absolutism was becoming a reality (Berend and Ránki, 1970, p. 33).

Statistical data for occupations reveal the extent to which agriculture shaped the ecomomic base of the Habsburg Monarchy. In 1869, 67.2 per cent of all workers in the already more developed western half of the Empire were active in agriculture and forestry; this percentage only fell slowly, namely to 62.4 per cent by 1890, to 58.2 per cent by 1900 and to 53.1 per cent by 1910. The share of those working in industry and trade was correspondingly slow to increase, with a more rapid increase in the number of workers only taking place in the tertiary sector. Agriculture's high share of the economically active population in 'Cisleithania' consti-tuted a fundamental difference to Germany, because there, in the second half of the nineteenth century, the share of the agricultural population fell by more than 30 per cent, while that of industrial workers rose by 37 per cent. Conversely, the corresponding figures for Austria are 20 per cent and 22 per cent, respectively, and therefore throw a very characteristic light on the different pace of development in the two states (Möller, 1974, p. 79).

The comparison is rather different if one only refers to the developed Alpine Lands and the Bohemian Lands (Bohemia, Moravia, Silesia). This would give us proportional figures of those in industry and trade in 1910 of 37.5 per cent in Germany, 27.1 per cent in the Austrian Alpine Lands and 35.2 per cent in the Bohemian Lands. This, however, only goes to underline the domestic disparity in the Danube Monarchy, because the share of the population in trade and industry was correspondingly low in the other regions.

All previous attempts to identify a Rostowian take-off or Gerschen-kronian spurt-like development in Austria can be described as relatively unconvincing. Some historians date the beginnings of industrialization in the Bohemian and Alpine regions as early as the turn of the eighteenth to the nineteenth century, and Komlos related the transition to industrial development and economic modernization to the Malthusian crisis at the end of the eighteenth century: the economic reforms of Maria Theresa and Joseph II ended the age-old Malthusian demographic cycles and initi-ated an irreversible upswing in the western regions of the Empire (Komlos, 1989, p. 198). Freudenberger summarized the results of his research in a similar way: 'By 1770 a momentum had been achieved in the Habsburg Monarchy that provided it with an economic and even political basis with which it was able to operate fairly successfully for about another 40 years' (Freudenberger, 1978, p. 339). Others, however, date the breakthrough to industrialization as taking place in the middle of the nineteenth century and relate it to the economic reforms of the so-called era of neo-Absolutism from 1848 to 1859, which functioned as a kind of 'revolution from above' (März, 1968). This dating accords the modern banking system particular influence as a specialized institutional factor in the mobilization of capital. The Austrian banks, however, partic-ularly after the crisis of 1873, have been revealed to have acted overcau-tiously and conservatively; they were involved more in the business of making loans than in the finance of industry and railways, and they were neither entrepreneurial nor enamoured with industrial finance, especially when compared to their counterparts in Germany.

With the arrival of 'cliometric' research towards the end of the 1960s, quantitative data have been used as an aid in the attempt to solve the problem of dating. On the one hand, the boom period of 1867–73 and the accelerated rate of economic growth at the end of the nineteenth century were regarded as candiates for a Rostowian 'take-off' or Gerschenkronian 'spurt'. Later, however, 'cliometric' research put back the date of the start of modern economic growth still further, namely into the early nineteenth century. On the basis of various indices of industrial production a credible argument was put forward that Austria had already achieved the breakthrough to modern economic growth during the so-called *Vormärz*, that is, in the period from 1815 to the Revolution of 1848.

By way of conclusion and summary it may be stated that the controversial discussion concerning the start, precise dating and pace of modern economic growth in the Habsburg Monarchy will certainly continue in the future. It is, however, relatively clear that the concept of a 'take-off' or 'great spurt' must be regarded as inadequate to describe the Austrian pattern of industrialization. It has therefore with justification been suggested that, in the case of the Habsburg Monarchy (as in the case of France), it is best to talk in terms of a 'slow, but relatively constant process of growth'. Its beginnings must be dated as having already taken place by the 1820s at the latest, a period in which the first of many cyclical upturns can be identified which were not subsequently to be destroyed by a longer phase of stagnation.

TURNING-POINTS OF CYCLICAL ECONOMIC DEVELOPMENT

The turning-points of cyclical economic development can be analysed as a means of dividing the economic history of Austria in the nineteenth century into periods. The theory of 'long waves' related to endogenous economic factors which was founded by Nikolai Kondratieff, Arthur Spiethoff, Joseph A. Schumpeter, and others defines for the nineteenth century phase of upturn from 1787/93 to 1810/17, then from 1844/51 to 1870/75, and 1890/96 to 1913/20, and a down-turn from 1810/17 to 1844/51 and between 1870/75 and 1890/96. Whilst the Austrian pattern of development does indeed follow this course of long-term cyclical development, there are however remarkable divergences of detail, which require a more exact differentiation.

During the mercantilist era the government attempted to stimulate modernization with the aid of economic and social reforms. It had its greatest success in the sector of agricultural reform (*robot* – i.e. corvée – abolition, conversion of the peasants' dues and obligations to a money rent, improving the peasants' legal status), in the expansion of the infrastructure (regulating rivers, canal and road construction, the 'new port' in Trieste), in the fostering of human capital (compulsory general education, the religious Toleration Patent, widening the freedom of wage employment) and in the promotion of export trade (granting privileges for starting factories, abolishing most internal tariffs except the inner tariff barrier between Austria and Hungary). The reforms initiated economic growth by creating a legal environment conducive to capital accumulation and technological change. However in these instances, as in the case of the era of neo-Absolutism, one must be cautious not to confuse

economic policy with economic reality. A period of upturn lasting until
the financial crash of 1811 was followed by one of stubborn stagnation
which endured until 1825/6; this 'postNapoleonic depression' was
followed by an upturn in the cycle which started in 1825/6 and continued
until the mid-1840s, albeit already starting to weaken after 1830. Although
the politics of this period was characterized by the adherence to
Metternich's system of the 'Holy Alliance', economic life in Austria did
see a significant process of modernization: there was investment in the
infrastructure; new roads and the first railways were built; the two
Polytechnics of Prague (1807) and Vienna (1815) trained a whole new
generation of engineers, and Austria was soon to make significant contributions to innovations in the iron, sugar and brewing industries. The
number of steam engines used in agriculture, industry and transport
rapidly increased. This trend was strongest in the textile industry with the
introduction of mechanization to facilitate factory-based production; in
1841, the textile industry accounted for more than 40 per cent of total
industrial production. As far as the international economy was concerned,
approaches were made to the German Customs Union. The Metternich
regime sought to compensate, to a certain extent, the lack of freedom in
the political sphere by initiating economic reforms from above. These
efforts are summarized, with no little cynicism, in a poem by the Austrian
writer Franz Grillparzer:

> Sie wollen Freiheit
> nun wohlan, gebt ihnen eine Eisenbahn.
> Da können sie dann frei verkehren,
> der Schacher wird sie dienen lehren.

> They want freedom
> so let them play!
> let's give them a railway.
> Now they can move or stay
> but haggling will teach them to obey.

The phase which immediately preceded the Revolution of 1848 was,
on the other hand, characterized by a far-reaching and severe economic
depression, a situation which points to a connection between economic
and political developments, the outbreak of unrest in March 1848 was
related not least to the hunger revolt in Bohemia in 1846/7 and the
terrible economic conditions which prevailed in the big cities.

In spite of the 'reform from above' which began during the era of neo-
Absolutism in the decade following 1848–9 and which was predominantly
expressed in legal, administrative and infrastructural measures, the upturn
tendencies remained relatively weak until 1866/7; and they were contin-

ually undermined by various military interventions. Examples of these are
the upheaval and confusion of the Revolution of 1848/9; the policy of
'armed neutrality' during the Crimean War of 1853/6; the war with
France and Piedmont-Sardinia in 1859; the Schleswig-Holstein War of
1864, and the Austro-Prussian War and the war with Italy in 1866. These
conflicts were accompanied by disruption in the economic sphere. Above
all, it was the loss of the upper Italian provinces which brought the
greatest industrial setback; according to a census of 1833, there was a total
of 10,136 factories and manufactories in Austria, of which 8,452 were
located in Lombardy and Venetia, although the majority of these were
small and medium-sized firms involved in the silk industry. The state
policy of deflation had a negative effect and the Austrian Credit-Anstalt,
which was founded in 1854 and modelled on the Crédit Mobilier of Paris,
adopted a conspicuously low profile as far as providing finance for
industry was concerned. This was true of the Austrian banks in general,
which maintained relatively extensive funds, but restricted the capital
market for industry. It was only after 1866/7 that there was an amazing
upturn and boom in growth which continued unbroken until the outbreak
of the world economic crisis of 1873. The Great Depression of 1873 to
1896 – in Joseph Schumpeter's words the down-turn phase of the 'bourgeois Kondratieff' – was more strongly characterized by reductions in
money variables than in production volume – that is, the cut-backs in
investment, falling prices and the collapse of profits and yields on capital
were far greater than the various product lines.

Stronger signs of an upturn already began to appear after 1883, and from
1896 onwards the upturn tendencies were quite clearly dominant. Whereas
nominal gross national product only rose annually by 1.38 per cent (i.e. 0.59
per cent per capita) during the period 1872/4–1895/7, real per capita gross
national product rose by 1.51 per cent annually, the corresponding figures
for the period 1895/7–1911/1913 are 4.92 per cent and 2.46 per cent respectively. The banks began a new and increased involvement in the financing
of industry, and the state also subsidized the economic process via its rear-
mament programme. Nevertheless, the end of the nineteenth century saw
a renewed recession, although the economy did make a speedy recovery
experiencing, from 1904 onwards, the longest upturn of the so-called
Gründerzeit, or years of expansive commercial enterprise. The fiscal stimulation provided at that time by the 'Koerber Plan', which sought via investment in the infrastructure to accelerate the economy, may have had a
favourable influence on this development. The long-term economic developments can also be documented by, amongst other things, data for industrial production and the developments in the level of prices which, for the
most part, correspond to the pattern of the economic cycle.

THE LONG-TERM PATTERN OF INDUSTRIALIZATION

As early as the end of the eighteenth century several, initially for the most part unrelated proto-industrial 'export-trade landscapes' had taken shape, upon which the industrialization which also commenced in Austria at the beginning of the nineteenth century with the wide-scale mechanization of cotton spinning could build. It was also around this time that the regional division of labour between the more industrialized western and the more agricultural eastern regions, which is to be regarded as characteristic of the Habsburg territories in the nineteenth century, took place. In some 'advanced regions' (Baltzarek, 1979), participation in the Industrial Revolution was made possible not least by the import of know-how and human capital from more advanced Western European countries. Particularly in the Bohemian Lands, a rural proto-industry had already been able to asset itself in this way in the eighteenth century and a 'rural serf's industry' (Freudenberger and Mensch, 1975; Klíma, 1974) developed on a massive scale on some of the large estates or manors of the land-owning aristocracy. At the beginning of the nineteenth century, the Moravian capital, Brno, was rightly considered to be the 'Manchester of Central Europe' (Freudenberger and Mensch, 1975, pp. 44 and 55). It was not least the concentrated consumer demand of the capital city and Imperial residence of Vienna which resulted in numerous firms starting up in Vienna and the 'Vienna Basin'; amongst these were the large cotton-spinning mills, like the Pottendorf Yarn Manufacturing Company – founded in 1801 and the largest of its day on the European mainland – various cotton and silk-weaving mills, textile printers, chemical industry, paper mills and metal goods factories, raw sugar refineries, glass and mirror factories, factories for the production of building materials and engineering plants. The iron industry in Upper Styria, in Carinthia and in the Lower and Upper Austrian 'iron centres' constituted a second industrial zone, which underwent a process of concentration following the introduction of coal firing and then, above all, in the context of railway construction. In Vorarlberg, a smaller centre for textile manufacturing developed as a result of a spill-over effect from the textile industry in eastern Switzerland. Northern Bohemia for its part, was a preferred area for the production of linen, and, from the 1820s onwards, it became the leading centre of the cotton industry on account of the shift in conditions of location caused by the import of raw American cotton along the Elbe route. The availability of enormous reserves of coal favoured the establishment of heavy industry in Bohemia, whilst Moravia was able to consolidate its leading position in the woollen industry, in sugar production and in various branches of agriculture. The centre of gravity of the dynamics of industrialization, therefore, shifted to the northern regions, which were the leaders in terms of industrial production and productivity alike. The Rudohoři (Erzgebirge) region, for example, with its diverse industrial structure; the area around Prague; the industrial region of Kladno-Plzeň; the area extending from the Saxon border to northern Moravia with its extensive textile industry; the heavy industry in Moravská Ostrava, Bílovec, Frýdek, Fryštát and Těšín, and finally the area around Brno were all regions of industrial concentration on a scale only matched in the other provinces by the Vienna Basin, and, to a lesser extent, by the heavy industry in Upper Styria and the textile industry in Vorarlberg.

It must, however, be stressed when assessing the pattern of industrialization that once again the various levels of development of the individual states must be taken into consideration. Whereas large parts of the Alpine lands, Bohemia, Moravia and Silesia could already look back on a proto-industrial past, with the beginnings of a modern factory industry which can be dated as the start of the nineteenth century, Galicia, Bukovina, Dalmatia and the coastal provinces could be best described in today's terminology as 'peripheral regions'. This means, however, that a comparison of industrialization always faces a problem, not least because of the 'internal arithmetic' which is not necessarily reflected in the overall data, even in the case of rapid growth in the 'progressive regions'. Although greater socio-economic disproportions and a kind of west–east divide in the wake of the process of industrialization could also be discerned in the countries of Western Europe and Western Central Europe, they did not embrace such large, completely differently structured and socio-economically extremely heterogeneous territories as those 'Kingdoms and Lands represented in the Reichsrat'.

If one compares the economic situation in Austria at both the beginning and at the end of the nineteenth century with that which prevailed in the advanced Western European countries a particular economic weakness can be noted. The Austrian economy was relatively backward in the eighteenth century and, despite economic growth in the nineteenth century, remained so on the eve of the First World War, if compared to Western Europe. The issue is whether the gap widened or closed in the intervening time. The paltry available data suggest that this relative economic backwardness actually increased somewhat in the first half of the nineteenth century. Whereas in the eyes of many contemporaries, Austria did not lag very far behind Prussia and the German Customs Union in the 1840s and, in certain key industrial sectors, like cotton, pig-iron and coal production, the rates of growth were even higher than in Germany, Austria was subsequently to fall behind. The period 1849–57 was marked all over Europe by a vigorous upturn, but Austria was unable to participate to the same degree as other nations. As an industrial late-comer she remained for a long time dependent on Western European capital and technology and, for all the industrial progress made in some regions – Komlos (1983, pp. 106–9), for example, estimates that industrial output per capita increased at the respectable annual rate of 2.1 per cent in the period 1830–50 – Austria fell sharply behind when compared with Western Europe from the middle of the 1850s until the end of the 1860s. The boom of the 1850s was much weaker in Austria than in Germany, France or England, and the increase in growth in Austria was overtaken by that of the German Customs Union. Moreover, this occurred not only in the energy- and capital-intensive heavy industries, but also in the consumer-oriented textile and food industries. The breakdown in production and the cotton crisis which was a result of the American Civil War hit Austria much more severely than, for example Great Britain, Switzerland or Germany, because, like Sweden, she was especially vulnerable. The recession was exacerbated by the drastic deflationary policies which Austria introduced in the interests of her financial position following the lost war of 1859; of the 350,000 employed in the cotton industry in 1861, only 70,000 were still working by 1864. However, during the boom of 1867–73 and in the last three decades before the First World War, Austria and Hungary were able to rapidly catch up and the economy grew at a faster rate during these periods than in most Western European countries, with the result that the gap which had separated Austria from Great Britain, Belgium, France and, to a lesser extent, Germany began to narrow. Drawing on the international-comparative studies of Paul Bairoch (1976), Austria, with a real per capita GDP increasing at barely 0.5 per cent annually, would have been well below the European average, until 1870. In the phase prior to the First World War, however, Austria's annual rate of growth of 1.32 per cent enabled her to make up a lot of ground, being only clearly outstripped by that of Sweden and Denmark and, to a much lesser extent, of Germany. According to David Good's (1984) estimates, the Austrian half of the Empire would, in 1910, have had the eighth highest real per capita national product in an international comparison of standards, coming behind Great Britain, Belgium, Denmark, Holland, Switzerland, Germany and France, but ahead of Norway, Hungary, Sweden, Finland, Portugal, Italy, Spain, Greece and Russia. Nevertheless, Good's assertion is most certainly accurate: 'By 1914 the empire's position relative to Western Europe was no better and may have been somewhat worse than a century before and it had lost out to Germany for political dominance of Central Europe. But in its final four decades the empire began to 'catch up'' (Good, 1988, p. 15).

If the Habsburg Monarchy remained to its very end the model of an 'industrialized agricultural state', then this was also reflected in industry in the size of firms and the structure of production. Without doubt the production of consumer goods had pride of place; according to the census of factories in 1906, 32 per cent of all industrial workers were still employed in the textile and clothing industry, whereas, by comparison, the areas of raw materials and production goods industry which were disproportionately more significant for the intensity of industrialization employed only 18 per cent and 17 per cent respectively. Small and medium-sized firms predominated – 70 to 80 per cent of all firms fell into the category of having less than 100 employees, depending on the respective branch – although individual areas of production (e.g. mining, textiles and sugar) did indeed show a high degree of concentration (Matis and Bachinger, 1973, p. 214). In the iron and engineering industries there were, in addition to the smaller traditional plants, also large concerns which were the result of the mergers of smaller firms (e.g. the Alpine Mining Company and the Prague Iron Company), whilst large, individual, mostly German companies dominated the new electrical and chemical and pharmaceutical industries which sprang up in the 1880s.

The comparatively low degree of concentration as far as large firms are concerned was also partly connected to the anti-equity stance of the legislation which was introduced in Austria after the speculation crisis of 1873 and which discriminated against this rising form of financing capitalist industry; whereas there were still 536 industrial share companies in 1870 with capital of 1.23 billion crowns, the number of share companies had fallen to 490 with nominal capital of 1.46 billion crowns by 1910 (Somary, 1902, pp. 40–59). Nevertheless, during the 'Great Depression' of 1873–96 there was a significant process of concentration headed by the large banks, heavily involved in industry, and which saw horizontal and vertical integration and, above all, the creation of cartels. This creation of cartels was also related, without doubt, to the concentration in banking and the great importance of the credit apparatus for the long-term financing of industry in Austria. This enabled the banks to enjoy a strategically more important position than elsewhere and they supported the merger of industrial enterprises which came under their sphere of influence, whereby their interest and promotion was predominantly concentrated on those areas of production which appeared to be particularly conducive to the creation of cartels.

OUTLINES OF ECONOMIC POLICY

In describing the relationship between the state and the economy in the Habsburg Monarchy one can talk with justification in terms of the primacy of politics; economic considerations were not notably reflected in overall policy. Indeed, the neglect of economic possibilities, which not least revealed a discrepancy with the claims which the Monarchy had as a great power, often led to military and political errors with corresponding political effects on the domestic scene.

The lack of a strong line on economic policy contributed, for its part, to national disintegration and delayed modernization. Ultimately, the basic dilemma was that the economic power of the Empire was insufficient to support foreign policy, whilst conversely, the errors on the foreign policy front often contributed to the conservation of the relative economic backwardness. Moreover, domestic and foreign political interest ultimately won the day when the problem was confronted which, in the long term, also had a massive influence on the economic policy of the Danube Monarchy, namely the binding together of the Central European economic area and the integration of structurally extremely heterogeneous economic regions in a common internal market. At the beginning and the end of the period under review there were two notable attempts to solve these problems: Bruck's conception of Central Europe as an economic variation on the general foreign-policy strategy of Prime Minister Schwarzenberg, and the so-called 'Koerber Plan' to restrict nationality conflicts with the aid of concerted measures to improve the economic structure (canal and railway projects, the extension of the port of Trieste). Both attempts were to fail (Gerschenkron, 1977).

The project of the 'seventy-million Empire', as propagated by Prince Schwarzenberg and the Minister of Trade and Finance, Bruck, envisaged the creation of a large, common market in Central Europe and an economic zone under Austrian leadership. Many of the economic policies of the neo-Absolutist regime were directed towards this end. A centrally guided programme of reform was introduced in the decade after 1848. Its main pillar was the late-Josephinistic 'ideal of the welfare state' and a ministerial bureaucracy which was to be regarded as the supra-national conception of the state. Although the revolution had failed, it did ultimately lead to that irreversible process of modernization which has variously been characterized as a 'revolution from above'. Although the new regime remained dependent on traditionl policies to protect the interests of the Habsburg Monarchy, and the social dominance of the high aristocracy and the 'bastions of the old order' (Arno J. Mayer, 1981) remained firmly intact, concessions did have to be made to the aspiring bourgeoisie.

The dawning of the 'new age' had such major effects that an unconditional return to the maxims of the *Vormärz* period was out of the question. Many long-overdue reforms which had been originally planned under the *ancien régime* and then prevented by the political reaction to the French Revolution were now put into practice. Examples are the *Grundentlastung* (1848), that is, the emancipation of the peasantry, and abolition of the inner tariff barrier with Hungary (1851) and the introduction of freedom of commercial and industrial activities (1859). Above all the bourgeois desire for acquisition was, at the same time, given a relatively free rein in order to compensate for the lack of political participation, although the state did still reserve the right to restrict and channel these activities. To the same extent that neo-Absolutism, the institutional embodiment of the authoritarian state, had resisted granting constitutional rights, it also felt compelled to compensate for the lack of political freedom with the 'promotion of external welfare'. It was at this time that the foundations for a rebuilding of the Monarchy were laid in many areas of the economy, including administration, justice, finance, banking, credit institutions and education. Economic policy pursued the goal of internal and external integration and, with the aid of infrastructural measures, the establishment of a homogeneous economic zone for the Monarchy as a preliminary stage for a later Central European customs union.

The first aim was at least partly achieved, unlike the second which sought to combine the political claims to power in the German Confederation with plans for economic hegemony and which failed because it brought the Monarchy into fundamental opposition to Prussia, and, ultimately, because of a too-narrow economic base: the 'Little German' free-trade movement gained the upper hand against the 'Greater German' advocates of protective tolls. Austria's isolation on matters of trade policy, the growing internal nationality conflicts and the permanent constitutional crisis, together with the financial disaster which was greatest after the heavy losses of the war of 1859 and the deflationary policies which were introduced on the basis of a one-sided overestimation of currency stability, were all highly decisive factors which weakened the position of the Habsburg Monarchy in the struggle for hegemony in Germany.

The Austrian defeat at the battlefield of Königgrätz-Sadowa (Sadová near Hradeckrálové in Bohemia) led to a new orientation in domestic and foreign policy which was to have far-reaching effects; the withdrawal from the German Confederation led to a shift in emphasis in foreign policy towards Eastern Europe and the Balkans and, therefore, towards that fateful entanglement which was to culminate, in 1914, in the First World War. This eastwards orientation, however, meant that a solution to the

Hungarian question had to be found, which had been simmering since 1848–9. Indeed, in domestic policy in general, the problem of internal harmony became a more pressing one, particularly after the strengthening of the Reichsrat by the October Diploma of 1860 and the February Patent of 1861. Austria and Hungary had been bound together since the Compromise (1867) in the form of a union with a common monarch and 'common affairs' like foreign, finance and defence policies. In addition there was a number of dualistic matters including customs and trade policy, the fixing of the money system and coinage, the common railways and the commercial conduct of the state as a whole. Otherwise the Austro-Hungarian Compromise, valid for ten years, guaranteed autonomy in both parts of the Empire. This provided the basis for an independent Hungarian economic policy which was predominantly conducted in the interests of the Magyar upper classes. The conditions for a common policy in the western half of the Empire were, however, disproportionately more difficult, as was the balance of interests because of the *Proporz*, or the proportional representation of nationalities which had been sanctioned by the Reichsrat. Prevalent amongst the difficulties to confront the ten-yearly negotiations between the two Compromise 'delegations' were the domestic problems of 'Cisleithania', particularly in view of the so-called 'Quota', i.e. the respective share of common expenditure, with the result that the outside world often had the impression of a 'monarchy ruling on sufferance'.

There was at least some commonality of interest on matters of foreign policy, which, since the mid-1860s had been characterized by a movement towards a system of free trade bringing the Monarchy into open competition on the world market. In the main there were barely any difficulties, because both halves of the Empire adhered to the principle of free trade to an extent that one can talk in terms of a balance of interest between Hungarian agriculture and Austrian industry. On the foreign policy front *rapprochement* with France was sought until 1870–1. Not only was France amenable to Austrian requests for loans, it also offered Austria a preliminary treaty in 1867 with the Latin Monetary Union which she dominated.

A veritable boom commenced in Austria-Hungary in 1867: an unprecedented scale of economic expansion, triggered by a favourable agricultural economic situation in Hungary and which was nourished and fostered by railway construction, bold building projects in the run-up to the Vienna World Exhibition of 1873, and a bull market on the Vienna Stock Exchange. This boom was equated with the success of the liberal economic system. Only the drastic change in the economic climate following the stock-exchange crash of 9 May 1873 and the subsequent

Great Depression prompted a radical movement away from the values of the preceding epoch and ushered in an existential crisis for political and economic liberalism in Austria. Economic liberalism was unable to find a suitable and effective remedy to combat the crisis, whilst political liberalism was doomed to fail on account of its inherent contradiction, namely that its programmatic demands for increased democratization were, in the long term, aimed against itself (as a bourgeois party of dignitaries) and led to the strengthening of the movement towards modern mass political parties.

The shattering of the free-market economy, which was palpable during the economic collapse, awakened the need for social control and collective security in place of the liberal-individualistic principle of competition. The German Liberal Constitutional Party, which held a relative majority in the Reichsrat until 1879, had already been compelled to grant certain concessions to the anti-liberal movement. There were, for example, interventionist tendencies in the fields of transport, foreign trade and financial policy. The reform of the trade constitution had also been debated since 1874 and it was on this very question that the struggle between a liberal and controlled economic order was to be settled in Austria in favour of the latter. A period which had witnessed a relatively high degree of economic freedom was followed by a return to guild-based thinking, to strict state control and one-sided promotion of existing small firms as a product of a protectionism supported by the middle classes. The restoration of a 'Christian world order based on the balance of the classes' became one of the central tenets of a feudal conservative coalition, the so-called 'Iron Ring', during the 'Taaffe Era'. The new social classes which resulted from the emerging modern capitalism were to have their freedom of action restricted and combated. This development was expressed, amongst other things, in the phenomena of anti-capitalism, anti-Semitism and anti-liberalism which are interesting from the point of view of social psychology.

In 1879, Prime Minister Count Edward Taaffe's feudal conservatives came to power and formed a government, and this 'Iron Ring' attempted to establish the anti-liberal front in Austria on a broad basis, by seeking to integrate the newly enfranchised, so-called 'Five-Florins-Men' (for purposes of taxation) in the government following the change in the electoral law of 1882. The new government was committed to a 'solidarity' protectionism as an instrument to rule and stabilize the system, and its economic policy sought to combine economic growth with the protectionist promotion of the trades and the restoration of an agricultural state; its domestic policy sought to achieve a social and national balance, but was unable to counter existing discrepancies. This 'defensive strategy of the old elites' in order to maintain traditional positions enjoyed only partial success; the powers which it had unleashed were soon to take on a life of their own.

On the one hand, the petrification of the petit-bourgeois agricultural structure was favoured; the maintenance of a situation in which the government was not least interested for electoral reasons, whereas at the same time, on the political front, the new mass parties of the Christian Socialist and Social Democratic parties were founded; in the economic sector there were, however, also to emerge new collectivist groupings. The 'blessings of solidarity protectionism' (Rosenberg, 1967, pp. 66–8) which were aimed against the 'excesses of capitalism' were to be experienced not only by the farming classes and the independent artisans, but also by the exploited industrial working population of the day which was to enjoy the fruits of a system of social insurance. Social provisions and a partial social redistribution of wealth were conceived not only as a means of countering social tensions, but also as an instrument to promote trade and agricultural producers of consumer goods who, it was hoped, would benefit from the accompanying increase in the spending power of the masses.

A further expression of the 'collective desire for security' was the advent of a modern cooperative ethos (consumer and building cooperatives, the Raiffeisen and Schulze-Delitzsch organizations) as well as cartels, which, although initially aimed purely defensively at supporting prices and restricting competition, were later, under the control of 'finance capital' (Rudolf Hilferding, 1981), to strive towards a monopolistic position in the market. The protective tolls movement and the expansionist policies pursued by the Habsburg Monarchy from the beginning of the 1880s onwards, taking its lead from those of the greater European powers, corresponded to 'organized capitalism' and its interests and, from the point of view of foreign trade, complemented them. Problems which had been exacerbated not least as a result of the policy of restrictive tariffs (the 'Pig War' with Serbia, the Customs War with Romania) thus came to the fore. In the Balkans, the expansionary zones of Austria-Hungary and Russia overlapped on the dispute concerning the legacy of the Ottoman Empire. The temporary weakness of the Tsarist Empire after the war with Japan enabled an armed conflict to be narrowly avoided over the annexation of Bosnia and Hercegovina in 1908, and although Turkey was effectively driven out of Europe by the Balkans Conflict of 1912–13, a permanent solution to this problem, however, remained elusive, with the result that the reason for the impending First World War lay dormant in the zones of conflict.

On the domestic scene new ideas and political forces had taken up the legacy of liberalism in the 1880s. Economic policy also frequently served new social ideas and models. New parties with a social and national influence vehemently demanded their right to consultation, leading to an expansion of the basis for economic policy. At the same time a balance of interest was made more complicated by the numerous diverging special interests. In political practice, this resulted in a dispersal of resources, to the compulsion of the nationality *Proporz*, and to the desire of the government to gain the maximum political support via widespread compromises. To counter the particularist tendencies, which were the result of party-political, economic and national special interests, it was important that the civil service should assert itself as the decisive force and custodian of interests, whose prime principle was the state as a whole and the full maintenance of its traditions. After the collapse of the 'Iron Ring' (1894), nationality struggles and party wrangles, ultimately leading to the adjournment of the Reichsrat, soon resulted in the 'omnipotence of the bureaucracy', which had distinguished itself by its remarkable degree of stability. The inability of the parties to form a government or coalition, and the obstruction of individual national groups, resulted in the civil service being regarded as more capable of governing the state than the political powers.

With the increase in domestic contradictions, the integration of the internal market came to dominate economic policy. Prime Minister Koerber's economic plan, which similarly had its origins in the civil service pursued, via investment in the infrastructure (canal and railway investment, expansion of the port of Trieste), a concerted structural policy aimed at balancing the disparate levels of growth in the regions; it ultimately failed not least because of the ruling fiscalism. The expansion of state control and regimentation, together with the omnipotence of the bureaucracy which had already commenced towards the end of the nineteenth century, increased as a matter of course during the First World War. Although various attempts to balance domestic political and socio-economic inequalities failed, this was certainly not because of a conscious discrimination of individual peoples; rather, it was simply a matter of the inability to realize a systematic and comprehensive policy for development, and the missed opportunity to transform the multinational state into a new form which was acceptable to all its peoples (Fink, 1968).

It would, however, be equally erroneous to measure the special national legal and political situation which obtained in the former Habsburg Monarchy against the modern notion of a nation state. Similarly it would be wrong to assess the economic backwardness in the light of the ideals of today's theories of economic growth, without raising the question as to whether the strategies for development demanded by a modern state could have been realized in the specific historically determined structures of the multinational Empire. The main reason for the failure of the

Habsburg Empire is simply that it functioned in its own day as a living anachronism: on the one hand it was predominantly dynastic and, therefore, a historical relict and, on the other, as a multinational state, it was ahead of its time; whereby its dilemma was that its continued existence as a multinational, pluralistic society could not possibly be subordinated to a single, centralist and universally valid conception of a state under conditions of rising nationalism.

REFERENCES

Bairoch, Paul. 1976. 'Europe's Gross National Product: 1800–1975', *Journal of European Economic History*, 5, pp. 273–340

Baltzarek, Franz. 1979. 'Zu den regionalen Ansätzen der frühen Industrialisierung in Europa', in Herbert Knittler (ed.), *Wirtschafts- und sozialhistorische Beiträge. Festschrift für Alfred Hoffmann* (Vienna: Verlag für Geschichte und Politik)

Berend, Iván and Ránki, György. 1970. 'Nationaleinkommen und Kapitalakkumulation in Ungarn: 1867–1914, Social economic researches of the history of East-Central Europe'. *Acta Historica Academiae Scientiarum Hungaricae*, 62, (Budapest)

Bolognese-Leuchtenmüller, Birgit. 1978. 'Bevölkerungsentwicklung und Berufsstruktur, Gesundheits- und Fürsorgewesen in Österreich 1750–1918, in *Materialien zur Wirtschafts- und Sozialgeschichte* (Vienna: Verlag für Geschichte und Politik)

Butschek, Felix. 1985. *Die Österreichische Wirtschaft im 20. Jahrhundert* (Stuttgart: Gustav Fischer)

Fink, Krisztina. 1968. *Die österreichisch-ungarische Monarchie als Wirtschaftsgemeinschaft* (Munich: Rudolph Trofenik)

Freudenberger, Herman. 1978. 'Economic progress during the reign of Charles VI', in Jürgen Schneider (ed.), *Wirtschaftskräfte und Wirtschaftswege II: Wirtschaftskräfte der europäischen Expansion* (Nürnberg: Klett-Cotta)

Freudenberger, Herman and Mensch, Gerhard. 1975. *Von der Provinzstadt zur Industrieregion* (Göttingen: Vandenhoeck & Ruprecht)

Gerschenkron, Alexander. 1965. *Economic Backwardness in Historical Perspective* (New York: Frederick Praeger)

1977. *An Economic Spurt That Failed. Four Lectures in Austrian History* (Princeton, N.J.: Princeton University Press)

Good, David. 1984. *The Economic Rise of the Habsburg Empire: 1750–1914* (Berkeley: University of California Press)

1991. 'The economic development of Austria-Hungary', in Richard Sylla and Gianni Toniolo (eds.), *Patterns of European Industrialization in the Nineteenth Century* (London: Routledge)

Gross, Nachum. 1996. 'Industrialization in Austria in the Nineteenth Century'. Unpublished PhD thesis, University of California, Berkeley

Hilferding, Rudolf. 1981. *Finance capital – a study of the latest phase of capitalist development* (London)

Huertas, Thomas. 1977. *Economic Growth and Economic Policy in a Multinational Setting* (New York: Arno Press)

Kausel, Anton. 1979. 'Österreichs Volkseinkommen 1830 bis 1913', in *Geschichte und Ergebnisse der amtlichen Statistik in Österreich 1829–1979* (Vienna: Österreichisches Statistisches Zentralamt)

Kausel, Anton, Németh, N. and Seidel, H. 1965. 'Österreichs Volkseinkommen 1913 bis 1963', in *Monatsberichte des Österreichischen Instituts für Wirtschaftsforschung* 14 (Vienna: Institut für Wirtschaftsforschung)

Klíma, A. 1974. 'The role of rural domestic industry in Bohemia in the eighteenth century', *Economic History Review*, 27 (Feb. 1974), pp. 48–56.

Komlos, John. 1983. *The Habsburg Monarchy as a Customs Union. Economic Development in Austria-Hungary in the Nineteenth Century* (Chicago: University of Chicago Press)

1989. *Nutrition and Economic Development in the Eighteenth-Century Habsburg Monarchy* (Princeton, NJ: Princeton University Press)

Koren, Stephan. 1961. 'Die Industrialisierung Österreich', in Wilhelm Weber (ed.), *Österreichs Wirtschaftsstruktur gestern – heute – morgen*, vol. I (Berlin: Duncker & Humblot)

März, Eduard. 1968. *Österreichiche Industrie- und Bankpolitik in der Zeit Franz Josephs I. Am Beispiel der k.k. priv. Österreichischen Credit-Anstalt für Handel und Gewerbe* (Vienna: Europa Verlag)

Matis, Herbert. 1972. *Österreichichs Wirtschaft 1848–1913* (Berlin: Duncker & Humblot)

Matis, Herbert and Bachinger, Karl. 1973. 'Österreichs industrielle Entwicklung', in Adam Wandruszka and Peter Urbanitsch (eds.), *Die Habsburgermonarchie 1848–1918*, vol. I: *Die wirtschaftliche Entwicklung*, ed. by A. Brusatti, pp. 105–232 (Vienna: Verlag der Österreichischen Akademie der Wissenschaften)

Mayer, Arn J. 1981. *The Persistence of the Old Regime: Europe to the Great War* (New York: Pantheon Books)

Möller, Hasso. 1974. *Wandel der Berufsstruktur in Österreich zwischen 1869 und 1961* (Vienna: Österreichischer Bundesverlag)

Rosenberg, Hans. 1967. *Grosse Depression und Bismarckzeit* (Berlin: Walter de Gruyter)

Rudolph, Richard. 1976. *Banking and Industrialization in Austria-Hungary. The role of banks in the industrialization of the Czech Crownlands 1873–1914* (Cambridge: Cambridge University Press)

Sandgruber, Roman. 1978. *Österreichische Agrarstatistik 1750–1918* (Munich: Oldenbourg Verlag)

1972. 'Wirtschaftswachstum, Energie und Verkehr in Österreich 1840–1913', *Forschungen zur Sozial- und Wirtschafts-Geschichte*, 22 (Stuttgart: Gustav Fischer)

Somary, F. 1902. *Die Aktiengesellschaften in Österreich* (Vienna: Manz)

Wallerstein, Immanuel. 1974. *The Modern World System: Capitalist Agriculture and the Origins of the European World System in the Sixteenth Century* (New York: Acar Press)

Wysocki, Jose. 1975. *Infrastruktur und wachsende Staatsausgaben* (Stuttgart: Gustav Fischer)

ELEVEN

The Industrial Revolution: Bohemia, Moravia and Silesia

MILAN MYŠKA

I

SOURCES relating to the economic and social development of the Czech Lands in the eighteenth and nineteenth centuries reflect no awareness of the 'Industrial Revolution'.[1] Neither has old Czech historiography made use of this typological concept although the processes generally associated with it have been studied intensively.[2]

Only since the second half of the 1950s has the designation 'Industrial Revolution' become part of the conceptual terminology of Czech historians.[3] However, the reception of this concept assumed a specific character: although the term was taken over from its traditional use in Western European and American historiography, its structure and content became linked with the concept *promyshlennyi perevorot* ('industrial overturn'), derived from Soviet historiography.[4] It became apparent that the Industrial Revolution was comprehended as 'the process of transition from handicraft to mechanical production', basically as a process covering the technical sphere and production.

Due to this narrow and one-sided conception a number of problems, which historians of other countries studied in relation to the Industrial Revolution, eluded the attention of Czech historiography. As a result many questions posed by world historiography about the Industrial Revolution cannot be satisfactorily answered in the Czech national context. Also this study cannot overstep these limits and barriers.

Only recently have Czech historians tended to attempt a broader approach to the subject, as for instance that adopted by Carlo M. Cipolla and the Polish historian Kazimierz Piesowicz:[6] as a complex of economic, social and civilizatory changes connected with the rise of the factory system and modern technical civilization. This embraces the transition from handicraft to mechanical production, from an economy of stagnation based on tradition and routine to a dynamic economy subject to permanent change influenced by technical advance, from an agrarian society with the majority of population living on the land to an industrial society in which the greater part of the national income is produced by industry and the larger part of the population is engaged in industry and lives in towns.

The complex conception of the Industrial Revolution poses the question of the mutual relationship of this global process with the sphere of innovations in techniques and production which we shall call the 'techno-production revolution', the essence of which is the substitution of machines, thermo-chemical processes and factory organization of production for manual work.[7] We start out from the presupposition that the implementation of these changes is the key factor in the process which determines the essence of the Industrial Revolution and, in contradistinction to industrialization, is its unique content.[8]

II

During the nineteenth century the process of the Industrial Revolution was the qualitatively dominant phenomenon of economic and social development of the Czech Lands (that is, Bohemia, Moravia and the Austrian part of Silesia). Prior to 1918 the Czech Lands did not possess an autonomous economy but were part of the Habsburg Monarchy's economy. Their economic development was – apart from specific local conditions – crucially influenced by general factors operating in the Monarchy as a whole, such as the entire Austrian domestic market, the orientation of foreign trade and the economic policy of the state. Capitalist growth in the west of Europe had mainly been taking place in national states whereas in Central and South-east Europe capitalism developed in the framework of a multinational monarchy and this, to a considerable extent, created conflicting conditions. A fairly wide-ranging integration accompanied the expansion of capitalism in the Habsburg Monarchy during the nineteenth century providing the possibility of access to an extensive market for each province.[9] The enormous economic area and a common currency facilitated the financing of the economy and promoted conditions for take-off also in economically relatively backward provinces, whose own potential for accumulation was low and their local markets stagnant. Of additional significance were the possibilities created by wider regional integration for the development of an infrastructure (railway networks, credit systems, education, etc.). These improvements in relatively backward areas would not have been feasible without the capital participation of the economically stronger and more advanced parts of the Monarchy.[10] As a result of the existence of a common market, individual provinces did not have to aim at harmoniously developing all branches of the local economy, in respect of the industrial sector, but were able to concentrate their resources on expanding those branches which had a greater chance of success.

Consequently the economy of the Habsburg Monarchy was marked by great regional and structural disparity.[11] On the one hand, comparatively powerful industrial regions arose on the territory of the Monarchy (Lower Austria, Bohemia, Moravia, Silesia) during the course of the Industrial Revolution and, on the other hand, stagnation, backwardness and traditionalism were preserved in the less developed Alpine and eastern and south-eastern provinces. According to the laws of the capitalist market economy this pattern guaranteed the economically more advanced regions cheap industrial raw materials, good and favourable markets for their products in the traditional areas. This became fully evident in the industrialization process of the Czech Lands. Indeed, in relation to the European market this situation secured the Czech Lands a fair measure of independence.

At the beginning of the 1840s the gross national income of the Habsburg Monarchy amounted to *c.* 1,600 million Austrian gulden (florins). By 1880 it had risen to 8,573 million gulden, of which the Czech Lands' share was 20 to 22 per cent.[12] According to Fellner's calculations it reached 29 per cent between 1911 and 1913.[13] The industrial sector participated conspicuously in this growth which is evident, for instance, from data about the economically active population: at the beginning of the 1840s the following percentages of the population obtained their livelihood from agriculture and forestry: 54.4 per cent in Bohemia, 55 per cent in Moravia and 53 per cent in Silesia.[14] By the end of the century, with the completion of the techno-production revolution in the main branches of industry in the Czech Lands, significant macroeconomic structural changes had taken place: the Czech Lands had assumed an agricultural-industrial character. The economically active population in agriculture in 1880 accounted for 44.5 per cent, in industry for 32.2 per cent and in commerce and transport for 5 per cent.[15] By 1900 the share of agriculture had fallen to 41 per cent whilst industry had increased to 36 per cent and commerce, transport and finance had risen to 5.5 per cent.[16] At the beginning of the twentieth century Bohemia, Moravia and Silesia had not yet reached the character of a predominantly industrial economy. Nevertheless, within the framework of the Habsburg Monarchy these regions had attained the highest level of industrialization (not taking into account the small Vorarlberg).

The period from the 1830s to the 1880s represents a break in the industrial history of the Czech Lands. Notable quantitative changes took place which signified a transformation of relations between small-scale and large-scale production, between handicraft and mechanical production as well as in the structure of the branches of industry. According to rather inaccurate statistics relating to 1841, the annual value of industrial production (excluding mining) in the Czech Lands came to 231.7 million gulden, which accounted for 27.7 per cent of total industrial production in Austria and 31.7 per cent in Cisleithania. The gross per capita value of industrial production in the Czech Lands was estimated at 34.86 gulden.[17]

Until 1880 the gross value of industrial production rose to 753.6 million gulden, that is an increase of 225 per cent. Not only had quantitative growth taken place but also structural changes occurred within Cisleithania in favour of the Czech Lands. Here 63 per cent of the total gross value of Cisleithanian industrial output was produced by 1880.[18] Thus in the course of four to five decades differences in the level of industrialization deepened between the Czech Lands and the other provinces of Cisleithania. Above all Galicia, Bukovina and the economically stagnating Alpine provinces lagged behind. By 1880 the gross per capita value of industrial production in the Czech Lands had reached 91 gulden, that is a threefold increase in comparison with 1841.

My calculations of the average annual rate of growth substantiate the dynamic process of industrialization. This amounted to 3.07 per cent between 1841 and 1880, which was the highest rate of growth in Cisleithania (2.44 per cent) as well as in the entire Habsburg Monarchy. For Lower Austria the annual rate of growth for the same period was 2.66 per cent.[19]

The development of Czech industry within the framework of the strongly differentiated territories of the Monarchy was accompanied both by advantages and disadvantages. It was an obvious advantage that the production of Czech industry had access to a relatively large market, especially in those Austrian provinces where industry remained relatively backward. However, sales on Austrian markets had limits which were set, above all, by the very low purchasing power of the generally poverty-stricken population, especially in the backward provinces (Galicia, certain parts of Hungary and the Alpine provinces) and, in addition, by surviving traditions of previous centuries which notably included a high degree of economic self-sufficiency (natural economy). Moreover, the capacity of the Austrian market was unfavourably influenced by the character of production. In particular the range of the textile industry was brought into line with the demand of the poor strata of society, that is, the market determined that simple products of lesser quality were produced and, above all, at low prices.[20]

The extended territory of the Monarchy with its varied types of geographical and natural environment provided Czech industry with suitable raw materials for the textile industry (wool, flax) and the food industry as well as for branches of heavy industry (iron ore, mineral fuels). These advantages were, however, limited by transport conditions. The Czech Lands had very little opportunity to utilize inexpensive means of waterway transport (practically only parts of the rivers Vltava and Labe), and the railway network, the construction of which had begun in the 1830s but was still sparse until the period of local railway development in the 1870s. In addition, railway freight was expensive chiefly because of the tariff policy of private companies.

Structural changes in industry of the Czech Lands are of interest to us from two points of view: from the aspect of the mutual relation between large-scale and small-scale production, and from the aspect of changes in the branch structure of industry. We regard as decisive shifts between consumer-goods and producer-goods industries.

Extant evidence does not record quantitative relations between large- and small-scale production before the beginning of the 1840s. Then the shares in total value of production were 78.2 per cent for large-scale and 21.8 per cent for small-scale production.[21] However, this relatively high share of large-scale production cannot be interpreted as evidence for an equally strong presence of machine-based factory production. In the 1840s a substantial part of the value of industrial large-scale output was still produced by manufactories, by the putting-out system or by mining establishments based on handicraft and simple cooperation. About the changes which had been taking place until the 1880s we can, for the time being, merely advance a hypothesis: it seems that the relations between large- and small-scale production did not change, but changes occurred in the structure of large-scale production. It is, therefore, necessary to interpret data of the 1870s – the final phase of the Industrial Revolution – which show that out of the total number of industrial workers in the Czech Lands only 20 per cent worked in factories, 45 per cent in small-scale artisan production.[22]

The number of workers in the textile industry of Moravia and Silesia (and this applied also to other parts of the Czech Lands for which precise data are not available) accounted for by statisticians in 1891 was 85,377 of whom 45,284, that is 52 per cent, were employed outside the factory premises as a domestic workforce. Ten years later Moravia and Silesia accounted for 129,730 textile workers of whom 63,825, that is still 49 per cent, worked in their homes within the putting-out system. They were in different ways integrated into large-scale production and in various degrees dependent on entrepreneurs.[23]

There is ample evidence in the literature about the Industrial Revolution that the techno-production revolution proceeded unevenly in the individual branches of industry. Also in the Czech Lands, as shown by Purš,[24] the first phase of the Industrial Revolution (1800–30) was connected with the techno-production revolution in the textile industry, and only during the second (1830–50) and third stages (1850–80) did mechanization, chemical technology and factory organization begin to assert themselves in the food industry, in mining and metallurgy and in the engineering industry.

At the beginning of the 1840s the producer goods sector (sector A) accounted for approximately 12 per cent of the gross value of industrial production, while that of the consumer goods sector (sector B) came to 88 per cent. Structural change in industry until 1880 was from the point of view of the relation between sectors A and B of little significance: sector A's share in the total gross value of production rose only to 17 per cent, while the consumer goods sector maintained its strong predominance (83 per cent). If, however, the criterion of the number of workers employed is applied, sector A moves to a more favourable position in which it absorbed 29 per cent of the total number of workers employed in 1880. The lower indicators for sector A in comparison with sector B can be explained by the fact that equipment designed to economize on human labour spread mainly in branches of heavy industry and that values created by a worker – for instance at a blast-furnace – were substantially lower than for instance in textiles. A more favourable position for sector A emerges if the criterion of motive power of steam engines is applied: in 1852 sector A used 44 per cent of total motive power of steam engines in the Czech Lands and this percentage rose to 52 per cent in 1880. One of the reasons for these relationships between sectors A and B can be found in the territorial division of labour in the Habsburg Monarchy. At the end of the last stage of the Industrial Revolution sector A was more developed in the Alpine provinces due to the more advanced level of the Styrian and Carinthian iron industy and the Lower Austrian engineering industry, especially in Vienna and its surroundings.[25]

Thus until 1880 the development of producer-goods production in which the iron and mechanical engineering industries held key positions lagged behind the needs of industrialization in the Czech Lands. This became apparent when during the investment boom of 1867 and 1873 further advance in industrialization was almost paralysed and substantial amounts of producer goods had to be imported. Between 1868 and 1873 the average annual imports of iron and iron goods only amounted to 40.6 million gulden, while in the five years between 1861 and 1865 the sum of 5.8 million gulden met existing demand.[26]

Whereas the consumer-goods sector became increasingly decentralized, sector A displayed a strong tendency towards geographical and capital

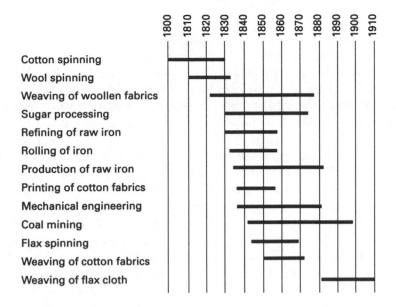

Fig. 11.1 The make-up of the techno-production revolution in the main branches of industry in the Czech Lands.
Source: Author's calculations.

concentration. Within the perimeter of four out of eight Czech Chambers of Commerce and Industry (Prague, Plzeň, Olomouc and Opava) the larger part of the total value of output of the following industries was concentrated: 67 per cent of mining production, 80 per cent of the metallurgy industry and almost 70 per cent of the engineering industry. Engineering was most strongly represented in the region of the Prague Chamber and mining and metallurgy in the region of the Olomouc Chamber (the Vítkovické horní a hutní těžířstvo, the Sobotínsko-štěpanovské horní a hutní těžířstvo, etc.).[27]

At the end of the 1870s the techno-production revolution was completed in iron metallurgy, the last of the branches to pass through the Industrial Revolution in the Czech Lands. Thus by the end of the 1870s and the beginning of the 1880s the process of the Industrial Revolution was accomplished in the Czech Lands, which became the first region of the Habsburg Monarchy to create an adequate technological and production-organizational basis for the factory stage of capitalism with all the consequences for the socio-economic structure of society.[28]

III

At the turn of the eighteenth and nineteenth centuries the Czech Lands belonged to the economically most developed areas of the Habsburg Monarchy. From the mid-eighteenth century a proto-industrialization had been taking place and a number of proto-industrial regions had arisen, where mainly rural inhabitants – but partly also inhabitants of towns – produced industrial goods using traditional handicraft techniques for the wider domestic markets and also for the foreign markets. The majority of the proto-industrial regions in the Czech Lands were engaged in textile production. They were chiefly situated along the northern border of Bohemia, Moravia and Silesia and belonged to the large proto-industrial Saxon–Czech–Silesian region, where the most advanced branches consisted of the linen, cotton and wool industries.[29] At the beginning of the 1790s within Bohemia alone 250,000 persons were employed in spinning flax, 56,000 in spinning wool and 34,000 in hand cotton-spinning; weaving of linen provided a livelihood to 59,000 persons, of wool to 9,000 and of cotton to 5,000 hand weavers; 4,000 persons were employed in glass making, 2,500 in iron metallurgy. Further, hundreds of thousands worked in various other branches of industry in Moravia and Silesia.[30]

The handicraft production of yarn and cloth was mainly organized according to a purchasing and putting-out system, while the decentralized and centralized manufactories were of lesser importance. Investment in production came above all from domestic capital provided by burghers and an important role was also played by capital from the merchant houses of Saxony, Prussian Silesia, Holland and England. A specific characteristic in the Czech Lands was the participation of the domestic nobility in industrial enterprises. These included textile, glass and iron production, that is, those industrial branches which were directly connected with their agricultural estates. At the same time, they took advantage of their seigneurial jurisdiction (forced regulation of the purchase of yarn, pre-emption rights, monopoly of the purchase of goods, etc.). In centralized manufactories some forced labour was employed at inequitable wages and in some instances corvée labour was also used.[31]

For the further development of the Industrial Revolution the expanding proto-industrialization was of decisive importance.[32] It furthered possibilities for capital accumulation, obtained foreign markets for Czech industry, became a 'school of entrepreneurship' for hundreds of factors and manufacturers and, last but not least, it taught the mass of producers professionalism and the discipline of industrial activity. Among others it fulfilled the function of a 'social learning process'.[33]

The dynamic expansion of capitalist production began only with the rise of large mechanized industry and factory organization. In the course of the Industrial Revolution mechanical production and new thermo-chemical processes replaced the traditional forms of proto-industrial production and in the closing decades of the nineteenth century they gained the decisive position in the economy of the Czech Lands.

The arrival of mechanical production set in motion significant structural changes. The existing sources of energy (human-, animal- and water-power) were no longer sufficient. The double-acting steam engine, which was independent of geographical and meteorological conditions and whose performance could be increased and regulated, became the new universal motor of industry. Steam power began to be applied in Czech industry during the 1820s. In 1841 there were 156 engines with an output of 1,384 kW in operation in the Czech Lands; by 1876 their number had risen to 5,244 with an output of 72,724 kW.[34]

Changes within the industrial structure also stimulated notable changes in transportation. The road network was improved; however, the most noteworthy transformation in the region where there was a lack of navigable rivers was the construction of a network of steam-engine railways. The main railway network leading from the Czech region was a part of the railway system of the Habsburg Monarchy and this influenced its orientation, above all, in the direction of Vienna which from the viewpoint of industrial development was not the most practical. The construction of the railways began in the 1830s. The main railway lines were completed during the 1870s. During the next phase, all efforts concentrated on the construction of railway lines of local importance. The construction of railways especially during the second and third phases of the Industrial Revolution became an important stimulating factor for industrial development, above all, mining, iron metallurgy and the machine-production industry.[35]

The transition to steam power, the implementation of new technology in ironworks, the development of the chemical industry and, last but not least, the expansion of railways caused radical changes in fuels and raw materials: wood and charcoal was replaced by coal and coke. Increasing demand for coal led to the rapid expansion of the coalfields of Ostrava, Kladno and Podkrušnohoří.[36] Steam power, mineral fuels and the expansion of rail transport influenced the location of industrial plants as well as of whole industrial centres and regions. While the significance of access to organic fuels (forests), to waterways with an adequate energy-producing flow and to raw materials declined, the importance of the proximity of coalfields and railway lines increased. This, among other factors, facilitated the concentration of industrial capacity in towns.[37] In the course of the Industrial Revolution a number of industrial regions of European significance arose in the Czech Lands: based on the textile and later also the engineering industry the industrial regions of Liberec[38] and Brno[39] arose; on the basis of mining, metallurgy and engineering the industrial region of Ostrava developed;[40] and the Prague industrial region displayed a multi-sectoral base.[41] Intensive population growth was characteristic for all these regions. The population of the industrial region of Prague increased from 121,000 inhabitants in 1843 to 356,000 in 1880, and to 566,000 in 1900. In the industrial region of Ostrava the population grew from 42,000 in 1849 to 97,500 in 1880 and to 222,000 in 1900.[42] This was not natural population growth but occurred through migration from rural areas where the main employment had been in agriculture and home industry, but also from more distant economically backward regions, such as Galicia to Ostrava.[43] This is substantiated by the population census from Moravská Ostrava where only 13 per cent of all inhabitants in Vítkovice in 1880 and only 6 per cent in 1890 were of local origin; the rest were immigrants.

As in a number of other countries in Western and Central Europe the techno-production revolution — that is, the introduction of working machines and factory organization into production — in the Czech Lands began in light industry, in our particular case in the textile industry. This was due to the fact that from the business point of view it was profitable to mechanize production designated for mass consumption. Furthermore, the required investments for the mechanization of light industry were substantially lower than, for instance, in mining and metallurgy, and also the capital turnover was much faster. However, the pace of this process was slowed down by the availability of an abundance of cheap labour in the Bohemian-Moravian region. Therefore the introduction of working machines — for instance, mechanical looms in the textile industry — was not profitable until well into the mid-nineteenth century and handicraft production was ousted very gradually.

The implementation of working machines and new thermo-chemical processes in the individual branches of industry progressed very unevenly. But also within any one branch the various stages of production did not develop uniformly (in the cotton industry, for example, there were differences between spinning, weaving and printing). In the majority of cases the reasons were not related to technical barriers but to general socio-economic conditions which were characteristic for the so-called non-initiating countries (*pays non-initiateurs*), as precisely formulated by Jan Pazdur: 'on peut introduire dans la pratique non pas ce que l'on sait mais ce que l'on peut'.[44]

In the Czech Lands the application of technical and organizational innovations, the pillars of the techno-production revolution, was not original but derived.[45] It began with the spinning of cotton and wool in the first years of the nineteenth century, and permeated into flax spinning only by the 1840s. During the second phase innovations were applied to the food industry, particularly in sugar-beet refining, and to iron metallurgy. Innovations in the last phase entered the engineering industry and the weaving stages of the textile industry: the weaving of linen began to be mechanized by the 1870s but the use of mechanical looms became predominant only at the beginning of the twentieth century. Particularly in this branch of the textile industry traditional handicrafts, proto-industrial forms of organization of production and mechanical factory production existed side by side. Handicraft production functioned partly as an independent segment of production and partly was subordinated to factories as a buffer during cyclical fluctuations.[46] The process of applying technical-organizational innovations to coal and iron mining took a long time to materialize.

In spite of the unevenness and phase shifts, the process of the techno-production revolution in the main branches of industry in the Czech Lands was completed around the turn of the 1870s and 1880s. Evidence for this is provided by the fact that prices of products were determined by the costs of mechanized industry, and goods produced by traditional handicraft techniques had to follow suit.

In a country with strongly developed proto-industrial forms of production the Industrial Revolution did not have the function of 'la création d'une industrie nouvelle' but of 'la transformation d'une industrie traditionelle existante',[47] that is, the function of qualitatively changing this industry. Therefore it is understandable that in this connection we pose the question: was there continuity between proto-industrialization and the Industrial Revolution?

If we look at the question of continuity from the point of view of the location of industrial activity we observe considerable differences between the individual branches: discontinuity prevailed in those branches of industry where technological innovation engendered structural change, as for instance in iron metallurgy and in most of the sections of the food industry. The old charcoal-based 'forest' ironworks became extinct or were converted to other types of production, while new works based on coke technology were established in the vicinity of coalfields. Contrary to this, textile factories were chiefly founded in localities and regions where previously a developed proto-industrial production had existed.[48] The tendency to shift textile factories into towns asserted itself only in the closing phase of the Industrial Revolution.

Unlike in other Central and Western European countries, in the Czech Lands the problem of continuity arose in relation to the person of the entrepreneur. Elements of discontinuity tended to predominate between entrepreneurs of the proto-industrial era and the entrepreneurs of the epoch of the Industrial Revolution. Only a small part of manufactory owners moved up into the ranks of factory owners. Particularly in the textile industry there was more frequent continuity between the putting-out system and the modern factory. Hypothetically the lack of continuity can be explained by the conditions of protectionism and Absolutist interventionism during the manufactory period which was far removed from economic liberalism and the market economy required by the advance of the Industrial Revolution. The differences of these economic-political conditions in the Habsburg Monarchy were so pervasive that old institutions and personages had hardly any chance of further development. If cases of continuity occurred at all, then they were exceptional.

Elements of discontinuity also predominated in the area of the direct producers – the workers. Continuity between the manufactory and the factory was mostly maintained for highly qualified workers. Whereas in the proto-industrial textile industry mainly men were employed and women predominated only in the spinning section, labour in the textile factories consisted chiefly of women and children because they constituted a cheaper work force. Thus, for example, during the 1860s four-fifths of the work force in the manufactories and putting-out enterprises in the cotton region of Frýdek-Místek were men, but two decades later male workers had shrunk to one-fifth to a fourth of the workforce in the cotton factories of this same region.[49]

During the Industrial Revolution in the Czech Lands neither the share of the state nor of joint-stock companies was important. It was the individual entrepreneur or the entrepreneurial family which played the decisive role. This was in spite of the fact that the techno-production revolution was ocurring at a time when the price of equipping factories with machinery was relatively much higher than it had been during the years this process was taking place in England or in Belgium. A further specific feature of industrial development in the Czech Lands was that, alongside bourgeois entrepreneurs, the true-born aristocracy was much more involved in entrepreneurship than elsewhere in Europe.[50] The nobility invested in industrial and mining enterprises, on the one hand, directly – especially after 1848, when it had acquired substantial capital (c. 72 million gulden) by being compensated for the loss of feudal dues, that is, by capitalization of the feudal rent – and on the other hand, by participation in joint-stock companies and banks.[51]

In iron metallurgy, not taking into account numerous state, municipal and ecclesiastical enterprises, bourgeois entrepreneurs owned merely 21 per cent of the total number of enterprises which produced 19 per cent of total output during the 1840s of the nineteenth century. At the end of the 1870s the share of this group rose to 24 per cent and 31 per cent respectively. The share of the true-born nobility in ownership of iron works was 59 per cent in the 1840s and fell to 37 per cent in the 1870s. However, the share of the true-born nobility in the total volume of production remained at two-thirds (!) throughout the whole Industrial Revolution. In reality the share of aristocratic capital was higher because part of it was hidden by share ownership in joint-stock companies and in Viennese banks which also invested in the mining and metallurgy industry. Not before the closing phase of the techno-production revolution did the capital of joint-stock companies in the hands of the bourgeoisie flow into the industry (in 1880 into approximately 30 per cent of the total number of enterprises). Thus the participation of the true-born aristocracy in enterprises in the iron metallurgy industry was extraordinarily high in the Czech Lands.

In the mining industry as well, the share of the true-born nobility was very large. Between 1831 and 1840 more than 30 per cent of all coal mines and 50 per cent of total output was in the hands of the aristocracy. Although this share was greatly reduced in the 1870s, the true-born aristocracy continued to hold a significant place in mining enterprises. Not until the 1890s was the aristocracy increasingly replaced by Austrian and foreign banking capital.[52]

Sugar-beet production became a new field for aristocratic enterprise. In the decade from 1831 to 1840 the true-born aristocracy owned 53 per cent (50 per cent of total output) of the newly established sugar refineries, leaving 47 per cent in non-aristocratic ownership. In the mid-1870s the share of the aristocratic owners fell to 29 per cent and bourgeois entrepreneurs owned 71 per cent, of which 40 per cent was owned by agricultural joint-stock companies.[53]

In the main branch of the industrial sector, the textile industry, aristocratic entrepreneurs were strongly present during the proto-industrial period. Their interest declined in the course of the Industrial Revolution and this branch became the province of entrepreneurs of bourgeois descent (merchants, owners of putting-out enterprises, wealthy town-craftsmen, etc.). For example, in 1841, out of eighty-one cotton-spinning factories only two belonged to aristocrats.

The relatively low share of joint-stock companies in the founding of industrial enterprises was caused by unfavourable Austrian commercial legislation. H. Matis and K. Bachinger[54] state that they were taxed at least twice to four times as highly as personal enterprises. Therefore the interest on the capital of these companies was also unsatisfactory.

The high participation of aristocratic capital in industrial enterprise in the Czech Lands is sometimes held to be responsible for the slow introduction of capital-intensive challenging technical and organizational innovations. Yet this is a one-sided view. We have sufficient evidence to show that a number of enterprises managed by aristocratic families were innovators in the technical advance of industry (the iron works of the Archduke Rudolph of Habsburg in Vítkovice, the sugar refineries and chemical factories of the Counts Salm, the Fürstenberg iron works, etc.).

From the socio-psychological point of view, the behaviour of Czech entrepreneurs exhibited certain specific features which are difficult to compare with other countries. The first generation of industrial entrepreneurs did not normally consider profit as the aim of their entrepreneurial activity but as a means of acquiring higher social prestige. They strove to gain a closer relationship with the true-born aristocracy: formally they attained this by being elevated by the Emperor into nobility, and effectively by adapting their lifestyle to that of the aristocracy. During the Industrial Revolution, sections of the bourgeois entrepreneurs who proclaimed their Czech nationality did not remain in their businesses for more than one or two generations; they usually invested their capital into land-ownership (following the pattern of the medieval burghers) and pursued other activities (arts, science, patronage).[55] This was one of the serious drains of accumulated capital out of industrial activity, which slowed down innovative investment

IV

What was the place of the Industrial Revolution in the development of the Czech Lands and their society? Before the beginning of the Industrial Revolution the complex of economic and social relations was integrated into the economic and legal structure of the aristocratic manorial system, from the basis of which sprang up economic as well as administrative and political functions. The Industrial Revolution, the greater part of which in the Czech Lands preceded the bourgeois revolution – that is, the political revolution – began to disturb these structural relations even in those areas where the new relationships were directly generated from them. It also manifested a tendency towards overcoming regional barriers and restrictions by creating new economic and social functions. This stimulated the rise of new manufacturing, commercial and also cultural and political centres, distinguished by a dynamism which contrasted with the obvious social, economic, technical, commercial, but also political, cultural and ideological stagnation of surviving elements of the patrimonial system based on agrarian production. It inspired the expansion of transport, was the cause of wide-ranging population shifts both spatially (through industrial centres and regions) and structurally (by sectoral shifts in industry, commerce and transport). The Industrial Revolution thus realized changes which in the Czech Lands resulted in the rise of modern industrial society.

NOTES

1 An exception is the first use of the concept 'Industrie-Revolution' in our connotation, within the area of the Habsburg Monarchy, by M. Fränzl, *Statistik*, III (Vienna, 1841), p. 318.

2 Cf., for instance, A. Salz, *Geschichte der Böhmischen Industrie in der Neuzeit* (Munich and Leipzig, 1913) and K. Hoch, *Čechy na prahu moderního hospodářství* (Bohemia on the Eve of Modern Economy) (Prague, 1936). The term was utilized without explaining its content by B. Mendl, *Hospodářský vývoj Evropy* (Economic Development of Europe) (Prague, 1931, 2nd edn 1947), p. 90.

3 J. Purš 'K otázce průmyslové revoluce v hlavních odvětvích textilního průmyslu v českých zemích' (On the question of the Industrial Revolution in the main branches of the textile industry in the Czech Lands), *Československý časopis historický*, 2 (1954), pp. 93–143. Discussed in more detail in the book J. Purš, *Průmyslová revoluce v českých zemích* (The Industrial Revolution in the Czech Lands) (Prague, 1960).

4 S. G. Strumilin, *Promyshlennyi perevorot v Rossii* (Industrial Revolution in Russia) (Moscow, 1944) and V. K. Yatsunsky, 'Promyshlennyi perevorot v Rossii' (Industrial Revolution in Russia), *Voprosy istorii*, 12 (1952), pp. 48–70.

5 C. M. Cipolla, 'The Industrial Revolution', introduction to C.M. Cipolla (ed.), *The Industrial Revolution* in *The Fontana Economic History of Europe* (London and Glasgow, 1973), vol. III, pp. 8, 12–13.

6 K. Piesowicz, *Powszechna historia gospodarcza* (General Economic History) (Warsaw, 1967), p. 184.

7 This concept is defined in more detail by M. Myška, *Die mährisch schlesische Eisenindustrie in der Industriellen Revolution* (Prague, 1970).

8 W. Jonas, 'Kritische Bemerkungen und Ergänzungen', in J. Kuczynski, *Vier Revolutionen der Produktivkräfte* (Berlin, 1975), pp. 147–53.

9 Brno as the centre of the textile industry can be given as an example. During the Industrial Revolution the production of woollen fabrics was here six times higher than the consumption of Moravia and Silesia required. See A. Špiesz, 'Priemyselná revolúcia v Anglicku a na území dnešného Čeckoslovenska' (The Industrial Revolution in England and on the territory of today's Czechoslovakia), *Historický časopis SAV*, 19 (1971), pp. 58–61.

10 I. Berend and Gy. Ránki, 'Ungarns wirtschaftliche Entwicklung 1848–1918' in A. Wandruszka and P. Urbanitsch (eds.), *Die Habsburgermonarchie 1848–1918*, vol. II. A. Brusatti (ed.) *Die wirtschaftliche Entwicklung* (Vienna, 1973), pp. 464–6.

11 H. Matis, *Österreichs Wirtschaft 1848–1913* (Berlin, 1972), pp. 28–30.

12 F. Fillunger, *Vergleichende Statistik über die Real- und Produktionswerthe* (Vienna, 1868) and F. X. Neumann-Spallart, *Die Ernten und der Wohlstand in Österreich-Ungarn* (Vienna, 1874).

13 F. v. Fellner, 'Die Verteilung des Volksvermögens und Volkseinkommens der Länder der Ungarischen Heiligen Krone zwischen dem heutigen Ungarn und

den Successions-Staaten' *Metron*, 3, 2 (1923), pp. 226–307, E. Waizner, 'Das Volkseinkommen Alt-Oesterreichs und seine Verteilung auf die Nachfolgestaaten', *Metron* 7, 4 (1928), pp. 97–182.

14 J. Hain, *Handbuch der Statistik des österreichischen Kaiserstaates*, vol. II (Vienna, 1853), pp. 373, 380–1.

15 Calculated according to 'Die Ergebnisse der Volkszählung und der mit derselben verbundenen Zählung der häuslichen Nutztiere vom 31. Dezember 1880 in den im Reichsrathe vertretenen Königreichen und Ländern', *Österreichische Statistik 1880*, vol. I (Vienna, 1882).

16 'Berufsstatistik nach den Ergebnissen der Volkszählung vom 31. Dezember 1900 in den im Reichrsrathe vertretenen Königreichen and Ländern', part 8: Böhmen, pp. 213–45; part 9: Mähren, pp. 96–131; part 10: Schlesien, pp. 46–63, in *Österreichische Statistik*, vol. 66 (Vienna, 1904).

17 C. Czoernig, *Statistisches Handbüchlein für die Österreichische Monarchie*, vol. I (Vienna, 3rd edn, 1861), pp. 72–3.

18 Calculations according to tables in the work of J. Purš, 'Použití parních strojů v průmyslu českých zemí v období nástupu imperialismu' ('Utilization of steam engines in industry in the Czech Lands in the period of the rise of imperialism'), *Československý časopis historický*, 3 (1955), pp. 268–69.

19 Calculated according to the method by N. Th. Gross, 'Industrialization in Austria in the nineteenth century', unpublished dissertation, University of California at Berkeley, 1966, p. 65 and 'Austrian industrial statistics 1880/85 and 1911/13', *Zeitschrift für die gesammte Staatswissenschaft*, 124 (1968), pp. 36–69.

20 F. Herz, 'Die Schwierigkeiten der industriellen Produktion zu Österreich', *Zeitschrift für Volkswirtschaft, Sozialpolitik und Verwaltung*, 19 (1910), pp. 693–7.

21 Czoernig, *Statistisches Handbüchlein*, pp. 72–3.

22 K. Novotný, 'Vytváření manufakturního dělnictva v českých zemích' (Formation of the manufactory working force in the Czech Lands), in *Hospodářské dějiny – Economic History*, vol. III (Prague, 1979), pp. 149–59.

23 H. Herz, *Die Heimarbeit und der Nothstand der Heimarbeiter in der mährischen Industrie* (Brünn, 1904), pp. 18–19.

24 Purš, *Průmyslová revoluce*, pp. 14–15.

25 M. Myška, 'Hutnictví železa v průmyslové revoluci. Výrobní odvětví v ekonomických souvislostech průmyslové revoluce v českých zemích a v habsburské monarchii' (Iron metallurgy in the Industrial Revolution. An industrial branch in the economic contexts of the Industrial Revolution in the Czech Lands and the Habsburg Monarchy) in *Z dějin hutnictví* (History of Metallurgy), vol. X (Prague, 1981), pp. 277–8.

26 M. Myška, 'Vliv výstavby železniční sítě na rozvoj hutnictví železa v habsburské monarchii a v českých zemích 1830–1914 (The impact of railway construction on the development of iron metallurgy in the Habsburg Monarchy and the Czech Lands) in *Z dějin hutnictví*, vol. XVIII (Prague, 1989), pp. 133–8.

27 Myška, 'Hutnictví železa', p. 278.

28 Cf. A. N. Chistozvonov, *Genezis kapitalizma: problemy metodologii* (Genesis of Capitalism: Methodological Problems) (Moscow, 1985), pp. 267–8.

29 See, for example, A. Klíma, 'Hausindustrie, Manufaktur und Frühindustrialisierung in Böhmen', *Österreichische Osthefte*, 30 (1988), pp. 528–41 and 'Probleme der Proto-Industrie in Böhmen zur Zeit Maria Theresias', in his *Economy, Industry and Society in Bohemia in the 17th–19th Centuries* (Prague, 1991), pp. 99–116.

30 K. Novotný, 'Průmyslová revoluce' (Industrial Revolution), in *Dějiny techniky za feudalismu* (History of Technology under Feudalism) (Prague, 1974), p. 48.

31 M. Myška, 'Pre-industrial iron-making in the Czech Lands: the labour force and production relations *circa* 1350–*circa* 1840', *Past & Present*, 82 (1979), pp. 44–72.

32 J. Komlos, 'Thoughts on the transition from proto-industrialization to modern industrialization in Bohemia', *East Central Europe*, 7 (1980), pp. 198–206.

33 H. Freudenberger, 'Die proto-industrielle Entwicklungsphase in Österreich. Proto-Industrialisierung als sozialer Lernprozess', in H. Matis (ed.), *Von der Glückseligkeit des Staates. Staat, Wirtschaft und Gesellschaft im Zeitalter des aufgeklärten Absolutismus* (Berlin, 1981), p. 355.

34 Novotný, 'Průmyslová revoluce', p. 49.

35 L. Kárníková, *Vývoj uhelného průmyslu v českých zemích do roku 1880* (Development of the coal mining industry in the Czech Lands up to 1880) (Prague, 1960).

36 Myška, 'Vliv výstavby železniční sítě, pp. 133.

37 J. Purš, 'Changes in the spatial organization of industry in Bohemia at the threshold of the Industrial Revolution' in *Historická geografie* (Historical Geography), vol. 19 (Prague, 1980), pp. 282. and J. Matějček, 'Rozmístění manufakturní a tovární výroby v českých zemích v letech 1780–1848' (Location of manufactory and factory production in the Czech Lands, 1780–1848), in *Z dějin textilu* (Textile History), vol. XI (1987), pp. 47–94. M. Myška, 'Facteurs de la localisation de la révolution industrielle', *Revue d'histoire des mines et de la métallurgie*, 1 (1969), pp. 45–74.

38 J. Joza, *Z minulosti textilního průmyslu v libereckém kraji* (From the Past of the Textile Industry in the Liberec Region) (Liberec, 1958).

39 J. Vytiska, 'Brněnská průmyslová oblast v první polovině 19. století' ('The Brno industrial region during the first half of the nineteenth century') in *Brno v minulosti a dnes*, (Brno in the Past and Today) vol. 5 (1963), pp. 313–89.

40 M. Myška (ed.), *Studie k vývoji ostravské průmyslové oblasti* (Studies in the Development of the Ostrava Industrial Region) (Ostrava, 1966).

41 Z. Míka, 'Počátky průmyslové výroby v Praze' (The beginnings of industrial production in Prague), in *Pražský sborník historický* (Prague Historical Collection), vol. XII (1980), pp. 85–169.

42 L. Kárníková, *Vývoj obyvatelstva v českých zemích 1754–1914* (The development of the population in the Czech Lands during 1754–1914) (Prague, 1965), pp. 109.

43 B. Pitronová, *Haličské migrace na Ostravsku* (Migration from Galicia to the Ostrava Region) (Opava, 1979).

44 J. Pazdur, 'Le progrès' technique dans la sidérurgie du royaume de Pologne en rapport avec la révolution technique en Angleterre (1760–1830 environ)' in *L'acquisition des techniques par les pays non-initiateurs* (Colloques internationaux du CNRS, 538) (Paris, 1973), p. 530.

45 See F. Redlich, 'Die Neuerung im Geschäftsleben' in F. Redlich, *Der Unternehmer* (Göttingen, 1964), pp. 125–7.

46 M. Myška, 'Opožděná industrializace. Proto-industriální výrobní formy a vztahy za průmyslové revoluce na příkladu lnářského průmyslu ve Slezsku' (Delayed industrialization. Proto-industrial production forms and relations during the Industrial Revolution illustated by the flax industry in Silesia), *Z dějin textilu*, vol. XI (1987), pp. 95–159.

47 F. Crouzet, 'Quelques problèmes de l'histoire de l'industrialisation au XIXe siècle', *Revue d'histoire économique et sociale*, 53 (1975), p. 529.

48 K. Novotný, 'Rozmístění manufakturní výroby v Čechách kolem roku 1790' (Location: of manufactory production in Bohemia around 1790), *Hospodářské dějiny – Economic History*, vol. XI (1983), p. 5.

49 Myška, 'Opožděná industrializace', pp. 95–159.

50 F. Redlich, 'Europäische Aristokratie und wirtschaftliche Entwicklung', in Redlich, *Der Unternehmer*, pp. 289–92.

51 M. Myška, 'Der Adel der Böhmischen Länder. Seine wirtschaftliche Basis und ihre Entwicklung', in A. V. Reden-Dohna and R. Melville (eds.), *Der Adel an der Schwelle des bürgerlichen Zeitalters 1780–1860* (Stuttgart, 1988), pp. 169–89.

52 M. Myška, 'Das Unternehmertum im Eisenhüttenwesen in den Böhmischen Ländern während der Industriellen Revolution', *Zeitschrift für Unternehmensgeschichte*, 28 (1983), pp. 98–119.

53 F. Dudek, *Vývoj cukrovarnického průmyslu v českých zemích do roku 1872* (The Development of the Sugar Industry in the Czech Lands to 1872) (Prague, 1979), pp. 44–8, 57, 138–40.

54 H. Matis and K. Bachinger, 'Österreichs industrielle Entwicklung' in Wandruszka and Urbanitsch (eds.), vol. I: Brusatti (ed.) *Die wirtschaftliche Entwicklung*, pp. 215–19. See also F. Wiesner, 'Die Besteuerung der Stadt und des Kapitals in Österreich', *Zeitschrift für Volkswirtschaft, Sozialpolitik und Verwaltung*, 16 (1907), pp. 209–10.

55 On the mentality of Czech entrepreneurs during the Industrial Revolution, see J. Mertl, 'Česká buržoazie (The Czech bourgeoisie), a manuscript in the archives of the National Technical Museum in Prague, inventory no. 1626.

———⊨=⟫∙◇∙⟨=⊨———

TWELVE

Hungary: a semi-successful peripheral industrialization

IVAN T. BEREND

INTRODUCTION

THE age of revolutions, the decades around the turn of the eighteenth and nineteenth centuries, dramatically changed the economy and society of Western Europe. A demographic revolution altered the traditional, thousand-year-long birth and death rates and caused a population explosion. An agricultural revolution expanded arable land and increased productivity and production. Mechanized industrial firms, the greatest invention of the age, transformed the entire economy, the occupational structure and even the landscape. New industrial cities emerged and began to concentrate the majority of the population. The traditional speed of transportation quadrupled when old horse-driven coaches were replaced by railways. The dramatically transformed economic and social structures are clearly reflected by the British figures of 1841: only 22 per cent of gross national product (GNP) was produced by agriculture while the contribution of industry rose to 34 per cent and of services to 44 per cent. Industrial economy generated a rapid growth and a growing gap between the first industrial nation (and the countries of Western Europe, which shortly followed the British pattern) and the European periphery. In the mid-nineteenth century the per capita GNP of Britain and the other earliest industrialized core countries were, respectively, 80 per cent and almost 50 per cent higher than that of the European average; compared to Eastern Europe, the core's level was about three times higher.[1]

As a peripheral country of Europe, Hungary could not follow the path of the industrializing West. The 'Dual Revolution' of Britain (industrial) and France (political) did not touch Hungary's rigid social-economic structures, which remained frozen into its traditional feudal state. Preserved noble privileges, reintroduced servile labour service (*robot*) created insurmountable barriers to modernization. The absence of the Industrial

Revolution is clearly shown by the unchanged role of agriculture until the last third of the nineteenth century. In 1865, 75 per cent of the gainfully employed population of Hungary still worked in agriculture and the contribution of industrial production to GNP remained as low as 15 per cent.[2]

The transforming West, however, challenged the rest of Europe by offering an unlimited market for traditional export goods as well as a pattern to emulate. Enlightened travellers to Britain from the backward countries recognized the importance of adjusting to a transforming world and became advocates for change in their native countries. Count István Széchenyi became a forerunner and advocate of reforms in Hungary: he strongly criticized the existing feudal institutions, including serf labour and the lack of modern credit system in his book *Hitel* (Credit), published in 1830. From 1825 on, the Hungarian Diet started to debate the possibility of reforms and initiate changes. Széchenyi himself became a prime mover who worked out plans for railway constructions, initiated intensive waterway improvements and established the first steam mill in the country. His reform movement got an even greater impetus during the 1840s when Lajos Kossuth's agitation mobilized the country. Kossuth adopted Friedrich List's ideas of protectionism, demanding an independent Hungarian tariff system against the more industrialized 'Cisleithanian' part of the Monarchy. In 1840, Hungary did not enter the age of industrialization. The bulk of the industrial population was made up of some 230,000 independent artisans and their 78,000 employees, whereas only 23,000 factory workers were employed in mechanized factories. The census of 1841 listed only nine steam engines in Hungary. The biggest industrial firm, the shipyard of Obuda, was established by the Austrian Danube Steam Ship Navigation Co. In 1846, the first railway of 46 kilometres between Pest and Vác, the very first part of the Pest–Vienna line, was opened. The first savings bank was established in 1836, followed by the first commercial bank five years later. The so-called Reform Age between 1825 and 1848, thus, attacked and attempted to reform the *ancien régime*, and initiated certain changes.

Half-hearted, delayed and ambiguous reforms on the one hand, and the deliberate effort of Absolutist Habsburg policy to conserve the existing status quo on the other, did not allow a breakthrough. The historical turning-point of the modern capitalist transformation of Hungary was bound up with the Revolution of 1848–9. The abolition of serfdom and of noble privileges, along with the introduction of legal equality and free access to land and offices, opened a new epoch and created an adequate prerequisite of modernization. An immediate economic modernization, however, did not follow. The 1848 Revolution, led by the lower nobility, preserved too many old institutions and customs. Medieval institutions, such as the system of latifundia, the guilds and traditional property rights of mines still stood in the way of rapid transformation. The grave consequences of the defeat of the revolutionary struggle against Austria also weighed heavily on the country. Although irreversible achievements of the Revolution, such as the liberation of the serfs, were confirmed by Imperial patent in 1853, and the customs duties between Hungary and the Austrian provinces were abolished in July 1851, the long years of military administration, the centralizing efforts of the Habsburgs and the unsettled political conditions of the country, including the stubborn passive resistance of the Hungarian political elite, blocked the road of modern industrialization.

The stormy years of Habsburg Absolutism, however, became a period of gradual transition. Exploiting the possibility of a dramatically enlarging food market in Austria and Bohemia, Hungarian agriculture expanded production. Merchant families of Pest-Buda diligently delivered agricultural products to the western part of the Monarchy and served as middlemen by selling Austrian industrial goods in the Hungarian market. Intermediate trade became the most profitable business in Hungary. Trade became a major source of capital accumulation and moderate prosperity during the early 1860s, when most of the rich grain merchants of Budapest started to invest in the flour-milling industry, laying the foundations of a world-famous export branch of Hungarian food processing.[3]

The Austro-Hungarian customs union and the striking increase of trade generated the need for modern transportation, which was also an Imperial interest. The decades-long dreams of the Hungarian reformers and revolutionaries, the plans of a Széchenyi and a Kossuth, thus, were realized by Austrian financial groups with the active collaboration of the Habsburg administration. After 1849, an almost entirely non-existent, 200 kilometre-long Hungarian railway 'system' expanded more than ten times, as first Vienna and Pest were linked by rail, and then, through Pest, new lines were built towards the great grain-producing and cattle-raising regions. By 1866, a railroad system totalling 2,160 kilometres in length connected Vienna–Pest–Szeged–Temesvár (now Timişoara in Romania) the most important grain-producing region) and Vienna–Pest– Szolnok–Debrecen (the centre for stock-raising east of the Tisza River). Gradual transition, in spite of unsettled political conditions, was also helped by a rather moderate development of banking. In 1866, about eighty financial institutions were in operation, mostly savings banks, as opposed to thirty-six in 1848; one of them, the Hungarian Land Credit Institute (Magyar Földhitel Intézet), established in 1863, was the first large bank of the country.[4] Bank credits were also accrued by the big Austrian banks.

In 1867 the Austro-Hungarian Compromise (*Ausgleich*) put an end to the period of uncertainty which had prevailed since 1849 and completed the creation of the most important prerequisites of transformation. Austria abandoned her efforts to centralize the Empire and the Compromise established a dualist state structure with two centres. Hungary formed its own government and civil administration. A new customs and trade agreement preserved the tariff union, while a uniform currency and the conversion of the Austrian National Bank into an Austro-Hungarian National Bank (1878) economically unified Austria-Hungary. A huge Empire and market with fifty million inhabitants and a self-sufficient Imperial unit created the stable conditions for Hungarian modernization for the coming half century. Hungary, with the background of the highly developed Austrian banking system and extensive Austrian capital investments in its infrastructure, emerged to the stage of prosperity and rapid capitalistic transformation. On this basis some element of the core's transformation gained ground and started to form a new framework for a modern economy. One of these elements was an emerging demographic revolution: with certain marked differences, Hungary's demographic trends followed the Western demographic revolution.

POPULATION EXPANSION, SOCIAL AND EDUCATION CHANGES

The population of the most developed countries of Western Europe which became the core of the world economic system in the early modern times increased from 45.1 million to 162.4 million – thus by 3.6 times – between 1800 and 1910. The European periphery, where the population more than trebled, showed a similar trend. In Central and Eastern Europe, the increase of population was 3.9 times.[5] Hungary, nevertheless, belonged to the 'slower' countries: according to the census of 1787, its population was 9.3 million, which increased to 13.8 million by 1850, and to 20.9 million by 1910. This moderate, 225 per cent increase was lower than the European average.

At the beginning of the twentieth century, 37 births per 1,000 inhabitants were more or less equal to the late-eighteenth-century birth rate in the European core. The death rate, however, dropped to 25.7 per 1,000, compared to 35–46 per 1,000 in the 1820s, and reached the highest rate in the West.[6] These figures reflected the ambiguity of modernization in Hungary. Birth rates still showed the characteristics of a rural, non-industrialized society, whereas death rates reflected the dramatic changes of the modern age. Life expectancy at birth had increased from 17–21 years to 39 years in one century.

The breakthrough of the modern demographic trend went side by side with an increase in mobility which strongly transformed the social base of the country. One of the most visible factors of increased mobility was mass emigration, mostly to the United States. In the last decade of the nineteenth century, roughly half a million people left the country and another 1.4 million followed them up to the end of the First World War.[7] Internal migration, however, was even greater. In 1910 roughly 6 million people, about one-third of the population, lived and worked in places other than the locality of their birth. Nearly 1 million people moved to the capital city. In the mid-nineteenth century the three independent settlements of Pest, Buda and Obuda had about 150,000 inhabitants. After the unification of the city in 1873, the newly founded Budapest rapidly developed and by 1913, with its satellite-settlements and industrial suburbs, its population surpassed the 1 million mark. Overall the urban population easily doubled during this period. In 1913 about one-quarter of the population lived in cities. This transformation expressed an ongoing modernization of the Hungarian society. The majority of the working population still lived in the countryside and worked in agriculture. The most important changes, however, took place in the middle strata of the society. In the traditional 'noble society', strongly and strictly hierarchical, the possibility of the rise of a modern middle class was practically absent. The nobility represented about 5 per cent of the population and remained rather closed. Upward mobility from the rank of the peasantry – with the exception of the church hierarchy – was excluded. The scarcely existing urban population could not fill the gap. During the second half of the century, however, the characteristic feudal rigidity started to melt. The gentry, the traditional noble middle stratum, rapidly lost ground. Before 1848 the number of families of the landed middle nobility was about 30,000 but around the turn of the century only 7,000. From the déclassé gentry, however, a bureaucratic–military elite emerged and occupied a great part of the ministerial and county administrations, and the military and legal posts in the country. The *office*, the famous, historical family names and, last but not least, important connections and family links still assured a kind of 'gentleman' status or at least an 'upper-class consciousness'.[8]

In spite of this legacy, a new middle class began to emerge. As a consequence, and partly as a survival of formal noble society, the peasantry, including even its well-to-do upper layers, remained excluded from society. Its access to middle-class positions, with very personal exceptions, remained closed. The gap, however, was partly filled by non-indigenous elements, immigrants from Austria and Bohemia and even Western European countries, and a mass Jewish immigration from the newly annexed Galician part of the Austro-Hungarian Monarchy. This latter immigration was relatively large. As a result of permanent immigration from Galicia, the number of Jews, which was 75,000 in 1785, increased to 851,000 in 1900. Before the First World War, roughly 5 per cent of the population of Hungary was Jewish. In Budapest the percentage reached nearly 25.[9] Since former restrictions banned Jewish landed property and, in spite of liberal political practice, any kind of occupation connected with the state remained an exception for Jews, the increasing and rapidly assimilating Hungarian Jewry started to fill the gap of the non-existent indigenous middle class. Though 35 per cent of the Jews became blue-collar workers, another third occupied white-collar posts: nearly two-thirds of the new business bureaucracy and half of the lawyers, medical doctors and journalists were recruited from their ranks. The remaining third made a living from trade, artisan work and business in general. From countryside pedlars to shopkeepers to pioneering entrepreneurs, fully half of the newly emerging middle class was Jewish. 'Jew' became a synonym for shopkeeper in the Hungarian countryside. The number of independent small entrepreneurs in industry, trade, transportation and intellectual positions almost doubled between 1870 and 1910 from more than 400,000 to more than 800,000 people.

The outstanding career of the Weiss family may be seen as a charac-teristic case of the birth of a successful entrepreneurial class. The first generation (Adolf) was a Jewish village artisan (pipe-maker), turned merchant, who moved to the capital and participated in the grain trade with Austria in the 1850s, and later invested in flour mills in the 1860s. The second generation (Berthold and Manfred), from the accumulated family wealth, established a tinned-food factory, and then gradually built up the largest engineering firm of the country employing 30,000 workers during the First World War.[10] Another striking case was the Chorin family, descended from a Moravian rabbi who immigrated and settled in Arad (now in Romania). The second generation (Ferenc) turned to jour-nalism and then to politics, and from there to entrepreneurial activity as the top manager of one of the biggest coal-mine companies, a partner in big-banking business and the founder of the Association of Hungarian Industrialists.[11]

Gaps in the ranks of the emerging middle class were also filled by immi-grants from Austria, Bohemia and even from Germany, Switzerland and other Western countries. The existence of the Monarchy, its huge terri-tory and open borders gave ground to what was at that time typical intra-national mobility. The dearth of highly qualified workers was filled by skilled labourers who settled in Hungary from the Czech Lands and Austrian territories. In the early period of industrialization a great part of the demand for skilled workers was satisfied by attracting labour from the western part of the Monarchy. In 1875, 25 per cent of the workers in Budapest and 35 per cent of the workers of the more sophisticated iron-and-engineering industry were non-Hungarians.[12] When the labour movement began, during the 1870–80s, even the language of the first workers' organizations was German and their newspaper (*Arbeiter Wochenkronik*) was published in German. The number of entrepreneurs who moved to and settled in Hungary was, of course, much smaller. The importance of their immigration, however, was especially great. The Austrians Dreher and Freund, the Swiss Haggenmacher and Ganz or the Bavarian Mechwart and the Norwegian Gregerson – to mention the most outstanding names – became the most successful pioneers of Hungarian industrialization.

An emerging middle class of assimilated Jewish, German, Czech and other entrepreneurs played an important role in providing a better response to the challenge of the industrialized western provinces. They helped Hungary to react better than many other peripheral countries of Europe. A further element of a more successful response was a pioneering liberal educational reform and a far more advanced educational system than in most of the European peripheries. Based on the result of the educational reform of Maria Theresa in the second half of the eighteenth century, the real turning-point occurred immediately after the Austro-Hungarian Compromise. Baron József Eötvös, the Minister of Education of the revolutionary government of 1848, and one of the leading figures in the reform movement, initiated the law of compulsory and free education for children from six to twelve in elementary schools and up to fifteen years of age in so-called Repeaters' Schools. In 1868, when the law was enacted, 68 per cent of the population of Hungary was illiterate and only 48 per cent school-age children attended schools. An extensive school-building and teacher-training programme helped to make the new law a success. In the school year of 1910–11, 89 per cent of the school-age generation attended school and illiteracy dropped to 32 per cent. The percentage among wage earners was 25 to 28 per cent. Illiteracy was restricted more and more to the older generations. Although secondary education remained an exclusive privilege of the children of the élite, and only 5 per cent of the secondary-school generation studied in German-type *Gymnasiums* (secondary schools) before the First World War, and higher education was available for only 10,000 to 14,000 students, the educational level of Hungary was dramatically elevated and efficiently served the country's interest in adjusting to a transformed Western Europe.[13] Special political and social conditions helped to generate a genuine internal modernization process in Hungary.

INVESTMENTS AND RAILWAYS

Industrialization of Hungary was generated by the 'pull effect' of the steeply increasing market possibilities, the increased demand or food and raw materials in the more developed western part of the Monarchy. Aiming to meet the needs and requirements of its rapid economic expansion, Austria and the Czech Lands directly contributed to Hungarian investments and input of know-how and expertise. Capital export from the Western core countries started in the early nineteenth century but gained a tremendous impetus after 1870. From $6 billion that year, its volume increased more than sevenfold to $46 billion by 1913. On the European periphery French and German capital played the prime role. Up to the 1890s, between 10 and 14 per cent of exported French capital was invested into the Monarchy. Nearly 23 per cent of German capital exported to Europe was channelled to Austria-Hungary.[14] Since Austrian capital accumulation rapidly increased, imported and exported capital was quite balanced in the western part of the Monarchy. Moreover, Austria and Bohemia invested huge amounts of capital in Hungary. From the 5.5 billion crowns of exported capital from Austria and Bohemia up to early twentieth century, 4.7 billion went to Hungary, and played a decisive part in financing the Hungarian economy. Between 1867 and 1913, 40 per cent of invested capital in Hungary came from west of the River Leitha. Extra-Hungarian sources dominated the finance of state loans. More than 55 per cent of them were held abroad, 23 per cent in Austria alone. Almost 55 per cent of municipal bonds and debentures, issued in Hungary, were held abroad, 27 per cent of them in Austria. Large investments financed Hungarian banks, mining and industrial companies through Austrian mortage loans to Hungary. The bulk (70 per cent) of railway bonds issued were sold outside Hungary, 37 per cent in Germany and 33 per cent in Austria.[15] The most spectacular contribution of Austrian and German investment in the Hungarian economy was financing the building of a modern transportation system. It had started in the 1850s and 1860s, but gained a tremendous impetus after the *Ausgleich*. Modernization of traditional water transportation was rapidly continued, especially after the Treaty of Berlin (1878), when the waterworks on the lower Danube was completed in five stages by 1896. The number of steamboats and barges – 135 and 532 respectively in 1867; 338 and 1,500 in 1913 – roughly trebled on the 3,500-kilometre-long navigable waterways during the half century before the First World War.[16]

In view of the limitation of water transport, however, railways seemed the main possible way of transporting huge export surpluses to the industrial centres of Cisleithania. After the first major lines were completed and

Table 12.1. *Length of railways in kilometres*

Year	Length
1850	222
1867	2,285
1873	6,253
1890	11,246
1900	17,108
1913	22,084

the relatively modest construction of 2,285 kilometres of lines were built by 1867, an unparalleled construction boom almost trebled the line length in six years, that is, between 1867 and 1873, when nearly twice as many lines were built than during the twenty years before the Compromise (see table 12.1). Most of these lines (84 per cent) were privately owned. The state, however, strongly supported construction by guaranteeing 5 per cent interest on capital invested if reported earnings did not reach that figure. This commitment was given, usually for ninety years, at the time when the government issued a concession. This institution opened the road for unparalleled speculation and profiteering. The government paid only 2 million crowns in 1870 but almost 32 million in 1874. The main financiers of railway building were twenty-one banks, fifteen of whom were Austrian and led by the Austrian Rothschilds, who also acted as intermediaries of French, German and English financial groups. After the Great Depression of 1873, which temporarily stopped railway construction, the state intervened again. In December 1877, Austria returned to a system of state railways, and Hungary soon followed. Most of the private lines were taken over by the state. At the turn of the century, only 3,000 kilometres remained in private hands and all of the new lines were built by the state.[17] The dramatic development of the Hungarian railway network resulted in a railway density of European standards (see table 12.2).[18]

Hungarian railway density was close to, and from a certain point of view even ahead of that of the West. Existing capacities, however, were much less exploited and reached only about one-third of the Western level. This fact clearly shows that railway construction was much more intensive than in countries of similar peripheral positions and financial possibilities. The reason for this stems from the practically 100 per cent Austrian and foreign investments along with Imperial economic and strategic interests. Consequently, a railway system was produced beyond the given economic need of the country. One can not, however, argue

Table 12.2. *Railways before the First World War*

	Hungary	European periphery, total	European core, total
Land area/1km line in sq.km.	15.73	157.66	10.14
Length of line/100,000 inhab. (in km)	110.0	59.4	90.2
Weight of goods transp./ inhab. (in 100,000t/annum)	3.00	1.66	8.18
No. of journeys/ inhab./annum	5.6	2.5	21.9

that the oversized transport facility was built at the expense of other branches. In reality it was through the railways that the country could build a strong and ever-growing economic relationship with Austria and the West. Transportation became the prime mover in generating an agricultural boom and contributing to the emergence of an export-led growth. Railways, in addition, acted as multipliers and had a tremendous influence on other branches of the economy, including the expansion of the labour market which enabled hundreds of thousands to become wage workers. It is hardly possible to overestimate its impact on industrialization as well.

THE FOUNDATION AND ROLE OF A MODERN BANKING SYSTEM

The establishment of a modern banking system was another striking legacy of the post-1867 Austrian capital inflow into Hungary. Eighty financial institutions, mostly small savings banks, which existed in 1866, represented a modest start. A turning-point was signalled in 1867 when the Austrian Rothschilds founded the Hungarian General Credit Bank (Magyar Általános Hitelbank) with the contribution of the Credit-Anstalt, the leading Vienna bank. The Hitelbank, together with four other Crédit Mobilier-type major Budapest banks, which were engaged in lending and speculative investments, participated in extensive foundation of joint-stock companies and stock-exchange speculation. Banks and savings institutions mushroomed during the *Gründerzeit*. Their numbers increased from 78 to 429, and their capital assets from 169 to 531 million crowns between 1867 and 1873. The great crash of the Vienna Exchange on 9 May 1873, however, stopped the growth of and partly even destroyed the Hungarian

Table 12.3. *Development of the Hungarian banking system*

Year	Number of institutions	Share and reserve funds	Deposits (in 100,000 crowns)	Bills of exchange in 1,000 crowns)	Mortgage stock
1848	36	3.7	19.1	2.7	17.3
1867	107	28.9	143.1	81.2	170.1
1873	637	199.6	348.4	267.6	333.7
1913	5,993	2,568.4	4,123.6	3,266.2	3,941.8

bank system. As a result, seventy-four credit institutions collapsed in Hungary, including four of the five big banks founded after the Compromise. Only the Rothschilds' Hitelbank survived and became one of the pillars of a newly emerging banking system during the 1880s. Austrian banks and French financial groups started to invest in existing but until that time relatively small-scale Hungarian banking institutions after 1879 and created the new big banks of the country. The Hungarian Discount and Exchange Bank (Magyar Leszámitoló és Pénzvalto Bank), the Hungarian Mortgage Credit Bank (Magyar Jelzáloghitel Bank), the historic Hungarian Commercial Bank of Pest (Pesti Magyar Kereskedelmi Bank) which was founded in 1841, and later (in 1890) the Hungarian Bank of Industry and Commerce (Magyar Ipar és Kereskedelmi Bank) formed the core of the financial system of Hungary. Besides these huge banks, a great number of savings banks, savings and loan associations and provincial banking houses appeared (see table 12.3).

The five leading banks before the First World War, together with their 153 affiliated credit institutions, controlled 58 per cent of the total capital resources of the Hungarian credit system. Meanwhile the predominantly Crédit Mobilier-type banks of the 1860s and 1870s were transformed into investment banks of the German type, and retained permanent control over a great part of Hungary's industry. The five biggest banks – especially the Commercial Bank (Kereskedelmi Bank) and the Credit Bank (Hitelbank), which owned fifty-nine and sixty-three industrial firms respectively – controlled 47 per cent of the shares of the Hungarian industrial share-holding companies in 1913. At the beginning of the twentieth century, 55 per cent of the shares of the leading Hungarian banks were abroad, 46 per cent in Austria. Around the big banks, however, the most influential groups of domestic entrepreneurs emerged: the Chorins, Fellners, Lánczy at the Commercial Bank, the Ullmans and Kornfelds at the Credit Bank.[19]

The banks in Hungary played a determinant intermediate role between the Austrian banks and the Hungarian financial market and became one of the prime movers of the modern economic transition of the country. Their role in the great spurt of industrialization, especially after 1890, was decisive. The extension of agricultural credit, however, was the most important activity of the banks throughout the entire period. In the second half of the nineteenth century, mortgages generally accounted for more than a half of the assets of the credit institutions. The credit supply of trade and industry was never as large, up to the time of the First World War, as mortgage credits to landed estates.

AGRICULTURAL DEVELOPMENT

On the European periphery one of the most important consequences of the core's Industrial Revolution was the rapidly increased market possibility for their traditional agricultural export goods. This characteristic feature of core–periphery relation was reproduced within the more or less self-sufficient Austro-Hungarian Monarchy. Market possibilities for Hungarian agriculture were especially favourable. West European and Cisleithanian markets offered unlimited export possibilities until the early 1870s, which became the strongest 'pull-effect' for modernization. The traditional landed-aristocratic elite sought to adjust to the new requirements of the European economy. Count István Széchenyi's clear recognition of the new needs and his extensive activity, the legislation of the 1848 Revolution and its acceptance by the Vienna government in the early 1850s, all prepared the way for the adjustment of Hungarian agriculture. The abolition of the *robot* system – three million of former leasehold serfs with a parcel of land they had cultivated before – left almost half of the estates in the hands of the landlords: 30.4 per cent of total land area belonged to 89 per cent of holdings with a plot between 0 to 20 hold (1 hold=1.4 acres), and almost 23 per cent of the land belonged to the 10 per cent well-to-do landowners with an estate of 20–100 holds. Nearly half (47.7 per cent) of the total land area, however, belonged to 1 per cent of all landowners – those with more than 100 holds.[20]

The modernization of agriculture in the effort to supply the industrializing West gained a great impetus around the *Ausgleich*. One of the prime movers of the transformation was the rapidly expanding credit supply: in 1867, Hungarian and foreign banks accrued 170 million crowns of mortgage loans; by 1900 this amount had increased by elevenfold and it doubled again a decade later to reach 3.8 billion crowns.[21] On this basis wage labour became general and modern technological transformation began in the 1860s. Better tools and animal-driven equipment were introduced. The greatest change, in this respect, was the appearance of steam-driven threshing machines. Their numbers were 2,500 in 1871, increasing to 30,000 up to the First World War. Threshing, the single agricultural operation, became completely mechanized. Horse-drawn seed-drills, reapers and harvesters also appeared in the Hungarian countryside and their numbers were multiplied in the last third of the century. One of the most important elements of technological progress was the introduction of the modern Norfolk rotation system. Fallow land, amounting to 22 per cent of the arable land in the first half of the 1870s, consequently dropped to 8 per cent before the First World War. Extensive reclamation works started in 1879, and by the time war broke out 2.5 million holds (roughly 4 million acres) were drained. The area under cultivation increased by nearly one-third between 1873 and 1913. This expansion was achieved primarily from the reduction of the area of unproductive soil and from the conversion of pasture and meadow land. The proportion of arable land in the country rose from 35 per cent in 1873 to nearly 46 per cent in 1913. As an element of a more intensive cultivation, the large and middle-sized estates started to collect and use substantial amounts of animal manure, which allowed fertilizing on average once every nine years. Artificial fertilizers also appeared about the end of the century: from 5.5 lb of artificial fertilizers used per hold of arable land in 1898, the figure rose to about 26.5 lb in 1913.[22]

As a consequence, production spectacularly increased: maize production rose by 3.6-fold, wheat production by 2.8-fold, potatoes by 7.5-fold and sugar beet by 21-fold between 1864–6 and 1911–13. This increase was partly a result of the expanded area under cultivation – the acreage under wheat, maize and grain fodder grew by 50 per cent – partly of a significant rise in average yields. During the half century before the First World War, the average yields of wheat, maize, rye and potatoes per hold increased by 66 per cent, 60 per cent, 71 per cent and 160 per cent respectively (see table 12.4).[23] Stock-breeding became another important factor of an impressive agricultural development (see table 12.5).

The development of stock-breeding, however, cannot be described in purely quantitative terms. During the half century before the war, a significant qualitative progress took place as well, especially from the 1890s on. In 1880, for example, more than 80 per cent of the cattle in the country were native Hungarian draught animals, giving low yields of meat and milk. By 1895, only two-thirds of the stock belonged to this type, and, by 1911, less than one-third. While in the early 1880s 37 per cent of the stock were cows, by 1911 already more than 46 per cent, which shows a significant changeover to a more intensive form of cattle-raising.

Around the turn of the century, 40 per cent of the income in agriculture originated from stock-breeding. The annual increase in production of animal products reached 1.7 per cent, and for non-animal crops 2 per

Table 12.4. *Production of main crops (in 10,000 tons)*[24]

	1864–6	1911–13	1911–13 as percentage of 1864–6
Wheat	17.2	49.1	285.5
Rye	11.2	13.2	117.9
Barley	6.7	16.8	250.7
Oats	6.2	13.6	219.4
Maize	13.4	48.5	361.9
Potatoes	7.3	54.9	752.0
Sugar beet	2.0	43.3	2,165.0

Table 12.5. *Animal stocks (in millions)*[25]

	1870–5	1910–14	1910–14 as percentage of 1870–5
Pigs	4.44	7.58	170.7
Cattle	5.28	7.32	138.6
Horses	1.67	2.20	131.7
Sheep	15.08	8.55	56.7

cent, between 1867 and 1913. The rate of growth in agriculture was impressive: yearly average growth was around 2 per cent – according to László Katus's calculation 1.8 per cent – between the *Ausgleich* and the First World War.[26]

Rapid agricultural development was a characteristic phenomenon of peripheral modernization in the era of the Industrial Revolution. The 'pull-effect' of the industrializing West – in the Hungarian case, most of all, the western provinces of the Austro-Hungarian Monarchy – was the prime-mover of the development of agriculture. Between 1850 and 1913, the value of Hungarian exports jumped from $30 million to $368 million. In just forty years preceding the First World War, exports increased more than threefold – that is, there was an annual growth of over 3 per cent. During the last two decades before the War, the average annual growth rate of European exports was 3.2 per cent, Hungary's export growth, however, reached 3.6 per cent. In 1910, the country's contribution to European trade reached 3 per cent, much more than the four Balkan countries together (2.1 per cent), and more than Spain's contribution (2.2 per cent).[27] Hungary's export boom was greatly aided by the huge and more or less self-sufficient entity of the Austro-Hungarian Monarchy. As well as the demand from the rapidly industrializing Austria and Bohemia, the protected market – which was surrounded by increasing tariff walls from the late 1870s – also contributed to the boom in Hungary. The latter enjoyed the upward trend of food prices on the European market until the flood of cheap American grain to Europe brought them down, but then could avoid the negative impact of declining agricultural prices. Grain prices on the world market fell drastically during the last quarter of the century; between 1855 and 1864 and 1885 and 1894 the price of wheat fell by one-third. Price movement in the safe market of the Monarchy, however, was different and, especially after the radical increase of tariffs for agricultural products at the beginning of the twentieth century, Hungary achieved a more than 20 per cent improvement in terms of trade.[28]

Hungary's export boom, unlike that of many other countries on the European peripheries, inspired much more than the expansion of the traditional agricultural branches. The strength of the domestic market, the strong financial and political ties with Austria, and, partly as a consequence of these, a relatively highly developed infrastructure along with internal social and educational advancement, all generated spin-off effects and the beginning of industrialization. Hungary's chief export item in the entire period was grain, which accounted for over 50 per cent of all exports. Grain, however, was considered a fortunate export item in all respects, at least up to the turn of the century. Besides the constantly growing demand and rising prices it offered a good and rather obvious way of turning towards processing. As early as the 1860s, Hungary began to exploit the industrial potential of being an exporter of grain. Unlike a great many agricultural products, grain was eminently suited to industrial processing. The manpower needs were rather cicumscribed in the milling industry, which required large-scale technological investments, a great deal of capital and a labour force which was skilled but not large. Though local milling industries were in operation throughout Europe, Hungary was practically the only European country which was able to transform the majority of its grain exports into the export of food products. Modern food processing gained a footing in 1836 when the Pest Rolling Mill Co. (Pesti Hengermalom Társaság), the first Hungarian steam mill, was founded by Count István Széchenyi. The first major boom-period of food processing, however, started only in the 1850–60s. In these decades, within the newly established customs union, investments in Hungary became rather lucrative. Even if unsettled political conditions blocked the path to massive industrial investments, more than a dozen huge sugar refineries were founded by Austrian entrepreneurs. A modern large-scale mechanized sugar industry became the first leading branch of the emerging food-processing industry in Hungary. The leading role, however, soon shifted to the flour-milling industry. The customs union offered a great possibility for trade of agricultural products and provided the main source of capital accumulation in the country. The best opportunities for profitable investment were offered by the flour-milling industry. Rich merchants hurried to exploit it in the 1860s. By 1867, fourteen big export mills were established in Budapest, and food processing continued to lead the advance after the Compromise: one-third of the newly founded joint-stock companies operated in the milling industry. In 1866, the mills of Budapest ground about 50,000 tons of wheat; by 1879 the figure had increased by eightfold, to 430,000 tons. Although the machinery which was used in the mills was partly imported, an important Hungarian invention – the roller mill – by András Merchwart of the Ganz Co., guaranteed technological superiority and thus the lead in quality and productivity for the Hungarian milling industry, which soon became an exporter on a world scale. Budapest's milling capacity was second in the world, behind the American Minneapolis. Consequently, the ratio of flour in Hungarian grain exports increased to two-thirds at the beginning of the twentieth century. It markedly differed from the Russian or Romanian exports, where grain was almost entirely (in Russia 98 per cent; in Romania 92 per cent) exported in unprocessed form.[29]

The rise of the Hungarian flour-milling industry was closely connected with the development of the engineering industry. One of the key elements of its success, the invention, patent and production of roller-mills, assured not only technological superiority for the Hungarian flour mills, but also contributed to the development of the Ganz works, which soon even exported its world-famous product. Agriculture offered a profitable market for other branches of engineering as well. The spin-off effect was already recognizable in the mid-nineteenth century when quite a few, relatively small factories such as Röck, Vidats, Schlick, Otl were founded and started to produce various kinds of agricultural implements. The second biggest branch of the Hungarian engineering industry produced machinery for agriculture and food processing. Domestic supply soon covered half of the demand.

Thus, a rapidly developing export-oriented agriculture unleashed a spin-off effect which generated a related industrial development. The same should be said about railway construction. It started entirely with foreign investments and served Imperial interests but also gave an initiative to some related industrial concerns. Coal mines, for example, were opened in Hungary by two big Austrian transportation companies, the Austrian State Railroad Co. and the Danube Steamship Co., which started extraction from the anthracite mines in Anina (Staierdorfanina) and Reşiţa-Doman (Transylvania) and in Pécs. Coal output basically covered the needs of the expanding railroads and increased to 0.7 tons by 1866, then more than doubled (to 1.6 million tons) during the next seven years. At the turn of the century coal production reached 13.9 million tons. Railway construction also had an impact on the iron, steel and engineering industries. One of the pioneers of these concerns was, again, the Austrian State Railroad Co., which built up a formidable industrial complex. At its south Transylvanian site moving from coal and iron-ore mining to crude iron, steel and rail production, the Resica firm became one of the most modern and largest factories in the country. This firm produced one-fifth of the Hungarian pig-iron production after the *Ausgleich*. The Ganz works, a small workshop, began to expand by 1854 when its patent of cast railway-carriage wheels led to an important enlargement of the work. The factory cast the 100,000th carriage wheel in 1867. Six years later the government opened the Hungarian State Railway Machine Works (MAVAG-Magyar Államvasutak Gépgyára), one of the largest engineering firms of the country, in Budapest. It developed and produced steam locomotives, and, from the last decades of the century, became able to supply the well-developed Hungarian railways. Rails and other equipment were produced by the Hungarian State Railway Machine Works in Diósgyör. During the first decades of railway construction Hungary imported practically everything from rails to locomotives but gradually developed a huge iron, steel and engineering industry and became self-sufficient in feeding her dense railway network. Around the end of the century two-thirds of the Hungarian output of machinery consisted of transport equipment.[30]

Hungary did not react to the increased agricultural export possibilities by a pure increase of its traditional agricultural sector as most of the peripheral countries of Europe did. An increased growth of agriculture, in most cases, did not generate structural changes in the backward economies. An industrial spurt began in Hungary. The half century before the First World War was, for the most part, an era of extensive Austrian and foreign capital investment with fully 40 per cent of invested capital originating from outside Hungary. The role of domestic accumulation, however, changed dramatically. During the first boom period, between 1867 and 1873, 60 per cent of investment came from outside the country; between 1900 and 1913, only 25 per cent.[31] Although Austrian and foreign investments increased, in absolute terms, the relative decline of the role of foreign investments shows the self-generating trend of domestic accumulation.

A MODERATE FOLLOW-UP INDUSTRIALIZATION

The British Industrial Revolution generated a process of rapid industrialization throughout the entire nineteenth century. Taking the level of Europe's industrial production in 1900 as 100, the significant figure in 1830 and in 1850, according to Paul Bairoch, was only 20 and 33 respectively. From this time, especially from the 1860s on, a rapid annual growth of about 3 per cent became characteristic. Europe's production consequently doubled in about two decades. Latecomers had a rather difficult task in trying to catch up. The responsive Hungarian economy, however, began to cope with the serious difficulties of latecomers and the lack of a 'proto-industrialization'. From the 1860s onward two major trends of industrial development emerged. First, as had been noted, the development of a genuine export flour-milling industry at Budapest. In addition, import substitution also gained an impetus. This development became characteristic in branches such as coal mining, iron and steel industry, rolling-stock manufacturing and agricultural machinery and equipment. From the end of the century the first results of import substitution appeared in industrial consumer-goods production such as textiles, leather, and paper goods – one-third of the domestic consumption was met by domestic output in 1910 – which were traditionally supplied by the Austrian and Bohemian industries. From the 1890s Hungary's annual industrial growth was nearly twice as fast as the European average: 6 per cent in the 1890s and 5 per cent after the turn of the century. These were the decades of the breakthrough of large manufacturing industries in Hungary. The spread of the steam engine became decisive from the 1860s onwards. The industrial census of 1863 reported that 8,100 horsepower capacity was in operation in the country. In the following twenty years until the next industrial census of 1884, the horsepower capacity of steam engines increased by eightfold, to 63,900 horsepower. Almost 60 per cent of the total capacity, however, was concentrated into food processing. The iron industry increased its steam engine capacity sixfold.[32] Modern technology appeared in this branch: charcoal was replaced by coke in the smelting process; water-wheels, which had formerly driven the bellows, were withdrawn from service. After the introduction of the Bessemer (1868) and Martin (1873) processes, a great many of the smaller old furnaces were closed down. Mechanized big industry concentrated in some limited branches while other industries remained at a small-scale artisan level. In 1880, Hungarian manufacturing industry employed only 110,000 workers, that is, only 21 per cent of all industrial workers. A survey on the main branches convincingly demonstrates the triumph of a developing industrialization in Hungary. The spread of machinery and

Table 12.6. *Horsepower capacity of machines in industry*[33]

Year	Horsepower (1,000s)	1863=1
1863	8	1.0
1884	81	10.1
1898	307	38.4
1913	886	110.8

the prevalence of large-scale mechanized industry became characteristic from the 1880s onwards (see table 12.6): between 1884 and 1898 the capacity of the steam engines used in industry increased more than four-fold and at the end of the century mechanized factories began to play a leading role in every branch of industry.

Between 1898 and 1913, when mechanization reached a turning-point, the number of factories rose from 2,700 to 5,500, and the number of employed workers from 302,000 to 563,000. More than half of the industrial workforce was already employed in mechanized big industry. Small-scale industry represented only one-quarter of the total industrial output before the war and was mostly limited to a few branches, such as food processing, construction and clothing.

By the last third of the nineteenth century, especially around the turn of the century, a successful adoption of the main results of the Industrial Revolution began to change the economic landscape of the country. Food processing, however, preserved its leading role. As an export industry, based on modern technology and the solid background of Hungarian grain-production and marketing capability in the western part of the Monarchy, food processing employed, in 1898 and 1913 respectively, 15.3 per cent and 14.5 per cent of those employed by the manufacturing industry in the country in 1898 and 1913 respectively. The value of food processing doubled in the last decade and a half before the First World War (from 646 million to 1,288 million crowns), which represented 44.1 per cent (in 1898), and 38.9 per cent (in 1913) of total value of production of the manufacturing industry in Hungary.[34]

Next to food processing, some branches of the so-called heavy industries also made an impressive advance. Coal mining gained a great impetus from the 1890s on when the Hungarian General Coal Mining Co. (Magyar Altalános Möszénbánya Rt) was founded with huge foreign investment to exploit one of the country's most important lignite fields near Tatabánya. The second largest coal operator was the Salgótarján Coal Mining Co., a joint venture which represented 29 per cent of total lignite extraction. Coal and lignite output rose rapidly, by more than three

Table 12.7. *Coal production in million tons*[35]

Year	Lignite	Coal	Total	1860=1
1860	2.4	2.4	4.8	1.0
1880	10.1	8.0	18.1	3.8
1900	52.1	13.7	65.8	13.9
1913	89.5	13.2	102.7	21.7

Table 12.8. *Iron and steel production*[36] *in thousand tons*

Year	Iron ore	Index	Pig-iron	Index	Steel	Index
1867	294	50.2	105	75.0	–	–
1880	586	100.0	140	100.0	16	100.0
1913	2,059	351.4	623	445.0	800	500.0

and a half times between 1880 and 1900, then increased by nearly another 60 per cent by 1913 (see table 12.7).

The modern iron and steel industry introduced the most advanced Western technology in Hungary from the 1870s and 1880s onwards. The regenerative heating furnace in Salgótarján (1872), the Lauth-trio in Zólyom (now Zvolen in Slovakia) (1875), the regenerative puddling machine (1878), and the introduction of the Bessemer and Martin processes in the same decade marked the road of the adaptation of the most advanced technology. The merging of the two biggest iron-makers, the Rimamurány Works and the Salgótarján Foundry, created the country's largest industrial enterprise. From the turn of the century the firm, which employed 16,000 workers, reorganized its production: Martin-steel production was concentrated at Ozd. The State Iron Works in Diósgyör installed a twin-steam engine of 4,150 horsepower in 1891.

Hungarian engineering belatedly followed the introduction of steam-engine construction and achieved its most advanced level after the 1880s. The first steam engine was produced in Hungary in 1858 (by the Röck engineering firm), and the Lang-firm constructed an engine of 1,000 horsepower capacity in 1885. Steam-locomotive construction was especially successful from the early seventies on. During the first twenty years, 500 locomotives, of the most advanced types, were turned out. At the end of the century, another 500 were produced in four years and the new construction of MAVAG's locomotive (with a speed of 100 kilometres per hour) gained the Grand Prix at the Paris World Exhibition in 1900.

All this shows the great ability and potential of the leading companies in the Hungarian iron and steel and engineering industries to adopt and even to improve modern technology. Among the more advanced lines, the electrical industry acquired a growing importance. It enjoyed the advantage of a late start: the new waves of technological innovation of the Age of Industrial Revolution (as some call the second and third Industrial Revolutions) arrived in Hungary without any major delay and without the devastating competition of earlier industrialized countries. One decade after the birth of the electrical industry (in 1867 with Werner Siemens) the Ganz Works produced its first electrification project and the National Theatre in Budapest was among the very first in Europe to introduce electric lights. In 1883 the exhibition of the electric industry in Vienna presented the sensation of Hungarian generators, and a Budapest show in 1885 exhibited a revolutionary invention, the alternating-current transformer, which opened the road to the development of high-powered electrical technology. The famous trio of Ganz-engineers, Károly Zipernowsky, Miklós Déri and Otto Bláthy, assured by their patent a competitive market for the newly established Ganz Electrical Works, which built the world's first alternating-current electric power station next to Lucerne in 1886. Ganz also built the alternating-current electric power station for Rome, and, in 1892, the Hungarian firm built the world's first electric transmission-line (from the Tivoli hydro-electric station for a 30-kilometre-long distance). In 1897 another Ganz engineer, Kálmán Kandó, began to experiment with the three-phase electric locomotive, and his name was linked with the construction of the continent's first electrified railway, the Valtellina line in Italy in 1902.[37]

Another leading firm, the United Incandescent Lamp Co. (Egyesült Izzólámpa Gyár) began manufacturing incandescent lamps and electric cables by the late 1880s. An important invention and patent of the Wolfram (tungsten)-lamp (1904) helped the Hungarian firm to achieve a huge export expansion. At the same time, a promising new pharmaceutical industry also emerged (with such firms as Chinion and Richter) as an export industry.

During the course of its expansion, by the end of the nineteenth century the enlarged domestic market served as an initiator of import substitution in the absent or backward consumer-goods industries. The textile industry, which was the leading branch of the British Industrial Revolution, had hardly developed in Hungary. As a consequence of the Austro-Hungarian common market, the highly developed Austrian and Bohemian textile firms dominated the Hungarian market. At the end of

Table 12.9. *Value of industrial production in constant prices*[38]

Year	1900 crowns (millions)	Index
1860	175	100
1900	1,400	800
1913	2,539	1,450

the century, Hungary had only 110,000 cotton spindles as compared to the 4.5 million in Cisleithania. The Hungarian textile industry met scarcely 14 per cent of domestic consumption. Output of woollens met not quite 10 per cent, and the production of cotton cloth slightly more than 3.5 per cent of domestic consumption. Between 1900 and 1913, however, Hungarian textile production grew three and a half times, and the number of spindles rose from 110,000 to nearly 500,000. Despite rapid growth, domestic textile manufacturing still satisfied only roughly 30 per cent of domestic consumption in 1913.[39] This was also true of the other branches of the consumer industries. Paper production more than trebled between 1900 and 1913, as did the leather and printing industry, while the wood industry doubled its output. All these branches together employed 21 per cent of industrial workers in 1898 and 31 per cent in 1913, but represented only 16 per cent and 20 per cent respectively of the value of production and satisfied only about one-third of domestic consumption.

Industrialization, nevertheless, gained an impetus, and the strong 'pull-effect' of Austrian and Bohemian industrial transformation generated not only the modernization of Hungarian agriculture, infrastructure and raw-material extraction, but challenged the entire Hungarian economy and led to structural changes. The rate of Hungarian industrialization was impressive (see table 12.9).

Yet, although industrialization had important results and the preponderance of agriculture was indeed diminishing, the peripheral character of modernization remained dominant. Hungary did not become industrialized, as did the core countries of Europe, and Hungary's old economic structure basically survived. At the time of the Austro-Hungarian *Ausgleich*, about 75 per cent of the gainfully occupied population worked in agriculture; by the First World War their share had declined to 64 per cent. Industrial population, on the other hand, increased from 9 per cent to 24 per cent. In the same period, agriculture, which provided 70 per cent of gross domestic product (GDP) in 1867, declined to 62 per cent by the early 1910s. The share of industry, consequently, had risen from 15 per cent to

26 per cent.[40] Hungary remained, thus, basically an agricultural country and industrialization could not break through. The process of catching up began but, as in the cases of some of the European peripheries, it remained far from being finished. The per capita gross national product increased from $230 to $372 (in 1960 value), that is, by 61 per cent during the half century before the First World War. As a result, the Hungarian level increased from 51 per cent to 58 per cent of the Western European average of GNP between 1867 and 1913.[41] In the era of the Industrial Revolution, Hungary represented the path of semi-successful economic modernization, a phenomenon quite common in the Central and Eastern European and Mediterranean regions, where far-reaching economic, social and political consequences strongly determined progress in the post-First World War years.

NOTES

1 P. Bairoch, 'Europe's Gross National Product: 1800-1975', *The Journal of European Economic History*, 5, 2 (1976), p. 279.

2 I. T. Berend and Gy. Ránki, *The European Periphery and Industrialization 1780–1914* (Cambridge University Press, 1982), p. 17.

3 V. Sándor, *Nagyipari fejlödés Magyarországon 1867–1900* (The development of the big industry in Hungary) (Budapest, Szikra, 1954).

4 Gy. Vargha, *A magyar hitelügy és hitelintézetek története* (The History of the Hungarian Banks and Crediting) (Budapest: Pesti Könyvnyomda Rt., 1896).

5 *The Fontana Economic History of Europe. The Emergence of Industrial Societies* (C. Cipolla), Part 2 (1973), pp. 747–8.

6 *Magyarország történeti demográfiája* (Historical Demography of Hungary), ed. J. Kovacsics (Budapest, Magyar, Statisztikai Hivatal, 1963); D. Danyi, 'Regionális fertilitási sémák Magyarországon a 19. század végén' (Regional fertility patterns in Hungary at the end of the 19th century), *Demográfia*, 2 (1969).

7 J. Puskás, *Emigration from Hungary to the United States before 1914* (Budapest: Akadémiai Kiadó, 1975).

8 Gy. Concha, 'A gentry', *Budapesti Szemle* (1910), vol. 142; P. Hanák, 'Vázlatok a századelö magyar társadalmáról' (Notes on the early 20th century Hungarian society), *Történeti Szemle* (1962), no. 2.

9 Gy. Szekfú, *Három nemzedék és ami utána következik* (Three Generations and After) (Budapest: Mecénás, 1989), pp. 153, 246–7.

10 I. T. Berend and Gy. Ránki, 'A Csepeli Vasmú rövid története' (A short history of the Csepel Ironworks) in *Csepel története* (A history of Csepel) (Budapest: Kossuth Könyvkiadó, 1965).

11 G. Deák, *The Economy and Polity in Early Twentieth Century Hungary. The Role of the National Association of Industrialists* (Boulder: East European Monographs, 1990).

12 I. T. Berend and M. Szuhay, *A tőkés gazdaság története Magyarországon 1848–1944* (A History of the Capitalist Economy in Hungary, 1848–1944) (Budapest: Kossuth Könyvkiadó, 1978), p. 152.

13 I. T. Berend, 'Economy, education and the social sciences', in I. T. Berend and Gy. Ránki, *Underdevelopment and Economic Growth. Studies in Hungarian Economic and Social History* (Budapest: Akadémiai Kiadó, 1979), pp. 48–50.

14 Berend and Ránki, *The European Periphery*, pp. 78–9.

15 I. T. Berend and Gy. Ránki, 'National income and capital accumulation in Hungary 1867–1914' in Berend and Ránki, *Underdevelopment and Economic Growth.*

16 I. T. Berend and Gy. Ránki, *Hungary. A Century of Economic Development* (Newton Abbot, David and Charles, 1974), pp. 38–9.

17 G. Ujhelyi, *A vasútügy története* (A history of the railways) (Budapest, 1910); L. Ruszicska, *A magyar vasútépítések története* (A history of railroad building in Hungary until 1914) (Budapest, 1914).

18 Berend and Ránki, *The European Periphery*, p. 100.

19 Berend and Ránki, *Hungary*, pp. 28–34.

20 Berend and Ránki, *Hungary*, pp. 42.

21 Berend and Szuhay, *A tőkés gazdaság története Magyarországon 1848–1944* (Hungary), p. 371.

22 Berend and Ránki, *Hungary*, pp. 44–5.

23 *Ibid.*, p. 46.

24 *Ibid.*, p. 46.

25 *Ibid.*, p. 47.

26 L. Katus, 'Economic growth in Hungary during the Age of Dualism', *Studia Historica*, 62 (1970); I. T. Berend and Gy. Ránki 'National income and capital accumulation in Hungary 1867–1914', in Berend and Ránki, *Underdevelopment and Economic Growth.*

27 P. Bairoch, 'European foreign trade in the 19th century: the development of the value and volume of exports', *Journal of Economic History* (1973); S. Eddie, 'The terms and patterns of Hungarian foreign trade 1882–1913', *Journal of Economic History*, 2 (1977); Berend and Ránki, *The European Periphery*, p. 115.

28 See L. Katus's chapter in *Magyarorság története* (A history of Hungary) vol. VII (Budapest: Akadémiai Kiadó, 1978); S. Eddie, 'Terms and patterns'.

29 I. T. Berend and Gy. Ránki, *Magyarország gyáripara 1900–1914.* (Hungarian Manufacturing Industry) (Budapest: Szikra, 1955), p. 190.

30 Berend and Ránki, *Hungary*, pp. 58–9.

31 Berend and Ránki, 'National income and capital accumulation'.

32 Berend and Ránki, *Hungary*, p. 54.

33 *Ibid.*, p. 60.

34 *Ibid.*, p. 63.

35 *Ibid.*, p. 56.

36 *Ibid.*, p. 57.

37 M. Gelléri, *A magyar ipar úttöröi* (Pioneers of Hungarian Industry) (Budapest, 1906).

38 Berend and Ránki, 'National income and capital accumulation', p. 78.

39 Berend and Ránki, *Hungary*, pp. 59–60.
40 Berend and Ránki, *The European Periphery*, p. 159.
41 Bairoch, 'Europe's Gross National Product', p. 286.

THIRTEEN

The Industrial Revolution and the countries of South-eastern Europe in the nineteenth and early twentieth centuries

LJUBEN BEROV

A NUMBER of difficulties are posed by the attempt to summarize the rates and scope of socio-economic change typical for the age of the Industrial Revolution in the countries of South-eastern Europe. Their origins are dual. In part they stem from existing differences in what individual authors understood by 'industrial revolution'.[1] European economic historians offer varying interpretations of some economic and political phenomena as essential components of the term. As a result views differ on the chronological framework for this revolution in each Balkan country, and some authors even doubt whether the Industrial Revolution took place at all. These problems are theoretical in nature; others are factual, stemming from an insufficiency of research into some important economic indicators from the eighteenth and nineteenth centuries which are significant for national historiographies of Balkan countries or ethnic regions. These factual difficulties are heightened by the fact that, where there are gaps in the economic history of a given nation in certain periods of the eighteenth, nineteenth and early twentieth centuries, analogies with known contemporary conditions in neighbouring countries cannot be relied upon. The usefulness of such analogies is limited by the differences in the historical fate of some nationalities in South-east Europe at the time (e.g., the chronology of their liberation from Ottoman domination), as well as their varying degrees of economic backwardness.

The emergence of varying views on the significance of the term 'Industrial Revolution' in the European literature on economic history dates back to the 1950s.[2] The first German and French authors to introduce the term 'Industrial Revolution' in scientific publications in the third quarter of the nineteenth century had based their discussions mainly on the British version of the phenomenon, without attempting a rigorous definition of the theoretical contents of the new term.[3]

In recent decades, certain economic historians, especially in the Balkans, have considered the most distinctive characteristics of the

Industrial Revolution as residing in the area of technology and in the difference effected in man's attitude to nature by the introduction of machines and steam-power. Hence, historians have concentrated on establishing the chronology of the chief technological innovations and their implementation in the industry of a given Balkan country, of the resulting replacement of outdated handicraft techniques, and of the establishment of some new industrial branches (e.g., the generation of electric power). In certain areas (Bulgaria, some regions of modern Yugoslavia, and to an extent in Romania), satisfactory research has been conducted on a national or regional scale into the decline of traditional branches of handicrafts in the last decades of the nineteenth century. Such research has relied upon the official annual reports of local administrative chiefs, town histories (written mainly in the first third of the twentieth century and based on memories of nineteenth-century contemporaries),[4] evidence from the first official census, etc. The value of such sources is, however, limited by the fact that in many cases the disintegration of the old branches of handicrafts and manufactory production resulted not from the establishment of local industrial production but from the competition presented by cheaper, higher-quality goods imported from Western and Central Europe. Reliable data on the quantitative parameters and evolution of these imports on a yearly basis can be found in the national statistics of the Balkan countries, and partly too in the statistics of Western European exporters themselves. However, evidence on the chronology of the establishment of industrial production in the Balkans, and especially of its quantitative parameters, is scarce. Detailed histories of larger enterprises, giving factual information on the evolution of annual output, the number of workers employed, or the capacity of main production machines and prime movers in the earlier stages of operation, are very rare.[5] Hence, it is difficult to estimate the correlation of production levels in industrial enterprises with those in manufactories and handicraft workshops in the period of transition before the final triumph of mechanical production. Poor artisans, through a maximal limitation of income along with low retail prices for their goods, managed for many years to exist side by side with still underdeveloped local industry. They also managed to cope with the largely detrimental effects of imported Western and Central European goods, whose prices had risen considerably, owing to high costs of primitive transport by cart-and-horse from the import-harbour to the consumer in the interior of the country.

This view of the content of the term 'Industrial Revolution' is complicated by the fact that the transition to machine technology did not occur simultaneously in the different branches of handicraft and manufactory production. It is for this reason that in some studies published in the (former) German Democratic Republic the chronology of industrial revolution in each country is based on the stages by which technical revolution occurred in the various branches of traditional handicraft production. The actual realization of such a chronology is, however, difficult for individual Balkan countries, because of the lack of evidence on the correlation between the output of handicraft-manufacture and large factory machine production in individual branches over the decades of the second half of the nineteenth century (statistical data are missing even for the beginning of the twentieth century).

H. Mottek has suggested reasonably that a country's transition from an agrarian to an agrarian-industrial state should be regarded as the end of the Industrial Revolution. This transition should be marked by the fact of industrial production gaining a value-prevalence over agrarian. When this principle is applied to the case of the Balkan countries, however, the historian encounters the obstacle that annual records for the value of national income in Bulgaria were not kept until 1924,[6] in Greece not until 1927 (and then only sporadically, with numerous imprecisions),[7] and in Turkey not until 1938.[8] In Yugoslavia records began in 1926 (to be terminated during the Second World War),[9] in Romania in 1928,[10] and in Albania as late as the end of the Second World War (approximate estimates exist for 1938).[11]

Economic historians working on the problems of the Industrial Revolution, by applying quantitative methods, focus mainly on rates of industrial development. They presume that we may talk of industrial revolution only in the case of an economic leap or an increase in the annual rate of production in processing and manufacturing industries, in contrast to the previous slow development of manufactory and handicraft production. The earliest studies of annual growth rates of industrial and handicraft production in the Balkan countries did not appear until the first decade of the twentieth century.[12]

Because of the lack of research, it should be noted that cross-country comparisons based on average rates of growth of industrial production in individual countries from the eighteenth to the nineteenth century are not entirely reliable. This is because in the initial stages of industrial development relatively high annual growth rates are not difficult to achieve. If, for example, the high (over 10 per cent per annum) rates of industrial growth achieved in the Balkan countries during the first decade of the twentieth century were to be compared with the respective rates in England over the first half of the nineteenth century, a distorted picture would be drawn – namely, that the characteristic traits of the Industrial Revolution in the Balkans were far more convincing than those in England. It should be mentioned, however, that there are no exhaustive data available on the rate of growth of factory industry in England, that is, data on the amount of annual industrial output or on the total number of factory workers employed over the last decades of the eighteenth century, while data for the beginning of the nineteenth century encompass both factory industry and crafts. The available data shed light only on the growth rates of individual branches of industry such as cotton textiles – which, however, yielded just 5 per cent of total industrial production in England at the end of the eighteenth century.[13]

Less frequently, authors emphasize national capital accumulation and investment as one of the main prerequisites for industrial revolution in a given country. A comparative study of Balkan countries from this aspect is rendered impossible, however, by the lack of the respective national studies on the scale and rates of capital accumulation.[14] Scholars sometimes take into account the fact that the Industrial Revolution of the eighteenth and nineteenth centuries had to be preceded by a revolution in agriculture. This enabled agricultural workers to be more productive and facilitated the redeployment of the excess agricultural labour force necessary for industrial development. The degree of industrial development attained by the end of the nineteenth century, however, did not always require more workers than those who were engaged in crafts or manufactories, and who were eventually replaced by machines. Historians also consider the demographic and psychological preconditions essential to guarantee the workforce needed for industrial development. Such considerations were less crucial for the Balkan countries during the early stages of their industrial development in the second half of the nineteenth century. There were few serious difficulties in recruiting industrial workers: conditions in agriculture produced a large surplus population amongst peasants; the birth rate was high in the villages and the number of impoverished peasant holdings was large.

Economic historians who have emphasized the part played by the Industrial Revolution in effecting those continuous changes in social relations which preceded the establishment of capitalism added an important aspect to the understanding of the process of industrialization. The chronological framework of those changes is often vague and open to dispute, even through more is known of the process of industrialization in the case of large Western European countries. Some authors, for example, arbitrarily take the beginning of the first economic cycle or of an important political event to mark the end of the period of industrial revolution. Thus, for instance, in the case of England the crisis of 1825, or the middle-class victory over the landed aristocracy in the passing of the Reform Act in 1832, constitutes such a terminal point. In France the economic crisis of 1838–9 or the political revolution of 1830 mark such a point. For most

Balkan countries, however, it is hard to choose a political or economic event from the end of the nineteenth or the beginning of the twentieth century to mark a precise historical date for the periodization of the Industrial Revolution and the emergence and victory of capitalism in each individual country. For that reason this chapter uses any such identification of the Industrial Revolution with the victory of capitalism tentatively and theoretically; this concept is not used as a basis for a definition of when the Industrial Revolution in a given country was completed.

Other authors insist that by the end of the period of Industrial Revolution the two antagonistic classes of bourgeois society should already have been formed – the proletariat and the bourgeoisie. This condition related logically to the theoretical assumption described above. Demonstrating such an argument, however, in the case of Balkan countries (and not only Balkan ones) presents certain difficulties when we attempt to establish the point at which the working class – as a numerous, organized social stratum of hired labour – was formed in a particular country. It is fairly clear when it can be claimed that an *individual* belongs to the working class; later and better-organized censuses in European countries provide statistical information about the numbers in this social stratum, because the occupational distribution of the population takes into account the social position of the employed.[15] Reliable statistical data from population censuses in Bulgaria first appear as late as 1900 (earlier figures were methodically flawed); in Yugoslavia and Greece they are available from the 1920s; in Turkey from the 1930s; while in Albania and Romania they are not available until after the Second World War. Nevertheless a question remains about the point at which we can declare that the working class in a particular country has been formed, since its numbers grow continuously, as we can see by looking at those countries where data are available from the nineteenth century until after the Second World War. What is the absolute number, or percentage, of the population that should be accepted as a minimum if we are to agree that the working class in a particular country has already been formed? When purely quantitative trends are also assessed qualitatively, such as for the presence of political organization or ideological and political awareness, statistical estimates inevitably become highly arbitrary. The formation of the first workers' political party in a particular country, for example, cannot serve as proof of a fully fledged working class if this party is few in number or has been joined by a great many intellectuals. It is even more difficult to establish accurately the exact moment when the bourgeois class was formed in various Balkan countries. Historical information on the emergence of a national bourgeoisie is considerably less plentiful than that available for the relatively well-studied history of the evolution of the working class and its organizations in Balkan countries. Population censuses provide evidence of the number of independent owners among the economically active population, but do not specify what capital they had. Comprehensive studies on the history of the formation of a national bourgeoisie in Balkan countries are indeed a rarity – they have been undertaken only for Romania and, in part, for Bulgaria.[16] Hence, in this discussion of the industrial revolution in the Balkan countries, assessments of the formation of the working lcass and bourgeoisie will be employed only as part of general theoretical considerations.

Some economic historians, perhaps influenced by W. W. Rostow, pay special attention to decreases in interest rates. Evidence available about the evolution of interest rates in individual Balkan countries during the eighteenth and nineteenth centuries is, however, sparse – apart from data on the interest rate of central issuing banks in some countries from the 1880s onwards.

It is still a matter of dispute whether the Industrial Revolution of the eighteenth to nineteenth centuries caused an increase or a decrease in real wages of hired workers in the respective countries. Despite the existence of richer archival and statistical sources in Western European countries, there is sufficient evidence to support conflicting theses on this issue.[17] It is much more difficult to answer this question precisely in the case of Balkan countries as the problem of the evolution of prices, and especially of workers' wages in the eighteenth and nineteenth centuries, has scarcely been investigated.[18]

From what has been said so far, it might be concluded that to attempt a comparative survey of the phenomenon known as 'industrial revolution' in the countries of South-eastern Europe, although it is the subject of numerous discussions, is considerably harder than it is for eonomically advanced European countries. It would be unfair to accuse Balkan economic historians of being unenterprising; however, many of them have witnessed upheavals in historiography during recent decades and, in addition, inadequate archival and other relevant information about the late eighteenth and the first three-quarters of the nineteenth century exacerbated their difficulties.

The problem of the Industrial Revolution in South-eastern Europe has not been comprehensively studied. A conference held in Hamburg in 1979 on these issues contributed very little to its elucidation. In fact, some studies and estimates of individual Balkan countries have been offered but often they are based on a variety of methodologies. Certain authors, such as R. Bičanić,[19] N. Vučo,[20] K. Serban,[21] O. Constantinescu and N. N. Constantinescu,[22] and I. Lungu,[23] definitely support the hypothesis that the Industrial Revolution occurred in their countries in the nineteenth century, while others do not mention it, or do not answer the question directly;[24] yet others give a qualifying answer.[25] Some well-known European economic historians also deny that features typical of the Industrial Resolution existed in the Balkan countries.[26] Soviet authors, studying the history of individual Balkan countries in the nineteenth century, employ the notion 'gradual industrial overturn'.[27] This notion, however, is based on a logical contradiction and amounts to an unsuccessful attempt to find a compromise between recognizing and denying the signs of industrial revolution in a particular country.

A general answer to the presence or absence in South-eastern Europe of traits which typify the controversial phenomenon of 'industrial revolution' should be based on an analysis of the specific economic situation in each country in this region during the eighteenth and nineteenth centuries. This is necessary because although all nations of South-eastern Europe were economically and socially backward during that period there were national differences – in degree of backwardness, in national structure, and in the timing of their liberation from Ottoman domination – which determined what constituted the main obstacles in each country's struggle for economic growth and development. I shall analyse the economic development of individual countries, taking into account their present-day state borders (before 1990 – eds.); this will avoid some long-standing disputes about ethnic claims to certain regions and the powers historically exercised over them by particular states.

Post-Second World War borders naturally do not always coincide with nineteenth-century borders, subject as they were to constant political change. As a result, some historical studies go beyond the geographical confines of today's state borders, but their findings can usually be sifted and reapportioned to sub-regions which correspond to present borders. It is only in the case of Yugoslavia that certain regions need to be analysed separately, because before the First World War (or until 1912) they differed considerably in their economic development and they were both politically and ethnically distinct from the other main regions of the post-1945 federated state, which is the entity discussed in this study. Such an approach would naturally also obtain in the case of Transylvania, which was outside Romania until the First World War.

It is quite natural that the survey of individual countries should start with those which offer ample information about the development of industry during the period under consideration (they have, for example, more official statistical data, a greater number and more specific studies in economic history, etc.). Accordingly, the economic history of Bulgaria, Romania, Croatia and Slovenia, and the former Serbia can be discussed on a comparatively more scientific basis. Treatment of this sort implies that greater attention should be paid to those Balkan countries where industrial development was more intensive during the nineteenth century and at the beginning of the twentieth century. These are also the countries which can provide evidence of whether their economies exhibited the main traits of an industrial revolution.

Bulgaria does not seem to have been the most highly industrialized region in the Balkans in the nineteenth and the early twentieth centuries, but it offeres more statistical data and a greater number of historical studies on the development of industry. The mechanization of handicraft and manufactory production in the country began in the nineteenth century in woollen textiles, and not in cotton textiles as was the case in eighteenth-century England. There were several underlying reasons. First, the cooler climate (compared with England) brought long, cold winters and stimulated the production of woollen, rather than cotton clothing. Second, woollen textiles were favoured by the fact that most of the coarse cloth and uniforms for army recruits consumed in the Ottoman Empire after 1829 was produced in the Bulgarian lands (though the uniforms themselves were generally tailored in Istanbul). Hence the production of coarse woollen cloth emerged as an important 'export' branch to the Bulgarian lands. The raw materials necessary for the production of cotton cloth were brought from Macedonia. This was unprofitable, given the cost of cart transport at the time: hence during the eighteenth and early nineteenth centuries prices for cotton cloth were about 50 per cent higher than those for woollens. After 1805–10,[28] and especially after the Napoleonic Wars, the competition presented by cheaper English cotton materials, initially imported via Thessaloniki and Istanbul, came to be seriously felt. Thus, after the Crimean War, handicraft domestic or even manufactory production of cotton materials ceased in Bulgaria.[29] In such a situation it was impossible for cotton textile production to lead the way in industrial mechanization during the nineteenth century.

The first industrial enterprise, equipped with machines, that appeared in the Bulgarian lands under Ottoman rule, was the woollen textile factory founded in Sliven in 1834 by Dobri Zheliazkov. It quickly became a state enterprise, catering mainly for the needs of the Turkish army. The factory's first, rather primitive, spinning looms were imported from Russia[30] and supplemented by copies made by local ironmasters. The Sliven factory was established only three decades after the first woollen textile factories in England, and preceded by several years the emergence of wool-spinning in the western regions of continental Europe (Alsace, 1838). The factory was considerably enlarged during the early 1840s, while in the 1850s and 1860s it was completely rebuilt, and re-equipped with superior English machines and water-driven devices. Production in the 1850s reached totals of 50,000 to 60,000 metres of cloth per year, while in the 1870s annual output rose to about 125,000 metres. The workforce through the 1860s and 1870s fluctuated around 330 persons.[31]

The Sliven factory could not satisfy the demand created by the Turkish army. Even after it was opened, a big manufactory for woollen cloth continued to exist in Plovdiv, owned by the brothers Atanas and Mihalaki Gümüsgerdan. They put out large quantities of wool among poor peasants in villages of the Central Rhodopes, who both worked on their land and were engaged in domestic spinning for which they were paid by the piece. The coarse cloth they produced was further processed in the firm's central dyeing and fulling workshop. In 1848–9 the brothers Gümüsgerdan built a second woollen textile factory in the village of Dermen dere (a district in today's Plovdiv) which, in the 1850s and 1860s, was gradually enlarged and equipped with water-driven Austrian and Czech spinning and weaving machines. This factory employed between forty-five and fifty-seven workers. Factory production initially accounted for only a quarter of the total amount of cloth provided for the Turkish army by Gümüsgerdan Brothers.[32]

This goes to show that by 1848 handicraft production of coarse woollen cloth had still not been entirely replaced by factory production, even for army orders. The requirements of the local population were still met almost exclusively by domestic production – whether by households providing for their own immediate needs or by domestic production in its commercial form, controlled by factors of decentralized manufactories. The difference between the market values of domestically produced coarse cloth and the cost of factory-produced cloth does not appear to have been great, which discouraged the establishment of private industrial enterprises – particularly in a context of administrative and financial arbitrariness on the part of the Ottoman rulers, who granted insufficient rights to the subjected Christian population. Capital accumulation among Bulgarian subjects was also limited, and this acted as an inhibiting factor, since newly accumulated capital was directed to trade and usury, which promised better returns than industrial production. All these factors ensured that the appearance of further woollen textile factories would be delayed by twenty-five years. It was not until 1873–4 that the building contractor Ivan Grozev established the third woollen textile factory in the town of Karlovo, employing between twenty-six and thirty workers. Meanwhile, the second, state-owned woollen textile factory was built in the village of Bali Efendi (in today's district of Kniazhevo, Sofia), employing forty workers. These enterprises functioned until 1877, when some of them were destroyed in military operations and by pillage.

Table 13.1. *Distribution of production on Bulgarian territory (estimates 1877)*

Sector	Million grošes	In %
Industrial production	13–19	0.7–1.0
Manufactory enterprises	7–10	0.3–0.5
Handicraft production	180	9.8–9.9
Agricultural production	1,620	88.7–89.1
Total	1,820–1,829	100

Just before the Russo-Turkish War of 1877–8 another three manufactories were preparing to turn to factory production (Ivan Kalpazanov in Gabrovo; Saraivanovi Partners, N. Popovich and the Kiuvlievi Brothers as well as Manolovi Brothers (predecessors of Kalovi Brothers) in Sliven). The war, however, spoilt their plans and their realization had to be postponed until the 1880s.

Even if we consider woollen textile production only, it is clear that the transition from handicraft to machine production in the Bulgarian lands had not been completed by 1878.[33] Moreover, some other factory enterprises were built, only to fail quickly owing to low import duties, the laxity of tax and administrative regulation, the underqualification of their proprietors, etc. During the 1860s and the first half of the 1870s, seven steam mills were opened, also two large silk-textile factories (afflicted by a disease of silkworms which spread in the 1860s), two small soap factories, a state-owned printing house, a small brewery, a small factory for the production of macaroni and vermicelli, a shoe-polish factory, a small distillery, etc. Around 1877 there were only twenty-five industrial enterprises, employing a total of 660–760 workers.[34] Just 0.1 per cent of the economically active population in the Bulgarian lands was employed in factory production. In 1877 the approximate breakdown of the main branches of material production in the Bulgarian lands within today's borders appears to have been as shown in table 13.1 (in million Turkish grošes and percentages of approximate total material production).[35]

The historical literature does not provide estimates for rates of annual growth in industrial production during the period from the establishment of the first factory in 1834 up to the war of 1877–8, but even if it did, the estimates would not be of any scientific value, given the small number and scale of the existing industrial production (with the exception of that in Sliven). Machine technology in woollen production was not yet complete; in other branches of artisanship it was only just beginning, while in most crafts there was a complete absence of industrial enterprises. The minimal share of industrial production and the lack of any mass transition from handicraft to machine production clearly indicate that we might talk only of the first steps towards an industrial revolution in the Bulgarian lands in the years preceding liberation from Ottoman rule in 1878.

During the first decade after liberation the development of factory production in Bulgaria was somewhat accelerated. Import duties remained relatively low, however; the national railway system was still under construction, while land transport continued to be expensive. Hence the home market was very limited. The capital available in the country was too small and was mainly directed into trade and usury. The results achieved in industrial development were modest, therefore, though they exceeded the results for 1834–77. By 1887 the country already had thirty-six large steam and water-mills, five textile factories, eight leather-processing plants, five distilleries, ten breweries, three soap factories, one cement factory, one dyeing plant and twenty-three small tobacco factories: a total of ninety-two enterprises in the processing industry.[36] To take only larger enterprises: 23 enterprises were founded between 1880 and 1884, 33 from 1885 to 1889, and another 54 from 1890 to 1894. In all, by 1894 there were 130 factories,[37] though many of these would later cease to operate. An unofficial census conducted by D. Yablanski reveals that by 1894 there were 72 larger and solidly functioning industrial enterprises, employing 3,027 workers.[38] When these data are compared with the figures from 1877, it can be seen that during this seventeen-year period a 4 to 4.5-fold increase in the number of industrial enterprises and workers had been achieved, equivalent to an average annual growth rate of 8.7 per cent. The reliability of this result should not, however, be overestimated since the relatively low base of the calculation might easily cause a distortion in the growth rate. Such a relatively high growth rate in factory production is not exceptional: it can be traced too in Russia during the initial stage of industrialization in the second half of the nineteenth century. The average annual growth rate in industrial production rose in Russia from 3.4 per cent in the period 1863–75 to 9 per cent in 1875–85, before dropping to 4.2 per cent from 1885 to 1891 and 4 per cent from 1890 to 1913.[39]

From the second half of the 1890s big advances were made in the development of Bulgarian industry, thanks to the gradual increase in import duties to a level of moderate protectionism, the passing in 1895 of a law for encouraging local industry, the gradual widening of the home market, and the decrease in what had initially been a prohibitively high rate of interest in the country. Hence usury ceased to attract the larger part of available capital and more of this was channelled into industry, where the rate of profit was increasing. The statistical data in table 13.2 might be cited to illustrate the development of large-scale industry, encouraged by

Table 13.2. *The development of industry in Bulgaria 1894–1921*

Year	Number of enterprises	Number of workers[a]	Fixed capital invested[b] (million gold leva)	Motive power hp	Annual output (million gold leva)
1894	72	3,027	10.91	–	–
1900	103[c]	4,716	19.82	–	–
1904	166	6,149	36.14	8,976	32.77
1909	266	12,943	66.03	17,677	78.31
1912	389[d]	15,560	94.95	32,421	115.08
1921	454[e]	17,282	180.85[f]	43,117	97.37

[a] Annual average number
[b] Machines, buildings and equipment
[c] These data do not include 236 smaller industrial enterprises which were not furthered by the state (employing fewer than 10 workers or with less than 20,000 gold leva of investments in machines, buildings or equipment), employing a total of 2,723 workers.
[d] The data do not include c. 400 smaller industrial enterprises, employing nearly 4,000 workers, whose annual output was valued 35.5 million gold leva.
[e] In addition, there existed a further 1,090 smaller industrial enterprises, belonging to branches of industry which were not furthered by the state (e.g. tobacco), with a total of 37,000 workers and an annual value of output of 131.6 million gold leva.
[f] Calculated from paper currency into gold leva at the rate of exchange for the Swiss franc in Sofia.

the state from the mid-1890s to the Balkan War of 1912–13.[40] Industrial growth before 1912 was interrupted between the autumn of 1912 until 1921–3, as Bulgaria went through three wars and a postwar economic crisis, owing to which industrial production in 1921 did not greatly exceed that of 1912. The data for 1912 lead to the conclusion that in the period 1894–1912, that is, in less than two decades, the number of larger industrial enterprises had grown along with the number of workers employed, more than fivefold, the sum of capital invested over eightfold, the value of annual production in fixed prices by about 4.3-fold,[41] and motive power almost 3.5-fold.

Calculating the growth of industrial production in fixed prices implies an annual growth rate of almost 10 per cent (except for the sub-period from 1904 to 1911 only, which had an average of 13 per cent). Between the two World Wars growth rates in factory production in Bulgaria dropped to an annual average of 6.4 per cent between 1921 and 1941. While in the sub-period 1924–9 the rates once again reached 12 per cent, in 1930–3 they fell to near zero in industry as a whole.[42] Thus, with its average annual growth of 10 per cent, the continuous increase in industrial output between 1894 and 1912 stands out clearly as the peak of Bulgaria's industrial advance under capitalist conditions.

At first glance, the average annual growth rate between 1894 and 1912 looks high, and seems to support the claim of an industrial revolution in the country. It definitely exceeds the average growth rate of industrial production in England in the first half of the nineteenth century, which fluctuated between 2.3 and 2.4 per cent, and reached 5.5 per cent only in 1820–5.[43] A similar situation obtained in the second half of the nineteenth century. Unfortunately, there are no similar figures on a national scale for the final decades of the eighteenth century.

Growth rates in industrial production for Bulgaria over the period 1894–1912 turn out to be three times those of Germany during its Industrial Revolution (at any rate during its last decade, it we are to accept Mottek's assumption that Germany's Industrial Revolution occurred between about 1834 and 1873). In 1860–80 the average annual growth in Germam industrial production amounted to 3 per cent, and it was only after the Industrial Revolution that it rose to an average of 4.5 per cent in 1880–94 and to 7.6 per cent in 1894–9, after which it fell to 3.5 per cent in 1900–13.[44] The difference is not substantial when compared with average growth rates in French industry during France's Industrial Revolution. Between 1845 and 1869 the average growth rate in France reached 7.9 per cent, falling to 2.9 per cent between 1870 and 1900 and 3.4 per cent between 1900 and 1913.[45] The difference is also smaller by comparison with average growth rates in the USA during the Industrial Revolution of the second half of the nineteenth century. There was an average rate of 8.5 per cent between 1839 and 1844; 10.6 per cent between 1844 and 1849; 7 per cent between 1849 and 1854 and then, after temporarily falling to 2.7 per cent between 1859 and 1869, the figure rose once more to stand at 9.8 per cent between 1869 and 1874 and 10.4 per cent between 1879 and 1884.[46] It should, however, be borne in mind that calculations for the rate of growth of industrial output in the nineteenth century include handicraft and manufactory, as well as industrial production.[47] These results are not, therefore, fully comparable to those for Bulgaria. There, if one were to take into account production growth not only in big, state-supported industry, but also in the crafts and smaller industrial enterprises, not encouraged by the state, considerably lower results would obtain. If we accept an average monthly income for an independent craftsman and his working family members as well as hired workers in his workshop of at least 50 leva per person employed in 1862 and 65 leva in 1912 (a little more than the income of an unskilled labourer, regularly employed, as registered by official statistics on average wages in the country), and if we assume that the value of raw materials used was approximately equal to the total payment of wages, the total value of handicraft production[48] would come to 205 million leva in 1892 and 210 million leva in 1912.[49] When the total value of factory production is added to these figures, the increase in the combined total value of handicraft and industrial production is obtained, which allows the Bulgarian data to be compared with those relating to England and the USA.

Calculated in this way a figure of 215 million leva emerges for 1892, rising to 325 million leva in 1912 – that is, a growth of 51 per cent over a period of twenty years. This equals an average annual growth rate of 2 per cent – lower than the results for England during the first half of the nineteenth century.

These comparisons indicate that the top achievements of Bulgaria during the period 1894–1912 do indeed come close to industrial growth rates in the advanced countries, though the differences in estimation methods do not allow more accurate conclusions to be drawn. The case of the USA (and to some extent that of Germany) shows that periods of high growth rates in production may even follow the Industrial Revolution. Taken by itself, therefore, this parameter is not sufficient for the drawing of reliable conclusions on the presence or absence of an industrial revolution in Bulgaria.

The second quantitative approach is that of the replacement of handicraft and manufactory production by the factory. In the branch of woollen textile production in Bulgaria, this process began in 1834 and was not completed until the 1890s.[50] In the cotton textile industry it occurred later, under pressure from cotton textile imports from western Europe (the first local cotton textile factories had yet to appear – in the period 1897–1906). In the areas of leather processing, lace production and textile dyeing, the process of replacement lasted through the second half of the 1880s and into the first half of the 1890s,[51] while in soap and candle production it continued well into the first decade of the twentieth century. Flour-milling had emerged as the second most important branch of capitalist industry in Bulgaria by 1912, yet it could not replace several thousand small village mills, driven by water or wind. In the metalworking industry the first factories appeared for the production of wire, nails, casts, agricultural implements, simple milling machines, the repair of locomotive engines, etc., but still handicraft production of metal goods was not superseded until 1912. A number of crafts were not affected by the advance of factory production. This was the case with the production of shoes, underwear, clothing, millinery, furriery, knitting, baking, the production of draught carts and most wooden wares. In the food industry handicraft production dominated until the Second World War, although there were attempts to establish factories in this field too. A number of new crafts appeared where there was a lack of factory competition (barbers and hairdressers, electricians, plumbers, etc.). For all these reasons, the overall number of persons employed in handicraft production in Bulgaria, after slumping by half in the 1880s, when a large part of the old traditional crafts went bankrupt, grew to around 150,000 to 173,000 persons at the end of the nineteenth century, falling again to around 115,000 to 135,000 persons by the 1920s.

It should also be remembered that the new spheres of heavy industry – such as mechanical and electrical engineering, the production of basic chemicals, etc. –developed only slowly and inconsistently. Ferrous metallurgy had yet to emerge, non-ferrous metallurgy took its first steps, organizing the production of copper concentrates. Coal production very nearly satisfied home demand, but the remaining branches of the mining industry were poorly developed or even absent. Advances in transport and communications were faster, but agriculture was still far from being mechanized.

By the time of the Balkan War, therefore, machine production had a long way to go before it could completely replace handicraft production. In 1911–12 the number of workers employed in factories (including smaller enterprises not supported by the state) was still six to six and a half times smaller than the number employed in handicrafts. This fact does not support the claims that a complete industrial revolution had taken place in Bulgaria by 1912. Neither was any sharp change witnessed in the period between the two World Wars, though large-scale industry did take a major step forward at this time and achieved a fivefold increase in production. It was not until 1939 that the number of factory workers to handicraftsmen approached a ratio of 3:2, or that the total national income from industrial production equalled that from handicraft production.[52]

Estimates for Bulgaria for another typical indicator of industrial revolution – the decrease in the rate of interest – are even less reliable. Shortly after the Liberation of 1878 the interest rate in the country was very high. Two state banks were founded, but were unable to satisfy the demand for credit. Given the high demand for loans among the peasants (especially when Turkish lands were to be bought over), non-regulated usury credit continued to play an important role. It was only about 1894–5, and especially after 1905, that the development of private banks took off, favouring a decrease in interest rates and a change in the ratio of demand to supply on the credit market. A trade law passed in 1897 fixed the legal rate of interest at 8 per cent.[53] In 1906 the National Bank of Bulgaria decreased interest on the credits it offered to 7 per cent (or 6 per cent for the large

Table 13.3. *Comparative per capita value of industrial output*

Country	Year	Value in French francs
England	1830	276
England	1850	448
USA	1869	497
France	1870	227
Germany	1873	306
Bulgaria	1911	36

private banks),[54] but private banks rarely granted advances below 8 per cent, while smaller banks lent at rates which could reach 10–12 per cent when the total interest was deducted from the credit granted in advance. According to this indicator, Bulgaria lagged far behind England, France and Germany, where the discount rate of the central issuing banks fluctuated around 4.5 per cent as early as 1857–65 and by the end of the century had dropped to 2.5 to 3.8 per cent.[55]

The results do not look any better if the presence of an industrial revolution is judged by the transition of a particular country's economy from an agricultural to an industrial one, or at least to an industrial–agrarian one (that is, with non-agrarian branches predominating over agrarian ones). In the specific conditions prevailing in Britain this situation was achieved as early as the 1830s; in the USA and Germany in the 1880s, and in France during the 1890s (a little behind the timescale historians traditionally offer for the Industrial Revolution). Agricultural production in Bulgaria for 1911, calculated by K. Popov, was three times as large as non-agrarian branches of material production (industry, handicraft, building, transport, communications),[56] and it was not until 1939 that this ratio dropped to around 2:1, as As. Chakalov reports (see note 6).

How much Bulgaria differed from the large capitalist countries in this regard can also be seen from estimates of the per capita industrial production (calculated in gold French francs).[57] If we accept that the Industrial Revolution in England had been completed by 1830–50, in the USA by 1869, in Germany by 1873, and in France by 1870,[58] the following picture emerges of industrial production per head of population in French francs (cf. Table 13.3).[59]

The results show that even after the Balkan War in 1911 Bulgarian industry lagged substantially behind those capitalist countries whose Industrial Revolution was completed in the nineteenth century. Once more, it is clear that we should not talk of an accomplished industrial revolution in Bulgaria even by the time of the First World War. When we consider comparable levels of industrial production per head of population it is evident that it was not until 1939 that Bulgaria came close to matching levels which had been achieved in the advanced countries at the time they had accomplished their Industrial Revolutions. It was only after a lag of almost a century, in the years following the Second World War, that Bulgaria exceeded this level.

As regards Romania, it is difficult to give a precise dating for the first introduction of machine technology into handicraft and manufactory production in the nineteenth century. Some authors cite as the first 'factory' on Romanian territory the textile manufactory in Potcoava,[60] founded in 1794 – incorrectly, since it is not clear when and to what extent this enterprise was equipped with machines. Others mention the existence of industrial workers in Romania in the 1840s,[61] though precise data concerning the mid-century – and even the 1860s – are sparse. It is true, however, that some large industrial enterprises were established in the middle of the nineteenth century, including T. Mehedincin's first petroleum-processing plant, the factories of M. Kogalniceanu, N. Baleanu and N. Kokulescu, etc.[62] In the 1870s – and especially after the first protectionist duty was introduced in 1875 and the Bank of Bucharest was founded – other large enterprises were established, such as the railway depot at Bucharest, two big sugar refineries, seven steam mills, and the 'Mandrea' factory in Bucharest, the Goetz enterprise, with branches in Galatz (Galaţi), Czernowitz (Cernăuti), Sulina and elsewhere. In the final account, however, these first decades of industrialization do not amount to much. Official data for 1866 show that the country had only 39 larger industrial enterprises,[63] of which only 18 met the requirements of the law for furthering local industry introduced in 1887.[64] In 1879 the number of larger factories reached 87, while in 1887 it came to 171,[65] only half of which were large, state-supported enterprises.

After the end of the 1880s the industrial development of Romania accelerated. Official data for 1866-77 show an average of eight large industrial enterprises founded per year, while in 1887–94 this figure had risen to nineteen. In the period from 1895 to 1904 it stood at seventeen, and between 1905 and 1915 it was fifty-nine. Most of the new enterprises came in the metalworking and chemical industries, while the number of new textile factories decreased, along with the initially favoured branches of milling, distilling, brewing and other food industries. The boom of 1905 was much assisted by the rapid emergence of the oil production and refining industries, in which mainly foreign capital was invested. The branch structure of pre-war Romanian industry was more varied than that of Bulgarian industry prior to 1912. A general view of the quantitative changes in industry can be found in table 13.4 which provides data

Table 13.4. *Industry in Romania, 1866–1915*

Year	Number of large enterprises	Number of persons[a] employed	Motive power hp	Annual output in million lei in current prices[b]	
				Processing industry	Extracting industry
1862–6[c]	39	–	–	90,2	10,0
1892	115	7,148	–	–	–
1901–2	625 (182)[d]	39,746	45,211	229,7	16,0
1904[e]	471 (294)[d]	37,635	49,766	273,1	–
1910	(472)[d]	56,338[f]	73,919	350,9	–
1912–13	–	74,894	–	518,9	105,0
1913[f]	–	–	–	971,8 (670,2)	225 (89[g])
1915	851 (847)[d]	60,937	126,666	584,1 (400,5)	– (83,9)

[a] Most of the persons employed were workers in 1902, for example, 37,325 workers were reported and only 2,421 employees and self-employed persons.

[b] Figures in brackets are based on prices of 1901–2 (calculated on the basis of M. Jackson, 'Industrial output in Romania and its historical regions 1800–1930' in State University of Arizona, *Department of Economics – EC 79–89* (Tempe, 1982), p. 26. From the end of the nineteenth century until 1910 the level of prices in Romania was generally steady.

[c] Based on M. Lupu's estimate (M. Lupu, 'Studii privind dezvoltarea economiei României în perioada capitalismului', *Studii şi cercetări economice*, 2 (1967), pp. 332–3).

[d] In brackets – only state-supported enterprises.

[e] Based on N. Paianu, *Industria mare 1866–1906* (Bucharest, 1906), pp. 49f.

[f] Incl. 10,338 persons in extracting industries.

[g] Based on not very reliable retrospective data of the industrial census of 1920. The data refer to a considerably larger number of enterprises (all enterprises employing over ten workers, while other sources include only enterprises with over twenty workers).

Sources: *Ancheta industrială din 1901–1902* (Bucharest, 1904); *Prima statistica industrială al României dupa primul război mondial* (Bucharest, 1922); *Anuarul statical României 1922* (Bucharest, 1923), pp. 200–6; N. P. Arcadian, *Industrializarea României* (Bucharest, 1936), pp. 130, 133.

on the number of persons employed, motive power and annual industrial output (though the data are not entirely comparable). The average percentage growth of annual production in fixed prices, calculated on the basis of the data presented in table 13.4, amounts to 2.8 per cent between 1866 and 1902, 5.3 per cent between 1902 and 1910 and 12 per cent between 1910 and 1915. Between the two World Wars growth rates in industrial production tended to decline. In the period 1919–29 an average annual growth rate of about 4 per cent was obtained, while between 1929 and 1938 it was 2.9 per cent.[66] It is clear that from the initial stage of industrialization in Romania during the 1860s up to the Second World War, there was no steady tendency of development in industry, except for the decade 1905–15.

If we take into account how fast handicraft and manufactory production was replaced by factory production, Romania appears to be somewhat ahead of Bulgaria in this respect. A number of crafts were replaced by the factory in the last third of the nineteenth century. In 1860, for example, there were thirty-six handicraft workshops for cloth production in Romania, whereas by 1901 only one was left.[67] The situation was similar in soap and fur production. In a number of branches, however, industrialization did not succeed in replacing handicraft and more primitive production entirely. As late as 1915, despite the existence of 98 more or less modern mills, there were still 4,816 small peasant water and wind mills, not supported by the state.[68] Despite the existence of 54 large wood-processing enterprises, another 778 small sawmills were still functioning.[69] The production of bread, clothing, shoes and other everyday articles was mainly performed by handicraftsmen.

Because of this and the emergence of new crafts, which were not threatened by factory competition, there was a large number of craftsmen in Romania during the decades at the turn of the century.[70] A census, covering 32 regions in 1902, reveals the existence of 53,589 independent master craftsmen, who employed 44,166 journeymen and apprentices, along with 7,000 members of their own families.[71] A later census from April 1908 shows a decrease in the number of independent craftsmen to 47,449, paralleling an increase in the number of journeymen and apprentices employed by them to 80,392[72] – a fact reflecting the emergence of a social group of well-to-do craftsmen. By 1900–2 there were 89 independent craftsmen per 10,000 persons in Romania, while in Bulgaria this number was 194. This fact also reflects traditional differences in the social structure of the two countries, that is that after 1878 a comparatively greater proportion of persons was engaged in handicraft production in Bulgaria.

Romania differed from Bulgaria in that as early as 1902 production levels achieved by industry were already far greater than those achieved by artisans. The total handicraft production in Romania (calculated by the method applied in the case of Bulgaria) amounted to 90–120 million lei in 1902,[73] or less than half the total of local industry's annual production. That handicraft production should be so comparatively slight during the early years of the twentieth century, when industrialization was still not very far advanced, may be because Romania imported many of its industrial goods from other, more advanced European countries. Recalculated official statistical data for 1900 show that 45.3 French francs per head of population were spent on foreign imported goods, while in Bulgaria this amount was only 21.8 French francs. Handicraft production seems to have prevailed only until the second half of the 1870s.[74]

Romania's performance in other aspects of the Industrial Revolution also deserved to be more highly rated. According to table 13.4, before the First World War Romania had come closer to a level of per capita industrial production more typical of advanced capitalist countries during their process of industrialization in the nineteenth century. In 1910 the average value of per capita production in large-scale industry amounted to 60 (in 1915 to about 61) gold French francs,[75] while in 1913 (when more detailed statistics were available) the figure had risen to 104 francs. According to these figures pre-war Romania was almost three times ahead of Bulgaria, but still twice to four and a half times behind the level reached by advanced capitalist countries in the nineteenth century.

Romania's industrialization also ranks higher than Bulgaria if rates of interest are compared. In the period 1901–14 the rate of interest in Romania generally fluctuated between 5 and 6.5 per cent and rarely reached 7 to 8 per cent (the average value for the period is 5.7 per cent for bills of exchange and 6.8 per cent for Lombard credit).[76]

Yet, by the time of the First World War Romania had not turned into an industrial or even agrarian–industrial country to a degree that would justify claiming that the Industrial Revolution had been accomplished. No estimates have been made of the national product of the country at that time, yet some approximate estimates might be attempted. If we take into account the amount of agrarian production in Bulgaria in 1911 (936.8 million gold French francs, as reported by K. Popov) and compare the amount of land cultivated in Romania and Bulgaria at the time (7.33 vs. 3.39 million ha), it might be expected that the agricultural produce of Romania in 1911–12 would amount to 2.03 billion lei.[77] This sum is two to three times greater than that provided by the country's industrial production. Even by 1939 the value of Romanian industrial production had still not reached that of its agriculture.

Transylvania – since 1921 part of the Romanian state – could not fulfil its industrial potential until the First World War. The first signs of industrial development in this mixed ethnic region were felt from 1867, after the Austro-Hungarian Compromise. Coal and iron deposits in Anina (Staierdorfanina) and Reşiţa–Doman were exploited. The mining and metallurgical base of the Braşov Mining and Blast Furnace Association was built along the Ziu river and in Kalani. The first big mill with an annual capacity exceeding 50,000 tons of flour was constructed in the early 1870s.[78] Transylvania approached Romanian levels of industrial development in the 1870s and 1880s, but later its rate of development declined. The number of big industrial enterprises in Transylvania in the years preceding the First World War (791 in 1910)[79] was somewhat lower than that of Romania. The absolute total value of industrial production (494 million lei in 1913)[80] in current prices, equal to about 370–412 million lei in prices for 1902) was also lower than that of Romania. In 1913 the per capita value of industrial production was 79–96 gold French francs comparable with prices from the first decade of the twentieth century.[81] The relative number of craftsmen in Transylvania was twice as high as that in Romania.

Other industrially developed regions in the Balkans in the nineteenth and early twentieth centuries are Croatia (including Vojvodina) and Slovenia, then part of Austria-Hungary. This region was known for the considerable development of manufactories in the second half of the eighteenth and the early nineteenth centuries.[82] The first steps towards industrialization date from the 1830s, when several big factories, equipped with machines, were built. In 1835 the first steam engine in the region was installed in the large paper factory of Andria Adamič in Rijeka, whose production in the 1840s reached 450,000 forints, and which employed 300–500 workers.[83] In 1836 the sugar factory in Čepinu was built. In 1838 the first ship in the region was launched in Sisak.

During the 1840s and 1850s the construction of large industrial enterprises took a big step forward.[84] In 1846 the first steam mill in Vukovar appeared, while in 1847 the first spinning factory in Varaždin was established.[85] Two big state monopoly factories were also built for tobacco products in Rijeka and Varaždin. In 1851 the first seven mechanical looms appeared in the textile factory in Rijeka, while in 1852 the first small chemical factory, employing 15 to 20 workers, was established in the same place. In 1854 Rijeka again housed the first large metalworking factory. In 1856 the production of threshing machines and other equipment was initiated in Osijek.[86] The growth of industry at that time might be judged by the fact that in 1835 there was only one steam engine working in Croatia, with a motive power of 18 hp, while in 1849 there were four such engines and in 1859 eighteen engines, with a combined motive power of 293 hp.[87]

During the 1860s the number of big industrial enterprises increased yet further. At the end of that decade Croatia and Slovenia (Carniola/Krain) could already boast a metallurgical plant for ferrous metals in Jesenice,[88] a lead plant in Idrija,[89] a woollen-textile and cotton-textile factory in Ljubljana,[90] a big glass factory in Varaždin, a cement plant in Split,[91] as well as a paper factory, two sugar refineries, three chemical factories, eight steam mills, two steam sawmills, two metal factories, six printing houses, etc., elsewhere.[92] Industrialization in the 1860s was strengthened by the construction of the first railway lines in the region which started in 1862. Foreign capital played an important part in these first decades of industrialization. Investment, however, was channelled into areas of enterprise which offered a high rate of profit. Many craftsmen from the old traditional occupations continued to work well into the 1880s.[93]

During the last three decades of the nineteenth century and the early years of the twentieth century there was an upsurge of industry in Croatia and Slovenia, even though it was interrupted for one to two years by the Great Depression of 1873 and the economic crisis of 1890. A number of new areas were opened up, the first of which was electric-power production.[94] A substantial number of large enterprises was established in previously existing trades, the large sugar factory in Rijeka, for example, the paper factory in Zagreb,[95] the machine building plant Djuro Djaković in Zagreb,[96] the cotton-textile plant in Tržić, a number of large mills, wood-processing enterprises, factories for metal goods, ceramics, hosiery, etc. In 1912–13 there were 712 industrial enterprises working in the region, each of which employed over 20 workers. In 1912 the value of their annual production amounted to 303 million French francs. With a population of 4.06 million this implied an average annual per capita value of output amounting to 77 French francs.[97] This sum is lower than the respective one for Romania, but it is twice as large as that for Bulgaria. It was only in the years leading up to the Second World War that the number of workers employed in industry became almost equal to that of persons employed in handicraft production.[98] The total value of industrial production, however, was still very much smaller than that of agricultural production. This indicates that the Industrial Revolution had not yet been completed. It was hindered by the relatively low rates of growth of industrial production in the newly formed Yugoslav state between the two World Wars (an annual average rate of 4 per cent for the country). In the industrialized of Croatia and Slovenia regions the growth rates were even lower, for two main reasons: the loss of free access to the large home market of the pre-war Austro-Hungarian Empire; and the competition of the ruling Serbian bourgeoisie.

In Serbia, despite early liberation from Ottoman domination, industrialization began several decades late, owing to the limited size of the home market, the incompleteness of the bourgeois revolution in the country, the slow accumulation of capital, etc. Among the first Serbian industrial enterprises were the state printing house in Belgrade (1836), a leather factory in Topčider (1839) a woollen textile mill in Belgrade (1852), and a military plant in Kragujevac (1853).[99] Through the 1860s and the first half of the 1870s, however, the economy was still dominated by handicraft production.[100]

It was only after 1878 that a partial step towards industrialization was taken in Serbia. By 1881 the country already had twenty-two industrial enterprises, but of these only two (the Kragujevac military plant and the Vaifert brewery in Belgrade) were large-scale operations.[101] In the 1880s and early 1890s nearly every successive year saw a new enterprise in the processing industry employing between 65 and 518 persons. Noteworthy among these were the electric power station in Belgrade, woollen textile mills in Paraćin, and Leskovac, a glass factory in Jagodin, a coke plant in Belgrade and others. Despite some sporadic attempts at exploiting coal and ore mines between 1837 and 1848, it was not until 1866–91 that the first large modernized enterprises – such as the mines and blast-furnaces for lead, silver, copper and zinc in Majdanpek, Rudna glava and Kučajna – began operating, along with the cinnabar mines at Avila, the mines near the villages of Brod, Ruplte, Vrška čuka, Zajčji vrh, Resava and Aleksinac. By the early 1890s the country already had 9,000 workers in the processing and extractive industries. The crafts, however, employed some 132,000 persons,[102] a fact which suggests that artisanship was far from being replaced by factory production in this period.

The end of the 1890s saw a dynamic phase in Serbian industrial development, given new impetus by the expansion of the country's railway system. Belgrade had been connected with the Austro-Hungarian network in 1883, with the Bulgarian one in 1886 and, in 1888, with the Istanbul–Thessaloniki–Skopje line. Industrial growth was further assisted by the newly evolved policy of protectionism and state support. The advance in industrial development is apparent in the data in table 13.5.[103] These reveal relatively high growth rates in industry (10 to 33 per cent per annum) in the first decade of the twentieth century,[104] which can be explained by the relatively low starting base. The level of industrialization achieved, however, remained very low – only 24 gold French francs per capita value of industrial output per annum.[105] Workers employed in industry accounted for less than 1 per cent of the country's population, while the value of total industrial output was less than a tenth that of agricultural output. In the period between the two World Wars Serbia's industrial development took a big step foward, but this still fell short of a full industrial revolution.

Greece's partial liberation fom Ottoman domination after 1821 did not immediately advance industrialization. Few industrial enterprises with

Table 13.5. *Number of enterprises and workers employed in Serbia, 1898–1910*

Year	Number of large enterprises	Workers employed
1898	28	1,702
1902	66	3,936
1906	110	5,624
1910	428	16,000

machine technology emerged during the 1830s and 1840s. By 1850 there were only seven 'factories' in the country, and these were manufactories rather than industrial enterprises based on machines.[106]

Industrialization accelerated only after the intensive domestic agrarian colonization of 1832–71[107] and after the first protectionist duties were introduced in the 1860s, along with the gradual improvement of the country's roads and the construction of its first railway lines in 1867. By that year Greece already had 68 enterprises with 7,300 workers.[108] To begin with, extractive industrial activity predominated, though most of these ventures were based on foreign capital.

Industrial development intensified after the end of the 1870s. By 1877 the number of persons employed in industry had reached 24,300, while in 1882 – after the annexation of Thessalia – it stood at over 40,000, including those in semi-craft workshops.[109] In 1893 the number of those employed in larger industrial enterprises alone was 17,152 as against 7,342 in 1873. Motive power in industry had reached 10,000 hp,[110] up from 296 hp in 1876. One of the largest enterprises in the country was the Lavrion Mining Company, with over 2,300 workers. The milling industry developed rapidly. Its foundation was laid in 1857 with the establishment of Alatini Brothers' large Thessaloniki mill, while in 1894, by which time the country had over forty steam mills, the first national monopolistic organization (syndicate) of the milling industry came into being. The textile industry lagged behind until the second half of the 1880s, and even then the large textile factory owned by Retsina Brothers enjoyed a monopoly in the branch.

Unfortunately, data on the total value of Greek industrial production in the nineteenth century are sporadic and not entirely comparable. S. Mrampanassis reports that official data for 1867 show the value of total industrial production to have amounted to 51 million drachmas, while P. Morajtinis's data for 1874 contain the figure of 166 million drachmas.[111] It is apparent from the text, however, that this figure includes 112 'big' enterprises, 75 small 'factories' and 'many other workshops', without precisely differentiating between handicraft production and industry. It might be deduced from the incomplete data on individual branches of industry that production from large enterprises in 1874 amounted to around 74 million gold drachmas (including extractive industries). Other evidence for 1892, however, suggests a figure of 42 million drachmas.[112]

Greek industrial development received significant promotion in the wake of the Balkan War and during the 1920s. A considerable number of new large enterprises appeared in the food and textile industries. The foundations of some new branches of heavy industry were laid after the big electric power stations in Athens and Thessaloniki were built in 1908. By 1907, industry and handicrafts employed 29.6 per cent of the economically active population, as against only 15.7 per cent in 1870.[113] Exhaustive statistical data for industry only are not available, but the annual growth rate for industrial production in the 1890s is estimated to have been 4.2 per cent.[114] In the first decade of the twentieth century it was higher, and in 1911–12 alone 66 new industrial enterprises were set up, with a capital of 230 million drachmas.[115] The political coup of 1909 played a favourable role, though it tends to be overestimated by some authors.[116] The territories newly annexed between 1912 and 1918 were of only limited significance, with 608 small handicraft enterprises. By 1920 Greece had already 2,905 enterprises employing more than 6 persons, providing work for some 65,000 persons and with a total motive power of 90,000 hp.[117] In 1921 the value of the country's industrial production amounted to 400 million pre-war gold French francs.[118] With a population of 5.56 million, this implies an average value of per capita industrial production of 72 gold French francs, that is only a third of the results for advanced economies at the time of the completion of their Industrial Revolutions in the nineteenth century.

During the 1920s Greek industry expanded more than twofold, while between 1929 and 1938 the expansion was only 15–20 per cent. Despite this advance, Greece lagged behind with respect to the value of per capita industrial output, and in 1938 it ranked below Bulgaria and Romania.[119] By the same year the total value of industrial output was already twice that of total handicraft output, but still lagged behind the total value of agricultural output. By this comparison, however, Greece in 1938 enjoyed a better position than Bulgaria, where the ratio of industrial to agricultural output stood at 1:7 (compared with only 1:2 in Romania).

Among the remaining Balkan regions and countries it is only Bosnia-Hercegovina which stands out: there industrial development in the nineteenth century equalled that in contemporary Bulgaria or Serbia. It received significant assistance from the Austro-Hungarian regional administration, which enjoyed considerable revenues from the output and export of high-stem timber from the region's large state-owned forests.

These were used in 1886–96 to establish the ironworks and blast-furnaces at Vareš, the wood distillery at Teslić, the metallurgical plant at Zenica, the sugar refinery at Uzora, the distillery at Tuzla, the brewery in Sarajevo and the coal mines in Kreka.[120] Industrial activity in the local private trade and usury credit was at first negligible. While it is true that, along with the appearance of the first capitalist manufactories in the period 1861–9, the first factory in the region was also built in 1860 (owned by a joint-stock company in Sarajevo), this worked successfully for only eight years. In the second half of the 1870s more industrial enterprises appeared, along with J. Feldbauer's Sarajevo brewery.

The last years of the nineteenth century, however, saw a marked increase in industrial development. By 1918, 121 industrial enterprises had been established, of which 28 were in the extractive industry.[121] F. Schmidt states that before the First World War 22,800 persons had been employed in industry as a whole in Bosnia-Hercegovina.[122] If we assume the annual value of production per worker to have been about 2,500 French francs the value of annual output can be estimated at 57 million French francs. As the population in the region was 1.89 million, this implies that the per capita value of industrial production amounted to 30 French francs.

Between the two World Wars Bosnia-Hercegovina lagged behind the other regions of the new Yugoslav state. By 1938 its share in the country's industry amounted to 11 per cent, as against 27 per cent for Croatia (without Dalmatia), 20 per cent for Serbia, 16 per cent for Vojvodina, 14 per cent for Slovenia and 5 per cent for Macedonia.[123]

Macedonian industry developed more slowly and falteringly. It is difficult to establish exact parameters before 1912 because of the lack of relevant Turkish statistics. Some historical studies show that in the third quarter of the nineteenth century, industrial development was confined to the Greek region (today's borders) of Macedonia, largely in Thessaloniki, and partly in Seres, Drama and Kavala. It was only in the final quarter of the century that industrial enterprises were established within the borders of FYROM (Former Yugoslav Republic of Macedonia). After the building of a tobacco factory in Prilep in 1873[124] and a chocolate factory in Skopje in 1882,[125] the first steam mills and textile factories were set up in Bitola, Prilep, Krušovo and Ohrid in the second half of the 1880s and the 1890s. In the first decade of the twentieth century (especially after 1903), further industrial enterprises appeared in Skopje, Štip, Veles, Kavadarci, Resen and elsewhere.[126] It was not until 1908 that the first electric power station was built, in Skopje. With the exception of chrome-ore extraction in the regions of Skopje, Tetovo, Kumanovo and Krivolak, other branches of heavy industry were not really developed.

Before the Balkan War there were seventy-four industrial enterprises on the territory of FYROM employing – if we accept what seems a rather exaggerated estimate[127] –some 10,000 workers. Average annual output per worker would have amounted (given the large share taken up by the food industry) to perhaps 1,800 to 2,000 French francs. Since the population of the region in 1911 was around 1.45 million, this presupposes an average per capita value of industrial output of about 12–13 French francs. Between the two World Wars the Yugoslavian part of Macedonia once again lagged behind its neighbouring countries.[128]

In fact, Turkey lagged even more. In 1913 it had 269 industrial enterprises with a motive power of over 5 hp, employing 16,975 workers.[129] Of these a large number was in the textile industry. Assuming an average annual value of production of 20 per cent below that of Bulgaria, the value for Turkey could be estimated at around 95 million French francs, based on 1910–11 prices. With a population of 19 million, this meant that the per capita value of industrial output was 6 French francs, a result several times lower than that for Bulgaria and Serbia.

Before the Balkan War, Montenegro (Crna Gora) took its first steps towards establishing a local industry (in 1912 the country had only six wood-processing enterprises).[130] The situation was still worse in Albania and in the region of Kosovo. Even as late as 1938, industry occupied only a very modest place in the Albanian economy: just 3.8 per cent of national income.[131]

This summary of economic data in the individual countries produces a number of conclusions about the chronology and nature of industrialization in the Balkans as a whole. The first thing to emerge clearly is that when compared with the advanced capitalist countries, industrialization was very much delayed because of the Balkans' general backwardness. If we ignore the first isolated attempts at establishing industrial enterprises, it is quite clear that the initial stage of Romanian, Croatian and Slovenian industrialization should be dated back to the 1860s; in Serbia it gained momentum in the 1880s; in Bulgaria, Greece and Bosnia-Hercegovina in the 1890s, as is also the case for Turkey; in Albania industrialization does not really begin until after the Second World War. If we rank the nations according to the average level of per capita industrial output we find that, around 1911, Romania leads, followed respectively by Croatia/Slovenia, Bulgaria, Bosnia-Hercegovina, Serbia, Macedonia, Turkey, Montenegro and Albania. All of them, however, lagged far behind the levels of per capita industrial output achieved by the advanced capitalist countries during their own Industrial Revolutions. Not a single Balkan country had managed to reach the economic stage of an advanced industrial country by the Second World War. This indicates that an industrial revolution had not been accomplished. We can only talk of an initial or uncompleted industrial revolution. Indeed, the term 'revolution' is not appropriate for processes which had continued for more than a century in the countries discussed here.

The Balkan states did not follow the British model of Industrial Revolution. The missing element was the preliminary mass exodus of the population from the land, typical for England. The building of industry developed at a slow pace and it was only after the Second World War that it intensified in some countries in the region. The centrality of the cotton industry, which was both the origin and the mainstay of the British Industrial Revolution, from the eighteenth to the nineteenth century, has no corresponding equivalent in the Balkans. In the beginning the leading branch in some countries was the woollen textile industry (Bulgaria, Turkey) or flour milling (Macedonia, Greece). In Serbia and Croatia/ Slovenia, however, the leading branches were different. The only exception seems to be Romania, where the textile industry was initially poorly developed (at the beginning of the twentieth century the country was still unable to abandon the import of textiles, which continued to supply 96 per cent of domestic demand). Extractive industries were also significant in the beginning, although ore production in various countries depended largely on the availability of natural resources. Wood-processing and leather industries, along with the production of building materials, were initially important, with the partial exception of Greece. Engineering was generally poorly developed. It was only Romania, and parts of Transylvania and Croatia, that made limited efforts in that respect, and they should not be overestimated.

The uncompleted Industrial Revolution in the Balkans evolved in conditions of lack of capital and low industrial output. In 1901 a state-supported enterprise in Transylvania had an average number of 98 workers, compared with 82–7 in Croatia/Slovenia, 63 in Romania, 54 in Serbia and 48 in Bulgaria (1909). Hence, criteria for state-support in Romania from 1887 and then between 1912 and 1920 stipulated enterprises employing over 25 workers, while the comparable law in Bulgaria included those employing over 10 workers.[132] Foreign capital played a significant role in the industrialization of the Balkans.

Balkan countries generally used imported machines, whose technical level was good. Competition among European engineering firms left no place for the domestic production of low-quality or outdated machines. Some branches (e.g., the oil industry in Romania) were set up with the most advanced technology available at the time.[133]

The Industrial Revolution in the Balkan countries, though incomplete by the Second World War, nevertheless played a positive role in their economic development. They became less dependent on imports, though that did not contribute much to a competitive decrease in prices of industrial goods, because of a moderate customs protectionism. It also had a positive impact on the increase of the average worker's pay, in that the average industrial wage in the Balkan countries was higher than the wages of agricultural labourers. The development of industry raised the demand for hired workers and thus promoted a general increase in workers' wages in the individual countries.

NOTES

1 In the 1930s, the Soviet literature on economics began to employ the term 'industrial overturn' (*promyshlenyi pereverot*) which, after the Second World War, was accepted in the Bulgarian historiography. See, for example, the textbook for the higher schools of economics, *Stopanska istoriia* (Industrial History) (3rd edn, Sofia, 1982), pp. 200–5. The meaning of this term actually overlaps with 'Industrial Revolution' (see *Bol'shaia sovetskaia entsiklopediia* (Great Soviet Encyclopaedia), vol. I (Moscow, 1959), pp. 626–7), but the very term suggests that the economic change was not a result of a revolutionary process.

2 See A. Toynbee, *Lectures on the Industrial Revolution* (London, 1950); C. Fohlen, *Qu'est-ce que la révolution industrielle?* (Paris, 1971); Ph. Deane, *The First Industrial Revolution* (Cambridge, 1969); P. Mantoux, *La révolution industrielle au XVIIIᵉ siècle. Essai sur les commencements de la grande industrie moderne en Angleterre* (Paris, 1959); J. Kuczynski, 'Zum Problem der industriellen Revolution', *Zeitschrift für Geschichtswissenschaften*, 3 (1956), pp. 501f.; P. Mathias, 'La révolution industrielle en Angleterre: un cas unique?', *Annales, Economies Sociétés Civilisations*, no. 1 (1972), pp. 33–46; R. Nolte, *Marxismus und industrielle Revolution* (Berlin, 1967); *Cambridge Economic History of Europe*, vol. VI, parts 1, 2 (Cambridge, 1966); K. Borchardt, *Die industrielle Revolution in Deutschland*, Foreword by C. M. Cipolla (Munich, 1972); H. Wehner, 'Deutschlands Weg zum Industriestaat. Einige Bemerkungen zu den Veröffentlichungen des Instituts für Wirtschaftsgeschichte der Hochschule für Ökonomie – Berlin zu Fragen der industriellen Revolution in Deutschland etc., *Jahrbuch für Wirtschaftsgeschichte*, part 1 (1969), pp. 349f.; H. Mottek, H. Blomberg, H. Wutzmer and W. Becker, *Studien zur Geschichte der industriellen Revolution in Deutschland*, vol. I (Berlin, 1960).

3 See Introduction, this volume.

4 N. Vučo, *Raspadanje esnafa u Srbiji* (The Decline of the Guilds in Serbia) 2 vols. (Belgrade, 1954); P. Tsonchev, *Iz stopanskoto minalo na Gabrovo* (The Industrial Past of Gabrovo) (Sofia, 1929).

5 The following, quite rare, exceptions should be mentioned: A. L. Lisac, *Razvoj industrije papira u Zagrubu* (The Evolution of the Paper Industry in Zagreb) (Zagreb, 1961); D. Klen, *Tvornica papira Rijeka* (The Rijeka Paper Mill) (Rijeka-Bolzano, 1971); Fr. Kresal, *Razvoj predionice Litija ob 75. obletnici* (75 Years' development of the Litija Spinning Works) (Litija, 1961); N. Todorov, *Balkanskiiat grad XV–XIX v.* (The Balkan Town During the Fifteenth–Nineteenth Centuries) (Sofia, 1972), pp. 225–50, 267–94.

6 As. Chakalov, *Natsionalniiat dohod i razhod na Bulgaria 1924–1945 g.* (State Income and Expenditure in Bulgaria, 1924–1945) (Sofia, 1946). For 1892 and 1911, only an estimation can be found, in K. Popov, *Stopanska Bulgaria prez 1911 g.* (Industrial Bulgaria in 1911) (Sofia, 1918), pp. 459, 455.

7 X. Zolotas, *Nomismatike statheropoiesis* (Monetary Stabilization) (Athens, 1929); P. Dertilis, 'To eisodema tes Hellados' (Greece's income) in *Arheion oikonomikon kai koinonikon espistimon* (Archives of Economic and Social Sciences) (Athens, 1932); Ch. Evelpides, 'To ethnikon eisodema' (The national income), *Agrotike Oikonomia* (Agrarian economy), no. 4 (1937), pp. 393–420.

8 *Turkiye milli geliri toplam harcanalari ve jatirimlari 1938–1948–1967* (Aggregate expenditure and revenues in the Turkish national income for the years 1938–1948–1967) (Ankara, 1968).

9 V. M. Čuričić, M. Tošaić, A. Vagner and P. Rudčenko, *Naša narodna privreda i nacionalni prikhod* (Our National Economy and National Income) (Belgrade, 1930); St. Stajič, 'Realni nacionalni dohodak Jugoslavije u periodima 1926–1939 i 1947–1956' (The real national income in Yugoslavia during 1926–1939, and 1947–1956), *Ekonomski problemi* (Economic Problems), no. 3 (1957), pp. 29–42.

10 D. N. Iordan, *Venitul national al României* (National Income of Romania) (Bucharest, 1930); M. Georgescu, 'Venitul national' (National income) in *Enciclopedia României* (The Encyclopaedia of Romania), vol. III (Bucharest, 1939), pp. 941–66.

11 *40 vjet Shqipëri socialiste. Të dhëna statistikore për zhvillimin e ekonomisë dhe të kulturës* (Forty years of Socialist Albania. Statistical data on the development of its economy and culture) (Tirana, 1984), p. 135.

12 L. Berov, 'Kâm vâprosa za tempovete na kapitalisticheskata industrializatsiia na Bulgaria' (On the question of the rate of capitalist industrialization of Bulgaria), *Izvestiia na ikonomicheskiia institut pri BAN* (Proceedings of the Institute of Economics at the Bulgarian Academy of Sciences), vol. VIII, no. 3–4 (1954), pp. 129–63. For additional information see an article by the same author in the periodical *Statistika* (Statistics), no. 3 (1960), pp. 30–47. For Romania, Yugoslavia, Greece and Turkey the annual rates of industrial production growth can only be assessed for the period after the First World War, but still only for some parts of the period. See *Protektsionizâm i konkurentsiia na Balkanite prez XX v.* (Protectionism and competition in the Balkans during the twentieth century) (Sofia, 1989), pp. 66–70.

13 B. R. Mitchell, *European Historical Statistics 1750–1975* (London, 1981), pp. 375–6; N. F. R. Crafts, *British Economic Growth during the Industrial Revolution* (Oxford, 1985), pp. 78–99.

14 About the changes in the annual amount of investment in Bulgaria there is only one, already quoted, work by L. Berov, but it concerns only the period after the 1890s. Research into the precise annual rate of accumulation of capital on a national scale is rare, even in Bulgarian historical publications and normally concerns a later period – during the Second World War. See L. Berov, 'Kapitaloobrazuvaneto v Bulgaria prez godinite na Vtorata svetovna

vojna' (The accumulation of capital in Bulgaria during the Second World War), *Trudove na Visshiia Ikonomicheski Institut 'Karl Marx' v Sofia)*, (Occasional Papers of the Institute of Economics 'Karl Marx' in Sofia), no. 2 (1971), pp. 11–47. In some specialized monographs by Bulgarian and Romanian authors the conditions for the accumulation of capital during the period of the established capitalism are mentioned, but such monographs provide only isolated examples and no precise quantitative indices. See, for example, G. Radulescu, 'Rata profitului in economia romaneasca în anii 1927–1938' (The profit rate in the Romanian economy in the years 1927–1938), *Studii şi cercetări economice* (Economic Studies and Research) no. 4 (1969), pp. 23–56.

15 Fragmentary data about the number of employed workers in the big industrial enterprises can be found in the statistics concerning the state-supported industries in some Balkan states shortly before the First World War. Such statistics constitute the main source of information that serves to distinguish the industrial workers from the workers employed in the handicraft industry, mentioned only as 'workers' in the mixed census registers.

16 See St. Zeletin, *Burghezia româna. Originea şi rolul ei în istorie* (The Romanian bourgeoisie. Its origin and role in history) (Bucharest, 1976), and C. C. Giurescu, *Contribuţiuni la studiul originelor şi dezvoltării burghezieia române pînă le 1848* (Contributions to the study of the origins and development of the Romanian Bourgeoisie up to 1848) (Bucharest, 1972); *Stopanska istoriia na Bulgaria 681–1981 g.* (Economic History of Bulgaria, 681–1981) (Sofia, 1981), p. 260; L. Berov, 'Klasova struktura na burzhoaznoto obshtestvo v Bulgaria v navecherieto na socialisticheskata revolyutsiia' (The class structure of the Bulgarian society on the eve of the socialist revolution), *Izvestiia na Instituta po istoriia pri BAN* (Proceedings of the Institute of History at the Bulgarian Academy of Sciences), vol. XXXI (1990).

17 See T. S. Ashton, 'The standard of life of workers in England 1790–1830', *Journal of Economic History*, 9 (supplement 1949), pp. 22–49; G. N. von Tunzelman, 'Trends in real wages 1750–1850', *Economic History Review*, 32 (February 1979), pp. 33–49; P. Stearns and D. Walkowitz, *Workers in the Industrial Revolution* (New Brunswick, 1974); J. Kuczynski, *A Short History of Labour Conditions under Industrial Capitalism*, vol. IV (London, 1946); P. Mantoux, *La révolution industrielle au XVIIIᵉ siècle* (Paris, 1959); E. W. Hunt and F. W. Botham, 'Wages in Britain during the Industrial Revolution', *Economic History Review*, 2nd series, 40, 3 (1987), pp. 380–400; *Histoire économique et sociale de la France*, vol. II (Paris, 1970), pp. 487–93.

18 See L. Berov 'Wages in the Balkan lands during manufacturing capitalism and the industrial capitalism', *Bulgarian Historical Review*, 4 (1978), pp. 39–58; 'Le salaire des ouvriers qualifiés dans les pays balkaniques au cours de la période du capitalisme manufacturier et de la révolution industrielle', *Etudes balkaniques*, 1 (1978), pp. 30–54; 'La salaire des fonctionnaires d'Etat et du secteur dans les pays balkaniques au cours de la période du capitalisme manufacturier et de la révolution industrielle', *Etudes balkaniques*, 2 (1980), pp. 58–86.

19 R. Bičanić, *Doba manufakture u Hrvatskoj i Slavoniji 1750–1860* (The manufactory

period in Croatia and Slavonia, 1750–1860) (Zagreb, 1951), p. 228. The author maintains that the Industrial Revolution in Croatia and Slavonia begins in the 1840s and ends at the end of the nineteenth century.

20 N. Vučo, 'Industrijska revolucija u jugoslovenskim zemljama' (The Industrial Revolution in the Yugoslav lands), *Acta Historico-oeconomica Iugoslaviae*, no. 1 (1974), pp. 9–15, and 'Industrijska revolucija u Srbiji u XIX veku' (The Industrial Revolution in Serbia in the nineteenth century), *Ekonomske anali* (Economic Annals), 56 (1977), pp. 58–70.

21 C. Şerban, 'Innovation technologique en Roumanie aux XIXe et XXe siècle et ses implications socio-économiques', *Revue romaine d'histoire*, 3 (1988), pp. 135–51.

22 O. Constantinescu and N. N. Constantinescu, *Cu privire la problema revoluţiei industriale în România* (On the Problem of the Industrial Revolution in Romania) (Bucharest, 1974). The authors are of the opinion that the Industrial Revolution in Romania begins at the end of the nineteenth century.

23 I. Lungu, 'Aspecte ale începuturilor revoluţiei industriale în mineritul din Valea Jiului' (Aspects of the beginnings of the Industrial Revolution in the mining industry in the Jiul Valley), *Sargetia*, 5 (1968), pp. 243–50.

24 See *Stopanska istoriia*, pp. 416–20; J. Šorn, 'Doprinos proučavanju problema industrijske revolucije u jugoslovenskim zemljama (s osobitim obzirom na Sloveniju)' (A contribution to the study of the question of the Industrial Revolution in the Yugoslav lands (with special regard to Slovenia)), *Acta historico-oeconomica Iugoslaviae* 1 (1974), pp. 141–5; D. Miroslava, *Industrija grad-janske Hrvatske 1860–1873* (The Industry of Civil Croatia) (Zagreb, 1970), p. 230.

25 See, for example, V. Panayotopoulos, 'La révolution industrielle et la Grèce 1832–1871', *Etudes balkaniques*, 3 (1977), pp. 92–7.

26 Kuczynski, 'Zum Problem der industriellen Revolution', pp. 523–4.

27 *Rumyniia 1848–1917 gg.* (Romania of 1848–1917) (Moscow, 1971), p. 177.

28 Tsonchev, *Iz stopanskoto minalo*, p. 281.

29 *Ibid.*, p. 280.

30 It is not at all clear whether these Russian machines copied original English models.

31 G. Kozarov, *Dobri Zheliazkov Fabrikadzhiiata* (Dobri Zheliazkov the Man-ufacturer) (Sofia, 1934); G. Danailov, 'Pârvata bâlgarska textilna fabrika' (The first Bulgarian textile mill), *Spisanie na bâlgarskoto ikonomichesko druzhestvo* (Bulletin of the Bulgarian Economic Society), 9 (1902), pp. 569f.

32 Todorov, *Balkanskiiat grad*, pp. 282–94.

33 The manufacturing of woollen braiding constitutes a special case. It was mechanized during the first two decades of the nineteenth century by the employment of simple iron cog-wheels moved by water power, but still remained a small-scale production. During the 1830s and the 1840s some of the richer producers of braidings attempted the establishing of bigger work-shops (actually, mini-factories, called 'rooms') which used very few cog-wheels (their number normally was ten to twenty). However, even before such facto-ries were properly established, in the 1880s they began to decline because the

braidings got out of fashion and the demand for them in Bulgaria, Serbia and some of the neighbouring countries fell off.

34 L. Berov, 'Ravnishte na ikonomicheskoto razvitie na bâlgarskite zemi po vreme na Osvobozhdenieto' (The level of the economic development in the Bulgarian lands during the period of the Liberation), *Trudove na Visshiia Ikonomicheski Institut 'Karl Marx'*, no. 1 (Sofia, 1970), p. 32.

35 *Ibid.*, pp. 28, 32. The value of 4.1 Turkish silver grošes at this time was equal to 1 gold French franc.

36 *Doklad na Minsterskiia sâvet do kniaz Ferdinand po sluchai dvadesetgodischninata 1887–1907* (Report of the Cabinet of Ministers to Prince Ferdinand on the Occasion of the Twentieth Anniversary 1887–1907) (Sofia, 1907), p. 8.

37 D. Todorov, 'Nasârchavanata industriia i industrialnata politika v Bulgaria' (The state-encouraged industry and the industrial politics in Bulgaria), *Stopanska misâl* (Economic Thought) 4 (1932/1933), p. 43.

38 D. M. Yablanski, 'Kakva triabva da bâde ikonomicheskata politika na Bulgaria' (What should be the economic politics of Bulgaria), *Spisanie na Bâlgarskoto ikonomichesko druzhestvo* (Bulletin of the Bulgarian Economic Society), nos. 4–5 (1901), pp. 214–24.

39 Calculated on the basis of data of the sum total of the production in current prices. Cf. A. A. Mendel'son, *Teoriia i istoriia ekonomicheskih krizisov i tsiklov* ('Theory and history of the economic crises and cycles'), vol. II (Moscow, 1959) and vol. III (Moscow, 1969), p. 524. The prices of the principal industrial products in Russia at the end of the nineteenth century were relatively stable but, although they went up in 1873, their predominant tendency was to fall. It means that the growth of the physical capacity of the production was only a little bigger than the growth of the nominal sum of the production.

40 For 1894 and 1900, see D. M. Yablanski, 'Kakva triabva da bâde ikonomicheskata politika', pp. 214–24; for 1904, see D. Yordanov, 'Prebroiavane na industriite nasârchavani ot dârzhavata' (An account of the state-supported industries), *Spisanie na Bâlgarskoto ikonomichesko druzhestvo* (Bulletin of the Bulgarian Economic Society), 5 (1906), pp. 295–329, and 6 (1906), pp. 412–43; for 1909, see *Anketa na nasârchavanata ot dârzhavata industriia prez 1909 g. Obsht pregled* (An inquiry into the state-supported industry in 1909. A general survey) (Sofia, 1912); for 1911–12, see *Statisticheski godishnik na Bâlgarskoto Tsarstvo. IV. 1912* (Annual statistics of the Bulgarian Kingdom, IV, 1912) (Sofia, 1915), pp. 181–99; for 1921, see *Statisticheski godishnik na Bâlgarskoto Tsarstvo 1925 g.* (Annual Statistics of the Bulgarian Kingdom 1925) (Sofia, 1926), pp. 170–1.

41 The nominal growth for 1894–1904 most probably doubled annually (if we accept that the average productivity of a worker has not changed during this period), and between 1904 and 1912 the growth was 3.5 times. It should, however, be taken into consideration that after a long period of monetary stability the market prices in Bulgaria in 1912 were about 40 per cent higher than at the turn of the nineteenth and the twentieth centuries. If the value of the growth rate of the industrial production is calculated in fixed prices, then for 1904–1912 it will be about 2.18 times.

42 *Protektsionizâm i konkurentsiia*, p. 68.

43 Calculated on the basis of data in B. R. Mitchell, *Historical Statistics 1750–1975* (London, 1982), p. 375.

44 Calculated according to the general index of the industrial production in *Statistisches Jahrbuch für das Deutsche Reich 1929* (Berlin, 1930), p. 146. The earliest available data concerning Austria-Hungary and Belgium are for 1900–13, and show a medium rate of industrial production growth in fixed prices; these are, accordingly, 3 per cent and 4 per cent, but in a period that is decades later than the time Industrial Revolution took place in these countries.

45 Calculated on the basis of *Annuaire statistique de la France*, vol. LVIII, 1951 (1952), pp. 127–36. For 1845–69 the calculations reflect the installed capacity of the stationary steam engines (if we accept that this capacity grew at approximately the same rate as the production) according to the data in *Annuaire statistique de la France, 1937. Résumé rétrospectif* (Paris, 1938), p. 89.

46 Calculated on the basis of data in A. Gallman in fixed prices, cf. *Cambridge Economic History*, vol. VI, part 2 (Cambridge, 1966), p. 673.

47 The economic statistics in the USA until 1899 include all enterprises with annual production over $500 (the equivalent of 2,600 French gold francs or golden leva). The figure is the same as the average annual income of a medium-rank state servant or a richer craftsman in Bulgaria at the end of the nineteenth century.

48 Including the production of the bigger handicraft workshops and the smaller state-supported industrial establishments which were half way between handicraft and industry.

49 Based on the numbers of active persons engaged in handicrafts as shown in the official census-records for 1892 and 1910 (172,000 and 135,000 respectively). The estimates of K. Popov of the national income in 1892 and 1911, in his, *Stopanska Bulgaria prez 1911 g.*, p. 459, do not provide separate data about the handicrafts and contain a number of inaccuracies, particularly as concerns 1892.

50 Tsonchev, *Iz stopanskoto minalo*, pp. 58–9. The author means the home production of woollen yarn and coarse cloths, since the manufacturing of such articles had died away much earlier.

51 Br. Gâbenski, *Istoriia na gabrovskite vâstaniia* (History of the Uprisings in Gabrovo) (Sofia, 1903), p. 43. In 1892, one-fifth of the original number of the handicraft workshops in these three branches still worked, but these were only workshops which produced on order such special articles as were unsuitable for industrial manufacturing because of the low demand.

52 Calculation based on data in As. Chakalov, *Natsionalniiat dohod i razhod*, pp. 63, 65, 68.

53 *Dârzhaven vestnik*, no. 114, 29 May 1897.

54 *Yubileen sbornik na BNBanka* (An Anniversary Collection of the Bulgarian National Bank) (Sofia, 1928), pp. 73, 101–2, 112.

55 E. Y. Bregel', *Kredit i kreditnaia sistema kapitalizma* (Credit and credit system under capitalism) (Moscow, 1948), p. 105.

324 LJUBEN BEROV

56 Popov, *Stopanska Bulgaria prez 1911*, p. 459
57 Calculated by the author on the basis of data concerning the nominal sum of the industrial production in 1913, data in the relevant national annual statistics, in indices of the capacity (volume) of the national industry reduced to 1913=100, as well as data concerning the numbers of the population towards the end of the national Industrial Revolution according to official censuses, about the average dollar exchange (5.2 French francs for $1, 25.2 French francs for £1, and 1 French franc for one Bulgarian lev).
58 The reason is the lack of earlier data on the general index of the industrial production.
59 Including the unsupported enterprises. The calculations of P. Bairoch, *Commerce extérieur et développement économique de l'Europe* (Paris, 1976), pp. 137–8, are not always accurate. For example, according to Bairoch it appears that the ratio between Bulgaria and Britain for 1900 is only 1:7.6.
60 N. N. Constantinescu, *Din istoricul formării si dezvoltării clasei muncitoare în România pînă la primul râzboi mondial* (On the History of the Formation and Development of the Working Class in Romania up to the First World War) (Bucharest, 1959), p. 21.
61 Şerban, 'Innovation technologique en Roumanie', pp. 135–51.
62 N. I. Angelescu, *Din începuturile industriei româneşti* (On the beginnings of Romanian industry) (Bucharest, 1934), p. 7.
63 G. Zane, *L'industrie roumaine au cours de la seconde moitié du XIXᵉ siècle* (Bucharest, 1973), p. 188.
64 The law required that there should be at least twenty-five employed workers, and over 50,000 gold leva of capital investment.
65 Based on data in *Ancheta industriala din 1901–1902* (Industrial Survey from 1901–2), Part 1 (Bucharest, 1904).
66 *Protektsionizâm i konkurentsiia*, p. 70.
67 Zane, *L'industrie roumaine*, p. 173.
68 N. Arcadian, *Industrializarea României* (The Industrialization of Romania) (Bucharest, 1936), p. 138.
69 *Istoriia Rumynii 1848–1917* (History of Romania) (Moscow, 1971), p. 341.
70 While craftsmen in Britain, USA, Germany and France stayed in business after the nineteenth-century Industrial Revolution, their relative number decreased.
71 Arcadian, *Industrializarea României*, p. 86.
72 *Ibid.*, p. 88.
73 Based on the average wage of the industrial workers in 1902, 2.2 lei (estimate based on the average figure of the statistical intervals as shown in *Anuarul statistic al României 1912* (Annual Statistics of Romania 1912) (Bucharest, 1912), p. 385.
74 According to M. A. Lupu, 'Studii privind dezvoltarea economiei României în perioada capitalismuli' (Studies regarding the development of the Romanian economy in the period of capitalism) in *Studii şi cercetări economice* (Economic Studies and Research) (1967), pp. 325–33, the sum of the industrial produc-

tion was bigger than the sum of the handicraft production as early as 1862–6. M. Lupu's data, however, also include, among the others, bigger handicraft enterprises or industrial establishments which had less than twenty workers. Such enterprises were not considered by the industrial statistics at the time.

75 Recalculated from current prices into prices for 1901–2, assuming that the index of the industrial prices in 1915 was 145 given that 1902=100. See M. Jackson, 'Industrial output in Romania and its historical regions 1880–1930' in *State University of Arizona. Department of Economics – EC 79–89* (Tempe, 1982), pp. 25–6. The prices of some basic foodstuffs in 1914–15 were 50 to 60 per cent above the level of the prices in 1901–2.

76 Calculation based on data in C. C. Kiriţescu, *Sistemul bănesc al leulei şi precursorii lui* (The Monetary System of the Leu and its Precursors), vol. II (Bucharest, 1967), pp. 552–3.

77 This sum should be considered as the maximum, since the share of the stock-breeding and the agricultural cultivation in the Romanian agricultural production was lower.

78 E. Tandler, *Die industrielle Entwicklung Siebenbürgens* (Kronstadt [Braşov], 1909), p. 49.

79 Including Banat and the Krisçana-Maramureş area.

80 Jackson, 'Industrial output in Romania', p. 66. The amount is rounded to 500 million lei in L. Vajda, 'Despre siţuatia economică şi social-politică în Transilvania în primele anii de sec. XX lea' (Concerning the economic and socio-political situation of Transylvania in the early years of the twentieth century) in *Studii şi materiale de istorie modernă* (Studies and Materials of Modern History), I (Bucharest, 1957), pp. 300–5.

81 Other authors point at a result of 118 French francs. See, for example, J. R. Lampe and M. R. Jackson, *Balkan Economic History, 1550–1950* (Bloomington, 1982), p. 311.

82 Iv. Slokar, 'Zgodovina steklarske industrije na Goriškem' (The glass industry in Goriška), *Kronika* (Annals), no. 12 (1964), pp. 62f.; R. Bičanić, *Doba manufakture*, pp. 180–1; Iv. Slokar, 'Začétky kemične industrije v Ljubljani i nieni okolici' (The beginnings of the chemical industry in Ljubljana and its neighbouring areas), *Kronika*, no. 12 (1964), pp. 30–2; St. Mezei, 'Razvoj industrije u Bačkoj' (Industrial development in Bačka) in *Prilozi novijoj ekonomsko-socijalnoj istoriji* (The applications of the new economic and social history), vol. II (Novi Sad, 1959), pp. 92f.

83 Klen, *Tvornica papira*, pp. 28–50.

84 Some authors accept 1850 or 1858 as the beginning of the Croatian industry. See I. Karaman, 'Počeci industrijske privrede u Slavoniji' (The beginnings of industrial economy in Slavonia), *Odsjek za povijest* (Department of History), 6 (Zagreb, 1968), pp. 97–109; N. Juranović, 'Industrija u Hrvatskoj u razvoju od 100 godina' (100 Years of Croatian industrial development), *Ekonomski pregled* (Economic Review), 3–4 (1958), pp. 264–75.

85 Iv. Kurtali, 'Postanak i razvoj varaždinske tekstilne industrije' (The beginnings and the evolution of the textile industry in Varaždin), *Godišnjak gradskog muzeja Varaždin* (Annual of the Town Museum in Varaždin), no. 1 (1961), pp. 67–74.

86 K. Firinger, 'Počeci manufakture i industrije u Osijeku' (The beginnings of manufactory and industry in Osijek), *Osiječki zbornik* (Osijek Collection), no. 6 (1958), pp. 143–69.

87 Bičanić, *Doba manufakture*, p. 214.

88 J. Varl, 'Ob stoletnici železarne' (On the centenary of an ironworks) in *Jeklo in ljudje. Jeseniški zbornik* (Jesenice Collection), vol. XI (Jesenice, 1969), pp. 7–12.

89 J. Šorn, 'Proizvodnja svinca v osrednji Slovenii med leti 1840 in 1918' (The production of lead in central Slovenia between 1840 and 1918), *Zgodovinski časopis*, 16 (1962), pp. 55–79.

90 F. Kresal, *Tekstilna industrija v Sloveniji* (Textile industry in Slovenia) (Ljubljana, 1976), pp. 129f.; I. Slokar, 'Bombažna industrija v Ljubljani do leta 1860' (Cotton industry in Ljubljana up to 1860), *Kronika*, no. 1 (1972), pp. 13–16; I. Slokar, 'Ljubljanska suknarna' (The Ljubljana cloth mill), *Zgodovinski časopis*, 16 (1962), pp. 55–79.

91 J. Morpurgo, *Dalmacija cement 1865–1965* (Dalmatian Cement, 1865–1965) (Split, 1965), pp. 16f.

92 Despot, *Industrija gradjanske Hrvatske*, pp. 137–77; I. Karaman, 'Osvrt na stanje obrtničko-industrijske privrede u osamdesetim godinama 19. st. na području sjeverne Hrvatske' (Looking back at the state of the handicraft–industrial economy in northern Croatia in the 1880s) in *Acta historico-oeconomica Iugoslaviae*, no. 2 (1975), pp. 55–66.

93 T. Hočevar, *The Structure of the Slovenian Economy 1848–1963* (New York, 1965), pp. 24–5.

94 Fr. Strajnar, 'Razvoj elektrogospodarstva v LRS' (The evolution of power production in the Slovene People's Republic), *Kronika*, no. 2 (1954), pp. 131–4.

95 A. Lisac, *Razvoj industrije papira u Zagrebu* (The Development of the Paper Industry in Zagreb) (Zagreb, 1961), pp. 28f.

96 Dr. Jović and Br. Andjelko, '*Djuro Djaković' – industrija šinskih vozila, industrijskih i energetskih postrojenja i čeličnih konstrukcija* (Djuro Djaković – The production of rolling stock, of industrial and power equipment and structural steel) (Zagreb, 1971), pp. 12f

97 Calculation based on I. Karaman, 'Osnovna obilježja razvitke industrijske privrede u sjevernoj Hrvatskoj do provog svetskog rata' (The main features of industrial economy in northern Croatia up to the First World War) in *Acta historico-oeconomica Iugoslaviae*, 1 (1974), pp. 48–53; Hočevar, *The Structure*, pp. 44–7, 116; R. Signjar, *Statistički atlas Kr. Hrvatske i Slavonje 1875–1915* (Statistical atlas of Croatia and Slavonia) (Zagreb, 1915), pp. 48–9.

98 *Protektsionizâm i konkurentsiia*, p. 69.

99 L. Protić, *Razvitak industrije i promet dobara u Srbiji za vreme prve vlade kneza Miloša* (The Development of Industry and the Circulation of Capital in Serbia during Prince Miloš's First Rule) (Belgrade, 1953), pp. 28ff.; L. Cvijetić, 'Fabrika čohe u Topčideru. Prva beogradska fabrika' (The broadcloth factory in Topčider. The first factory in Belgrade), *Ekonomski anali* (Economic Annals) (1970), pp. 31–2, 63–84.

100 V. Karasev, 'Osnovnye cherty social'no-ekonomicheskogo razvitiia Serbii v kontse 60-h-nachale 70-h godov XIX v.' (The main features of the social and

economic development of Serbia at the end of the 1860s and the beginning of the 1870s), *Uchenye zapiski instituta slavianovedeniia* (Learned Papers of the Institute of Slavonic Studies), vol. V (Moscow, 1952), p. 212.

101 *Istorija srbskog naroda* (History of the Serbian People) (Belgrade, 1983) vol. VI, p. 10.

102 Vučo, *Raspadanje esnafa.*

103 M. Mirković, *Ekonomska historija Jugoslavije* (Economic History of Yugoslavia) (Zagreb, 1958), p. 277; Vl. Vukmanovič, *Radnička klasa Srbije u drugoj polovini XIX veka* (The Working Class of Serbia in the Second Half of the Nineteenth Century) (Belgrade, 1972), p. 81. Early sources disagree to some extent about the number of the industrial enterprises in Serbia. About 1898, V. Levy speaks of over 156 bigger establishments of the extractive and the processing industries. See V. Levy, *Coup d'oeil économique sur la Serbie actuelle* (Vienna and Brussels, 1899), p. 9.

104 M. Naumović, 'Razvitak industrije u Srbiji na početku XX veka' (The development of industry in Serbia at the beginning of the twentieth century) in *Zbornik radova Mašinskog fakulteta u Novom Sadu* (Proceedings of the Faculty of Engineering at Novi Sad), no. 7 (Novi Sad, 1971), pp. 1–8.

105 For the annual production 71 million dinars and 2.91 million population.

106 M. Nikolinakos, 'Materialen zur kapitalistischen Entwicklung in Griechenland', *Das Argument*, 57 (1970), p. 178.

107 The reform acts Tanzimat and the Hatti-humayün in Turkey in 1839 and 1856 respectively had a retarding impact on the economic development. As a result, the Greek merchants in Istanbul and the port-towns of Asia Minor lost the stimulus to move to the liberated part of Greece and to transfer their capital. Only after the lowering of the profit-norm in Western Europe in the 1870s, a number of rich Greeks began to move to Greece from Egypt, Asia Minor, Russia, Romania and so forth.

108 St. Mrampanasis, 'I exelixis tou hellinikou kapitalismou stofos tou leninismou', *Komunistiki Epitheorisi*, no. 4 (1970), p. 41.

109 A. Panajotis, 'Zur Entwicklung des Kapitalismus in Griechenland bis zum Zweiten Weltkrieg', *Jahrbuch für Wirtschaftsgeschichte*, no. 2 (1973), p. 47.

110 Other authors mention only 5,588 hp in 1889. See N. Svoronos, *Histoire de la Grèce moderne* (Paris, 1953), p. 74.

111 P. Moraitinis, *La Grèce telle qu'elle est* (Paris, 1877), pp. 296f.

112 Other authors mention 42 million drachmas in 1892. See *Historia tou hellenikou ethnous* (Athens, 1977), XIV, p. 55.

113 L. Kordatos, *Historia tes neoteres Helladas* (Athens, 1958), p. 160.

114 *Historia tou hellenikou ethnous*, XIV, p. 81.

115 X. Zolotas, *Griechenland auf den Weg zur Industrialisierung* (Leipzig and Berlin, 1926), pp. 23, 102–3.

116 M. Nikolivakoa, *Meletes pano helleniko kapitalismo* (Athens, 1976), p. 23.

117 Based on G. Koutsoumaris, *I morphologia tes hellenikis viomechanias* (Athens, 1962), p. 381; *Avgi*, 23.7.1964.

118 A. Andreades, *Les effets économiques et sociaux de la guerre en Grèce* (New Haven, 1926), p. 12.

119 *Protektsionizâm i konkurentsiia*, p. 73. It would be difficult to work out a similar comparison for 1911, because of the lack of clear data about Greece, but it should be expected that at the time the value of per capita industrial production in Greece was higher than its value in Bulgaria.

120 F. Hauptmann, *Die österreich-ungarische Herrschaft in Bosnien und der Herzegovina 1878–1918* (Graz, 1983), pp. 2, 42–9, 55–61.

121 *Statistika industrije Kraljevne Jugoslavije* (Statistics of the Industry of the Kingdom of Yugoslavia) (Belgrade, 1941), p. 73; K. Hrejla, *Industrija Bosne i Hercegovine do kraja prvog svjetskog rata* (The Industries of Bosnia and Hercegovina up to the End of the First World War) (Belgrade, 1965), pp. 24f.

122 F. Schmidt, *Bosnien und die Herzegowina* (Leipzig, 1914), p. 541.

123 Bičanić, *Doba manufakture*, p. 14.

124 *Tutunov kombinat Prilep 1873–1958* (The Tobacco Factory in Prilep 1873–1958) (Prilep, 1958), pp. 16f.

125 D. Zografski, *Razvitokot na kapitalistichkite elementi vo Makedonija za vreme na turskoto vladeene* (The evolution of capitalist elements in Macedonia during the period of Turkish rule) (Skopje, 1967), pp. 237–45, 482–515, 525.

126 L. Doklestić, 'O razvoju preradivačke industrije u Makedoniji na kraju XIX i na početku XX stoljeca' (On the evolution of the oil-refining industry in Macedonia at the end of the nineteenth and the beginning of the twentieth centuries), *Radovi Filozofskog fakulteta – Odsjek za povjest* (Occasional Papers of the Faculty of Philosophy – History Department), no. 6 (Zagreb, 1968), pp. 138–60.

127 L. Sokolov, *Industrijata vo NR Makedonija* (The Industry in the People's Republic of Macedonia) (Skopje, 1961), pp. 23–5.

128 K. Sidovski, *Razvitokot na industrijata vo NR Makedonija vo periodot medu dvete svetski vojni 1918–1941* (The industrial development in the People's Republic of Macedonia between the two World Wars, 1918–1941) (Skopje, 1960), pp. 309–11.

129 D. Novichev, *Ocherki ekonomiki Turtsii do mirovoi voiny* (Essays on the Economy of Turkey up to the World War) (Moscow, 1937), p. 272.

130 Mirković, *Ekonomska historija*, p. 271.

131 *40 viet Shqipëri socialiste*, p. 135.

132 Cf. *Monitorul official*, 110 (12.5.1887), and *Dârzhaven vestnik*, no. 22 (28.1.1895).

133 K. Grinvald, *Rumyniia. Ekonomicheskii ocherk* (Romania. An Essay on Economics) (St Petersburg, 1917), p. 3.

FOURTEEN

Industrial revolution in Russia[1]

ROGER MUNTING

THE concept of industrial revolution remains indefinite; even the very term has been challenged as a misnomer.[2] But the term conjures an image of an era of rapid and radical change involving the application of mechanical power, new sources of energy and raw materials and new or markedly changed forms of industrial organization. Thus would the artisan be separated from his tools to adopt a regime of work dictated by the machine: factories would transform peasant into proletarian. Social transformation would, in such perception, be at least as momentous as technological. Such images are often at odds with reality: industrial transformation has been more evolutionary than revolutionary. Ironically, industrial change in Tsarist Russia has often been interpreted as truly revolutionary: a reluctant inert peasant economy dragged and beaten into the industrial age by a centalized state for its own political reasons. Similar reasoning has been applied to the era of Stalin.

The long-standing historiographical theme of industry in Russia is of 'backwardness', an image of a largely peasant society, heavily dependent on technologically inefficient agriculture. Accompanying this was widespread poverty and ignorance, social and political conservatism, restricted social mobility and enterprise. This is at best a distorted picture, for the restrictions and conservatism of the Tsarist era spawned industrial development comparable in tempo and intensity to the generally accepted experiences in Western Europe.[3] An 'industrial revolution' in Russia has been identified at various points from the eighteenth century of Peter the Great to the 'Stalinist' industrialization drive of the 1930s. In the view of this essay the real industrial developments between the abolition of serfdom in 1861 and the First World War may be viewed as an 'industrial revolution', though one limited in depth and particularly in social impact. It is further argued that this revolutionary development was not 'forced' by government; it was not wholly or largely dependent on the initiatives or custom of the state apparatus but was essentially an autonomous function of the market.

By 1914 Russia had become a major industrial power. Particularly fast rates of growth of industry occurred in the 1880s and 1890s, a twenty-year period which has been taken to signal the 'take-off' into self-sustained growth.[4] Over a slightly longer time-scale, the later nineteenth century is often seen as witnessing the development of capitalism in Russia.[5] It was in those years that Russia began to reduce, but not overcome, her relative industrial backwardness. Throughout these years the perception of 'backwardness' remained strongly influential upon economic policy. Measurements or assessments of this 'backwardness' are difficult, however.

International comparison is full of methodological problems for it is rarely possible to compare like with like. Despite such methodological inexactitude it is nonetheless valuable to consider the comparative studies made by Paul Bairoch. These show that Russia ranked sixth in industrial output on a world scale in 1860 (behind Britain, China and India – each with a large labour-intensive textile sector – France and the United States). By 1913 Russia had moved into fourth place, albeit some way behind the three leading industrial powers: the USA, Germany and Britain.[6] Some further points must be made to illustrate the real advances of industry in Russia. In 1860 most manufacturing used well-established technologies; there was a high weighting to textiles and iron production. In the late nineteenth century major innovations were made in manufacturing (as, for instance, in steel making) and new products were introduced (as in chemicals, non-ferrous metals, electrical engineering, automobiles). Index numbers of manufacturing in 1913 have a high weighting given to goods based on new or recent technologies. It is for this reason that China and India slipped down the table; they remained large producers of the 'old' industries (primarily textiles) but did not experience technological changes associated with Industrial Revolution. Russia, however, enhanced her position in these same years. By 1913 she produced more steel than France, had become a major manufacturer of industrial machinery (fourth in the world) and was second in oil production.[7] Russia even had a nascent aeroplane industry in 1913.[8]

Further, between 1860 and 1913 the world's total manufacturing output increased by four times in volume. Thus Russian industry grew rapidly to take a larger share of a fast-growing world total. This stood at 7 per cent in 1860 and 8.8 per cent in 1900, falling back a little to 8.2 per cent in 1913 (the major increases were shown by the USA and Germany; Britain and France fell significantly).[9] Broadening the comparison beyond industry *per se*, data prepared by Paul Gregory show that in 1861 Russian national income (NI) stood at approximately half the level of the USA, 80 per cent of that of Britain or Germany and was roughly equal to that of France. By 1913 it was still well below American levels and only 80 per cent of German levels, but comparable to Britain and well above France.[10]

These points bear qualification. Russia had become a major industrial producer by the end of the nineteenth century, but was a long way short of social transformation. In some respects, therefore, the country would bear comparison with the economies of Latin America today,[11] in that industry, although quantitatively significant, was limited in its broader social impact. The overwhelming majority of the Russian population continued to earn their living from agriculture. As late as 1913 there were 3.1 million wage-earners in factories and mines (2.3 million in factories, as defined by factory acts, alone) from a population of over 170 million, of which over 50 million were economically active.[12] Industry provided a small part of national income: factory-based manufacture produced 15 per cent of NI in 1913, factories, handicrafts and construction together, 32.3 per cent.[13] Further, agricultural products provided 75 per cent of export earnings. However, even in the industrially more advanced Western economies industry was slow to achieve social change. It was not until 1851 that the urban population exceeded the rural in Britain, by then the 'workshop of the world'. (The Russian state reached this position a century later, well after the Stalinist phase of industrialization.) Employment in agriculture exceeded that in manufacturing in France as late as 1926 (39 per cent of the active population compared with 36 per cent). Even in the USA a higher proportion of the workforce was employed in agriculture (31 per cent) than in manufacturing (30 per cent) as late as 1910.[14] In addition because of the widespread dependence on off-farm income among peasant households in Russia, industrial or non-agricultural employment provided a share of income for a larger proportion of the population than might appear to be the case at first sight. It was impossible to distinguish between peasant and wage-earner at the margin, for individuals fell into both categories at different periods.

A further point of qualification is the level of per capita product and income. Low levels of per capita income have been the basis for much of the emphasis on the backwardness of Tsarist Russia, a point which has tended to underline the industrial achievements of the Soviet period. According to the data prepared by Bairoch, Russia's international ranking in terms of per capita industrial product even declined between 1860 and 1913, from fifteenth to seventeenth place. Other data, comparing gross national product per head, expressed in 1970 US dollars, show figures of $236 in 1860 in Russia compared with $804 for Britain, $481 for Germany. In 1910 the figures were $398 for Russia, $1,302 for Britain, $958 for Germany.[15] Although these figures show a slight advance, in relative per capita income Russia remained at the bottom of the rankings.

Table 14.1. *Annual average rates of growth of industrial production (per cent)*

1885–9	6.10
1890–9	8.03
1900–6	1.43
1907–14	6.25
Average	5.72

Such data, however, undervalue or ignore the real welfare or income benefits of agricultural production, in which Russia had a comparative advantage. It is unlikely that the average Briton had a consumption level three times higher than the average Russian.

It is also questionable how much emphasis should be placed on per capita product, as against aggregates, when examining the development of industry. In the period being considered Switzerland had a higher per capita income and industrial product than Germany but a very much lower aggregate output. The USSR, acknowledged as the second industrial producer after the USA in 1980 (notwithstanding revealed industrial problems and decline since that time), ranked only sixteenth in per capita terms in Bairoch's calculations.

Before 1914 industrial development in Russia was far from smooth. Rates of growth followed a cyclical pattern throughout Europe; in Russia it seemed that the amplitudes were deeper than elsewhere. Figures prepared by Gerschenkron, and long accepted by most observers, suggest considerable variations (see table 14.1).[16] The steep fluctuation in the rate of growth revealed by these figures is, however, in part a function of the over-representation of heavy metallurgical and engineering industries in Gerschenkron's index, and the corresponding under-representation of light industries. Although the capital goods sectors were leaders in growth, the largest industries remained textiles and food processing which experienced no great decline in development in the years of industrial 'crisis' about the turn of the century.[17] In 1902, the worst year of recession at this time, the most serious decline was shown in ferrous metallurgy, mining (especially of oil and ores), building materials and some consumer sectors: leather shoes, tobacco, wine and spirits (*vinokurenie*). The value of textile production increased by 7.6 per cent, between 1901 and 1903, food processing by 5.6 per cent.[18] Cotton textiles and sugar production had been the fastest-growing industries in the early nineteenth century and these remained in aggregate important throughout.[19]

From the last quarter of the nineteenth century, however, the dynamics of industrial change were more directly linked to new industries, in particular railways and related engineering and metallurgy. Railways provided both a source of demand for largely new industrial products and, as important, a means of integrating the domestic market. There were two great railway building periods, the 1870s and the 1890s. In the first, the major economic results could be seen to bring a degree of unity to the market, albeit incomplete. In these years the basis of the railway network in European Russia was laid. In the 1890s railways were more closely linked to the development of heavy industry.[20] Backward linkages in manufacturing were created, with Russia meeting part of the growing demand for rails and locomotives and other inputs. Throughout the years before the First World War, however, a major economic function of railways was to reduce the cost of agricultural freight.[21] One of the earliest major lines was the Moscow–St Petersburg line, opened in 1854. This made a major contribution to the growth of the capital as an industrial centre. St Petersburg was unusual in being both an industrial and cultural centre as well as a capital city – the famous Putilov armaments and engineering works was opened in 1873. More typically industries grew up away from established towns. Between 1861 and 1880 the rail network increased fourteenfold; in the same years cotton production grew by 400 per cent.[22] In subsequent years, the 1880s and 1890s, industrial growth was most evident in 'new' industrial regions. The Ekaterinoslav railway was opened in 1870, linking the iron resources of Krivoi Rog with the coal of the Donets basin.

Rapid industrialization from the 1880s thus saw the exploitation of natural resources and the establishment of major industries. It was in these years that Russia acquired a modern steel industry, engineering production which was, in many respects, technolgically comparable with leading Western European producers. Indeed much new production was by foreign owned firms. The southern Ukraine almost became Russia's equivalent of the Ruhr, overtaking the long established iron-producing region of the Urals. By 1900 52 per cent of the Empire's (including Poland) pig-iron was made in the southern Ukraine.[23] But the Ukraine was by no means the only centre of new industrial advance. Also from the 1880s the established oil industry in Baku took on a new lease of life. Crude-oil production multiplied tenfold: from 60 million puds in 1883 to 601 million puds in 1900 (one pud was equivalent to 16.4 kg). Exports boomed, to the extent that Russian kerosene accounted for 30 per cent of world demand as early as 1890–1.[24] In the well-established regions around Moscow, the Baltic, and Warsaw and Łódź in Tsarist Poland, industrial production also continued to increase.

Industrial transformation was limited regionally as well as socially. In many cases domestic resources remained under-exploited and in some major industries, chemicals for instance (the exception being rubber processing – galoshes were exported),[25] Russia remained backward. A considerable portion of consumer demand continued to be served by handicraft industries, urban artisans or, more commonly, rural domestic industries (*kustar*) often carried on by peasant households as a seasonal occupation or one otherwise ancillary to agriculture. The distribution of their products through tradesmen or fairs brought such goods well beyond a local market, and regional specialisms were well known. In the later nineteenth century, however, factory-based industry made inroads on such domestic handicrafts with cotton textiles replacing domestically produced linens, for instance. Peasant handicrafts were not simply superseded by larger-scale industry, however, for factories also helped extend or adapt demand for rural domestic industry through a put-out system. Kaufman has calculated that, by 1913, such craft industries produced 34 per cent of total industrial output.[26]

In aggregate and in the production of the most important industries, Russia had become one of the world's leading producers by the end of the nineteenth century. Output continued to grow thereafter. Between 1900 and 1913 total industrial production increased by 75 per cent, and over 46 per cent per capita. How can the spectacular development of industry in Tsarist Russia be explained? For many years the explanation was placed very much on the role of the state. The state was judged to be the prime mover in economic initiatives. By this thinking it was the state which provided the will to industrialize, in the absence of a dynamic entrepreneurial class. It was the state which mobilized capital through fiscal policy, in the absence of a rich mercantile class or well-developed banking system, and it was the state which encouraged the import of foreign expertise through tariffs and other means. Such an emphasis is most readily associated with misleading comparisons between the aspirations and policies of Witte (Minister of Finance to Nicholas II) and Stalin, and with the brilliant and seductive theory of Alexander Gerschenkron, though it has also been maintained by many others.[27] It is not without foundation. The state was enormously important in economic life to a degree extreme by the standards of much of Europe or North America. But it is difficult to maintain that the state bore prime or exclusive responsibility for industrial developments, both because state actions had negative as well as positive effects and because there is considerable evidence of autonomous developments in which the state played no part.

Direct state involvement in the industrial economy was extremely limited. Government guaranteed returns for early railway investors, foreign and domestic, and, from the 1890s, undertook much railway building itself but this was not unusual in European terms and anyway constituted a small part of total public expenditure. Defence was much more important, and became more so in the build up to the First World War. Thus, the state was directly or indirectly an important source of demand. State purchases, particularly for defence, as well as railway building, were of especial importance in the heavy engineering and metallurgical sectors.

It is more appropriate to consider broader economic policies associated with ministers of finance who, in varying ways, tried to give encouragement to industry – particularly Reutern, K. Bunge and, perhaps best known, Sergei Witte. However, there was little consistency between them. Reutern provided guarantees for railway investors, Bunge set out to assist industry by making it easier for joint-stock companies to be formed, reforming the tax system and encouraging bank reform. Witte is more often associated with direct encouragement to industry. He came to adopt a dynamic industrial policy in the late 1890s having achieved the elusive goal of his precedessors, a stable exchange rate in 1894. In 1897 the rouble joined the Gold Standard, one of the last major currencies to do so. It was thought thereby that foreign investors, in manufacturing as well as government bonds, would be better attracted by secure returns in gold. Similarly, the high tariffs introduced by Witte's immediate predecessor, I. A. Vyshnegradsky, in 1891, and revised in 1898, could be seen as having a protective function for Russian manufacture, and providing a further incentive for foreign investment.

The association of government intent with apparent effect on a *post hoc propter hoc* basis of reasoning has been a seductive path of explanation for many historians. Detailed empirical analysis has questioned the direct effectiveness of the state in industrialization, however. As we have seen, the state undertook little directly. Some 'indirect' policies were of questionable effectiveness as well. Tariffs were imposed largely for revenue raising rather than protection *per se*. Customs receipts accounted for one-third of ordinary revenue by 1900.[28] Russian tariffs were the highest in Europe and highest of all on foodstuffs! However, the differential introduced in 1898, which reduced duties on manufactures that did not compete with Russian-made products, can be seen as protective in character. But positive effects were modest. Tariffs put up domestic costs for raw materials, machinery, components and spare parts. This was a frequent complaint of foreign businessmen. Indeed, German entrepreneurs were not attracted by the promise of high levels of protection,[29] but rather by the size of the market. Further, high tariffs protected domestic inefficiency and enabled monopolistic practices to be adopted. Many cartels were formed about the turn of the century. The best-known were the steel producers *Prodamet* and the coal-mining cartel *Produgol*, though the first had been a combine of sugar producers formed in 1887.

It must be remembered that government policies were always primarily directed towards the strengthening of the state and maintaining the political status quo and not the generation of bourgeois capitalism. Indeed the state was reluctant to allow genuine economic freedom, limiting mobility and hedging around commercial activity with bureaucratic constraint.[30] An essential aspect of maintaining state apparatus was revenue raising; fiscal policy always dominated economic policy. It has been argued that fiscal policy, in effecting 'forced savings' in the economy, restricted or reduced popular consumption and therefore market demand. Although this is by no means a universally accepted judgement − Olga Crisp has maintained that fiscal policy had a neutral effect on consumption in rural areas[31] − Arcadius Kahan has presented convincing arguments that very little of the 'forced saving' was transferred from agriculture to industry. Most went to financing government expenditures in which industry did not figure highly.[32]

Yet the activities of the state were universally recognized and acknowledged. Foreign businessmen frequently complained at interference from local representatives of the state apparatus.[33] It is necessary to distinguish, therefore, between the state functions manifest in government policies which impinged directly or indirectly on the industrial economy and the lower administrative apparatus, the day-to-day functioning of bureaucracy, police and customs officers who often made life hard for foreign businesses. Bribery and corruption were commonplace; internal mobility was limited and the legal system seemed to conspire against foreign nationals.[34] Karl Siemens, who ran the Russian branch of the German firm, experienced many such problems as a foreigner, even though he had adopted Finnish nationality.[35]

But the importance of state policies should not be underestimated. On the whole the state played a more indirect than direct role in industrial development in Tsarist Russia, but nonetheless a vital one. It can be seen as influential in attracting the foreign capital and expertise to which these experiences refer. Undoubtedly direct foreign capital investment was important in Russian industry, especially in the 'new' industrial sectors and regions. French capital played an important role in engineering and metallurgy, German capital in chemical and electrical industries, British capital in oil extraction and so on. The figures of such investment have been difficult to determine with precision and have in some cases been subject to exaggeration and distortion. Pavel Ol', for instance, whose extensive tabulations continue to form the basis for records of joint-stock investment, was determined to show that Russian industry was falling into alien hands.[36] His figures are generally regarded as being too high.[37] An examination of balance of payments data gives a different position, showing that there was a net flow of capital into Russia only after 1893,[38] becoming increasingly important after 1897, when the currency was joined to the gold standard. By far the greater part of foreign capital lending was to government, rather than direct to industrial concerns, at never lower than three-quarters of the total.[39] Before 1893, important as direct foreign investment was, it was more than offset by net capital outflow, particularly of luxury expenditures by the well-to-do. This implies that domestic sources of capital were sufficient for industrial investment but were not channelled to that purpose. Thus foreign savings served to counterbalance consumption expenditures abroad. Foreign capital made up a large proportion of total industrial investment, especially after 1897. In the 1880s 41 per cent of new investment in industry came from abroad; this grew to 87 per cent in 1903–5, 50 per cent in 1909–13.[40] Further, many foreign-owned companies re-invested profits in Russia, thus adding to the stock of domestic capital.

More important than investment was the transfer of technology and expertise that accompanied capital flows. Whole industries were introduced to Russia: telephones by Bell of the USA or Ericsson of Sweden, Singer sewing machines, International Harvester machinery, Siemens telegraphic equipment, and many more.[41] The French company, Société de Terrenoire, established the famous Alexandrovsk steel works in 1877, using the most up-to-date technology. In 1896 the Hartmann Machine Company opened a locomotive plant in Lugansk. By 1907 the firm was able to export some of its products.[42] By such means up-to-date technology was brought into Russia. McKay notes that German-owned chemical works in Russia were little different from those in Germany.[43] One great advantage for the Russian branch of a foreign company was that research and development was almost invariably conducted in the home country, saving costs for the Russian producer,[44] but also reducing the educational benefits of such research. This is a major point of qualification. Technical progress made an important contribution to industrial development; for the source of much of such progress to be outside the country was an area of weakness for Russia. Russia had produced great and original thinkers in science but had been slow to exploit the productive potential of ideas; this was often forthcoming from foreign organizations. In 1898 the Nobel company, which was already operating in oil mining, set up a business to produce diesel engines. In fact the firm, 'Russkii Diesel' was based in Germany with manufacturing licences sold to several Russian factories.[45] However, there is at least one proven case of a German steel company providing its Russian factory with second-hand plant, replacing it at home with brand new equipment.[46] It is unlikely that this is an isolated case; it nonetheless represents a net flow of modern technology to Russia. McKay goes further in his examination of the influence of foreign capitalists, emphasizing the 'demonstration effect' to Russian businessmen and the value of demand for ancillary services within Russia.

The stress on the state and on foreign businesses in much of the literature has tended to understate the real value of native entrepreneurship. The entrepreneur, the risk-bearing businessman, the innovator, was and is a product of his time, made by events rather than determining them. It should come as no surprise that individuals set out to make money; where there was business to be done there were invariably businessmen to do it. But in Russian society, with an apparently rigid social structure, there was no obvious 'bourgeoisie', generally accepted as the social seed-bed of commercial and industrial entrepreneurship. It is for this reason that the state has been judged by many to have undertaken industrial initiatives. On the other hand, one of the foremost historians of Russia has stressed how the actions of a dominant and dogmatic state over centuries squashed the emergence of a bourgeoisie,[47] and, by implication, restricted private commercial activities.

This, however, is a far from universal assessment; to quote a leading expert on the subject:

> It would be a mistake to conclude from the failure of the merchantry (*kupechestvo*) to become the core of a Russian bourgeoisie that indigenous Russian capitalists made no significant contribution to the great industrial spurt.[48]

Who were these entrepreneurs? Well-known examples from religious sects, excluded from the mainstream of professional life, have been noted. The best known were the Orthodox schismatics, the Old Believers, who took a leading part in the cotton textile industry in the Moscow region from the early nineteenth century.[49] Although, with few exceptions they were confined to the 'Pale' of western Russia, Jews, as Kahan has shown,[50] played an important part in the development of industry within this area. And the 'Pale' included some of the most industrially advanced parts of Poland and the sugar-producing regions of the Ukraine. Jews were active in textiles, sugar trading and refining, but not in the production of raw sugar.

It was not only amongst religious minorities that industrialists were to be found but also, as it were, within the social fabric. Armenians were well established as traders, particularly in Transcaucasia. There were peasant traders and manufacturers in plenty though they operated on a small scale; it has long been argued, for example, that kulaks constituted a nascent capitalist class. Less frequently alluded to, though probably more significant quantitatively, are those of gentry status (*dvoryanstvo*) and the small stratum of merchants. Factories on gentry estates were well established in the era of serfdom and can hardly be said to characterize industrial revolution but some, like those in the village of Ivanovo on one of the Sheremet'ev estates, survived and prospered into the age of capitalism. The production of sugar from beet developed as an industry in the early nineteenth century and was almost totally confined to gentry estates. In the later part of the century Russia became one of the major beet-sugar producers in the world and a significant exporter. The initiative here lay with gentry estate farmers, such as Count A. A. Bobrinksy, who was also a pioneer in technical innovations.[51] State attitudes were ambivalent and foreign interest virtually absent.

Industrial interests of the gentry were not confined to processing agricultural products, though this was important.[52] In the 1860s and 1870s gentry, such as P. G. von Derviz, K. F. von Meck, Baron K. K. Ungern-Sternberg, were amongst the leading railway concessionaires. There was also an increase in the number of new factories in the 1880s and 1890s, suggesting new industrial enterprises rather than an extension of the old.[53] Industrial interests were manifest in a variety of products which had no connection with agriculture. Anfimov has identified numerous gentry interests in engineering (*mashinostroenie*), oil extraction, shipping and other areas in the First World War.[54] L. P. Minarik, found that, at the turn of the century, 82 of the 102 richest (by size of landholding) gentry families had industrial interests, as sole or part owner. Altogether these numbered 500 factories.[55] A survey of 1,482 joint-stock companies of 1901–2 in Russia revealed that no fewer than 800 had members of the hereditary gentry in post as directors or board members.[56]

Many merchants, especially in the lower guilds, continued to display characteristics in the later nineteenth century more associated with 'pre-industrial' culture than capitalism. Further, most mercantile activity was in trade rather than manufacturing. However, there had been considerable merchant interest in industry, especially cotton textiles, early in the century.[57] In the later nineteenth century many merchants used the money made from textiles to invest in other industries, including the new metallurgical sectors. It would be hard to maintain that such a group constituted a social class but it is significant that they had escaped the guild mentality (though guild membership remained a legal requirement) in that they ceased to have a commitment to a specific industry or trade. This stratum of merchants was by no means dependent on state leadership; rather they were able to form pressure groups to influence state policy. The Association of Southern Coal and Steel Producers lobbied government to protect locally produced coal and iron.[58] The Russian

Industrial Society was founded in 1867, and acted as a pressure group on government to favour economic development.[59] 'Indigenous capitalists contributed as much to the great industrial spurt as did foreign entrepreneurs and the state.'[60]

Economic change in general, and industrial growth in particular, are attributable to autonomous factors in the economy rather than to politically determined state leadership. Sources of autonomous change in demand can most readily be identified in a growing population. In Russia population increased at a rate almost unmatched in Europe, the figure for the Empire (excluding Finland and Poland) moving from 68 million in 1858 to 163 million in 1914. Because of losses in war and, more especially, territorial change, the 1926 census revealed a real figure of 147 million.[61] Population growth does not in itself necessarily constitute a stimulus to demand. Some of the poorest countries have large and rapidly growing populations. There is thus no clear and direct correlation between population growth and industrialization,[62] in the absence of other causative factors. However, the marked and accelerating expansion of populations in Europe from the mid-eighteenth to the twentieth centuries marked what Cameron has called the 'third logistic' of economic growth,[63] which coincided with major periods of European industrialization. Thus the Industrial Revolutions of Western Europe, from the eighteenth century, can be interpreted as providing the means of breaking away from a 'Malthusian' demographic regime[64] wherein population growth was constrained by economic resources. Similar reasoning can apply to Russia in the nineteenth century. A rapidly growing population brought benefits for industrial growth, where other necessary factors were present: a growing labour supply, pressures making for urbanization and the acquisition of knowledge,[65] as well as a real or potential increase in aggregate demand even though modest in per capita terms. In Russia per capita income remained low but, as may be judged from statistical analyses, showed no secular fall in the period under review. In general the increase in labour productivity in industry was slower than the growth of total production and therefore depended on the increase in the supply of labour.

But a growing population must be fed. In Britain and some other parts of Western Europe much of the increase in food supply came from imports; in Russia this was not so. Indeed Russia was a major food exporter before 1914. Net food supplies increased sufficiently to feed a rapidly growing population as well as providing an important source of exports. Per capita net supply of basic grains increased in the years before the First World War, from 10.8 puds (177 kg) per head in the period 1886–90, to 13 puds (213.2 kg) in 1896–1900 and 16.3 puds (267.3 kg) in

1909–13.[66] In addition there was an increasing variety in the diet as non-grain crops became more widely available. Peasant consumption for the most part was based on bread grains, often with high calorific values. Peasant budget data from thirteen provinces in the early twentieth century show average consumption levels of 4,477 calories per head per day.[67] Other data presented by A. V. Chayanov suggest that the peasant diet was high in carbohydrates but often below daily minimum require-ments (according to contemporary physiologists) in protein and fats.[68]

In the nineteenth century new products such as potatoes, tea and sugar entered the common diet. On average urban living standards were higher than rural. The gains in real wages reinforced the attraction of labour to enter the cultural discipline of the industrial workplace, another charac-teristic of 'industrial revolution'. Town-dwellers ate more fish, meat and dairy produce, as well as consuming more alcohol than peasants in the countryside.[69] This marginal but real shift in dietary structure underlines the net upward trend in consumption; diet may not be judged by bread alone, even in Russia. There were very large regional variations and fluc-tuations over time, but the measured average consumption levels did not imply abject misery or deprivation, even by international standards.[70]

This is a subject of enormous controversy for there were innumerable contemporary accounts of peasant misery and poverty and declining living standards. Further, the threat of famine was not removed in Russia until the 1950s. No serious commentator would seek to deny such factors. Aggregate data conceal any number of fluctuations and tell us nothing about short-term deficits in food supply, regional imbalances or social inequalities in income distribution. However, those findings do most clearly suggest that there was no long-term suppression of popular living standards (as was suggested by Gerschenkron), and certainly no decline in consumption *caused by* industrialization. The share of consumption in national income did fall (from 83.5 per cent in the period 1885–9 to 79.6 per cent in 1909–13) but aggregate product grew fast enough to more than offset this fall. Agricultural output and agricultural labour productivity grew throughout the period 1883–1913 (production by an average annual rate of 2.8 per cent per annum, productivity by 1.4 per cent).[71]

The productivity of labour probably grew faster in industry than in agriculture. All of this implies upward trends, though low absolute levels, in per capita income. Overall, Gregory estimates that this increased by 1.7 per cent per annum between 1883 and 1913 though significantly more quickly before 1900 (2.3 per cent per annum) than after (1 per cent per annum).[72] Olga Crisp has noted that there was a small improvement in real industrial wages between 1900 and 1913,[73] a trend comparable with other continental countries. It is easy to speculate that the modesty of the increase may have contributed to workers' discontent, and it should be noted that food prices were tending to rise in these years which would have limited the effective increase in income. But it is clear that more than wages contributed to workers' protests; hours were long and living and working conditions sometimes squalid. Factory acts, introduced in the 1880s, were frequently ignored and, despite its paternalism, the state was usually intolerant and oppressive of workers' protests. This is too large a question to be explored here. It is evident that the social and political structure of the old regime was unable to absorb pressures for change and eventually crumbled. However, it is important to remember that nowhere in Europe were political and economic rights readily granted to working people; nowhere were free labour organizations able to secure significant advances in consumption at the cost of saving and investment. Although it was unlikely to have been a preconceived state policy governments, by stopping the share of greater production being passed on in wages, were instrumental in ensuring that savings and investment increased. The improvement in real incomes resulted from a more rapid growth of national income.

The vital role of agriculture in industrialization is well attested. But the part played by agriculture in pre-revolutionary Russia has often been misconstrued, with emphasis being placed on the weakness of this sector rather than its strengths. Consequently much of the established literature on pre-revolutionary Russia has understated the real contribution of agriculture to a rapidly developing industrial economy. Agricultural Russia was important not simply because it was exploited as a source of savings; it was also a dynamic sector. Not only was the farm sector able to feed a growing population; it was a source of industrial raw materials (flax, hemp, cotton, tobacco, timber, leather and sugar). Agriculture also provided a source of investment capital, through accumulated profits or, and in this case more likely, a share of 'forced savings'. This accumulation was achieved largely through market exchange rather than through taxation. Part of new capital investment, as has been shown, came from foreign borrowing which was in turn funded by predominantly agricultural exports. Further, it was the agricultural population which provided a pool of labour for industry – in turn released as a result of growing productivity.

Aggregate agricultural production increased more because of intensification, producing higher yields, than an extension of cultivated area, though both factors were important. There was also an increase in the diversification of production. These developments were by no means confined to large estates or capitalist farms but were evident also on peasant land and within the traditional peasant social and economic units. This must cast doubt on the assumption that peasant economic institutions, in particular the village commune (*obshchina*), did in themselves inhibit qualitative advance in agriculture. There were, however, regional imbalances and an extension of regional specializations in the two generations down to the First World War. In the Baltic provinces there was some specialization in livestock and dairy farming, serving growing urban and export markets.[74] In western Siberia a dairy industry heavily oriented to export markets was developed entirely on peasant land and based on marketing cooperatives. The southern provinces of European Russia became more associated with extensive grain farming.

Total exports increased dramatically, though they accounted for a small proportion of the total harvest (rarely over 5 per cent). For some particular crops, like wheat and barley, the exported proportion was very much larger (25 to 50 per cent of wheat crop being frequent). By 1913 Russia had become the world's largest exporter of wheat.

The experience of the industrial development in Imperial Russia was the result of characteristics and forces that have, until recently, often been understated in much scholarly literature. In particular it is evident that the state did not play an unusually central role directly in industrial initiatives. Industrialization was autonomous, a result of growing demand which in turn was a function of growing population and of rising average real incomes. An important contribution to this general trend was the secular improvement in total agricultural production and agricultural labour productivity. Such developments by no means eliminated poverty; per capita incomes remained amongst the lowest in Europe, income distribution was extremely inequitable and the mass of the population remained dependent on the size of the harvest, rather than the price, and suffered extreme deprivation from periodic famine. Domestic savings were achieved at the cost of foregone consumption (in the absence of astronomical productivity rises this is inevitable) and some of this transfer was achieved through taxation. But there is little evidence to support notions that average living standards were reduced in order to achieve industrialization or as a direct result of government policies. Industrial development was essentially capitalist in character, comparable with other European nations. Foreign capital investment was increasingly important as a source of new capital formation in industry – and especially in some new industries – from the mid to late 1890s.

War, October Revolution and Civil War caused economic turmoil. Industrial dislocation rather than wholesale destruction, resulted in a catastrophic fall in total production, and incomes. Further, territorial losses (principally Poland and the Baltic States) had a disproportionate influence on industry, resulting in a contraction of about 20 per cent of pre-war industrial capacity. In addition the redistribution of land and resources in the agricultural revolution dispossessed the most commercially oriented peasants and privately owned estates. In the short term, serious famine followed the extreme procurement policies of the Civil War and localized drought.[75] In many respects the country that the new Communist Party leadership found themselves governing in the early 1920s was less industrialized than that which had gone to war under the Imperial banner in 1914. Yet the new regime was ideologically committed to industry and the industrial working class – a social stratum that had all but disappeared in the tempestuous months of Revolution. This contradiction was to be of profound influence on the political leaders and their various policies in the 1920s.

Economic policy was especially important, for the new rulers had very quickly developed a unique idea of economic planning. Although the central Five-year Plans of what later came to be known as the 'Stalinist system' dated formally from 1928 the idea of planning was as old as the Revolution (but no older – the word 'planning' entered the political vocabulary after the October Revolution). Planning as a form of economic management remained for the time being uncertain. Little was done in the short term beyond widespread and haphazard nationalization. Economic control became much more centralized, in the Civil War of 1918 to 1920 under the system of 'War Communism', a totalitarian system of rationing of resources. It was not yet planning in any real sense. The New Economic Policy (NEP) from 1921 represented a retreat of direct state administrative control with limited de-nationalization and a return to legal market exchange. But the state retained extensive and extraordinary influence. The Supreme Economic Council (VSNKh) which had been set up in November 1917 remained; a state planning committee (Gosplan) was instituted in 1921. In what was to become a famous phrase, the state was said to have retained control of the 'commanding heights' of the economy – the central bank, the budget, large-scale industry, which remained nationalized, and foreign trade, which continued to be a state monopoly. There was a clear political and ideological determination to direct the operation of the economy from the centre, though it was by no means certain how it was to be undertaken in detail.

The state was to be important for practical reasons also. The Revolution had brought profound social change. The small, rich luxury-consuming class of Imperial Russia had been dispossessed. Their expenditure abroad before 1914 had accounted for about 10 per cent of imports. However, these social changes had also effectively wiped out sources of domestic saving. Domestic capital formation could no longer be supplemented by foreign borrowing. With the nationalization of private property formerly in foreign ownership and the abrogation of the Tsarist government debt it proved impossible to raise further loans. There was in any event an ideological objection to allowing foreign capitalists freedom of operation in the country when domestic capitalists had been dispossessed by the Revolution, though attempts were made to secure foreign credits. In addition to these points it is well known that the agricultural sector had been profoundly affected by revolutionary change. The supply of basic foodstuffs, above all grain, was lower than in 1913. Taxation as a means of raising supplies from the peasant population became much more important in the 1920s than it had been in the Tsarist period. The state was thus forced by circumstance, as well as directed by ideology, to take on the burden of mobilizing investment resources.

It was in 1926 that the political shift to a new, second 'industrial revolution' was made, with ambitious investment targets drawn up by the Supreme Economic Council and the responsibility passed to Gosplan for drafting comprehensive national economic plans.[76] It was now that the state took on the responsibility for tackling the relative economic backwardness of the Russian economy. In doing so the state in succeeding years adopted methods of control and direction hitherto untried. The social and political costs involved and the dubiety of the economic benefits have been the subject of extensive academic concern and continue to be so. It is clear, however, that the pursuit of industrial growth involved both a reduction in average consumption levels and a concentration of resources on capital goods to meet the demands of the state rather than autonomous market forces. All these were characteristics which in the past have been erroneously attributed to the industrialization of Tsarist Russia.

NOTES

1 I am extremely grateful to Bill Albert formerly of the University of East Anglia and Robert Bideleux of University College, Swansea, for their helpful comments on earlier drafts of this paper.

2 Rondo Cameron, *A Concise Economic History of the World* (London, 1989), pp. 163–4. See also W. N. Parker, 'Agrarian and Industrial Revolutions', in R. Porter and M. Teich (eds.), *Revolution in History* (Cambridge, 1986), p. 167.

3 The best general survey of the period is P. Gatrell, *The Tsarist Economy, 1850–1917* (London, 1986). Considerable detail on the period under review can be found in R. W. Davies (ed.), *From Tsarism to the New Economic Policy* (London, 1990).

4 W. W. Rostow, *The Stages of Economic Growth* (Cambridge, 1965), p. 38.

5 The idea was advocated by V. I. Lenin in *Development of Capitalism in Russia*, first published in 1899. Partly because of the author the theme became established as historical orthodoxy in the USSR.

6 Paul Bairoch, 'International industrialization levels from 1750 to 1980', *Journal of European Economic History*, 11 (1982), pp. 269–334.

7 K. Thalheim, 'Russia's economic development' in G. Katkov, E. Oberländer, N. Poppe and G. von Rauch (eds.), *Russia Enters the Twentieth Century* (London, 1971), p. 95.

8 A. C. Sutton, *Western Technology and Soviet Economic Development*, vol. 1: *1917–1930* (Stanford, 1968), p. 259.

9 Bairoch, 'International Industrialization', p. 296.

10 Paul Gregory, *Russian National Income 1880–1913* (Cambridge, 1982), p. 158.

11 The point is elaborated by T. Shanin in *Russia as a Developing Society*, 2 vols. (London, 1986). However, Shanin's comparison of Russia with 'Third World' economies seems to be exaggerated.

12 A. G. Rashin, *Formirovanie rabochego klassa v Rossii* (The Formation of the Working Class in Russia) (Moscow, 1958), p. 42. The 'economically active' population is the author's estimate.

13 Gregory, *Russian National Income*, p. 73.

14 S. Kuznets, 'Industrial distribution of national product and labour force', *Economic Development and Cultural Change*, 5, (1957), appendix 3, pp. 84, 85, 93.

15 N. G. Crafts, 'Patterns of development in nineteenth century Europe', *Oxford Economic Papers*, 36 (1984), p. 440.

16 A. Gerschenkron, 'The rate of industrial growth in Russia since 1885', *Journal of Economic History*, supplement 7 (1947), p. 146.

17 Olga Crisp, *Studies in the Russian Economy before 1914* (London, 1978), pp. 34–5. The crisis was real enough: the number of factories (*predpriyatii*) closed was 550 in 1900, 1,016 in 1901, 840 in 1902 and 882 in 1903. See I. S. Golubnichii, *Narodnoe khozyaistvo SSSR v tsifrakh, 1861–1938* (The National Economy of the USSR in Figures, 1861–1938) (Moscow, 1940), p. 17.

18 V. I. Bovykin, *Formirovanie finansogo kapitala v Rossii* (The formation of financial capital in Russia) (Moscow, 1984), pp. 28–9.

19 W. L. Blackwell, *The Beginnings of Russian Industrialization, 1800–1860* (Princeton, 1968), chap. 2.

20 A. M. Solov'eva, *Zheleznodorozhnyi transport Rossii vo vtoroi polovine xix veka* (Russian railway transport in the second half of the nineteenth century) (Moscow, 1975), p. 293.

21 Crisp, *Studies*, p. 28.

22 A. M. Solov'eva, 'Promyshlennaya revolyutsiya v Rossii' ('Industrial Revolution in Russia'), in V. I. Bovykin and K. Nussbaum (eds.), *Proizvoditel'nye sily i monopolisticheskii kapital v Rossii i Germanii v kontse xix i nachale xx vv* (Productive forces and monopoly capital in Russia and Germany at the end of the 19th and beginning of the 20th centuries) (Moscow, 1986), pp. 12, 14.

23 P. I. Khromov, *Ekonomicheskoe razvitie Rossii xix-xx vv.* (The economic development of Russia, 19–20th centuries) (Moscow, 1950), p. 195.

24 J. P. McKay, 'Restructuring the Russian petroleum industry in the 1890s: government policy and market forces', in Linda Edmondson and Peter Waldron (eds.), *Economy and Society in Russia and the Soviet Union. Essays for Olga Crisp* (London, 1992), pp. 94–6.

25 K. Thalheim, 'Russia's economic development', p. 96.
26 Data from A. Kaufman, *Small Scale Industry in the Soviet Union* (New York, 1962), reproduced in R. Bideleux, *Communism and Development* (London, 1985), p. 147.
27 A. Gerschenkron, *Economic Backwardness in Historical Perspective* (Cambridge, 1958); T. H. Von Laue, *Sergei Witte and the Industrialization of Russia* (New York, 1963). An interesting biographical portrait of Witte can be found in V. V. Atan'ich and R. Sh. Ganalin, 'Istoricheskie portrety. Sergei Ul'evich Vitte' (Historical portraits. Sergei Yul'evich Vitte), *Voprosy istorii*, 8 (1990), pp. 32–53.
28 Crisp, *Studies*, p. 27.
29 W. Kirchner, 'Russian tariffs and foreign industries before 1914: the German entrepreneurs' perspective', *Journal of Economic History*, 41 (1981), pp. 361–79.
30 T. C. Owen, 'The Russian industrial society and Tsarist economic policy 1867–1905', *Journal of Economic History*, 45 (1985), p. 600.
31 Crisp, *Studies*, p. 28.
32 A. Kahan, *Russian Economic History, The Nineteenth Century* (London, 1989), p. 96.
33 Kirchner, 'Russian tariffs', p. 372.
34 E. C. Pickering, 'The International Harvester Company in Russia,' unpublished PhD thesis, Princeton University, 1974, p. 24.
35 W. Kirchner, 'The industrialization of Russian and the Siemens Firm, 1853–1880', *Jahrbücher für Geschichte Osteuropas*, 22 (1974), pp. 326, 350–1.
36 P. Ol', *Inostrannye kapitaly v Rossii* (Foreign Capital in Russia) (Petrograd, 1922).
37 V. I. Bovykin, *Formirovanie finansogo*, pp. 164–5, is far from dismissive of Ol's figures. F. Carstensen, 'Numbers and reality: a critique of foreign investment estimates in Tsarist Russia', in M. Lévy-Leboyer (ed.), *La position internationale de la France* (Paris, 1977), pp. 275–83, on the other hand, argues strongly against the validity of such estimates.
38 P. Gregory, *Russian National Income*, p. 129.
39 V. I. Bovykin, 'K voprosu o roli inostrannogo kapitala v Rossii' (On the question of the role of foreign capital in Russia), *Vestnik Moskovskogo universiteta, Istoriya* (1964), p. 70. Bovykin uses Ol's data for his calculations.
40 J. P. McKay, *Pioneers for Profit. Foreign Entrepreneurship and Russian Industrialization 1885–1913* (Chicago, 1970), pp. 26–8. Gregory is more cautious but acknowledges that in 1913 40 per cent of all industry was financed by foreign capital.
41 McKay, *Pioneers*; Kirchner, 'Siemens firm'; F. Carstensen, *American Enterprise in Foreign Markets: Singer and International Harvester in Imperial Russia* (London, 1984).
42 McKay, *Pioneers*, pp. 170–1.
43 *Ibid.*, p. 172.
44 Kirchner, 'Siemens firm', p. 349.
45 I. A. D'yakonova, 'E. Nobel' i dizelestroenie v Rossii' (E. Nobel and diesel making in Russia), in *Monopolii i ekonomicheskaya politika tsarizma v kontse xix i nachale xx vv.* (Monopolies and the economic policies of Tsarism at the end of the 19th and beginning of the 20th centuries) (Leningrad, 1987), pp. 83–6.
46 I am grateful to Professor Uli Wengenroth of the University of Munich for passing this information to me.
47 R. Pipes, *Russia under the Old Regime* (Harmondsworth, 1974), chap. 8.
48 A. J. Rieber, *Merchants and Entrepreneurs in Imperial Russia* (Chapel Hill, 1982).

49 W. L. Blackwell, 'The Old Believers and the rise of private industrial enterprise in early nineteenth century Moscow', *Slavic Review* (1965), pp. 407–24.

50 Kahan, *Russian Economic History*, chap. 1.

51 *Proizvodstvo sakhara na zavodakh Grafov Bobrinskikh* (Sugar production in the factories of Count Bobrinsky) (Kiev, 1896), p. 548.

52 A. P. Korelin, 'Dvoryanstvo i torgovo-promyshlennoe predprinimatel'stvo v poreformennoi Rossii' (The gentry and commercial–industrial entrepreneurship in post-reform Russia), *Istoricheskie zapiski*, 102 (Moscow, 1978), p. 132.

53 *Ibid.*, pp. 133, 137.

54 A. M. Anfimov, *Rossiiskaya derevnya v gody pervoi mirovoi voiny* (The Russian countryside in the Years of the First World War) (Moscow, 1962), p. 184.

55 L. P. Minarik, 'O svyazakh krupneishikh zemel'nykh sobstvennikov Rossii s promyshlennost'yu k nachalu xx v.' (On the links of the largest landowners in Russia with industry at the beginning of the 20th century), in *Ezhegodnik po agrarnoi istorii vostochnoi Evropy za 1971 g.* (Vilnius, 1974), pp. 307–18.

56 Korelin, 'Dvoryanstvo', p. 139.

57 R. Portal, 'Muscovite industrialists: the cotton sector (1861–1914)', in W. L. Blackwell (ed.), *Russian Economic Development from Peter the Great to Stalin* (New York, 1974), pp. 161–96.

58 Rieber, *Merchants*, p. 234.

59 Owen, 'Russian industrial society', pp. 587–606.

60 Rieber, *Merchants*, p. 415.

61 Y. E. Vodarskii, *Naselenie Rossii za 400 let* (The population of Russia over 400 years) (Moscow, 1973), p. 104; F. Lorrimer, *The Population of the Soviet Union* (Geneva, 1946), pp. 44ff.

62 Cameron, *A Concise Economic History*, p. 192.

63 *Ibid.*, p. 16.

64 J. Komlos, 'Thinking about the Industrial Revolution', *Journal of European Economic History*, 18 (1989), pp. 191–206.

65 These ideas are those of Boserup quoted in *ibid.*

66 Calculated from Gregory, *Russian National Income*, pp. 232–3 and Khromov, *Ekonomicheskoe razvitie*, pp. 452–4.

67 S. A. Klepnikov, *Pitanie russkogo krest'yanstva*, part 1, *Normy potrebleniya glavneishikh pishevykh producktov* (Feeding the Russian peasantry, part 1: Consumption norms of the major food products) (Moscow, 1920), p. 12.

68 A. V. Chayanov, *Normy prodovol'stviya sel'skogo naseleniya Rossii po dannym byudzhetnykh issledovanii* (Food supply norms to the Rural Population of Russia according to studies of Budget Data) (St Petersburg, 1915), pp. 19–20.

69 R. E. F. Smith and D. Christian, *Bread and Salt* (Cambridge, 1984), p. 356.

70 Chayanov, *Normy*, p. 57.

71 Data are from Gregory, *Russian National Income*, pp. 127–32, 135.

72 *Ibid.*

73 O. Crisp, 'Labour and industrialization in Russia', in *Cambridge Economic History of Europe*, vol. VII, part 2 (Cambridge, 1978), p. 407.

74 'Molochnoe khozyaistvo' (Dairy farming), *Sel'skoe khozyaistvo i lesovodstvo* (St

Petersburg, 1893), pp. 298–300 and V. Kovolevskii and I. Levitskii, *Statisiticheskii ocherk molochnogo khozyaistva v severnykh i srednykh polosakh Evropeiskoi Rossii* (A statistical essay on dairy farming in the Northern and Central Zones of European Russia) (St Petersburg, 1879), p. 3.

75 The Revolution and background are well documented by R. Service, *The Russian Revolution, 1900–1927* (London, 1986).

76 The economic history of the early Soviet period is perhaps most thoroughly covered in A. Nove, *An Economic History of the USSR* (Harmondsworth, 1969).

FIFTEEN

Revolutions and continuities in American development

WILLIAM N. PARKER

For aught that I could ever read,
Could ever hear by tale or history,
The course of true love never did run smooth.

W. Shakespeare, *A Midsummer Night's Dream*,
Act I, Scene I, 132–4

I

THE human experience in all its aspects, both over time and across space, occurred in North America during the nineteenth century largely within a capitalist culture, borne on the back of mercantile trade, and moving readily into the economic activities of land settlement, minerals discovery and agricultural and mining exploitation.[1] The continent was penetrated in the sixteenth century at opposite corners by peoples who spoke the Latin languages – the social, religious and economic institutions of the late European Middle Ages. Renaissance and North European capitalism entered with the Dutch and English chartered settlement and colonization companies – partnerships or joint-stock enterprises – in the seventeenth and early eighteenth centuries, or through grants made to various noble persons or corporations, virtually in fee simple, with only the slenderest of feudal restrictions. These were then transferred largely through sale to individual settlers and cultivators.[2]

Diagonally then, across the continent, from southeast to northwest, between Quebec and New Mexico, pushing in from its Atlantic coast after 1600 and its Pacific coast after 1840, migration and occupation by Anglo-Saxon and Gaelic (Scotch-Irish) and Welsh settlers – Protestant by religion, predominantly English by political, legal and literary culture – slid the institutions, that is, the behaviour patterns, the government and the intellectual and commercial values composing what Marx saw as bourgeois capitalism, as if on a great sheet under the continent's rich natural resources – its soils, forests, waters and minerals, its geography and topography. Within these institutions and physical conditions, the settlers – farmers and their ambitious wives and families, emancipated European peasants, small craftsmen, merchants and labourers – moved, took root, planted homesteads and created the farming enterprises, over 2 million in number by 1860, growing to over 6 million in the USA alone by 1920. Joined even during their creation by the links of transport, law and commerce, and supplemented by the industrial activities ancillary to agricultural life and production, these farming enterprises produced the continent's abundant and extensive agricultural production, and its interconnecting net of commercial, financial and small-scale mercantile enterprise.

Mineral rushes and agricultural revolutions

Accompanying the settlement of the frontier and generally just preceding it, and so pulling it along, were the discoveries of minerals, producing notable examples of local 'revolutions' in limited regions and in the time frame of a half a decade. In Central and South America, the whole dramatic early story of Mexico and Peru might be termed an extended minerals 'rush', induced by the peculiarly obvious hoards and deposits of the precious metals in a world where religious ornamentation, a royal treasury and mercantile trade were all prominent features. The nineteenth century's classic gold rushes in North America and beyond – from Georgia through Colorado, California, Idaho to Alaska – might be taken, together with the strikes in Australia and South Africa, as the last unwinding of an intensely specialized form of capitalist enterprise. Rushes into deposits of fuels – coal and oil – of iron and the non-ferrous metals, awaited the spread and increasing density of settlement, the resulting frequency of random sightings, a growth of the consciousness of their potential value and the increase in that value with transport improvement and industrial markets. In each nineteenth-century case – in Pennsylvania coal and oil, Michigan copper, Missouri and Illinois lead, most notably in the Lake Superior iron ores, in all the metals buried in the rich veins found in the Rockies, and finally, at the century's turn, across the mid-continent oil field in Texas and Oklahoma – rumours, a strike, the hectic rush, the further exploration, and at last the more or less orderly exploitation created volatile mining regions, making the West a land of recurring mining excitements.[3] The regions, attracting miners of wide ethnic diversity, set up the insubstantial frame buildings and rough culture of the mining town, to last a few decades while the deposit, sometimes with occasional discoveries of new extensions and with improvements in techniques of mining and recovery, eventually wore itself out.

In America, before the tractor – except for the replacement of the hoe and the sickle by mechanical horse-drawn equipment – there were no 'agricultural revolutions' related to the rising productivity which occurred steadily after 1840 through the movement on to new soils and terrains and through myriad small adaptations of practices to crops and markets. Similarly, except in the war that ended the bondage of the African-descended slaves, there was no need, as in Europe, for a revolutionary freeing of white peasants from the soil or the enclosure of commons or the consolidation of strips, nor were there the nets of rural industrial workers across the north-eastern countryside to be displaced by the factories when they came. American farm youth, ambitious or desperate, and the craftsmen, peasants, miners and manual labourers arriving in successive waves from Quebec, Ireland, Britain, Scandinavia and Eastern and Southern Europe took care of the industrial labour supply. The growth in numbers of new productive enterprises in farming occurred, indeed, at uneven rates, though less so perhaps than in industry. Sometimes military victory, followed by the pacification of the Indians, opened up large areas and brought the rushes of new settlement. The development of new regions for arable or pastoral farming nearly always entailed technical changes in farming practices, in genetic stock and even in implements, the latter made possible by the industrial development occurring contemporaneously.

Some of the specialized agricultural regions, it is true, appeared at the outset with a burst – the tobacco culture of eastern Maryland and tidewater Virginia, the rice culture of South Carolina and Louisiana, including Louisiana's modest contribution to the Caribbean sugar economy, and the famous, immense and fatal stimulus that came with the cotton gin. The spread of upland cotton in the south-eastern Piedmont and coastal plain went with a rush, and a second wave brought in the rich alluvial lands along the Mississippi to Arkansas and western Tennessee. In the grains and livestock belts of the interior, specialization was less sudden and generally less intense even as the mid-nineteenth-century corn-hog enterprises developed, first in Kentucky and Tennessee, then across the flat areas of the north central states from central Ohio to Iowa and Nebraska, followed by wheat to the immediate West, and at last by the great cattle kingdoms of the Plains and the extensive sheep farming higher up.[4]

Apart from cotton, the most significant case of an agriculture of marked regional characteristics, related to a few 'revolutionary' technical changes, was in the opening of the Great Plains, the drier, unforested steppes of the mid-continent from Texas through the Dakotas and on to the Arctic Circle in the four decades after 1850. Walter Prescott Webb's masterly book, *The Great Plains* (New York, 1931), tells the story. But within the forested areas to the east and west of the Plains, and even within the Great Plains area itself, settlement occurred more or less steadily once it began. Technical change then took the form of an adaptive evolution and the great specialized agricultural regions were formed by the spread of settlers and the growth and configuration of markets. Penetration by the railroad after 1840, of course, left a trail of commercialization and some growth of market towns and small urban places wherever it went.

Related to the development of these specialized agricultural regions were ethnic movements of two very different sorts. A black slave population was imported from West Africa in the eighteenth century, and given an immense stimulus to its continued multiplication after 1800 by the demands and lands of the cotton culture. Following that, after 1840 came the quite different, final, North European migrations of German, Central European and Scandinavian peoples to the wheat and dairy regions into the Prairies and Great Plains and to the states immediately to the west of the Great Lakes. With the Scandinavian migrations of the 1870s and the Ukrainian to Canada in the 1890s, the drawing power of the North American agricultural expansion on the populations of the Old World was exhausted. The charm, in a sense, was wound up and, overlapping it, all was prepared for the continuous thickening of the industrial and urban overlay that began to cover rural North America, its fields and forests.

II

In economic historiography, the concept 'Industrial Revolution' lies like a sheet of ice over a brook beneath which the waters are forever flowing. The term was standardized by Arnold Toynbee in his *Lectures on the Industrial Revolution* (London, 1864), then taken up by the Hammonds and other Fabians, adapting Marx's treatment of the sixteenth-century enclosures to the case of the eighteenth-century enclosures and the early nineteenth-century factory system. Major responsibility must be borne too by Paul Mantoux, in his classic book, *The Industrial Revolution of the Eighteenth Century* (London, 1905; New York, 1961) and that sturdy Tory, Lillian C. A. Knowles, who staged her presentation around three 'revolutions' – agrarian, commercial and industrial – to bring her from 1500 to 1900: *The Industrial and Commercial Revolution in Great Britain* (4th edn, London, 1926). T. S. Ashton's beautifully balanced little book, *The Industrial Revolution* (New York, 1964), and the equally thoughtful contributions by Lancelot Beales, *The Industrial Revolution, 1750–1850* (London, 1928) and the late Michael Flinn, *Origins of the Industrial Revolution* (London, 1966) added, in the generation of my teaching, to the life and popularity of the concept.[5]

In some American and British circles in the 1950s, as 'quantification' and 'development' began to obsess our consciences, it came to seem necessary that the idea be given some empirical content in the form of an acceleration in an industry's output, or in the index of industrial production for a country or a region, or, best of all, in a discontinuity upward in the rate of growth of the national product. Two economists in America benefited most from this taste of aggregation – W. W. Rostow, with his idea of a 'take-off' into self-sustained growth, and Alexander Gerschenkron, with his finding of a 'great spurt', not in the English case indeed, but in later industrializers, benefiting from the incentive of 'relative backwardness'. The concept lost then any tangible connection with specific industries (although Rostow did speak of 'leading sectors'), or indeed with an 'industrial' revolution as such, as distinct from rapid acceleration in the pace of something called 'economic growth'. Like a promontory on the sea coast, the sudden bulges disappear as the scale is enlarged and the history is seen in one mass and in the very long run from the loftier heights of *Weltgeschichte*.

Two regional episodes in American industrialization would seem particularly to qualify for comparison with the classic English story. Most obvious is the burst of growth of factory textiles in New England and, intertwined with it, an evident mushrooming of machinery and machine tool production before 1860, and thence the 'American system' of parts manufacture and assembly that careened across the century to the automobile plants in Detroit. A second, heavy-industrial revolution may be discerned in the rapid growth of large-scale coke-smelting, steel-making, and heavy-machinery construction in the area from Pittsburgh to Cleveland, in the decades 1850–1880, with an 'echo effect' south of Lake Michigan around 1900. Each of these 'revolutions' had its later echo in the upper South, in the blossoming of the Southern textile mills in the Carolina and Georgia Piedmont in the period from 1880 to 1910, and in the iron-and-steel works at Birmingham, Alabama, in the 1890s.

Both these sequences show the features that would seem to qualify them for the title – whether honourable or not – of 'revolutionary'. Both had a vigorous expansion in a cluster of related industries within a few decades, with a tapering off thereafter, and both had further effects spreading far out into the structure of production. Both – like the classic English revolution – had a revolutionary effect on the conditions of labour in their respective industries. Moreover, as a 'revolution' is a compression in time, so an industrial 'region' is a compression in space. Each helps to create the other, facilitating its development through the easier conditions of communication that they involve. The eastern and southern New England areas, and far up into the streams tributary to the Merrimac and the Connecticut Rivers, and to Long Island Sound, could be thought of as such a region in 1840. Similarly the upper Ohio valley and the small streams, canals and rail net across to Cleveland and Chicago formed a truly industrialized strip by 1900.

New England: a revolution in light industry[6]

Even more than in Britain, the concept of 'Industrial Revolution' has been attached most commonly in the American continent's industrial history – as if in a kind of 'original meaning' – to the adoption of machine methods and factory organization in the production of cotton textiles in southern New England at the turn of the eighteenth century, carrying on down to the 1830s, or even on to the 1850s. In Britain in that period, beginning slightly earlier, steam power also was being introduced, and the metal trades, thickly clustered at Birmingham, and the smelters at the Yorkshire, Scottish and Welsh coal-fields formed an integral part of the whole history. But in southern New England in these decades, the water-wheel furnished nearly all the factory power, and the industrial developments, both those adjacent to the cotton mills in the Providence–Worcester and Merrimac valley areas and those to the west in the Connecticut, Housatonic and Naugatuck valleys, were of a distinctly light-industrial nature. Clock mechanisms – machined from wood until well after 1830 – firearms, brass and tin-wares, shoes, rubber wares, fashioned in artisan shops or small factories, were the commodities sold in the shops or exported.

New England's 'revolution' came in the production of consumer goods with an extensive rural market, i.e., textiles and two universal domestic 'machines' – clocks and guns. Yet with astonishing speed and thoroughness, this 'revolution' came to produce both its own machinery for all its light industries, and the machine tools by which that machinery could be turned out. The cotton industry remained, in a sense, an enclave – as today in Korea or Peru – processing an imported raw material and exporting the product, without significant tangible linkages to a wider industrialization except through its use of machinery. The textile mills depended at the outset on the collection of mechanical inventions springing into activity in Britain, as instanced by Slater's and Lowell's well-advertised reproductions of the English machinery they had viewed. But the interruption of trade between 1795 and 1815 threw the rising industry on to its own resources. The Industrial Revolution in New England resided then not in the cotton mills, for all their effects on the labour force and the organization of capital; they were indeed little more than extensions of merchant capital to another area of organization.

Technically, the 'Revolution' derived from the machine-tool plants – Brown and Sharpe, the Whitten Works, and the Saco-Newton-Lowell amalgam in the East, and on the Connecticut River, Jones and Lamson at Springfield, Vermont, the famous federal Armory at Springfield, Massachusetts, Pratt-Whitney at Hartford, North at Middletown and Whitney's domain in Hamden, Connecticut. Machinery and the ability to make machinery cheaply was at the heart of the 'American system', by which a complex manufacture and its tasks of production were broken down to a series of small, easily repeated operations on parts, each machined as closely as possible so as to be nearly interchangeable with its counterparts. That technique went on then to be applied in every direction with a thoroughness characteristic perhaps – as a mental habit – of a regional culture only just emerging from the dominance of the exacting theology of an obsessive religion.

Pittsburgh to Chicago: a 'heavy' industrial revolution[7]

Nineteenth-century America's second true Industrial Revolution, that of western Pennsylvania and north-eastern Ohio, opened in the 1850s with two notable mineral finds – the unexpected discovery of oil deposits north of Pittsburgh and the full exploration of the immense soft coal reserves, in the continuation of the Pittsburgh bed on into south-eastern Ohio and south into West Virginia and Kentucky. There can be no question that the railway was a catalyst of this movement, although within the mineral area itself the rivers clustering at Pittsburgh, and the canals rather quickly built to Lake Erie carried much oil, coal and ore. The railway linked the West to the developed East far more effectively than the clumsy Pennsylvania portage canal had done, bringing in the East's miscellaneous manufactures and the grains of the rich central Pennsylvania region, and delivering to the eastern seaboard the West's agricultural and heavy industrial staples. More important for the construction of an inland empire, the railway permitted easy immigration and trade into northern Ohio, to the lake ports – ultimately to Milwaukee and Chicago. At the same time, the railway was by far the largest single consumer of iron and coal, and its machine shops like those deriving from the textile factories in New England became a centre and a source of machinists able in separate establishments to develop railway and steel-making equipment, and the earth-moving machinery in which – even before the harnessing of the gasoline engine – America became a world leader.

The 'revolution' appearing in both of these regions had its technical centre. In the New England case, this lay in the obsessive application of machinery and organizational efficiency as far out in as many lines of production as it would go. In the Pittsburgh–Cleveland revolution, the roots lay rather in the flourishing pre-existing iron industry and the use of anthracite replacing charcoal after 1840, then after 1870 of coke, for which specially large seams of bituminous coking coal in the Pittsburgh basin were ideally suited. Compared to the developing use of bituminous coal in western Pennsylvania, the whole anthracite mining and smelting development in the East in the 1830s and 1840s was, in a sense, simply a late appendage to charcoal iron. Throughout the state, after 1850, coal- or coke-smelted iron, using local ores and a trickle of imports, was shaped in forges and rolling mills with ample use of abundant power from water-mills and coal-fired steam engines. Tiny amounts of steel, by the ancient cementation or crucible techniques were produced. Pennsylvania, and after 1840, the Pittsburgh basin, then recapitulated in a few decades the whole technical history of the English iron industry from late medieval times to the late nineteenth century. Despite some skilful innovation in furnace construction, this development served simply as the opening act to the truly 'revolutionary' metallurgical development after the introduction of the Bessemer process and the immense ore discoveries that fed into the western region in its burst to heavy industry.

The heavy-industrial revolution of 1870–1900, then, was built on cheap steel pouring from Carnegie's J. Edgar Thompson plant after 1875 and those of Carnegie's companions, imitators, and competitors in Pittsburgh, Youngstown and Cleveland. With cheap steel, mining machinery and steel-making plant itself cheapened and by 1890 steel was replacing iron in rails and all structural uses.[8] The region, containing, as it did, Rockefeller's oil refineries, and lodged between rich coal deposits and access to the lake trade, developed strongly between 1870 and 1900, forming its own infrastructure, multiplying and strengthening its links with East and West and within itself. Then, between 1880 and 1910, it threw out three spurs which, taken together, created what the world for the next half century knew as the dominant industrial Middle West.

First, as we have seen, was the uncovering of the Minnesota–Wisconsin iron ore deposits after about 1885. The scenes exhibited forty years earlier when rich copper deposits became known in northern Michigan – the accidental discovery, the rushes of frenzied speculators, finally the settling down to steady exploitation – all this was reproduced on a gigantic scale as a stream of ore shipments by lake barges began to flow across the 600 or so miles to the mills. Second, just after 1900 steel had invaded the southern shore of Lake Michigan where a rich market had already long appeared in the railway, urban construction, and the farm-machinery industry around the McCormick plant. The giant steel works in Gary, Indiana, built between 1906 and 1908, were no mere whim of the United

States Steel Corporation when Morgan and Schwab put together that gigantic amalgamation. It holds an almost symbolic significance by marking a western boundary of the area over which the Minnesota ores and West Virginia coals could be economically assembled.

Chicago has, of course, a history and an urbanization all its own, made possible by its location at a point of tangency of the Great Lakes and the Prairies and Plains into which the railway could penetrate.[9] But a third development closer in spirit to the earlier history of Pittsburgh and Cleveland showed at last the interweaving of America's light-industrial and heavy-industrial revolutions, enlisting machine shops, the many small parts manufacturing plants, and the new sources of fuel for the internal combustion engine – no longer simply in Oil City, Pennsylvania, but at several locations in Ohio and Illinois, and, beginning in 1900, with spectacular 'gushers' in Oklahoma and Texas, the mid-continent oil field. The final development in this sequence occurred, of course, when the automobile assembly plants – which had had a flicker of life in Connecticut and northern Ohio – settled in Detroit. In the automobile industry, the light machinery skills and the techniques of plant organization already developed in New England were married to the heavy-equipment industries, and the steel-and-rubber works of the Pittsburgh–Cleveland region to create the prototypical American industry, the climax of America's two Industrial Revolutions.

III

The three great productive sectors in American development as shown in figure 15.1 – mining, farming and manufactures – exhibit then quite different time paths as they unfolded in the century and a half of continental settlement before 1940. Yet there are undeniable structural similarities, isomorphisms, in their historical records. Each sectoral history, taken by itself shows the rhythms characteristic of all human activity. In each, the development of routine, of repetitive patterns of behaviour, was formalized into sets of production organizations with continuing, or continually replacing, lives. But in each, the continuity is compounded with bursts of speed, even of frenzy, in which the activity accelerated. One who surveys American economic history across the whole spectrum of economic and social behaviour from the early days of the federal union to the 1930s and the Second World War – wherein so many of the earlier patterns were broken and transformed – must ask why these unevennesses, these revolutionary bursts, recur within steady growth, and what were their effects.

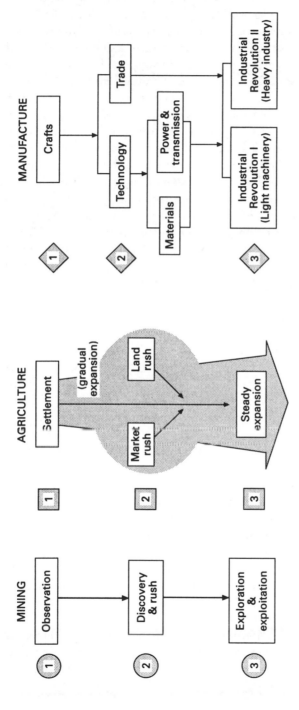

Fig. 15.1 Continuity and discontinuities in sectoral expansions (United States, nineteenth century).

At the outset in both mining and manufacturing, the path of the development lay at the outset deeply hidden. Minerals lie beneath the soil, and only outcrops or seepages hint at their presence. Discovery and exploitation of a deposit required the presence of a known market, either nearby or accessible by water or overland transport. Discoveries made too far in advance of possible economic exploitation remained mere observations, curious pieces of knowledge, usually lost or forgotten. When once the discovery had been made and the 'rush' had occurred, the days of the prospectors at that deposit were over, and rational exploitation got underway. Thereafter exploitation required continual, but more deliberate exploration, as veins or seams were followed and new shafts sunk. An important residue of a succession of minerals 'rushes' in the nineteenth century was, then, a cadre of prospectors to form a volatile mass ready to move on rumours of new discoveries, from one remote new region to another all across the West. But all this is not much different from the process of technical discovery in manufactures. Indeed, the earth's subsoil is in a sense a visible embodiment of the opportunities for novelty and wealth that lie hidden within the folds of technical knowledge. Here, as Schumpeter observed, a 'strike' can be accompanied by a certain period of extraordinary profits, attracting a 'swarm of entrepreneurs' until all the production sites and markets in some large portion of the earth's surface are used up to the limits of costs and knowledge.

The history of mining excitements teaches then the possibilities of surprise, of sudden 'revolutionary' explosions of opportunity in the course of the development of an economic sector. The history of agriculture, too, is not devoid of sensational 'rushes' through the opening of new lands or new portions of the markets. But its major lesson is of the opposite sort; it teaches the importance of routine, and of measured deliberate expansion, year after year, as a growing population occupies the soil, reproducing the techniques, the practices, the habit patterns, the family roles in a local society, that one generation teaches to the next. Uncertainty was endemic to the occupation, generated beyond control, both by the weather and natural catastrophe and by markets. But unlike mining, the immense capital stock of a nation's agriculture renews itself with the recurrent seasons. On American farms, crop yields under only very moderately conservative practices, could still be very high, particularly on lands of original forest cover in the first years of settlement. It was the possibility of such yields that kept settlement flowing. But after an initially high pay-off to a new region, yields commonly settled down to a level sustainable under the crops and practices which a generation's experience had shown were suitable to the location.

Now industrial activity shares in both the 'creative destruction' of the mining sector and the steady reproduction possible to farming. Before

1800 in the United States, industrial development was nowhere particularly rapid. Hand crafts, simple tools and a very modest use of water power and metals left colonial markets open to the industrial exports of the mother country. In the half-dozen port towns from Boston to Baltimore, the population showed the clustering conducive to the activities of a small artisan population. Outside of them, trade was hardly possible except along rivers or by itinerant peddlers, distributing a few simple staples or novelties. The result was that industrial activity, like charity, began at home, in farm families, in local neighbourhoods, or on the tidewater plantations. In the decades between the Revolution and the Civil War, in the Middle Colonies with their richer soils and easier conditions of life, opportunity presented itself where industrial resources, particularly the numerous small iron deposits and, by the 1830s, the eastern Pennsylvania anthracite coal deposits, were found or could be economically made available.

In contrast to the development west of Boston and up the Connecticut River, the industrial development in the Philadelphia–New York coastal economies, being closely linked with those two rival ports, is hard to subsume in the concept of 'revolution'. Here, well before 1790, two large commercial cities had developed, each being – unlike Boston in New England – a funnel for goods from deep in the interior, beginning with furs and timber, then grain and meats, transportable to Southern Europe and the sugar islands of the Caribbean. The migration of skilled craftsmen in a variety of urban trades – wood and metal-working, shoe-making, craft-shop textiles, printing and, most notably, money-changing and mercantile banking – all created the conditions for further industrial development. Between 1780 and 1880 in the region north and south of Philadelphia along the Delaware River and in the city itself, textile establishments, workshops and factories, though individually not on the New England scale, sprang up in abundance, producing generally fabrics of better quality than the Yankee mills. Inevitably numerous machine-tool shops also appeared, as well as a few notable engineers – Oliver Evans, who built an automated flour mill in 1792, and 'Mad' John Fitch who designed and built several steamboats before Robert Fulton's celebrated successes on the Hudson. Ripple effects of the growth in the urban 'heartland' – the tri-city area of Baltimore, Philadelphia and New York – were felt far out into the surrounding area.[10] As far south as Richmond a notable ironworks operated to become later a principal armoury of the Confederacy, and both Richmond in the south and Rochester far north on Lake Ontario became important flour-milling centres in the 1830s and the sites of a secondary urbanization. Along the Mohawk River, west from Troy and Albany, a chain of small towns began to grow into small cities after the Erie Canal was dug in 1825, beginning at Troy and Albany, touching Utica and Schenectady, causing Rochester to spring to life and ending in the lake port, Buffalo. All these benefited from the movement of heavy goods east and people west on the canal till 1870. After 1870, Buffalo shared in the oil and iron revolution at the eastern end of Lake Erie, and Rochester developed its notable optical and camera industries.

The industry of Pennsylvania east of the mountains between 1750 and 1840 and that of the New York interior along the Erie Canal after 1825 showed a steady development. Pennsylvania's varied industries were as large as New England's in total value added, but except to a degree in the iron industry, they showed none of the coherent inter-related technical development that made the discernible 'revolution' in the latter's network of factories and workshops. As we have been, Pennsylvania's development had a 'heavy' industry component, which became marked as the anthracite coal-fields beyond Reading and around Wilkes-Barre and Scranton opened up after 1830. It was into the centre of this mining, lumbering, rich farming area that the railway appeared and pushed the industry forward, especially after 1855, when the link to Pittsburgh was made.

Pittsburgh, founded at the head of the Ohio valley as a fort by the French in the early eighteenth century, was ceded to Britain with the whole of the Western area up to the Mississippi by the Peace of Paris (1763). After 1800, it assumed a growing economic importance as the terminus to the sizeable river trade that went through Marietta to the growing city of Cincinnati up into the valley of the Miami, and on to Cairo, Illinois, where it joined the Mississippi just below St Louis, where the Missouri came in from the West. In all these towns appeared trade, transport and even some manufactory development, similar to that which the Atlantic ports had called into being. Furs, grains, meats, whisky – the staples of Western commerce – were supplemented by some craft industry, mercantile services and much banking and lawyering in connection with the transfers of goods and land. But the laying of the canals between 1825 and 1845 through the mountains in three parallel tracks, to New York, Baltimore and Philadelphia, then north and south in Ohio, began to drain off the surplus produce from the Northern tier of counties in the old North-west. When these were paralleled in turn by the speedier and more flexible railways, the possibilities of a sizeable industrial growth southward along the banks of the Ohio and Mississippi River system were eliminated.

In the interior of the Old North-west before 1860, the river, lake and canal system similarly allowed for some growth of very modest town clusters. But sixty per cent or more of the population was farmers, many of them possessing some industrial tools and skills, and off the farm, the industrial arts were lodged in small town workshops to which was available the labour of the farmers and their families in the off-season. Within this framework, to be sure, an intensely commercial spirit – one may surely say, a capitalist spirit, an enterprising spirit – dominated life, thought, and ambition of farmers and villagers alike. In the decades before 1860, it was this condition of life, of economy and of aspiration which had been reproducing itself all across the north. The situation of small farmers in the south, who formed the vast bulk of the free population, might have been not greatly different, but there the industrial opportunity was limited by the low farm income derived from the generally relatively poorer land, the ameliorating and debilitating effects of a semitropical climate, and, in the prime areas of commercial farm production, the poisoned social atmosphere of black Slavery.

Revolutions and their 'linkages'

From such underlying physical conditions, what then was responsible for the two 'revolutionary' episodes which, the one feeding into the other after 1860, created the formidable industrial machine which catapulted the United States into the twentieth century, and developed further and faster in the two decades up to 1929?

The short answer seems evident. In New England after 1810, stemming both from the Providence-Lowell textiles and the Connecticut valley's guns and clocks, sequences of technical change were initiated, or imitated, in the production of machinery and in the application of water and steam power, and thence in the organization of tasks within a plant and the development of the characteristic form of the American factory and production line. And in Pittsburgh and the area to its immediate Northwest – Connecticut's 'Western Reserve' in Ohio – the introduction of coke-smelting and Bessemer and open-hearth steel had a similar chain reaction in the steel-using industries, in the presence of the immense transport possibilities of the railway and shipment on the Great Lakes.

These technical and economic elements in the historical process and their manifestations are subsumed by development economists under the intriguing heading – 'Linkages'.[11] A complete detailing of all the branches of the family would resemble the branching out of a family tree, and would be of no general interest in the absence of specific historical instances that detailed research into the local histories of our two 'revolutionary' episodes could develop. The concept of 'development linkages' furnishes a hold on the notions of both 'Industrial Revolution' and 'Industrial Region' where a compression of the responses and the appearances of the opportunities, of the 'feedbacks' in both time and space, is recognized to have occurred. The image has an attractive, mechanical quality. Like so much of what would pass for explanation in modern economics, it uses the metaphor of a mechanical, or hydraulic system. Explanation then runs in terms of 'structures', 'flows' and 'pressures'. 'Revolutionary' changes in the structure itself are not easily handled, except by placing them into a still larger structure – the 'economy' inside the 'political' system – and ultimately both placed within a relatively unspecified 'social' system.

Continuities and culture shift

But technological changes, revolutionary though they may be, can only spread urbanization and industrialization in the presence of certain permissive factors, in a favourable climate, as it were, and on soil already fertilized and tilled. Indeed it may be argued that technological change itself – though its history is dotted with seemingly 'random' discoveries – can exhibit a continuity and a connection both with fundamental scientific knowledge and with a flourishing economy only when *its* 'soil and climate' are prepared in those portions of an historical record labelled 'intellectual' and 'economic'. A group of intellectual and behavioural 'linkages' worth following as we reflect on the history, seeking both knowledge of its detail and an 'explanation' of what are seen as its massive structural movements, its cloud formations of periods and epochs, is perhaps best expressed by a word and concept shared by the biologist and sociologist, but even more often found in the anthropologist's writings and heard, too, occasionally among old-fashioned humanists: the concept of 'Culture'. It is the word, it may be recalled, on the hearing of which the Nazi leader, Hermann Goering, cocked his revolver. Nonetheless, it may perhaps be enlisted for 'purely scientific purposes' – or at least for purely descriptive and interpretive ones – without fatal emotional connotations.[12]

There can be no doubt that farming in America, in the presence of a free market in land, and property rights in a farm lodged unrestrictedly in the cultivator, converted the world's most ancient occupation – the material base of social and political order since earliest civilized times – into an economic asset, an object of commercial investment, an opportunity for profitable, even speculative, enterprise. But the American farm was also the seat of family life, of a group of human beings bound by ties of affection, of sexual gratification, of religion and social approval and – most important – of joint labour in shared tasks, and a non-market division of labour. Despite debt and tenancy, speculative ambitions and commercial incompetence, the correspondence, the nice fit, between the family farm's social scale and its economic effectiveness as a functioning, producing economic organism, viable on an intensely competitive capital market – gave the system, despite the inroads on it by debt and tenancy, or by speculative ambitions and commercial incompetence – its staying power, its tremendous strength as the central socio-economic institution of nineteenth-century American society.

Industry organized in households, in small, merchant-linked networks, or even in small partnerships and family-centred firms, fits easily in a society of family-centred farm-based enterprises. But, beginning with the railway and the spread of mechanization, two features of the environment produced a sharp social differentiation in scale between farming and industrial organization. One was the development of the markets and forms of capitalist finance, permitting the financial control and direction of even larger blocs of capital and labour beyond the family and work-shop level. The other was the rigid persistence of land, of space, of nature and the seasons as necessary ingredients of the agricultural production function, with the attendant difficulties of transport, travel and social communication, and of labour management and direction. The existence in industrial activities of economies of scale and spatial clustering, evidently enforced by the technology, in the mode in which it developed, gave opportunities for organizational and spatial concentration, for bureaucracy and urbanization, as forms of industrial culture. Farming still sturdily resisted till long after the telegraph, the railway, the automobile and the telephone. And the appreciation or evaluation of a rural environment, and a slim margin of entrepreneurial independence in the rural culture, made farming unprofitable as the locus for investment by massed corporate capital. But the social and economic organization of the industrial and financial arts readily yielded to the opportunities offered by concentration, formal organization and spatial agglomeration, and its quantitative weight in the national life steadily increased. Sometime, perhaps most clearly in the 1890s and certainly by the 1920s, the two cultures, lying like two overlapping documents on a computer screen, changed places. The urban-industrial culture came out from under and spread out on top. It was not at the push of a button, or the click of a 'mouse' – History does not often function with electronic abruptness – but by 1940 the United States of America was no longer a predominantly agricultural country. It had passed completely through the great Industrial Revolutions of the nineteenth century.

Between 1870 and 1940, then, the American national culture was the interwoven sum of these two variants of capitalist culture – the rural-agricultural and the urban-industrial. Its farms were still 'petty-bourgeois' commodity producers, consonant with an economy of small artisans and small firms. And the agricultural production function still resisted, with a certain amount of government support, amalgamation into the industrial sector, while its increasing productivity made room in the national economy for the growing dominance of a large manufacturing and financial establishment. The Harvard business historian, Alfred Chandler, in massive volumes, has vividly and compendiously illustrated for us the 'economies of scale and scope' that permitted, or even perhaps made inevitable, the development of the forms and arts of corporate management and the wide presence of oligopoly just inside the technological frontier.[13]

Yet Culture, based on occupation and the relative strength of affectionate and market elements in the separate economic sectors of competitive industries, is only another way of looking at the social whole. Unlike 'linkages', it is not a mechanical, but a biological, even an agrarian, metaphor. 'Linkages' emphasizes connections, the transmission of energy, and so helps us to define and analyse 'revolutions'. Yet they imply stability and continuity in the chains of links once formed. 'Culture' describes careful nurturing, the cultivation of a complex biological organism, containing the germ of life, and its maturing and flowering suddenly into new form. The blooming of a flower, the hatching of an egg, the bursting of the butterfly from its chrysalis – are examples of 'revolution', of moments of apparent, bewildering chaos, from which, or after which, for a time, a stable new order appears. As scientific observation, instrumentation, and theory themselves continue on their course of development, the 'linkages' in cultural transformation, not merely mechanical but microscopic and chemical in nature, can be simulated and even observed. The assimilation of agriculture within the body of industrial culture, in America and in Western Europe since 1940, permits the culture of that whole intercontinental portion of the globe to be seen as an evolving unit. Whether one then speaks of continuities or of recurrent, local, or temporary 'industrial revolutions' in such a history depends, of course, on the level, the scope in space and time, of the observing historian's vision.

NOTES

Acknowledgement is due to the Mellon-West European Project in the Yale Council on West European Studies (Yale Center for International and Area Studies) for space and support staff in a series of studies, of which this forms a part. Oral presentations at the economic history workshops at Yale, UCLA and Cal Tech helped to sharpen the ideas, as did also a useful reading by Carol Heim (University of Massachusetts, Amherst) and the encouragement of David Weiman (Yale). Fig. 15.1 is due to the stimulus and technical skills of Heather Salome (Yale, CWES-YCIAS).

1 W. T. Easterbrook, *North American Patterns of Growth and Development: The Continental Context* (Toronto, 1990), intelligently edited by Ian Parker, offers one of the few treatments of North American settlement in a continental context. With subtlety and originality, if with occasional obscurity, Easterbrook combined the lines of thought of Harold A. Innis and those of the group of Harvard-centred entrepreneurial historians formed by Arthur H. Cole, and acknowledging Schumpeter as their intellectual sponsor. D. W. Meinig's comprehensive treatment of the geographical lines of settlement and culture also breaks much new ground. See his *The Shaping of America: A Geographical Perspective on 500 Years of History*, vol. 1 (New Haven, 1986).

2 The European theory, enforced here as later in Africa, gave the European monarchs ownership of the land by right of 'discovery', while the tenures of non-Christian peoples were in practice transformed, if at all, to a 'right of occupancy' until by purchase, treaty or military action such rights were abrogated. In this respect, the United States government was simply the revolutionary successor of the British Crown. Its possession was maintained and then extended west of the Mississippi by purchase from France and by imposed treaty with Mexico. These rights, thus transferred, were then maintained against the evicted Indian populations by military force and by the sheer migrating pressure of the superior fertility of a population of farmers over that of the pre-neolithic cultures of hunter-gatherers, or very primitive agriculturists. See M. Harris, *Origin of the Land Tenure System in the United States* (Ames, Ia., 1953), ch. 11.

3 The experience of minerals exploration is summarized in my chapter 4 in L. Davis, R. Easterlin and W. Parker, *American Economic Growth* (New York, 1972). Richard R. Nelson and Gavin Wright, 'The rise and fall of American technological leadership', *Journal of Economic Literature*, 30 (December 1990), pp. 1931–64, develop these lines of thought, along with many new insights, in the treatment of the sources and consequences of America's resource abundance.

4 Except for cotton, many of the tropical world's plantation crops – tobacco, sugar, coffee, tea, cocoa – were addictive. A burst of demand followed their spread into a new market, as an existing population acquired the new taste or habit. Prices, very high at first, fell as supplies increased, and demand fell back within the limits of the growth of the addicted population. In the case of cotton, the trigger point for a burst of demand came when – in response to the mechanical inventions and the opening up of new supplying regions, the price of cotton cloth fell to a relatively low and steady level and, being a preferred commodity in most climates, took over the market from the other fibres – wool and flax – which yielded less readily to machine-processing. This de-industrialization of rural households and villages was favoured also by the rise in commercial uses for farm and plantation labour, and in America, at least, by an increased value placed on female and child labour, both with the increase in its factory employment and with a growth of farm money incomes and possibly by the development of a new self-image and social role of women and children in the farm family. After this point, in all the regions, growth

and the establishment of cropping patterns became matters of evolutionary development as crops and varieties best suited to soil, factor supplies and markets prospered and prevailed. The coincidence of the plantation form in a commercial setting with this phenomenon of a 'revolutionary' burst of demand may not be wholly accidental, since a period of high initial profits helped to provide the set-up costs of assembling the land and labour on plantation scale.

5 Bibliographical references to this literature as well as a compendious treatment of the historiography are given in David Cannadine, 'The present and the past in the English Industrial Revolution, 1880–1980', *Past and Present*, 103 (May 1984), pp. 132–72. Cannadine discerns four periods, in each of which the treatment of the 1770–1830 'revolution' is dominated by the principal economic concern of the period, i.e. (1) the social question, 1880–1920 (Toynbee, the Webbs, the Hammonds vs. Clapham); (2) cycles and the depression of the 1930s (Mostly by US historians); (3) economic growth, 1950–70 (Rostow, Ashton, Mathias, Deane, Landes); (4) the stagflation since 1970 (various cliometricians). Cannadine's distinctions, I think, are accurate and nearly all the relevant literature is surveyed. However, he does not do justice to the Usher/Schumpeter technological sequences of the nineteenth century (coal and iron, steel and railways and electricity-chemistry) in which the 'first' (1770–1830) Industrial Revolution can be fitted rather nicely. Curiously enough, both general historians and quantitative scholars tend to look at the *size* of the industries affected by the new technology in the context of the growth of the whole economy, including agriculture and services. Historians, especially, look at the revolution in the very long run, i.e., from 1650. This drowns out the early burst of machine technology in cotton textiles, iron-making and machinery, although these linked changes truly primed the pump for the series of continuous, drastic transformations of *industrial* operations which have appeared in clusters in various parts of the industrial matrix down. The late Donald Coleman made a thoughtful treatment of the term and concept as myth and history the subject of his Creighton Trust lecture at the University of London, on 30 October 1989.

6 This section is based on the research and analysis contained in my essay, 'New England's early industrialization: a sketch', published with selective bibliography in P. Kilby (ed.), *Quantity and Quiddity* (Middletown, Conn., 1987), pp. 17–46. See also a vigorous effort to quantify the growth of the industries, individually and as a group, from the reports and manuscripts of the US Census: Kenneth Sokoloff, 'Productivity growth in manufacturing during early industrialization; evidence from the American Northeast, 1820–1860', in S. Engerman and R. Gallman (eds.), *Long-term Factors in American Economic Growth*, NBER Studies in Income and Wealth, vol. LI (Chicago, 1986).

7 This section is based on my essay, 'The industrial civilization of the Midwest', published with selective bibliography in D. C. Klingaman and R. K. Vedder (eds.), *Essays on the Economy of the Old Northwest* (Athens, 1987), chap. 11, pp. 243–74; republished in somewhat extended form in W. N. Parker, *Europe, America, and the Wider World*, vol. II (Cambridge, 1991), chap. 12, pp. 215–57.

8 The economic history of steel in this area between 1860 and 1900 is most satisfactorily treated in two earlier books, Peter Temin, *Iron and Steel in Nineteenth-
Century America* (Cambridge, Mass., 1964), and in the five-volume work of
Father William T. Hogan, *Economic History of the Iron and Steel Industry in the
United States* (Lexington, Mass., 1971), vols. I and II. Still the picture as to
processes, ore sources and products is not crystal clear. The price of steel rails,
deflated by the commodity price index, fell in the period 1867-1913 by roughly
65 per cent on an 1867-9 base. (See US Census, *Historical Census of the United
States*, Series E130, E2, E40.)

9 The material and geographical foundations are well displayed in the recent
(1991) study by William Cronon (New York, 1991).

10 To say this is to grant an economic and social logic, to me still unclear, to the
concepts of Pred, Conzen, Meyer and other urban historians, and geographers regarding a 'system of cities'. See Allan Pred, *City-Systems in Advanced
Economies* (London, 1977). Michael P. Conzen, 'The maturing urban system in
the United States, 1840–1910', *Annals of the Association of American Geographers*,
vol. 67, no. 1, March 1977; Allan Pred, *Urban Growth and City Systems in the US
1840–1860* (Cambridge, Mass., 1980); David R. Meyer, 'Emergence of the
American manufacturing belt: an interpretation', *Journal of Historical Geography*,
9, 2 (1983).

On the early Pennsylvania development, T. C. Cochran, *Frontiers of Change*
(New York, 1981), offers a judicious introduction. Among the many detailed
or local studies, Diane Lindstrom's well-known work, *Economic Development of
the Philadelphia Region* (New York, 1978) can be supplemented by valuable and
sensitive studies by R. F. Passkoff, *Industrial Evolution: Organization, Structure, and
Growth of the Pennsylvania Iron Industry, 1750–1860* (Baltimore, 1983), Philip
Scranton, *Proprietory Capitalism: The Textile Manufacture at Philadelphia,
1800–1885* (Cambridge and New York, 1983), and Anthony F. C. Wallace,
Rockdale: The Growth of an American Village in the Early Industrial Revolution (New
York, 1980). For the industrial development of towns along the Hudson,
Mohawk and Ohio Rivers, reliance must be placed on the rather numerous
local histories. An excellent example of the latter is offered for the Troy, N.Y.,
complex by Thomas Phelan, *The Hudson–Mohawk Gateway: An Illustrated History*
(Troy, N.Y., and Northridge, Calif., 1985).

11 Following Albert Hirschman's original treatment in *The Strategy of Economic
Development* (New Haven, 1958), pp. 98–120.

12 The increasing attention given to the concept of 'culture' derives from the
French *Annales* school, and particularly from a long tradition in anthropology,
exhibited most recently in the essays of Clifford Geertz. See especially Clifford
Geertz, *The Interpretation of Cultures* (New York, 1973). The term and concept
are also expounded in reformulations of Veblenian 'institutionalist'
economics, an effort to be sharply distinguished from the neoclassically
derived neo-institutionalism developed with ingenuity and some scope by O.
E. Williamson and D. C. North. See the very thoughtful essay by Anne
Mayhew, 'Culture: core concept under attack', *Journal of Economic Issues*, 21
(June 1987), pp. 587–609. The subject is considered also in various original

and well-considered papers given at the meetings of the Social Science History Association at Chicago, Oct.–Nov. 1987, and published in *Historical Methods*, vol. 21, no. 4 (Fall 1987). See espeically the valuable and the thought-provoking contribution of S. Ryan Johansson on the 'computer paradigm' of a social system, and Gregory Clark's clever, sympathetic and, in the end, despairingly hard-headed observations on the problem offered to economists by the concept.

13 Chandler's work has been rather sketchily surveyed, with bibliographical references, in a review article by W. N. Parker, 'The scale and scope of Alfred D. Chandler, Jr.', *Journal of Economic History*, 51 (Dec. 1991), pp. 958–63.

SIXTEEN

The Industrial Revolution – an overview

SIDNEY POLLARD

IT is a common failing of economic historians that they are familiar, at best, with one or two countries only, and have to take their knowledge of areas outside those from secondary sources without necessarily fully understanding the workings of the societies to which they apply. If a larger area, such as Europe, is to be investigated, one widely used method of getting over this difficulty is to assemble a group of scholars, of whom each is a specialist in his own or at most one other country, to produce a collective work. The problem which then tends to arise is that in their different national contexts, words have slightly different meanings because they describe relationships having a different legal and social history. Moreover, the different timing of similar events, such as for example the introduction of the steam engine, means that the subject itself has been transformed with the passage of time.

These problems also faced the editors of this volume, but they had the advantage that their theme, the 'Industrial Revolution', is well understood all over Europe. If the bundle of economic and social changes usually subsumed by that term should differ in detail in different parts of the continent, it was the hope and precisely one of the objects of the authors to trace and explain the idiosyncrasies of their countries and thus help to assemble a European history in all its rich variety, yet grouped around a single development. Therein lies the justification for this book.

However, although the term 'Industrial Revolution' is widely used in common parlance and understood in many languages, it has not been without its critics. Coined originally for Britain, in a conscious parallel with the political upheavals across the Channel known as the French Revolution, it should, in the eyes of some, have continued to be applied to the British Isles only. Indeed, recently a number of critics have been of the opinion that the term is inappropriate even for Britain and, *a fortiori*, undesirable for other countries.

The main cause of this scepticism is precisely the implicit comparison with the contemporaneous French Revolution. Unlike the latter, the

(British) Industrial Revolution was not steered, or planned, or forced through:[1] it happened as a result of the uncoordinated actions of thousands, perhaps hundreds of thousands of people. It had no clear beginning, unlike the Paris Revolution, and no discernible end. Not one of the appropriate sets of statistics, such as national income or output per head, the proportion of people working in industry, or the investment ratio – even if reliable statistical series could be firmly established – shows a discernible break at any point in time. The available data show, at best, a smooth change in rates of growth over a longish period. Even if sophisticated statistical methods are used to find a break where the eye sees only a smooth curve, such a break depends on the formula used, and different formulae find different turning-points. It is therefore not surprising that one of the most marked aspects of the essays assembled here, is that not only in Britain, but everywhere else, there is disagreement on the exact dating of the 'Industrial Revolution', even though at the same time scholars in each of these countries agree that a breakthrough of this kind occurred, and that it could be dated. But they also agree that at the end of this period of change, breakthrough or 'take-off' there were still large areas of the economy which had a traditional shape, including small-scale handicraft industry, rural industry and possibly peasant agriculture, which had survived side by side with the modern factories and mines and the associated transport sector. Moreover, as against the short, sharp events making the French, or for that matter, the Bolshevik revolutions, the time spans of industrial revolutions are counted in decades, rather than in weeks. All this has persuaded some that the whole concept is inappropriate and that the Industrial Revolution is a 'myth'.[2]

Nevertheless, the term has remained popular, and none of the contributors to this volume doubts its usefulness. They are all agreed on its varied and many-sided impact, and out of the elements stressed by them individually to characterize the experience of their own countries, it should be possible to construct a composite picture of what was significant in the Industrial Revolution in Europe.

Possibly the most widely accepted ingredient of the complex of changes which are discussed in the chapters on the individual European countries, was the transformation which occurred within industry itself. Critical in each case were the technical innovations, characterized by the introduction of new types of machinery and of chemical processes.

There had, of course, been technical inventions and innovations in previous ages. The fulling mill, the stocking frame, the two-stage process of iron-making were examples of quite complicated, and in part even capital-intensive inventions which had improved the productive potential of certain industries in earlier centuries. What was different now was the emergence of an unbroken chain of inventions, or rather several chains, of much wider impact, leading to much more significant increases in productivity as well as the creation of new products altogether, but above all, introducing a mechanism contriving continuous, unending, irreversible improvements.

There were at least two aspects to this. On the one hand, the process of technical innovation itself was, in a sense, institutionalized. Inventors and tinkerers were not only welcomed and, in principle, assured of protection by the evolving patent laws, but, within engineering works and elsewhere, improvements and innovations almost became part of their daily lives. Similarly, still on the supply side, there occurred a veritable revolution in science, depending in part on the very discoveries made in workshops, but also, in turn, suggesting new paths, as well as setting limitations, to what the technicians could think up. The discovery of discovery itself became a commonplace and a major driving force. It is also evident that, as soon as inventions became widespread rather than isolated, they provided mutual support for each other, such that each could proceed only after others had been made elsewhere. Thus, deeper coal mines needed steam pumps, and the steam engine, once it was modified and put on wheels, drove railways, which in turn depended on cheap mass-produced iron but also made possible the exploitation of the coal mines which had provided the initial impetus for the improvement of the steam engine. Technology had 'taken off', and it was frequently the sheer technology to be found in Britain, rather than its precise cost effectiveness, which impressed foreign visitors and governments and induced them to try and imitate the progress of the advanced countries.

There were, at the same time, important changes in the market on the demand side. Rising productivity led to rising incomes which, in turn, assured innovators that there would be a market for their new products and processes. Technical changes in the means of transport – among the most important of the age – allowed cheaper raw material to reach the industrialists, while allowing their products to open up new markets. Thus it was, in turn, the invasion of the less-developed markets in Central and later Eastern and Southern Europe which forced their more traditional industrialists to innovate, or go under.

Thus industry, not surprisingly, holds the limelight in all the national accounts, but the role of agriculture is not neglected, not least because in most cases, as is repeatedly stressed, agriculture employed considerably more people, not merely at the beginning of the industrialization process, but even at its end. In some countries, notably The Netherlands and Britain, a highly efficient agricultural sector, modernized in essence before the industrial breakthrough, helped the process by raising national incomes, providing a market for industrial products, increasing the flow of raw materials to the towns, and giving up labour to man the factories and workshops. In France, by contrast, a satisfied and immobile peasantry may well have slowed down the opportunities open to potential industrial entrepreneurs, at least in the first half of the nineteenth century.

Germany was in a special position. While her western and southern peasant farms failed, like their French counterparts, to offer much of a stimulus to industry, it was the large East-Elbian estates – only gradually forced to give up some of their archaic features – which yet improved their productivity and by their exports provided much of the foreign exchange that tided Germany over the difficult years of early industrialization. Only in the later nineteenth century did technical improvements on the farms of the rest of Germany raise agrarian productivity there.

In the periphery, in Spain, Hungary, Italy and Russia, inefficient and poverty-stricken agricultural sectors undoubtedly retarded the onset of industrialization. But at the same time, the rural over-population could find no employment in nearby industry there, and millions emigrated overseas. Only some of the peasants from the Italian Mezzogiorno, and most of the surplus labour from the German East-Elbian lands, were able to move to industrial regions within their own countries.

Next to the technical changes, it is the industrial organization which receives most attention as a significant aspect of the industrial revolution in the national accounts: it is the factory system which caught the eye of contemporary observers as well as of historians. The factory could make more use of inanimate motive power, such as water-wheels and steam engines; it allowed a more logical division of labour, where necessary; and it gave the employer power to enforce a much greater degree of discipline and quality control than in the preceding domestic or putting-out system of 'proto-industry'. Factories not merely opened up greater opportunities for the introduction of new technologies, but also for innovation in labour organization, material saving and, above all, mass production.

It was mass production, the repetitive output of identical items, which was behind much of the increase in productivity that characterized the Industrial Revolution. Cotton and woollen yarn, and later cloth and stamped or cast metal goods, were typical products which were immensely cheapened by such processes. Other places that were not designated 'factories' worked on the same principle of the increase in quantities handled. Thus coke smelting and puddling greatly enlarged the quantities of iron turned out by individual works, and steam pumps and mechanical transport similarly raised the output of coal mines.

Factories, ironworks and mines required large concentrations of capital. Several of the studies concern themselves with the sources of that capital, and the social origins of the entrepreneurs who managed to mobilize their own or other people's savings for such purposes. Even larger sums were required for building up the necessary infrastructure, especially improved means of transport. In the early industrializing countries, this was found from existing private wealth. Later ones required government guarantees before venture capital, which had to jump several stages of development that the pioneer countries had gone through, was forthcoming. Those who came later still, including Russia, Sweden, Hungary and Spain, made use of much foreign capital, without which their industrialization would inevitably have been slowed.

Factories and other heavily capitalized places of large-scale employment changed the social relations between worker and employer, creating new social classes in the process. Instead of the simple personal relationship between the typical handicraft master and his journeyman, or the private, family-based working conditions of domestic industry, the factory was public, impersonal and limited to a pure wage nexus. Patterns of behaviour possible in earlier forms of employment, such as chatting or singing at work, taking an occasional break, idling on Mondays and speeding on Fridays and Saturdays, came under a prohibitive ban. Children worked away from their parents, there were often no skills imparted even when there were formal 'apprenticeship' contracts, and the withering away of mutual obligation of employer and worker was symbolized by mass sackings in slumps, and mass strikes as a method of collective bargaining.

The issue of skills is complex. Some traditional skills were devalued as machines took over performing tasks formerly undertaken by hand. But new skills had to be developed in their place, and it was frequently the lack of skills to be found in the workforce, including the intuitive understanding of how machines worked or how metals behaved, which made the transfer of technology from the advanced countries to the others so difficult.

But although the factory, the mine or metal works are at the centre of attention, all the contributions emphasize that these, at best, were important only in a few industries and even there they were rarely dominant. Even in 1851, when the Industrial Revolution phase was certainly over in Britain, factory employment dominated at most in the cotton and woollen textile trades and nowhere else. The 'typical' British worker, if numbers are to be taken as a guide, was still an agricultural labourer, a domestic servant or a tailor, rather than an engineer or cotton spinner. Large areas of industrial employment remained of the handicraft type and small scale even by the end of the century.[3]

Next to the slow pace of change, it is this apparently partial nature of industrialization which has helped to raise much recent doubt whether an industrial revolution can be said to have occurred at all, even in Britain, the 'classic' case. But this criticism misunderstands the nature of an industrialized society. Even today small, handicraft-type enterprises have a vital role to play: indeed, they are a necessary accompaniment of the automated factory. The archetypal modern mass-production industry, the motor-car industry, may serve as an example. To be sure, a few giant factories dominate the world scene of car manufacture, but they could not exist if it were not for the thousands of small, local, repair garages.

In the period of the Industrial Revolution, ever larger sections of industry were converted to the large-scale, factory type of enterprise in a mutually reinforcing process. What was possibly most significant was that the process had become irreversible, both because technical and scientific knowledge, once gained, could not be lost, and also because its products were cheaper than those made by traditional methods and as long as some kind of trade, some kind of free market existed in Europe, producers who failed to adopt the innovations and brought their products to market at a higher price, were bound to be driven out sooner or later.

As far as Britain was concerned, contemporaries had no difficulty in recognizing that a new power and a new historical phase had arisen in these islands. A country which, a hundred years before, had scarcely stood out from the European ruck, had by its economic strength helped materially to defeat the might of Napoleon; had amassed a huge colonial empire, captured one overseas market after another, shown an unprecedented rate of urbanization and, most significant of all, was able to produce, in a whole series of key sectors, as much as the rest of the world put together. Clearly there was a force at work here that was not comparable to any that had gone before.[4] If 'industrial revolution' is considered an inappropriate name, as some say, some other term would have to be found for what was an unmistakable phenomenon of world importance; but any other term would have the disadvantage that it would lack the universal acceptance of the traditional one.

It is theoretically conceivable that the bundle of technological, organizational and social changes that we collectively term the 'Industrial Revolution' might have sprung up simultaneously in many areas of Western Europe which were in terms of craft skill, scientific knowledge and accumulation of savings at a similar stage of development. France in particular, might have been thought a fertile ground for such early shoots of industrial innovation.[5] Yet such polycentric growth clearly did not occur.

Instead, despite some scattered promising initiatives elsewhere, change on a broad front occurred in one country only for the space of about half a century, before others began, with more or less conscious deliberation, to take over what had been created in Britain. It may well be that, in view of the relative poverty of European society in the eighteenth century and the limitation of world markets, it needed the concentration within a single area (rather like the necessary concentration in turn *within* Britain in a limited number of industrial regions), to economize on resources and by mutual support and a range of external economies speed a process which otherwise would have been too feeble to take off altogether. But the unicentric start had important consequences for Britain as well as for Europe as a whole.

Some of the reasons why Britain was first are enumerated in Deane's contribution. Among the consequences of the country's lone pioneer role was not merely a path and a character of economic change which differed from those of others, but also a particular relationship between Britain and the rest of Europe, and a unique role of the British economy in Europe for most of the nineteenth century.

Unlike the experience of the follower countries which were faced with a fairly comprehensive package of mutually reinforcing changes, the British evolution was slow, piecemeal and unconscious, in the sense of being unperceived as a whole. Innovations would start first in one distant corner, then possibly independently in another. Coal output rose in the north-east of England, then in other areas; tramroads and canals were built to link the coal with other waterways and more distant markets. Meanwhile, in other parts of the country, coke blast-furnaces cheapened the cost of ironmaking and allowed large quantities of home ores to be smelted, while elsewhere the reverberatory furnace reduced the costs of non-ferrous metals. In other parts still, spinning machines, first made largely of wood and driven by water power, lowered the costs of yarn. The list could be extended.

Several of these innovations led to spectacular increases in output, as well as to reductions in cost, but each took years to develop fully, and each covered only a small sector of the economy. It is clear that even if a sector which accounted for, say, 1 per cent of gross output, doubled its production in three years — a truly prodigious change — it would scarcely show up in the national output curve, and this would be true for similar performances by other sectors elsewhere, if they occurred some years later. Thus it was that spectacular, 'revolutionary' changes in one sector of the British industrial economy after another failed for a long time to show up significantly in the national output statistics.[6] But after a while two parallel changes would make the impact of these increases be felt with accelerating force. On the one hand, ever new sectors would experience revolutionary technical change, to add to the existing upward drive. But secondly, their accelerated growth rate would ensure that the modernized

sectors formed an ever larger segment of the economy as a whole so that
their growth rate, even if it increased no further, would have an ever
larger impact on the national figures. Here is one explanation for the fact
that in Britain so many of the qualitative technical changes occurred in
the late eighteenth century, while the fast quantitative growth rates are
discernible only by the middle of the nineteenth. It is a phenomenon
clearly observable also in Sweden, Germany, Italy and other countries.
But on the whole, follower countries could achieve faster growth even in
the early stages of industrialization than could be expected to occur in
Britain.

Secondly, because of her pioneer role, and also her preceding role in
world commerce which may have contributed to the pioneer role itself,
the structure of Britain's economy itself took on a different shape from
that of most European countries. For one thing, agricultural employment
declined much faster, in part because its rising efficiency had been a
precondition of Britain's take-off not necessarily matched elsewhere, but
in part also because the success of British exports and her colonization
allowed her to replace home food production by imports, paid for by
manufactures and by services. Yet agricultural productivity was higher
than elsewhere, and the 'productivity gap' between it and industrial
productivity much less. Services, including shipping, finance and insurance, formed a larger source of income and, for a country of her size,
foreign trade formed a larger proportion of her national income. Also, the
proportion of the labour force in industry was higher, urbanization was
more strongly marked, home investment was lower while foreign investment was much higher, the share of personal consumption was higher
and finally, if the statistics are to be trusted, school enrolment was much
lower in England and Wales than in other Western European countries
at similar levels of national income.[7]

Thirdly, while British developments occurred largely spontaneously, the
only competition to be feared being that of other British producers, developments on the continent were clearly influenced by the pre-existing
British Industrial Revolution, as source of help, as threat and as model.
This is noted in the chapters on France, Switzerland, Hungary and
Sweden, but is implicit in most of the others. For countries arriving last
on the path to industrialization, including Russia and Spain, it was the
whole of industrialized Europe and no longer Britain alone which
appeared in the combined roles of mentor and menace.

If Britain was thus, in some way, the odd man out, it follows that there
were differences of some significance between the course of the Industrial
Revolution here and in the rest of Europe. But it is evident that even
among the continental countries themselves, there were great differences

in the nature and character of the transformation which they went through. The question thus arises whether we can usefully speak of a single phenomenon at all, or if we simply have a series of different national histories which show some likeness in certain cases. It is a nice question which has aroused some controversy.

Readers of the individual country chapters will note that among the early followers, including Belgium, France, Switzerland, Germany and the Czech Lands, and to some extent also in Austria and The Netherlands, as well as in the United States, there was an obvious similarity in the industries which were modernized first, and in the technical and organizational changes, the factories, ironworks, coal mines and the machines installed in them. These were, until at least the middle of the nineteenth century, simply taken over from Britain. Similarly, where technical changes did occur elsewhere first, as in the case of the Jacquard loom, the Girard flax spinning process or the Heilmann wool-combing machine, they were adopted across all the frontiers, wherever modern entrepreneurship existed, including Britain. Further, technical considerations imposed certain similarities of organization. There were factory buildings and factory discipline, wage-payment systems, the provision of workers' housing in rural factory locations, and in due course also protective factory legislation and safety precautions in mines, which bore a close likeness everywhere. Conversely, there were no substitutes for British technology where some necessary ingredients were missing, such as coal or iron ore, though these were developed quite quickly in the following phase, such as the water turbine technology developed in parts of France in which coal remained expensive. The United States, however, formed a significant exception to this rule.

That said, it is clear that in other respects, developments took quite different turns in different countries. We can discern differences in the speed and success of adaptation; differences in the detailed sequence in which technology and the industrial sectors were modernized; and differences in the social origins of the entrepreneurial classes, and the sources of their capital. It is impossible to ignore differences in the legislative framework and the government economic policies, within which national entrepreneurship could develop, and differences in the extent to which the wishes of the industrialists could overcome the opposing interests of the traditional ruling agrarian elites.

One attempt to impose some sort of order on the variety of European responses to the wave of industrialization spreading outward from the British Isles is associated with the name of Alexander Gerschenkron, who saw regularities derived from the timing of the great 'spurt' which according to him characterized a key phase in the Industrial Revolution.

Earlier industrializers differed from later ones in a logical manner, largely because they had a less wide gap to bridge. It was the last arrivals who had to depend on strong government initiative, and government funds, on a powerful ideology of modernization, on up-to-date technology and large firms, among other differences, all of which gave their industrialization phase a markedly different character.

Gerschenkron's thesis has been influential, and has recently been re-examined overall and on a country-by-country basis by a group of experts.[8] In some respects, it was found to have stood up quite well to more recent research, but, in the end, it was judged to have failed to take account of the many varieties of historical experience, legal tradition, resource endowment and commercial linkages with the outside world to be found in different countries. A similar criticism may also be levied on W. G. Hoffmann's earlier attempt to characterize the sequence of industrialization as one moving from consumption to capital goods industries,[9] and it may be supported also by the essays assembled in this volume. The conclusion lies near, and it has been put forward from time to time[10] that there can be no generic phenomenon of an industrial revolution. Even if such a term might be applied to Great Britain, it would by that very fact not be applicable elsewhere.

The question necessarily turns on how much family likeness there has to be before the existence of a family is recognized. It is a semantic, or classificatory issue, and therefore in essence rather barren. It is more profitable to study instead the different ways in which different countries actually did cross that necessary stage between the 'traditional' economic structure of domestic and handicraft industry, of low agricultural output, limited foreign trade, little fixed capital and unprogressive science and technology, to arrive at the modern era with its factories and railways, its high and rising output and large cities, its large fixed investments and high-yield agriculture. These different ways will be affected by each country's geographical location within Europe, and especially in relation to Britain, and by the phase in history at which the process of industrialization began. But they will also be affected by national and regional traditions, by skills and experience, and by natural resources, among other things.

Many explanations have been offered for the particular path taken by the French economy. A large and relatively wealthy country, with numerous sophisticated and advanced industrial plants and a workforce skilled in traditional craftsmanship, France yet found herself unable to compete directly with Britain after the Peace of 1815. Among the reasons were poor coal supplies and an unfavourable geographical structure especially in relation to internal transport costs, the loss of her colonies, a

backward agriculture and possibly also the misguided policies of an interventionist government. To these has to be added the proximity to the
economy across the Channel which had gained an enormous lead in the
war years, when France was cut off from easy access to the latest technological innovations. Direct competition with the strengths of the British
economy was evidently unpromising; instead, France built on her own
strengths, supplying high-quality and fashion goods to wealthier markets,
rather than cheap mass-produced commodities to low income groups and
colonial areas. Thus France had few of the imposing mills and giant ironworks that were a hallmark of the British Industrial Revolution. Yet, in
the equivalent phase of her development, she registered a significant rise
in total output and incomes, a railway and canal network was built up,
and there were always some favourably placed centres, including above
all Paris itself, in which the latest technology was not only known and
used, but often also improved on by French technical skill and originality.
The country never lost touch with the industrial leaders of Europe.[11]

In the case of Belgium, locational proximity to Britain (as well as to
prosperous areas of France, Germany and The Netherlands across the
border) may have helped rather than hindered the Industrial Revolution,
the first and in some way the most thorough on the continent. Building
on their long traditions in the textile and metal trades, the Belgian industrialists followed the British example very closely in some respects, but
went their own way in others. Coal mines, ironworks and engineering
works, concentrated on the coal–iron belt, were among the earliest copies
of their British equivalents. Railways also came early. On the other hand,
the cotton industry, though it did establish itself in Ghent, was less important. Possibly the greatest difference lay in the direct long-term investment
in industry provided by the banks, and in the more positive attitude to
industrial progress on the part of the Brussels government, which was far
less dominated by the traditional landed classes than the British one.

The Dutch economy, equally close to the British in a geographical
sense, yet developed few of the outward symbols of the new industrialism.
Its advantages lay in its efficient agriculture and transport network, built
up in an earlier age, in a skilled workforce, a sophisticated financial sector
and a rich colonial empire. Without developing much 'modern' industry
until the 1890s at the earliest, The Netherlands nevertheless showed a
steady rise in incomes, from a high starting level, on the basis of a
balanced rather than a lead-sector development, in which traditional agricultural processing industries played a major part.

The Swiss economy was probably the earliest after the Belgian one to
follow and adopt British innovations. This is all the more surprising, since
quite apart from its poor resource endowment and difficult terrain, as well

as its poor bargaining strength in a protectionist world, the country lacked even the most elementary economic unity until the mid-nineteenth century. To these challenges the Swiss found a two-pronged answer, building in both its aspects on an exceptionally well-educated and skilled, yet low-wage, workforce. The watch-making industry, world-beaters on the basis of skill, taste, and the careful organization of an elaborate division of labour in the place of machinery, applied something like the French method of survival; the textile industry, on the other hand, which had a long tradition on a domestic putting-out basis, adopted something like the German model, making use of the import of cheap British yarn and adding later stages of weaving, printing and embroidery until such time as skill here too was replaced by machinery. The subsequent successes of the tertiary sectors of finance and tourism, benefited both by traditional skills and a natural resource.

The German process of industrialization possibly bears next to the Belgian the closest resemblance to the British, being based on similar resources (coal, iron ore and mixed farming in a northern climate). Since it occurred later, its leading sectors were the railways and the heavy industries rather than textiles, and their breakthrough into modernity was, if anything, even faster and more spectacular than the British, while being similarly regionally concentrated. In the intervening period, when Britain had been modernized but the German states still possessed traditional economies, German manufacturers made good use of cheap British semi-manufactures as inputs, including textile yarns and pig-iron, to be worked up by themselves on the basis of inherited skills and low wages.

Unlike Britain, however, Germany was an association of continental countries (collaborating economically in the Zollverein) without overseas colonies. The links of the more advanced regions within them were with Britain on the one hand, but also with the less-developed regions of Eastern Europe, including some inside the German Confederation itself, on the other. While their trade with Britain provided them with machinery and models of machinery, as well as cheap inputs, their Eastern trade provided easily available markets, as well as some raw materials such as flax and flax seeds, and food. The particular role of the big banks in the German Industrial Revolution, differing from Britain where much of the capital came from the industrial sector itself, but also distinguished from later comers like Russia, where much of it was channelled through the government, forms a key element in the Gerschenkron structure of the European sequence of industrialization.

The multinational, multi-faceted Austro-Hungarian Empire is, not unreasonably, treated in three separate chapters in this volume: the Czech Lands, including the most advanced modern industrial sectors of the

Empire, the Austrian lands, possessing some developed industry around Vienna and Vorarlberg as well as some agrarian Alpine regions, and the mostly agrarian Hungarian half of the Empire.

The Czech Lands show some similarities to the Anglo-German models. On early domestic textile industries were superimposed, in due course, the heavy industry centres based on good coal and iron supplies. In some respects, the existence of the Empire was of advantage in the earlier stages since it provided both sources of capital and a protected market, though that, in the end, was to prove a limited one because of the povety of most of its population. The different social base, compared with Western Europe, was highlighted by the prominent position taken by some noble landowner in the building-up of industry, in a manner not entirely dissimilar from the Silesian example across the border.

For the German-Austrian provinces, as for the Empire as a whole, the survival of traditional aristocratic power and its influence on government policy had less favourable consequences. Together with the enormous diversity of social traditions and levels of economic development, it proved a delaying factor in Austria's industrialization, though the financial strength and the market opportunities of Vienna encouraged at least an early rise of successful consumer- and luxury-goods production there. Hungary, on the other hand, definitely belonged to the European, even the Austrian periphery. The country gained by access to western, Cisleithanian Austrian capital and markets, and it boasted some advanced successful industrial sectors, including flour milling and electrical engineering; but even by 1914, its modernization was, at best, 'semi-successful'.

The pace of industrialization in Italy was not dissimilar. Here, also, there were immense differences between regions, between the advanced north-west and the largely stagnating and poverty-stricken south, and they could not be bridged even after unification. From a long and distinguished urban and industrial tradition, a flourishing silk industry, with its pioneer 'throwing' factories formed a bridge to the modern age. Other textile sectors, using water power, also emerged in the nineteenth century, but in the absence of coal, and with little iron ore, there was little development among the heavy industries. It was only from the 1890s onwards that, aided by the purposeful action of government and German-inspired banks, a rapid spurt — which included the metal industries and engineering and shipbuilding — could be said to have propelled Italy into the industrial age.

The European periphery had two paths open to it. The Swedish path, which might perhaps be taken as representative of the rest of Scandinavia, broke through from poverty and backwardness to modernity and high incomes in a remarkably short period, or rather in two phases, 1830–80 and 1880–1910, which it would be churlish not to designate as Industrial Revolutions. Of critical importance were a raw-material base (timber, iron ore), a well-educated population within a modern social and legal framework and the luck and skill in finding export markets and foreign capital at the right time, though the latter effect may possibly have been exaggerated in the past.

The alternative path, exemplified by Spain, Russia and the Balkan countries, was to develop as suppliers of food and raw materials to the advanced parts of Europe. Such industrial enterprises as existed, which were often quite efficiently run, remained isolated enclaves, unable to break out and spread among the poor, backward agricultural regions surrounding them. A variety of both geographical but above all social and political factors may be made responsible for the sluggish development of these deadweight regions. The Eastern European economies were ultimately industrialized on the basis of Marxist-inspired governmental crash programmes.[12]

Among the factors imposing their own national characteristics on what was, from one point of view, a European experience, must be the policies and the influence of governments. In national historiography these are often taken for granted and therefore treated only cursorily or omitted altogether; a European comparison, however, cannot avoid examining their role among other explanatory factors.

The influence of the political authority worked at many levels. Possibly the most important was the legal framework within which entrepreneurs were permitted to operate; its effects were often reinforced by the social esteem enjoyed by businessmen, and the public attitude towards commercial ethics. In this respect the entrepreneurs of the Low Countries and of Great Britain were said to operate in a favourable environment, while societies in which the landed nobility continued to enforce rigid rules on landownership, in which forms of serfdom survived and political power lay in the hands of an autocrat – modified at most by a council representing the 'estates' in which the majority of the population failed to be adequately represented – were deemed to be hostile. Much of Eastern Europe was in that position at the beginning of the industrialization process. It may, however, be asked how far the changeover from a 'hostile' to a 'favourable' environment, in that sense, was a cause or a consequence of the rise of commercial and industrial entrepreneurship.

Another kind of impact of the political framework on the course of the Industrial Revolution was provided by the wars of the period. Not all wars had an entirely negative effect, particularly in the victorious countries, and some industries, such as the iron industry, armaments manufacture and the mass production of uniforms, as well as the mechanisms evolved in the mobilization of capital and the training in seamanship, may well have benefited the British economy in the seventeenth and eighteenth centuries. On the other hand, the French economy was very severely damaged and held back by the Revolutionary and Napoleonic Wars. The acquisition of colonies, and colonial policy including the denial of access to merchants of other nations, may be classified under the same heading.

At a different level still, governments could affect the process of industrialization by policies of protection, of taxation, subsidies and interest guarantees, by patent laws and by commercial treaties, among others. These have received much attention in the literature, though there is no agreement on their significance. Even where a powerful state, as in Russia, attempted to exert a direct influence, its impact remained limited and industrial development was still dependent on the actions of myriads of entrepreneurs. At the opposite end of the spectrum, some of the most successful economies, including those of Britain, The Netherlands and Switzerland, received relatively little direct help from state initiatives. This may lend some support to the traditional saying that that state governs best which governs least, though here, too, it is not easy to separate cause and effect, and a low degree of government activity or a free trade regime may simply reflect the fact that a successful economy is in less need of protection. On the other hand, some specific measures, such as a closely targeted subsidy or prohibitive duty, or help with the introduction of a foreign technology at a strategic time or place, may have had a significant influence for good or ill.

Whatever the sum total of these favourable and unfavourable factors, the 'Industrial Revolution' was everywhere a lengthy process. Even among the late-comers, such as the Scandinavian countries, who could jump some intervening stages and absorb complete packages, and even in the case of the forced industrialization of Eastern Europe after the Second World War (essentially not treated in this volume), the process took several decades at the least.

One aspect of this extended transitional stage which is noted in virtually every essay, was the appearance of a 'dual economy' — a modernized, mechanized, usually also heavily capitalized sector coexisting with unchanged traditional sectors in some industries and in agriculture. There is a general tendency to describe this as a proof of incomplete or in some way failed industrialization, a sign of relative backwardness or of misplaced traditionalism.

In fact, however, no economy has ever been completely 'modernized', not even in the late twentieth century. This is not only because, as noted above, mass production needs appropriate service and adjustment trades to fit identical products and services to differing individual needs, nor is it merely a reflection of the uneven developments, the different pace at which mechanization and large-scale organization become available, or are economically sensible, for different branches of economic activity. It also reflects the impact of rising incomes on the structure of demand, as families, whose real income has gone up precisely because of the cheapening of their purchases through mechanization, have sufficient surplus thereby to be able to demand personally tailored services and hand-made craftsmanship.

Morcover, no economy of any size has ever had much more than half of its working population engaged in 'industry', and usually it has been well below the 50 per cent level. At the same time, there have been significant changes in the other two components of a nation's employment: agriculture and the services. While the agricultural sector has had its share drastically reduced, even in countries exporting mainly agrarian products in the international division of labour, the tertiary sector consisting of 'services' has continued to expand, as the main beneficiary of the changes introduced by the Industrial Revolution. In the process, its composition has drastically changed. Whereas in the early stages of industrialization it consisted largely of personal services, including domestic service, portering and small-scale shopkeeping, in later phases it was professional services, office-work and employment in large-scale transport and distributive enterprises which made up the bulk of its numbers. In any case, the traditional three-sector division has turned out to be misleading in various respects: people employed in drawing offices, for example, and those who teach the worker who later will man the machines, are in a way as much a part of the 'industrial' sector as those actually employed in the factories; similarly, the makers of tractors, and the producers of artificial fertilizers, should be considered as much a part of the agricultural sector as the men and women who actually work in the fields.

To sum up, it will be seen that the term 'revolution' has often been misunderstood. Nothing like the drastic turnaround and sanguinary violence of the typical political revolution was ever intended to be conveyed by it. Rather, it was meant, from the beginning, to indicate a significant break with the past, a new constellation of factors, a pervasive change affecting all aspects of social life.

One of its most significant components, arguably the most significant, consisted of 'revolutionary' changes in manufacturing industry, in mining and related transport undertakings – which justified the description of 'industrial' revolution in the first place. As noted above, at its heart were technical innovations, new machines and processes, which greatly reduced the costs, and increased the output, of the commodities produced. These, in turn, required larger concentrations of men and capital, new forms of organization and employment, a labour force of a different composition and with different skills and training. The process was usually accompanied by a rapidly rising population which was drawn into cities and towns and therefore posed its own challenges of consequential technical and organizational change. The long-term result, after a period of declining health and life expectation, was improved public hygiene, the eradication of several types of epidemics and advances in medicine which generally prolonged human life.

The demographic revolution which followed owed much to rising standards of living which percolated down to all classes of society and which, itself, provided one of the main driving forces, and the most significant result, of the Industrial Revolution. Another consequence was a better-educated population, as training and literacy were needed for many of the new processes; at the same time rising incomes were translated by ambitious parents and by caring communities into expanding educational provisions for ever larger numbers. An educated, better-off population was also inclined to demand a more responsible and responsive government, though the link between industrialization and the rise of democracy is by no means clear.

Inevitably, beyond the tinkering and practical step-by-step improvements which characterized the early phases, the later stages of the Industrial Revolution required an ever-widening scientific understanding of the way in which materials and the environment behaved, while science itself was fed both by the experience in industry itself and by the increasing resources made available for it, encouraged by the economic benefits which it brought. Here lies, perhaps, the most significant difference between the Industrial Revolution and all other earlier historical changes: its irreversibility. Those who refused to adopt it were left behind, and could not turn back the wheel: no population will in the long run accept more expensive products when cheaper ones, of the same kind, are available. In this simple economic phenomenon lay the irresistible force of the Industrial Revolution as it swept across the European continent after breaking out of its north-western corner from the middle of the eighteenth century onwards. The timing, the sequence, the paths and the human costs were different in each country, and the political framework, indeed, could differ widely, but the shape which society took at the end of the process was remarkably similar in all parts of Europe.

NOTES

1 Peter Burke, 'Revolution in Popular Culture', in Roy Porter and Mikuláš Teich (eds.), *Revolution in History* (Cambridge 1986), pp. 220–1.

2 Michael Fores, 'The myth of the British Industrial Revolution', *History*, 66 (1981), pp. 181–98.

3 Raphael Samuel, 'The workshop of the world: steam power and hand technology in mid-Victorian Britain', *History Workshop*, 3 (1977), pp. 6–72; Maxine Berg and Pat Hudson, 'Rehabilitating the Industrial Revolution', *Economic History Review*, 45 (1992), pp. 24–50.

4 D. C. Coleman, 'Industrial growth and Industrial Revolutions', *Economica*, 23/89 (1956), pp. 1–22; David Landes, 'The Fable of the Dead Horse; or, the Industrial Revolution revisited', p. 163, and C. Knick Harley, 'Reassessing the Industrial Revolution: a macro view', pp. 196–7, both in Joel Mokyr (ed.), *The British Industrial Revolution: An Economic Perspective* (Boulder, 1993).

5 N. F. R. Crafts, 'Industrial Revolution in England and France: some thoughts on the question: why was England first?', *Economic History Review*, 30 (1977), pp. 429–41; François Crouzet, 'England and France in the eighteenth century: a comparative analysis of the economic growths', in his *Britain Ascendant: Comparative Studies in Franco-British Economic History* (Cambridge 1990), pp. 12–43.

6 Joel Mokyr, 'The new economic history and the Industrial Revolution', in Mokyr, *British Industrial Revolution*, pp. 10–11.

7 N. F. R. Crafts, *British Economic Growth during the Industrial Revolution* (Oxford 1985), chapter 3; N. F. R. Crafts, 'British industrialization in an international Context', *Journal of Interdisciplinary History*, 19 (1989), pp. 415–28; N. F. R. Crafts, 'Patterns of development in nineteenth-century Europe', *Oxford Economic Papers*, 36 (1984), pp. 438–58.

8 Richard Sylla and Gianni Toniolo (eds.), *Patterns of European Industrialization: in the Nineteenth Century* (London and New York 1991); Alexander Gerschenkron, *Economic Backwardness in Historical Perspective* (Cambridge, Mass., 1962).

9 Walther G. Hoffmann, *The Growth of Industrial Economies* (Manchester 1958).

10 Rondo Cameron, 'A new view of European Industrialization', *Economic History Review*, 38 (1985), pp. 1–23; Rondo Cameron 'The Industrial Revolution: a misnomer', in Jürgen Schneider (ed.), *Wirtschaftskräfte und Wirtschaftswege*, Festschrift Hermann Kellenbenz (Stuttgart, 1981), vol. V, pp. 367–76; Rondo Cameron, 'Was England really superior to France?', *Journal of Economic History*, 46 (1986), pp. 1031–9; Richard Roehl, 'French industrialization: a reconsideration', *Explorations in Economic History*, 13 (1976), pp. 233–81; Peter Stearns, 'British industry through the eyes of French industrialists (1820–1848)', *Journal of Modern History*, 37 (1965), pp. 50–61.

11 Colin Heywood, *The Development of the French Economy 1750–1914* (London 1992).

12 Crafts, 'Patterns', generalizes these two paths by describing one as based on developing exports on the basis of (Ricardian) comparative advantage, the other as industrialization achieved by government initiative and stimulation.

Index